MW01392028

Lessons on the Road to PEACE

Lessons on the Road to PEACE

Photographs and text by John Noltner

For all those who believe that something better is possible.

For the ones who keep showing up to get us there.

The Facts of Life
by Pádraig Ó Tuama

That you were born
and you will die.

That you will sometimes love enough
and sometimes not.

That you will lie
if only to yourself.

That you will get tired.

That you will learn most from the situations
you did not choose.

That there will be some things that move you
more than you can say.

That you will live
that you must be loved.

That you will avoid questions most urgently in need of
your attention.

That you began as the fusion of a sperm and an egg
of two people who once were strangers
and may well still be.

That life isn't fair.
That life is sometimes good
and sometimes even better than good.

That life is often not so good.

That life is real
and if you can survive it, well,
survive it well
with love
and art
and meaning given
where meaning's scarce.

That you will learn to live with regret.
That you will learn to live with respect.

That the structures that constrict you
may not be permanently constricting.

That you will probably be okay.

That you must accept change
before you die
but you will die anyway.

So you might as well live
and you might as well love.
You might as well love.
You might as well love.

"The Facts of Life" from *Sorry For Your Troubles* by Pádraig Ó Tuama © 2018 by Pádraig Ó Tuama.
Published by Canterbury Press. Used with permission of my friend, the poet.

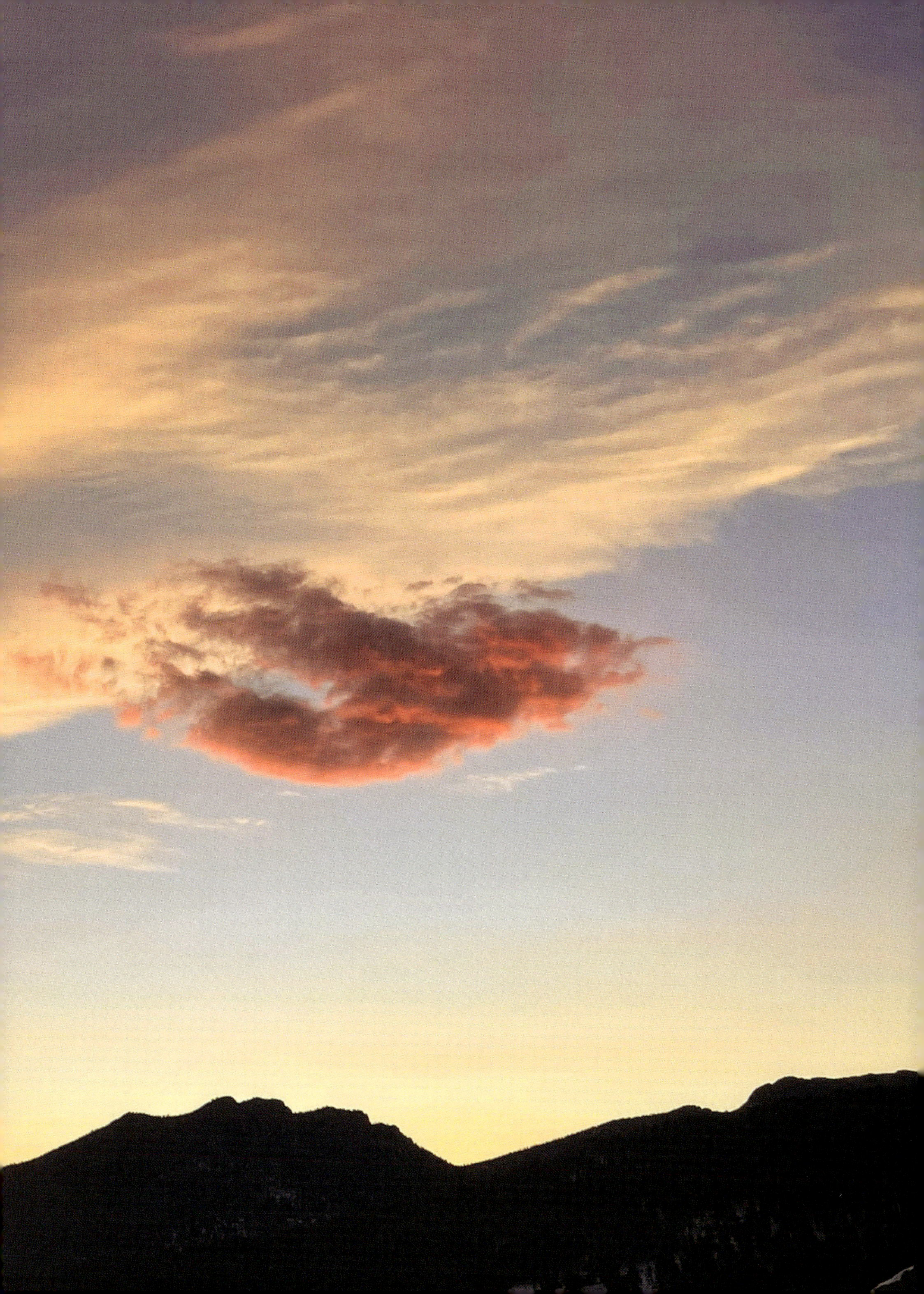

"Listen Deeply.
Challenge your own expectations.
And stay at the table."
 —John Noltner

Artist's introduction

An epic road trip with a mission.
900 days.
93,000 miles. 140 interviews.
One purpose: to rediscover what connects us.

This journey was born out of a difficult season and the desire to remember the beauty and wisdom that is all around us. The COVID-19 pandemic had shut down the world. Minneapolis police officers killed George Floyd just 11.6 miles north of my house, setting off waves of grief and unrest at home and around the world. The election cycle was defined by tension and venom.

Since 2008, I had been developing a storytelling project called *A Peace of My Mind* that uses portraits and personal stories to bridge divides and build community. In a divided world, I wanted to rediscover the common humanity that connects us. My efforts were rooted in a concern for the increasing polarization in our country and, as the project grew, so did the animosity and culture wars.

But something else emerged in the midst of the bitterness. Hope. Everywhere I looked, I found good people working on creative solutions to some of our most challenging issues. When ugliness reared its head, beauty responded. For every shooting, there was an outpouring of support. For every act of hate, a response of compassion. What if we could shift our focus to those efforts? What if we could boldly amplify our stories of courage, compassion, and connection and use those to light the way?

Something was stirring. COVID-19 changed our world. It disrupted supply chains and relationships. It exposed and exacerbated inequity and separation. The pandemic affected our wallets, our heads, and our hearts. But it also offered us a chance to explore new possibilities.

If we learned anything through the disruption, it's that we are more vulnerable than we ever knew, and we are more deeply connected than we ever understood.

In the fall of 2020, my wife, Karen, and I sold our home in Minnesota and hit the road full time to gather new stories for *A Peace of My Mind*. Karen will tell you that this is John's project and John's and Karen's journey, but I'm not sure that's true. Nobody does something like this alone.

We set out to find stories of hope, healing, and transformation. Our goal was to meet people who were affected by and engaged with the issues of the day. We wanted to learn more about the complexities of the world, to mourn our deep wounds, and to celebrate our spirit of resilience.

This journey was deep and wide and incomplete. When you leave behind all you know—when you untether yourself from life's usual routines and connections and expectations—you see the world in a new light.

You don't have to drive 93,000 miles to find stories like these. There is wisdom and beauty all around us if we choose to see it. Listen deeply. Challenge your own expectations and be willing to stay at the table.

I had turned off my phone because the pandemic headlines were consuming me. I wanted to pause the doom scrolling that had filled my idle hours imposed by the lockdown.

Just before dinner on Tuesday, May 26, I glanced at social media and saw that Minneapolis police officer Derek Chauvin had killed George Floyd the day before. Floyd died at the intersection of 38th Street and Chicago Avenue—11.6 miles north of my house.

I was tired. From a long day. From worrying about my own finances. From the steady stream of painful news. From social distancing. I considered just turning my phone back off.

But silence is violence. I've seen bumper stickers that say that. I believed that social distancing was good public policy and we were following those rules. But I also knew I needed to respond to Floyd's murder in an active way. I needed to go to that intersection.

I visited early the next morning, trying to avoid crowds of people. I wanted to be there, if only for a moment. A few dozen people gathered around the seeds of a makeshift memorial that would take root and grow in the coming days and weeks. We were a mix of Black, white, Asian, Hispanic, and Indigenous people. Some of us brought flowers. Some took photos. Others stood quietly.

A few activists passed around a megaphone and addressed the crowd with a quiet, early-morning simmer of anger, frustration, and grief. One Black woman took the megaphone and said, "Thank you to the white people who showed up today. We need you, white people. You still hold the majority power. You still call the shots. Slaves weren't freed until the white people chose to make them free. Women didn't get the vote until men changed the rules and let them. The Civil Rights Act didn't happen until the white people in power voted for it. Tell your white friends we need them, too. We need them now. Because this has got to stop."

It was a call for solidarity. A plea for allyship.

Sometimes you just have to show up. Bear witness. Acknowledge that whether the problems are over here or over there, us or them, you or me, 11.6 miles away or just around the corner, they are our problems. And we need to fix them together.

I am not the one to lead. But I'll stand with people who are hurting. I'll listen. I'll learn. And I'll keep showing up. Draw your lines where you like, but we are all in this together.

CUP FOODS
STAMPS KEYS PHONES & ACCESSORIES BUS CARDS
PRE-EXISTING CONDITION:
BEING BLACK IN AMERICA
GEORGE FLOYD

E 38th St
Speedway
Speedway
Screen time just got healthy.
25

On Thursday I returned to the intersection of 38th Street and Chicago Avenue with a bare studio kit, set up on the sidewalk, and asked a simple question: "What do you want to say?" The memorial at the intersection had grown since the previous day. The street was covered in messages of grief, determination, and hope. Artists had started painting a mural of George Floyd on the exterior south wall of Cup Foods. Cars blocked the streets. Families brought their children to teach, to yell, to support, and to grieve.

The crowd was a mix of activists, onlookers, clergy, mourners, and artists.

Some people didn't want to talk to me. Many did. Some of the most painful stories were too raw for people to share publicly. In those cases, I just set my camera down and we visited off the record.

"What do you want to say?"

There was an air of urgency, anger, and tension. We knew that the evening protests would be large. We knew that the city would burn, and it did.

Dr. King said, "In the final analysis, a riot is the language of the unheard. And what is it that America has failed to hear?"

People were crying out to be heard. I wanted to listen. When all else fails, we can at least do that.

I went back to that intersection the next day. And the next. And the next. I was tired, but my fatigue paled in the face of the soul-crushing weariness I saw in my brothers and sisters on the street.

My distress was manageable compared to the frustration I heard in their voices.

My exhaustion was no excuse when weighed against the heavy burden that they have carried for generations. Years of calling out and not being heard.

I was tired, but maybe I could offer to hold a little bit of that collective weight so that others didn't have to carry it alone.

I was tired, but maybe I could try to amplify the voices of the people I heard.

I see you. I hear you. And you matter.

White SILENCE IS White VIOLENCE
GEORGE
4-Eva
George
USE FRONT DOOR

GEORGE FLOYD
I CAN BREATHE NOW
LIFE

"What do you want to say?"

George Floyd studio

Why is being black in America a death sentence?

Stop pinning the acts of one person on an entire race.

There is power in the people, in numbers, and together we will rise. It's our job to use our voices and speak for those who lost theirs.

I don't care who you are or what you look like; you don't have the right to hurt anybody.

If we don't change the law, we don't change the condition.

I am numb. I don't feel angry, I don't feel sad, just numb. It's at the point where police brutality against African Americans is expected.

See it. Believe it. Work for it daily. This ain't over. My heart hurts.

I don't want to be filled with fear every time me or my brothers go outside. I don't want to worry about whether our lives are at risk just for doing things that everyone else does.

sam's sweet-talk thickens the suppression of my worth. My Words Will Conquer.

What you tolerate today becomes commonplace tomorrow. To create a brighter future we must make a stand today.

America will never be great until all races love each other and all people come together to stop the brutality of Black Americans and minorities. And I hope today changes somebody's heart to do the right thing because love conquors all.

People of color are sick and tired of being sick and tired. We're not asking for justice any more. We're demanding it. And we're not asking for equality any more. We're demanding it.

I want justice and I want to be part of the solution. I'm here to show solidarity and pick up the pieces.

Am I next?

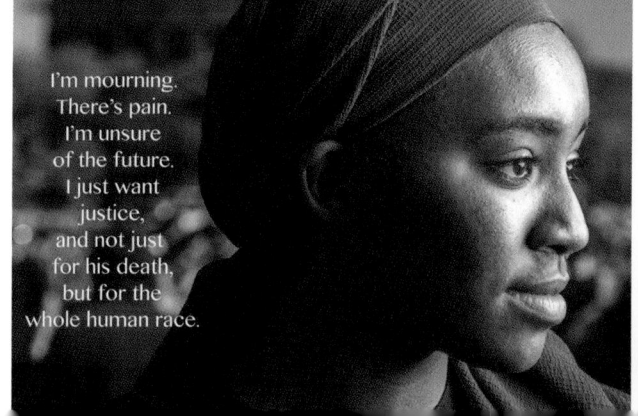

I'm mourning. There's pain. I'm unsure of the future. I just want justice, and not just for his death, but for the whole human race.

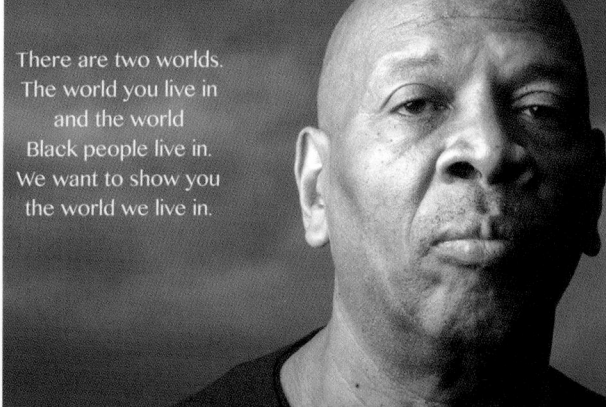

There are two worlds. The world you live in and the world Black people live in. We want to show you the world we live in.

We had gathered a powerful and important collection of stories, but couldn't share them in any of our usual ways. Because of the pandemic, we couldn't gather publicly, and so I struggled to have them seen. I could sense a collective desire in the community to talk openly about issues of race and equity, to build the muscles of dialogue, but many of us didn't have the tools to do it well. Many of us weren't sure where to start.

Just a dozen blocks north of 38th Street and Chicago Avenue, Our Saviour's Lutheran Church had an enormous exterior north-facing wall. I'd seen it before and imagined a public projection of images but never found the right reason to pursue it. As the city continued to wrestle with a difficult summer, I approached the church with this collection of stories and they agreed to let me project the images on that wall.

    Each night for ten nights, I climbed a wobbly extension ladder to reach the roof over the church's entry. I tied a rope to the cases for my projector and laptop and hauled them up with me. I ran an extension cord to the roof so I could project these stories 20' x 30' high on the sanctuary's exterior wall and say to the community, "We see you, we hear you, and you matter."

Something new

The pandemic had shut down *A Peace of My Mind*'s programming, but I found ways to gather new stories. We could work outside. We could set up microphones that were spread 20 feet apart. We could practice social distancing on the road just as well as we could at home.

It was a time of uncertainty, so why not try something new? A current of circumstances pulled at us. The world had shifted and we found ourselves in a unique moment in our personal history, as well as in our country's history.

We saw a window of opportunity where people could see and hear things in new ways. Collectively, we felt isolated and hungry for connection. We wanted to explore new ways to move forward together.

Karen and I are empty nesters. Our kids, Jordan and Grey, are grown. The house where we raised them had served its purpose and we were ready for something new. In the familiar boom and bust cycle of a freelancer's life, the economy had once again handed us some free time. Karen and I were restless and looking for meaning and purpose in the midst of the lockdown.

A Peace of My Mind had begun as an independent arts project, but it wouldn't survive the pandemic that way. Programming fees had kept us afloat and without them, we would quickly sink. With the help of friends, we retooled the project as a nonprofit. We built a donor base of people who believed that stories could bridge divides and build community. A small core of dedicated people knew and supported the work. I tapped into a broad network of contacts who offered to help connect us to interesting stories in communities across the country, and we decided to step into that tenuous space.

There was uncertainty on every level, but maybe, out of the ashes of this unsettled season, something new could grow.

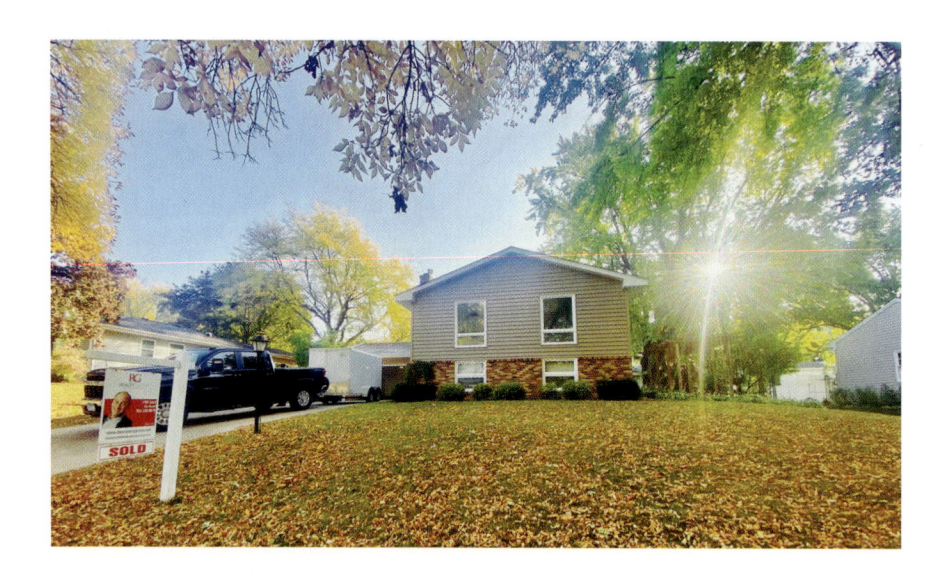

We began an exercise in letting go. We spent the summer getting our house ready for market. We painted the kitchen cabinets, upgraded interior doors, remodeled a bathroom, refinished worn hardwood floors. We did all the things we should have done years before, and now for someone else's benefit.

We made the choice to jump out of a perfectly good airplane. We were surrounded by friends and family members who loved us, and we loved them back. But it was time for something new.

Letting go is hard. We sold or gave away most of our household belongings. Boxes of memories and what little else remained, we put in storage. Karen and I sat on our neighbor's front porch, sipping cocktails and watching prospective buyers walk through our house. One of them would be living there soon and we floated theories about which one it might be. Forty-eight hours later, we had a signed purchase agreement and things started to get real.

21

10.04.2020

On a cold October morning, friends and family members gathered in our driveway to see us off. We had imposed a COVID-19–era "no hugging" rule that we promptly disregarded. We cried. We were eager to hit the road, but we were reluctant to drive away.

Our musician friends Quillan and Kim Roe led us in an acapella version of Woody Guthrie's "This Land is Your Land" to see us off. We cried some more. Not tears of sadness exactly, but a rolling wave of emotion. It felt big.

Karen and I said goodbye to Grey and Jordan and his girlfriend, Tiffany. Our beloved Cocker Spaniel Bailey settled into the spot between us on the truck's front seat.

We drove east toward West Virginia. My cousin Kathy and her husband, Bob, planned to travel from their home in suburban Chicago to meet us in the Mountain State. Seasoned RVers, they wanted to mentor us in trailer life, but even before we left, our plans hit a snag. We had ordered a 34' travel trailer in June with assurances it would be delivered by the end of summer, but COVID-19 supply chain issues delayed delivery. Kathy and Bob offered to visit with us for a few days and then leave their camper in West Virginia, so we could use it until ours was ready.

We said yes and thank you. We learned how to live small, how to live with uncertainty, and how to live close to nature. We found that the oddest part about this enormous life transition is that it didn't feel odd at all.

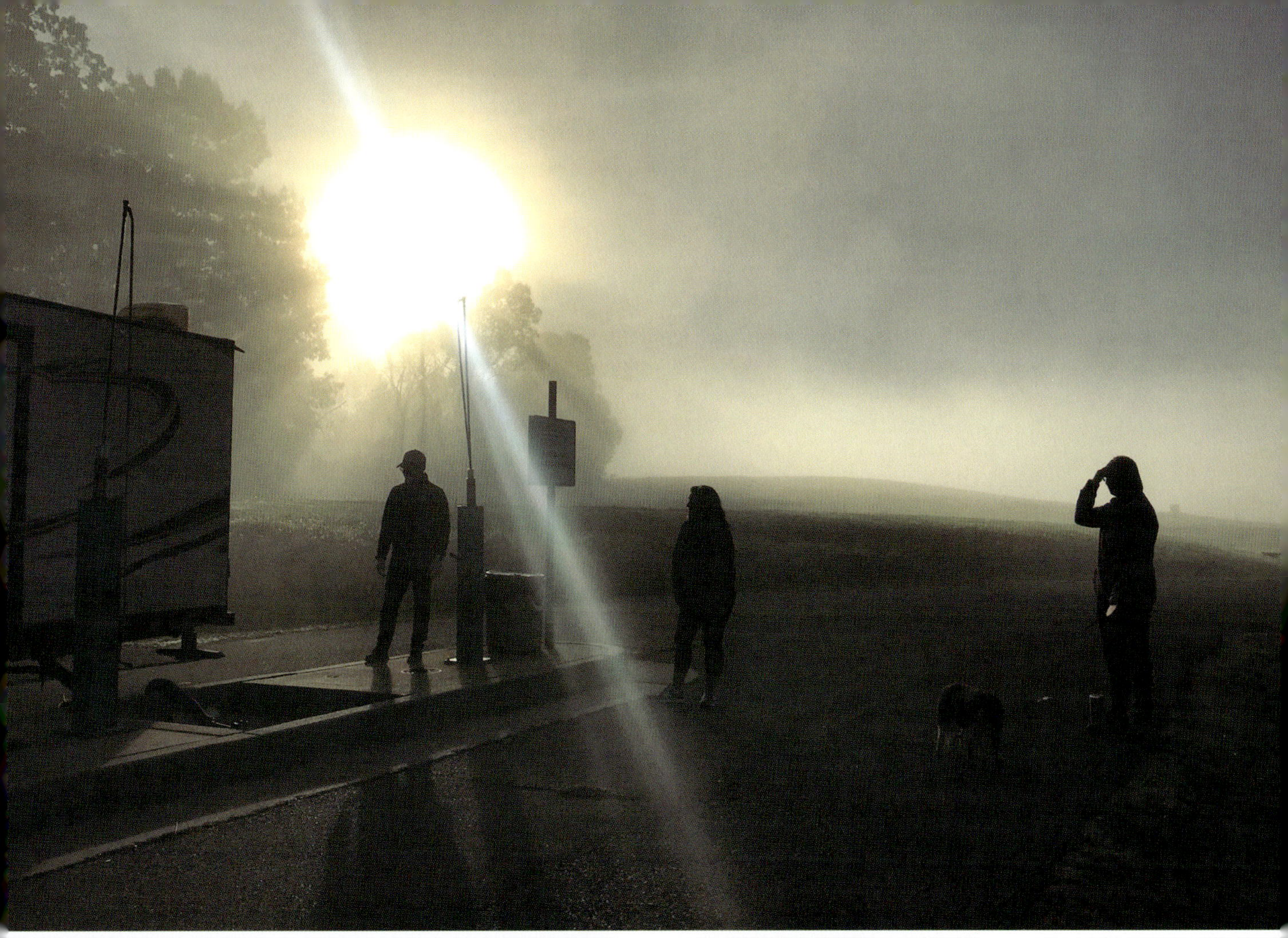

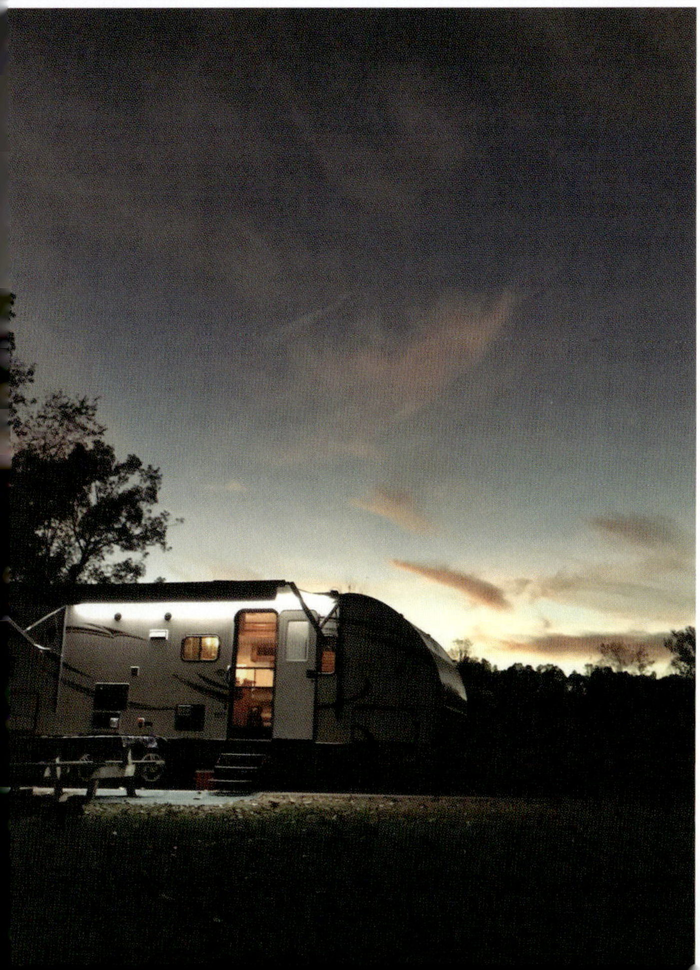

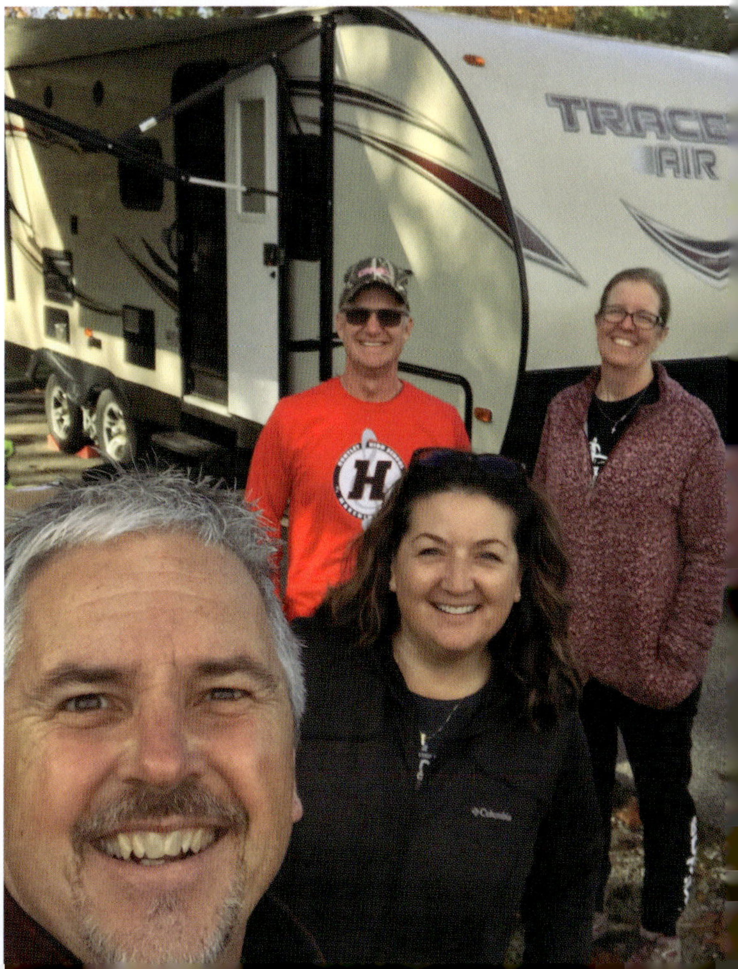
TRACE
AIR

Journey to West Virginia

Our rolling home was about 300 square feet and the small size pushed us outside more often. With COVID-19 still imposing a lockdown, our choices and activities were limited but we could still spend time in nature. We could still hike. That's often how we spent our free time pre-pandemic, and it quickly became our routine.

It was campaign season and there were flags and signs everywhere. Trump won West Virginia with 68.5 percent of the vote in 2016. It was his widest margin in the nation and it was the Democrat's worst performance ever in the state. Based on poll results and an informal survey of "Fuck Biden" yard signs, it looked like 2020 was on track for a repeat performance. I didn't plan on voting for Trump—and this election was contentious on a whole new level—so I wasn't sure how we would be received in that state.

The nights were getting cold and the fair-weather campers had gone home for the season. Including us and the campground hosts, only five of the State Park campsites were occupied. One vehicle displayed a confederate flag. Another had a license plate holder that read, "Certified American Terrorist Hunter."

West Virginia was in difficult times. Economic trends had decimated the coal towns. The opioid epidemic had ravaged the state. Yet there was a physical beauty to the landscape. A resilient pride in the people. And we were welcomed everywhere we went.

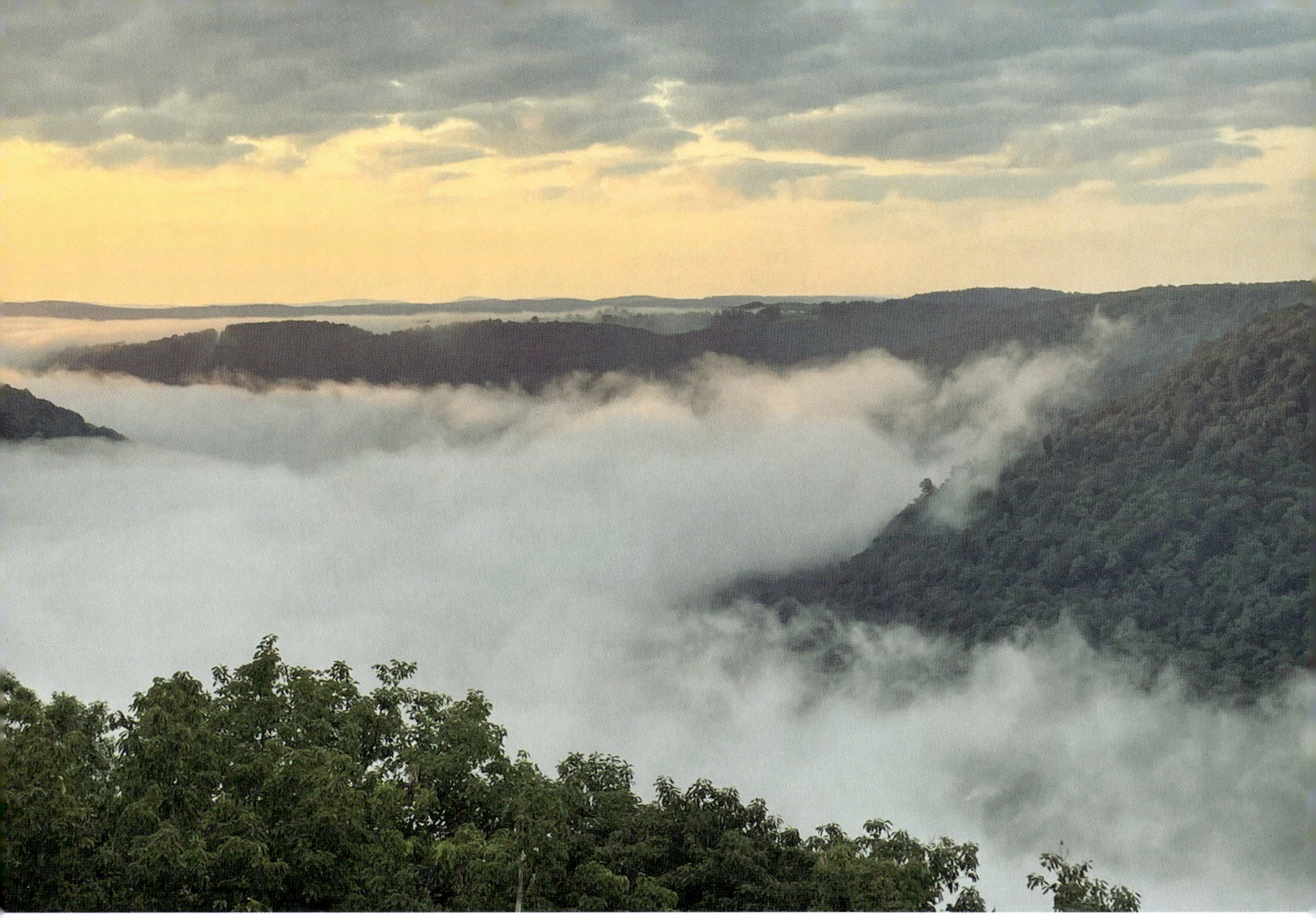

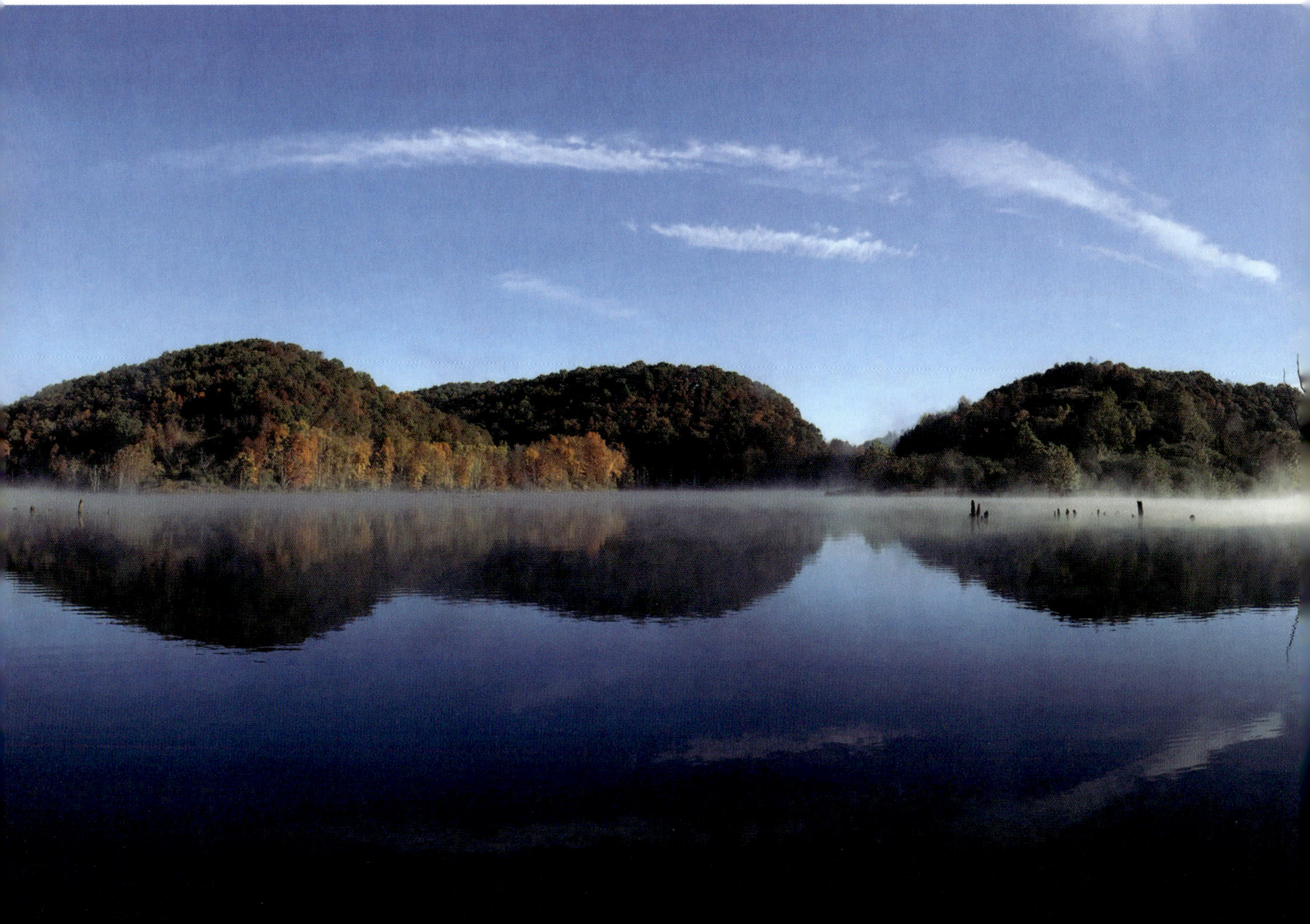

West Virginia studio

We found a rhythm to gathering stories and living a smaller life.
We organized a series of studio sessions in Parkersburg, West Virginia, and asked,

"When have you found strength in the midst of struggle?"

This year's struggles have shown me that our community's greatest strengths are our abilities to be resilient, to persevere and be supportive of one another!

Hard times are inevitable, and hard people are as well! But I know to be successful, your persistence has to be consistent against resistance.

I find my strength in the ones I love and care for because without them I would struggle in life. There've been times where I haven't been myself but being around the ones I love helps me out the most.

Once a broken woman, today I stand whole, complete. I have found peace, serenity, hope, faith, grace, courage but most importantly, self-love through facing my fears.

I found my strength in God. I hit a point where he was the only thing I had to help me. God has taken a broken, suicidal girl and turned me into the happiest person I've ever been.

Work hard.

I bake and get joy in giving it away.

Smiling at most people I come in contact with every day tends to make my days brighter, and my life more worthwhile, irrespective of my struggles.

26

Grief and depression were palpable when my father died. I looked at my daughter and realized the next steps I took would define how she will remember her mother. Giving up was no longer an option.

I find strength in my inner self, because you don't know how strong you truly are until all you have left is your will to survive.

When I found out my mom had cancer I was devastated and didn't think I was strong enough. But my wife and 3 boys supported me at my lowest.

In the midst of a struggle, I remind myself I am not alone. Someone I know has faced the same struggle and I shouldn't be afraid to ask for help.

I have found my strength from within. No matter what, I want to get back up and fight and push until I succeed.

I have always looked to myself for strength. I believe that the only person who can change my life is me.

From the depths of grief over the loss of my father I realized his voice is within me offering encouragement; providing me strength and peace.

When I am struggling I look for those who are overcoming. We all have different battles, but I find inspiration in seeing others succeed.

Moving into public spaces felt vulnerable. Social distancing and masks were common for some, but a rising public battle turned the masks into a shorthand for politics. Some people judged you if you wore a mask, others judged you if you didn't.

Everything felt off-balance. The local newspaper ran a story of a militia member who showed up to protect Black Lives Matter protesters after George Floyd was killed. But that same militia member's wife was arrested at a high school football game for refusing to wear a mask. A Trump train convoy passed through the state. Trump started claiming publicly that the only way he could lose is if the Democrats cheated. Everything felt off-balance.

COVID-19 variants emerged and in-person events shifted back online. Small groups and personal interactions were easier to manage than larger gatherings. We improvised. We felt our way through the dark. We tried to push more interactions outside.

The Smoot Theater in Parkersburg was a century-old Vaudeville house, then a Warner Brothers movie theater, and is now restored as a community performing arts venue. It had a lovely blank wall facing a parking lot and we cobbled together a low-tech method to project images there. I set a projector on the roof of my truck, powered it off a battery, and invited the community to gather outside for a viewing of their stories at dusk.

West Virginia University, which had invited me to town, printed posters of the stories we gathered and we hung them in the storefronts along Market Street, one of Parkersburg's main thoroughfares. More than 100 local stories were on display and, even in the midst of COVID-19, people could walk through town and see themselves and their neighbors lining the way.

Always
do your best,
believe
and never,
never, never
give up.

"Maybe we're going through a dark time, but I feel like our best is yet to come."
—Amanda Stevens

Amanda Stevens is executive director of Artsbridge and a musician from Parkersburg, West Virginia. She used to tour as a country singer, opening for stars like Tanya Tucker, Charlie Daniels, and Darryl Worley, but set that lifestyle aside when she started a family. Now her musical outlet is to dress up as a princess and sing at parties for children to bring a little magic to their lives.

I've always been optimistic. My kids asked me what joy meant, and I said, happiness can come and go. But joy is something that you can have, even when you're sad or feeling down. And I feel like I've always just had joy.

I had just left working for my dad's company. I didn't have a plan. I just knew I wanted to do something different. I missed the theater. I missed singing. So I started Princess Parties by Amanda. I ordered Cinderella dresses and I started doing birthday parties, tea parties.

I love little kids. And the best part of that is when they believe that you are really that person and you see that twinkle in their eye and you think, I am creating a little bit of magic right now. I tell my kids that I believe in magic, because I feel like I've seen it.

One time, a friend called and she said, a friend of mine, her little girl is dying. And I was wondering if you would go spend some time with her on New Year's Eve as Belle. She loves Belle.

I had never done anything like that before, where it wasn't like a joyous celebration. And I said, yeah, I'll do that.

Not fully realizing what the impact was gonna be. So I put on the Belle costume and I go to the house and her hospital bed was in the living room. And there she laid in her bed in a Belle gown. And she had her hair curled and she had her Belle toys and she was so excited.

I already have the music playing to create the ambiance and I kind of twirl around. In this moment, normally the kids jump up and they run up and dance with me and it just hit me like a ton of bricks. She's not gonna get out of that bed and come and dance with me.

So I just went over and sat beside her on the bed and I held her hands and we kind of danced like that. And she wanted me to sing it over and over again. That was different than anything I'd ever done. It wasn't about the performance. I wasn't worried like I had always been in the past about I hope I don't forget the words. I hope my makeup doesn't look bad. I hope my costume's okay.

The only thing in my brain was how sweet this little girl was and how much fun we were having together. And I felt a little bit of joy in knowing that for that brief period of time, she forgot that she was laying there in a hospital bed. She forgot that she was sick. And it changed me.

Ron Teska is an artist. A stone carver. He and his wife lived in Marshall County, West Virginia, for 40 years, but moved when fracking arrived and changed the character of his rural community.

We're in Wood County, West Virginia, along the Ohio River in a little town called Belleville. My wife and I have been here for four or five years. The move here was not out of choice. It was out of necessity, because the fracking came into the west end of Green County, Pennsylvania, and Marshall County near Cameron, West Virginia. And it just changed the whole area.

My wife and I both have master's degrees, and we could have had jobs making a quarter million dollars a year sitting behind a desk.

We happened to buy a farm in Marshall County in West Virginia that was so cheap, and life was so easy that all the folks living around there were rich folks with no money. And we joined them because we saw the benefits and the fact that all the children were eating organic pork because everyone's raising and butchering. And that's when we went into raising pigs, milk goats, and 125 blueberry plants. I developed a spring to feed 'em. And life was easy. And we didn't owe anybody. Never did owe a dime to anybody. That's the way everybody lived there.

Fracking came in and just like what happens in the Middle East. What happens in South and Latin America. What happens in Indigenous communities across this country. It happened to us. And that was the colonization of people for the benefit of the corporate fossil fuel industry. And the area just went down. I mean, the rents went from $200 a month to $1,600 per worker. People were kicking their family out of rental units to rent to the workers. The gasoline was up 50 cents higher than anywhere else. Used to pay $2 for a bale of straw. Now it's $16 a bale because of the corporate credit card and right of ways that they need to cover.

So a few folks were making out monetarily, a little bit of boomtown. It's the way it is in all communities, but the end result is there's no care for the way of life. There's no care for the water, air, and land. They become toxic. And the biggest benefactors are the corporate CEOs. And don't get me wrong, the local folks that made out with $300,000 because their minerals were bought by these companies, it's not worth it. It just ruined that whole area. That whole way of life is gone.

> "Marshall County was a place where people didn't need or have a lot of money to live. But they were happier than people who have many times more money than they have."
> —Ron Teska

Home for the harvest

The camper we ordered was finally ready back in Minnesota, so we towed Kathy and Bob's trailer back to Chicago and returned to the Midwest.

It was late fall, and Karen and I still own a Christmas tree farm in western Wisconsin. We had 1,000 trees to cut and stack for shipping. From the road we coordinated a crew of family members and friends and we met them at our farm for a long weekend of hard labor and reconnection.

It was a tough harvest. A little cold and a lot windy. Everything that could possibly break, broke. Sometimes twice. But the neighbors rallied. Daryl from next door fixed the chain drive on our tree baler. Tom down the road had an extra belt for our cutter. Friends from the city hauled trees and stacked them. We may support different politicians, but when there is work to be done, we show up and do it together. How have we moved so far away from that?

We squeezed in a Thanksgiving meal with Jordan and Tiffany. Grey joined via Facetime, with a phone screen propped up in their place at the table.

We picked up our trailer and stocked it for the drive to Charleston, South Carolina. It was a 1,300-mile tutorial in nomadic life.

First stop was Lake Mills, Wisconsin, to say goodbye to Karen's family. We parked in the driveway of a neighbor who was out of town, plugged our trailer into an exterior outlet, and promptly blew a circuit breaker in their locked house. It was a cold night without heat.

Our transit stops were guided by an app called Harvest Hosts. Farms, vineyards, distilleries, and museums allow Harvest Hosts members to spend the night in their lots if their rigs are self-contained. You can stay one night for free and in exchange, they hope you'll buy a little of what they are selling.

We stopped at a horse ranch in Kentucky, owned by a talkative man who had just installed 50-amp electrical service for his visitors. Turns out we only bought a 30-amp adapter, so it was another cold night without heat.

It snowed overnight and, for some reason I imagined that when I pulled in the trailer's slider, the rubber gasket on top would wipe all the snow away. That's not how it works. Cold and in a hurry, I retracted the dining room extension and the snow on the roof came inside with it. As we drove down the highway, the snow all melted inside the camper causing a modest flood in our brand new home.

We spent night three at a distillery in Durham, North Carolina, with no electricity at all. We parked next to a row of shipping containers in the gravel lot and ran the heater off our battery. Sometime around 2:00 a.m. the carbon monoxide detector went off. We knew to open the windows and abandon ship if that ever happened, so we loaded Bailey into the truck and drove to the nearest Walmart parking lot to troubleshoot. After an hour of reading online forums and manuals, we learned that running your battery too low also sets off the carbon monoxide detector.

Our learning curve was straight up, but we laughed. It all felt like an adventure.

This journey was never going to be a straight line.

Journey to Charleston

George Floyd's death had changed the narrative in our country. It was a difficult process, but new voices had become more interested in conversations about racial inequities. Charleston had been forced into those conversations earlier than most of us when in 2015 Dylann Roof shot and killed nine people at Mother Emanuel church. I wanted to explore the ways the city was grappling with the historical ramifications of slavery and to learn how those dynamics continued to ripple out today.

Magnolia Plantation was founded by the Drayton family in 1676. At times they claimed as many as 148 enslaved people as their property.

Magnolia was open to the public as a museum and seemed to be making an intentional effort to broaden their narrative to include the stories of the people who were enslaved there. They aimed to shed light on the problematic structures of an economic system that was built around the ownership of human beings and the theft of their labor and talents.

History was not being rewritten so much as it was being retold. The narrative of "the conqueror" was an incomplete story and as Magnolia wove other voices into the mix, it created a richer fabric, with new colors and textures that presented a fuller understanding of the truth.

We were invited to stay at the writer's cottage on the property, surrounded by ancient live oaks, their broad limbs draped with moss. Just down the road from the big house, we slept within view of the slave quarters that remained.

I woke up before dawn to walk the grounds alone, before the bustle of visitors would disturb the damp, still air. I walked through the gardens. Along the river. Beside the swamp and between the slave quarters, listening for whatever whispers of history remained in the place.

35

Joseph McGill showed up at the writer's cottage about 8:00 a.m. We sat on the screened porch with a space heater pointed in his direction. I was from Minnesota and accustomed to the morning chill in a way he was not.

Joe is the history and cultural coordinator for Magnolia Plantation and founder of The Slave Dwelling Project. In 2010 he started spending the night in historic slave quarters and has slept at more than 150 such sites across the country. He uses the experience to talk about the importance of preserving these historic structures so that we might have more complete conversations about our country's past. He facilitates groups in the overnight experience and leads campfire conversations so that others can find a new understanding of our shared history.

We tell ourselves a story that lets us off the hook. The narrative at these [plantations] didn't include the people from whom I derived my DNA. They were talking about the happy slaves and the benevolent slave owners. That—in my research—is not real. That's why we as African Americans need to embrace these places and become a part of the narrative.

[Magnolia Plantation] was a swamp. To engineer a swamp, to grow rice, takes skills, takes knowledge. And the Africans from West Africa—where rice grew, where the topography was similar—were taken from there and enslaved here for their knowledge of growing rice. They applied it here amongst the alligators, snakes, mosquitoes, snapping turtles, leeches. They enabled the Draytons to become the rich white planters that they did. [The model] lasted up to the Civil War, because during the Civil War, the free labor went away.

"When you're uncomfortable, that's when the learning starts."
—Joseph McGill

To deny that [reality] is just to continue to teach that education that I got when I was coming up and being educated about our history: the white male narrative that these founding fathers were God-like deities. These men were human. Twelve of our former presidents were slave owners. Twenty-five signers of our constitution were slave owners. Forty-one signers of our Declaration of Independence were slave owners. To say otherwise, we're lying to ourselves.

You think about enslaved people who inhabited those spaces. You think about mothers giving birth to children, and the law of that period took that child away from her. You think about those who ran away. Now it's our turn to represent them. We have to be their voice.

Joe told me about the first night he stayed in a slave cottage. As the daylight faded and his visitors made their way home, he explored the cabin and found small depressions in some of the bricks of the fireplace. He placed his fingers in the depressions but they were too small to fit his fingers. He realized that they were the fingerprints of enslaved children who were forced to make the bricks. If they pulled them out of the molds before they were completely dry, their fingers would sink into the soft bricks and now we can still see those prints 150 to 200 years later. Joe calls them the echoes of humanity and they continue to ring out, it seems, in so many ways today.

Johns Island is the largest island in South Carolina and sits just south of Charleston. The roads are narrow and flanked by live oaks, embracing you in their low country, deliberate, rural cadence. Rev. DeMett Jenkins agreed to meet me at the Moving Star Praise Hall, a modest wood-frame structure that holds memories of faith, family, and community gatherings for her. The praise hall was a sanctuary that offered both strength and shelter when times were hard.

DeMett is the granddaughter of businessman, preacher, and civil rights activist Esau Jenkins. She works as the Lilly Director of Education and Engagement for Faith-Based Communities for the International African American Museum in Charleston.

My grandfather was born in 1910. He came out of the womb fighting for justice like it was in his DNA. He always found ways to be bold and courageous, especially during a time when he could be killed for that. And here I am, 53 years old, fighting for the same thing. It's still police brutality, it's still prejudice, it's still discrimination and injustices. Here we are 30, 40, 50 years later and this is the same exact fight. Not a different fight, the same exact one.

[The Constitution was] not even written for me. 'We hold these truths to be self-evident, that all men are created equal.' No, that wasn't written with me in mind. All things need to be changed, all things need to be redone. We just took down John C. Calhoun's statue [in Charleston] but we still have Calhoun Street. Taking down the statue hasn't taken away what he represented. If we're going to make these changes, it has to be gut-wrenching changes like names of streets, buildings, schools. All of those were named after people who discriminated against Black people, who owned slaves.

I hope to empower my nieces and nephews and our kids so that they can continue the same way my grandfather instilled in us, that we've got to stand up for what's right.

The Moving Star Hall was a place of community where

Photograph of Esau Jenkins' van door on display at the National Museum of African American History and Culture in Washington, DC.

"Our whole history is wrapped around discriminating against people who look different from white people. We have to reinvent the world. We have a long way to go."

—Reverend DeMett Jenkins

African and African American people gathered to love and support one another. It is one of the oldest praise houses in the Carolinas. My cousin is now pastoring her small church out of that building, so the legacy continues. Our ancestors continue to uplift us as we think about who they were, what they've done, and what they've accomplished.

At one point in our conversation, DeMett said that she had grown up learning not to trust white people. An understandable lesson given the time and the place. Even now, she said, she needs to check her reaction at times. She needs to recognize her own response and challenge it so that she can judge people on their merits. I felt myself become a little defensive as we talked and, like her, I had to check my reaction.

I needed to recognize the historical currents that had made her experience true. I needed to sit with my discomfort in order to not only challenge my own expectations, but also to be patient with hers. If we are going to unravel our long and difficult history, we will have to sit with those truths, set our egos aside, and listen.

After we finished the interview and the portrait, I shared with DeMett that I was trying to connect with someone from Mother Emanuel church. She said, "Hang on," and dialed a number. I heard her say, "I have a guy who wants to talk to you." She handed me the phone: "It's Lee Bennett." Lee is the historian at Mother Emanuel and agreed to make time later that week.

It was that simple. The pace of our travels allowed us enough time to get to know a community and opened the possibility for new connections.

"I don't think your sermon comes from what you say, your sermon comes from what you do."
—Trudy Grant

Trudy Grant is a gospel singer, a civil rights activist, a mother, and a grandmother. She is the manager of Religious Affairs and External Relations for the National Action Network. I interviewed her in North Charleston at Charity Mission Baptist Church, where she serves as the assistant choir director.

I am not under the mindset that [civil rights] work is going to slow up or that it's going to be less difficult. That we still won't have police brutality. That we still won't have bias in education, bias in the pay gap, bias in other communities of color.

I'm not under the assumption that that's going to suddenly be okay. The work has to begin because what happens is, we had legislation in place, then there was a setback in legislation. Now we have to bring it back and then we have to move the needle forward. So we're starting at a place behind because we have to work to get it where it was. And then once we get it where it was, we have to ensure that it keeps on and it gets better. So, there's still going to be much-needed work.

My advice to folks is you can't become complacent when you know that something is not right. We have to remember that our voice, our vote, our conscience, all of those things matter. It's going to take a concerted effort and it's going to take all of those things pulling at you to make this world a better place. Your walk, your talk, all has to line up.

"There is power in learning from the past . . . the mistakes, the triumphs, and examples of inspiration and perseverance."
—Dr. Elijah Heyward III

Dr. Elijah Heyward III is the chief operating officer for the International African American Museum, built on the site of the historic Gadsen's Wharf, where up to 40 percent of enslaved Africans disembarked after their transatlantic journey.

Our mission is to honor the untold stories of the African American journey at one of our nation's most sacred sites.

My colleagues and I feel honored to be a part of a cultural landscape that's related to justice. The commitment to seeking justice through exposure to information and to the past.

In this moment there's a broad coalition of people who all seem to be on board in a way that feels really exciting. But that doesn't negate the need for difficult dialogue at times to offer proper contextualization, [and] also hope that there is a roadmap to a path forward that we can all benefit from as a collective society.

I think hope is all we have. The fact that I am a descendant of people who were brought here against their will, who had to figure out life in a new place that wasn't welcoming . . . I am the fulfillment of that hope.

"History must be told where it happened," Dr. Heyward said. There's something powerful about reclaiming a space with such a difficult history for such a healing purpose. As the museum was being built, I picked up a handful of concrete shards from the poured footings of the construction site and formed them into a peace sign on the wharf. It was an effort to create beauty where there once had been only pain. It was a meditation of sorts, a sign to others, a commitment to pay attention and to do better.

> "You're always reminded of being Black at its worst. It seems to almost be on purpose. And because that's what the world sees, that's how the world reacts to me or any other Black person."
> —Jonathan Green

Jonathan Green is an acclaimed American painter from Charleston, whose work centers on his Gullah tradition and the nearby community of Gardens Corner, where he grew up.

I paint about my people, my family, my community of Gardens Corner, South Carolina. I paint what I know, nothing else. I'm not trying to imagine anything. I'm not trying to impress anyone. I'm not trying to educate anyone about art. I'm just painting what I know, because my experience as a person of color, having been brought up in the era of segregation separation, I never saw people that looked like me on many walls. And when I did see any resemblance of me, it was usually distasteful, disrespectful, and a complete un-American attitude towards the people that have given 300 years of their lives without any reward of freedom. So I paint with a sense of dignity and respect for the people that nurtured me and inured me with enough knowledge to protect myself, navigating this world as an African American person.

It's difficult to talk about what representation means because you see so little of it. And what little you see of it, there isn't the most overwhelming, positive response around it.

I don't have any discomfort about history and what has happened or who has done what. I can trace my family heritage back some 250 years in this country. I know where they came from. I know what they have done. And I glorify the edifice of the plantation from the perspective, it's the work that my people did.

They cleared the land. They created the materials to build the houses, to maintain the houses, the gardens, to ensure the economic wealth of making Charleston the wealthiest city in America for over a hundred years due to rice, cotton, indigo. I know that. I know that when I walk throughout this peninsula, every home that has a historical marker on it was built by my people and maintained by my people until very, very recently. I know that. So as a Black, Southern, gay, independent thinker, I don't have any guilt.

Alphonso Brown is the founder and owner of Gullah Tours in Charleston. With a deep love for his city, Alphonso started a tour company dedicated to telling the stories of the many contributions Black Charlestonians made to the area.

Sometimes we think that whites should know, but they don't know. The main question is, what can we do now? We don't want to go down this path of racism. We want to talk to our neighbors and friends.

I can remember the very first tour that I did. At the end of the tour, I dropped people off at my house and a lady said, 'What about the Blacks? They haven't done anything here?' I stopped doing tours for about two to three weeks. I went around Charleston and studied Black history and it was like magic. I said, 'Lord, if you can help me through this . . . help me to find a route that would be perfect for Black history tours, I will promise you that out of everything I make, you'll get your 10 percent that you ask for.'

It's rare for me to have a busload of people who are all Black. I have lots of whites. These white people are not racist. They are people who are trying to get into heaven. They just want to do right.

"It's like my grandmother says, 'When you know better, you do better.'"

—Alphonso Brown

Denmark Vesey

The name Denmark Vesey kept coming up in conversations around town. I didn't know anything about him, so I started reading. Denmark Vesey was born into slavery but was able to purchase his freedom after winning the Charleston lottery in 1799. Although he had money left over, he was not allowed to buy the freedom of his wife or children, a situation that haunted him as he grew increasingly frustrated with the personal and societal injustices of slavery.

Vesey began to agitate. He planned an uprising for the summer of 1822, but when white authorities learned of his plans they hanged Vesey and 34 others. White mobs descended on the church that was Vesey's sanctuary (the precursor to Mother Emanuel's congregation) and burned it to the ground.

A statue honoring Vesey was erected in Charleston's Hampton Park in 2014. It was controversial. Critics charged that the monument was glorifying a terrorist, that Vesey was nothing more than a violent criminal. It's easy to find those comments on forums about the statue today. It's easy to find that sort of language in today's headlines as well.

Fifty years before Vesey planned to take up arms to fight for the freedom of his people, the founders of the United States did the same. They chafed at the rules imposed upon them by another power. They advocated for themselves. They fought for their liberation and independence and yet history remembers these agitators as freedom fighters, patriots, and founding fathers.

Denmark Vesey did the same for his people and was hanged as a terrorist.

How do we remember our history? Whose stories do we tell? And how do we connect that understanding to the headlines of today? We are still a young country, and there are lessons to learn as events from our past continue to ripple into our present.

Mother Emanuel

We stood in front of Mother Emanuel AME Church in Charleston, one of the oldest Black churches in America.

On June 17, 2015, Dylann Roof walked into a Wednesday evening Bible study as a guest. He was welcomed. He sat with the clergy and congregants for a full hour as they talked about their faith and studied the word of God. When everyone there closed their eyes to pray at the end of the evening, Roof pulled out a handgun and killed nine people. He was welcomed into a community of faith and he violated that trust in the most horrific way.

A gold cross stands to the side of the church as a memorial to those who were killed by an avowed white supremacist. Nine white doves represent the nine lives taken. As Karen and I stood quietly near the cross, a crowd of middle school students emptied out of vans and passed us on the sidewalk. All wearing jerseys, the students were, I guessed, members of a football team. A handful of coaches ushered them to the front of the church. All of them were Black. Just the two of us were white.

I wanted to hear how those Black men tried to explain to their Black youth what had happened at that church in 2015. How the weight of that story might have pressed down in the shadow of George Floyd's death just six months earlier. How do you put all of that into words?

I wished I could have mourned with them. I wished I could have said anything at all that would have made a difference. But we were on sacred ground. It wasn't our place to interrupt their pilgrimage and, for this moment, grieving in proximity was as close as we could get to grieving together.

Later that week I would return to the church to talk with Lee Bennett, thanks to that well-placed phone call from DeMett Jenkins. Lee would put that tragic day in the context of a larger historic struggle for justice that the church has been a part of for centuries.

47

Lee Bennett Jr. grew up a few blocks away from Mother Emanuel AME Church and is a longtime member of the congregation. A retired Army officer, Lee spent several years as deputy chief of staff of the White House Drug Control Policy Office and currently serves as a volunteer historian for his church.

A young man comes in to be a part of the Bible study and certainly he is invited in. He asked for the pastor, the pastor introduced himself and sat right next to him. The Bible study goes on for almost an hour and [the members], as they always do, rise in prayer, close their eyes. He shoots the pastor first and then continues shooting the others. When it was all over, he had killed nine people.

The church is downtown, so it wasn't unusual to have people who look different from us to be within the church. It's God's house, the doors of the church are always open. That has not changed. This is not the first time tragedy has knocked on the doors. This church is a resilient church. We lost nine people that time, we lost 35 others back in 1822; they were all hung. We are a resilient church and we're going to be around for another 200 years.

I'm hopeful. It's sometimes hurtful that it takes these sacrifices for [change] to happen. Nine lives lost [in order] to remove a flag over the Capitol? A man choked to death to remove it? That's a great price to pay to start these dialogues and to recognize the imbalance. So, I'm cautious with hope. Hope at a cost.

We owe it to ourselves to tell the truth and the church has a large part in that. As uncomfortable as it may be, the church has to take the responsibility to tell the truth. The most segregated day in the world is Sundays. People go their different ways. Who are your friends? Go to people's funerals and you look around and you see either everybody looks like me or everybody looks like you, when there should be some type of blending. We have to recognize our roles to fix things. It shouldn't be the burden of the oppressed people to say, "I got all the answers." We're all in this together.

At one point I asked Lee, "How is it that a person who looks like you can come to trust a person who looks like me after having that trust violated in such a horrific way?" And he said, "That's easy, John. This is not our house. This is the Lord's house, and we are here to welcome and love and serve everyone who walks through that door. We can't let the bad actions of one person change who we are." The grace of his response stunned me. What would happen if we could wash that across the land?

"It's amazing that we have to go through so much pain to make movement. It shouldn't take nine people losing their lives in a church to have a discussion about a confederate flag."
—Lee Bennett Jr.

We found a rhythm on the road. Interview, edit, explore, manage logistics. Even nomads have to do laundry from time to time. It was busy and in some ways it was hard, but in most ways it was good. We took a break along the coast at Edisto Beach State Park. Warm sun and cool breezes. Live oaks and palmetto trees. We breathed in the heavy scent of thick swamp and ocean air. I downloaded, edited, and wrote. We borrowed Wi-Fi in the parking lot of a local bookstore.

It was exotic and welcoming. We walked Bailey on the beaches and along the boardwalk that crossed the intertidal marshes. During low tide you could hear the tiny crabs clamoring across the muddy flats.

The landscape was healing and the days passed quickly. It was December. Campers hung Christmas lights from their awnings. Although we owned a Christmas tree farm up north, the only decoration we had was a battery-powered, lighted star we purchased at the local hardware store and set at the entry to our campsite.

We were born and raised in the Upper Midwest, and it didn't feel like Christmas when we were wearing shorts and sandals. We packed up to drive home for the holidays. The logistics were always a puzzle. We didn't want to winterize the trailer or haul it through the snow, so we arranged to drop it at a Dallas RV dealer for a few small repairs and then pick it up again in the new year. While we were driving across Louisiana, our world shifted.

Bailey had been a little under the weather. She hadn't been eating much. When we stopped at a gas station, Karen walked next door to buy her some KFC popcorn chicken, thinking that would get her attention. Normally, when I gassed up, Bailey would sit on the front seat watching me until I came back in the truck. But this time when I looked through the window, she was lying down at an odd angle. I opened the door and called her name and she looked at me, but didn't move. I reached down to pick her up and she was limp.

I called Karen. "You have to come back right now." She left without the food. I called a local vet. It was Saturday and they referred me to an emergency clinic 20 miles away. We started driving, but we knew it would be too late. We Facetimed the kids. It was pouring rain outside and pouring tears inside. Bailey slowly faded on the seat between us as we drove to the vet and she died before we got there.

Because of COVID-19, we weren't allowed inside. The vet collected her lifeless body from us at the door and we waited there under an awning to stay dry in the rain. We were wrecked. The vet returned and confirmed that Bailey was dead. She thought maybe a tumor on Bailey's spleen had ruptured.

They brought her body back outside to us and we sat in the truck with her, unwilling to close that chapter of our journey. We made arrangements for her cremated remains to be sent back to Jordan in Minnesota. We hung Bailey's collar on the rearview mirror and drove off without her, an empty spot on the seat between us and an enormous hole in our hearts.

51

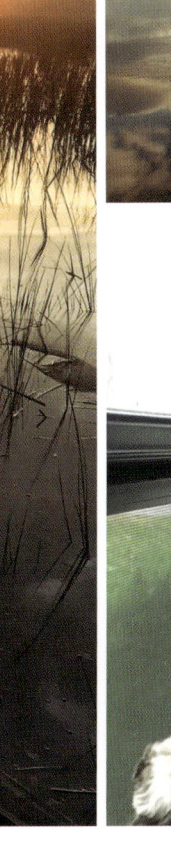

Christmas with family and missing Bailey

We dropped the trailer in Dallas as planned and kept driving north. A friend offered their cabin to us for our family Christmas. A cozy lakeside cottage for a few days in a yuletide blizzard. Shopping on the road was difficult, so we drew intentionally bad pictures to represent our gifts and wrapped those drawings with a bow. For a visual artist, my renditions were beyond awful, but it made for a good laugh. Amazon would deliver the real thing later.

It was a different sort of Christmas in so many ways. Bailey grew up with our kids and her absence loomed large. We no longer had our family home or the traditions that were attached to it. But we found our way in a donated home with photos of other people's memories on the walls. The company was good. Family time offered sunshine for the soul.

After a few days, we said goodbye and migrated south again. We spent New Year's Eve with friends in Dallas, picked up our trailer, and restocked for the road.

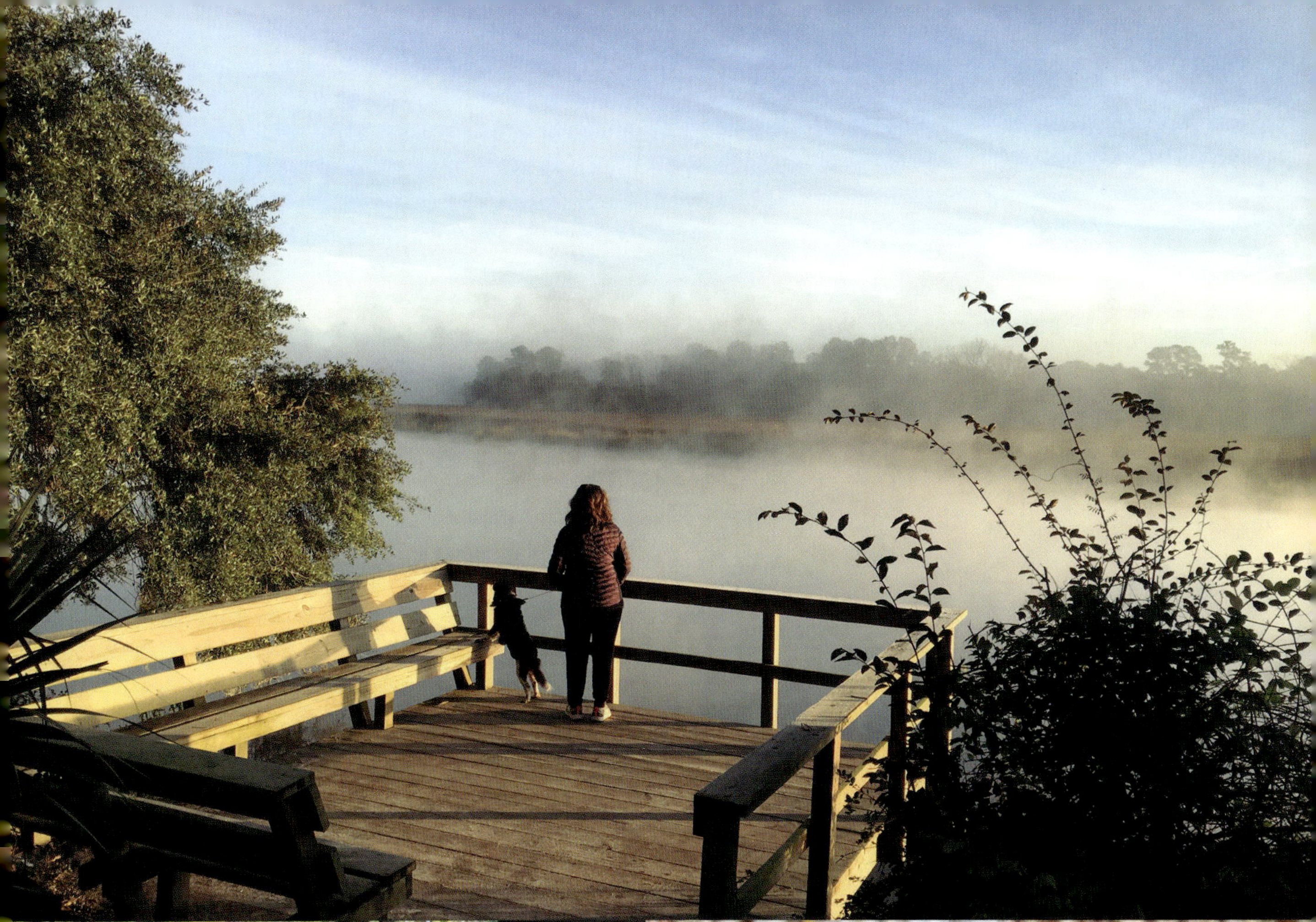

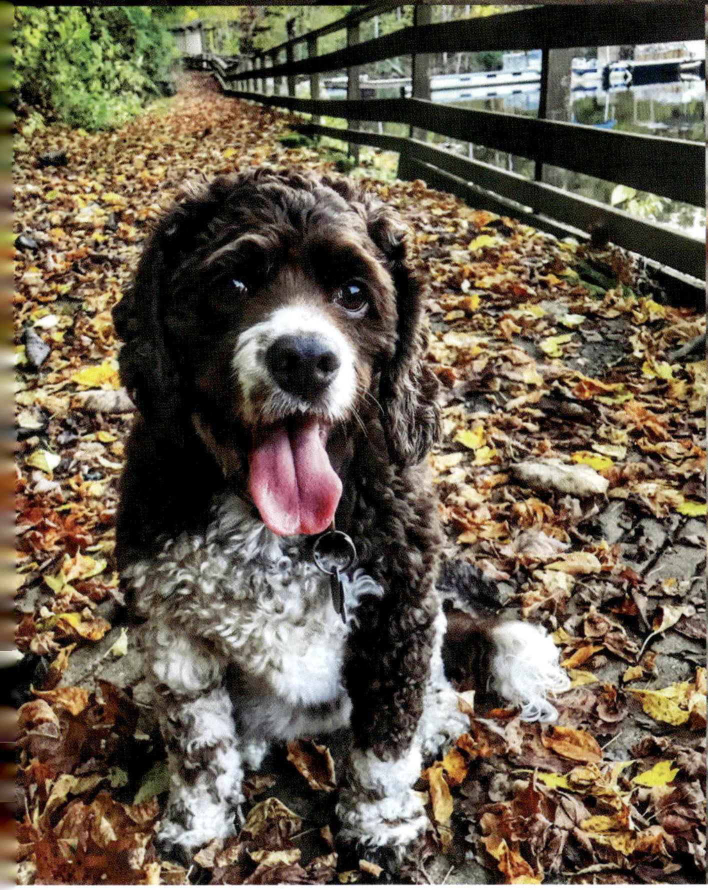

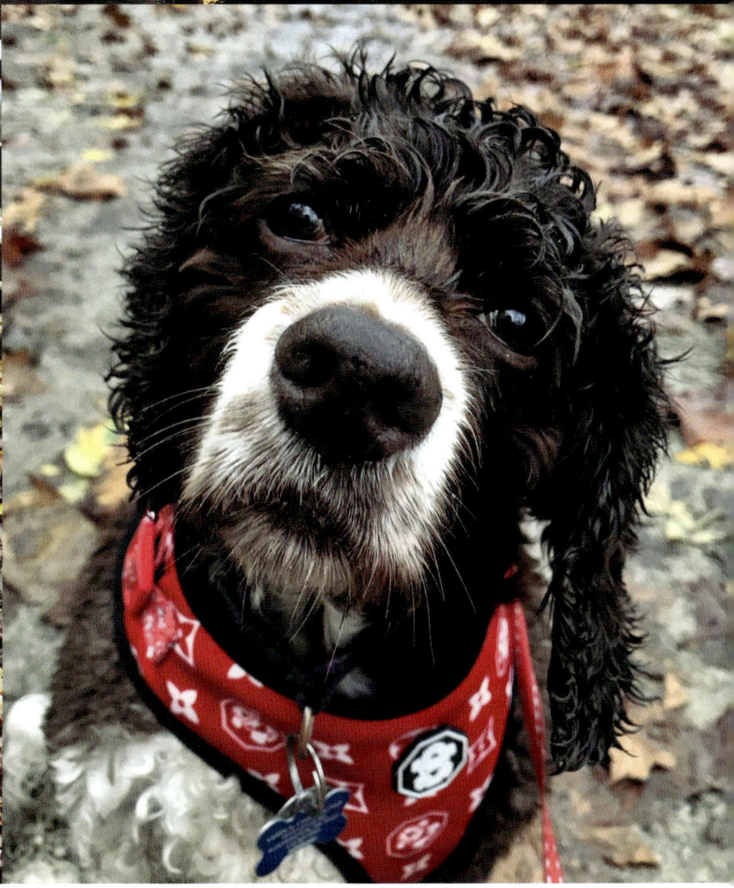

01.03.2021: Journey to Yuma

Our route was guided by the seasons, by the stories we hoped to tell, and by the doors that opened for us. To say we were in control of our schedule would be an overstatement, but we tried to nudge it when we could. Friends along the Arizona border offered to connect us to stories of immigration, so we headed that way.

COVID-19 cases were surging across the country, along with debates about masks and lockdowns. The world was waiting for a vaccine. New variants were emerging. At the time, the United States had confirmed more than 20 million cases of COVID-19, the highest number in the world. Half a million of those cases were in Arizona. Yuma County was one of the worst in the state and that's where we were headed.

We questioned our own judgment. We planned to stay isolated in our camper as much as possible. We would cook our own meals. I would do interviews outside. We could always turn around and leave if things felt too uncomfortable, but we had an opportunity and we wanted to try.

We drove through western Texas and spent a night at Davis Mountains State Park. We crossed the arid landscape of Arizona to the Gila Mountain RV Resort in Yuma, where we had reservations to stay for a week. Charlene Wicks was working the front desk.

"C'mon, hop in the golf cart and we'll go find you a spot," she said. "Just tell your wife you're on a hot date."

Charlene was a hoot and steamrolled any sense of reluctance I might have had. I didn't ask her right away, but I knew I wanted to interview her. Later that week, I had the chance.

Charlene is a snowbird. She's talkative. In her 70s and originally from Eugene, Oregon, Charlene has spent 23 years at the Gila Mountain RV Resort in Yuma, Arizona. She told me that in 2019 her husband, Bud, died in a motorhome accident as they were traveling from Yuma back to Eugene, but the

"Bud was pretty tidy. He hung up his dirty clothes. I'm a mess. I truly am. But he said, 'Where two people are alike, one of them isn't necessary.' He always said some pretty smart things."
—Charlene Wicks

people at the Gila Mountain RV Resort had become like family and Charlene continues to return each winter and now works there part time.

Bud hooked up the Mustang behind Fry's Grocery Store and I got some chicken wings to munch on. And I said, "I have a feeling of dread about this trip." He said, "We're going to be fine." We didn't get very far.

There was no traffic. Bud said, "What do you have to drink?" I gave him a bottle of water and he licked his lips and said, "I was really thirsty." But when he drank the water, he tipped his head back and I said, "You need a straw." And he said, "No, I don't."

I thought, "Yeah, you do," and crawled over the dog house. I took maybe two steps and he said, "What's this?" And he slammed on the brakes. And then a crash. It was like slow motion. This guy stopped in the middle of the highway to make a left-hand turn. Bud couldn't have stopped.

If I would have been sitting there—it pushed my chair back into the chair behind it—I would have been gone. I don't know how they got him out. Every bone in his body was broken and they revived him. The ambulance took him and I was sitting in the front of the ambulance. I didn't know my ankle was broken. That's what happens when you're in an accident.

My regret is I never said goodbye. I just couldn't. I knew Bud was going to go, but I couldn't say goodbye. I probably drove him crazy talking to him and told him I loved him. And I did tell him, "Don't worry about me. I'm going to be fine." I spent the night with him, but somewhere in the night he was gone. It was our 23rd anniversary.

I don't cry all the time. I'm getting better. If anything happened in that motorhome, we were supposed to go together, but it was just not my time. Bud was always a gentleman. You would have really liked him. I was sure proud of him. I had a star. I really did.

Doing research and lining up interviews before we got to an area made good sense, but so did a slow pace that allowed us to make informal connections and respond to unexpected circumstances. Sometimes what is unplanned is just as good or better than any strategy you can envision.

"This is my home. Yuma gave me the opportunity because [its residents] supported me. They trusted me. They believed in me."
—Teresa Reyes

Teresa Reyes was born in El Salvador and came to the United States in 1999 when she was 17 years old, nine months pregnant, and spoke only Spanish. As she established herself in her new home, she packed lettuce in farm fields, worked in slaughterhouses, and taught herself English. She eventually put herself through college and now works as an environmental scientist.

I was born in 1982 in El Salvador during the civil war. [The rebels killed my uncle] and my mom had to migrate to the United States. My grandma came first and then she sent the money to bring my mom and eventually all her kids. So when my mom decided to come here, she left me with my grandparents and my dad. It was a hard decision for her. I don't ask too many questions because it's very emotional for her, I just pay attention when she is able to open up.

I don't blame her, but sometimes people ask, "Why do you leave your kids?" Or why do you do this? But to be honest, I have kids. I've been an immigrant. I've been put in that situation where I have to leave my kids with my mom for a short period of time, so I can start having a better job. So I'm sure that she had to go through all of that. She didn't have her daughter for 17 years. I met her when I was 17.

The United States is what I needed, what I imagined. But you have to work hard. The idea that many people have back in my country is that you come to the United States and you just open your hands and the dollars come through. It's not true. You have to make sacrifices. For me, it took eight years, but after eight years, I have what I was looking for.

Teresa was matter of fact as she described her journey. But the whole time we talked, I wondered, what is the biggest risk I've ever taken? What is the biggest sacrifice I've ever had to make?

Erica Hernandez works as a youth minister in Yuma, Arizona, and volunteers for PFLAG, an advocacy group that offers support to LGBTQ+ people and their parents, family, and allies. She is a parent of a trans child.

His name is Cecil. He went to a private Christian school—and he started asking his classmates, "What do you think of someone who's this? Would you be friends with them? Would you approach them at all?" Trying to figure out, if I were to come out, am I safe? Are you a safe person that I can talk to? And so parents caught wind of it. Administration caught wind of it. And they said, "This isn't the place to discuss those things." He got expelled.

This was all new territory even though I was bisexual. I wasn't within the community. I didn't know the lingo. And so he really educated me and that's the first time I ever heard pansexual. "You know, maybe I'm pansexual." Ok, what is that? So he really took the time to explain it to us and I'm like, that makes sense. I can understand why you think that.

I want to get rid of the stigma that comes with being LGBTQ. We have to show them that we are worthy of love, just like anybody else. We have and need and deserve the same rights as everybody else.

[I want people to know] it's going to be okay. You are loved more than you know and it's going to be okay. Support comes in so many different forms. Reach out and figure out how we can help you. You can go to PFLAG, they can find a local chapter. There may be other support groups, where people are going through the exact same thing that you're going through. It's

"In fifth grade, he was still identifying as she, and so she asked, 'What would you do if I told you I was a lesbian?' I looked at her, and she was crying. And I said, 'Well, what would you do if I told you I was bisexual?' "
—Erica Hernandez

going to be okay. It won't be easy, but it's gonna be okay.

The love of a parent is unconditional. It's not that it should be. It is unconditional. As a parent, I don't see how you could not welcome your child with open arms. Any time they come through the door, any time they come to you, put your phone down, put the book down, let that call go to voicemail. Be there 100 percent for your children. Love is unconditional.

At the end of our interview, I asked Erica, "If Cecil were listening to this interview, what would you want to say to him?" and Erica replied, "Let's go get ice cream. Let's just make memories. Let's keep on living life to the fullest."

Life doesn't come in tidy boxes. I traveled to the border to talk about immigration and in the first few interviews, I encountered stories about parenting, loss, struggle, faith, economics, and gender identity. I suppose the word I should use is intersectionality, but the word that keeps coming to mind is simply *human*.

Alma and Juan Bosco Sandigo live on a ranch in Yuma, Arizona, where they raise Peruvian Paso horses. Alma was born in Mexico City and Juan Bosco grew up in the green coastal mountains of Nicaragua. They both immigrated to the United States decades ago and have become U. S. citizens. When Juan Bosco first moved to Yuma, he struggled to fall in love with the flat, arid landscape. He said he was too focused on what Yuma was not. It took years, but he eventually shifted his attention to what Yuma was and came to see and appreciate the beauty that surrounded him all along.

Alma

Who has the right to put the flag outside? If you test me, you can see that I am a good citizen. I have fulfilled my civic duties and I don't run away from paying taxes. I pushed my family to go forward. But it seems that all of those values are diminished because I may not [be] the right color or have the right accent to be called American.

Juan Bosco

It feels like you [have] to prove yourself to be a worthy citizen. When somebody adopts an individual into their family, after a time, they don't question if [that person is] now part of the family. It is just family, end of the story. It's not the same with immigrants.

Alma

It's because they don't see me as part of their group, [not that] I don't see myself as an American. We visited Germany. We were looking at each other, speaking Spanish to each other. A German [man] comes down and says, "Hey, you Americans." Why is it easier for people from other countries to say, "Hey, you Americans" than here in the United States?

Juan Bosco

In the States we're always foreigners. Outside the States, we're always Americans.

"My daughter is second generation. Her heart is in Yuma and this is her place and so it makes her an American, but she will always be [seen as] a Hispanic American."

—Alma and Juan Bosco Sandigo

Alma
Even in [Mexico], I go back to my place and they don't see me as being local anymore. I have to be careful when I speak so they don't treat me like a tourist. You belong to the community where you are. I'm an American and this is my community. My history has been created in the last 27 years and I have my part in creating the history of Yuma.

Juan Bosco
When you [plant] a tree in the desert, you aren't sure if it will make it until the new leaves come in the spring. A lot of times we lose hope. We don't see the results. Continue to work through the drought. Don't turn back. You will eventually see the fruits of your labor.

Juan Bosco invited me to return one evening to grill steak and to ride horses in the desert. His nephew asked me what sort of experience I had and I said, "I've ridden." But the horses I'd ridden were tourist-trained trail horses. He sized me up and saddled the "tame" horse for me. These were not trail horses. The animal felt like a coiled spring. A powerful beast. "Don't let him think you are afraid," he said. But I was afraid. How do you hide that from a clairvoyant wild creature? Hundreds of pounds of powerful muscle ready to explode. "Let's just ride around the arena first," he said. We never left the arena.

Journey to the desert

The Colorado River cuts a lush green line through Yuma's brown landscape. We walked along the riverbank and watched the abundant birdlife. I am not a desert person. I like Midwestern vegetation, so the water and the growth along the bank offered a welcome oasis. I resonated with Juan Bosco's lesson of learning how to see the beauty of this new place.

We traced the path of irrigation canals that siphoned water off the Colorado to sustain huge fields of lettuce, broccoli, and melons in the valley. We saw recommissioned school buses that carried laborers to the fields, each pulling a trailer with portable restrooms behind it.

We hiked up Telegraph Pass in the rugged mountain range just east of town. We found a taco truck for dinner, ice cream for dessert. We drove past the local high school and noticed that their team name is the Criminals.

We took a day trip to explore the Imperial Dunes. Just across the California state line, in a place that felt like the end of the world, we found the quirky roadside attraction known as the Center of the World, built by French parachutist Jacques-André Istel. He established the town of Felicity in 1986, named after his wife, and built a 21-foot-tall pyramid in the Sonoran Desert, a chapel on a hill, and a spiral staircase to nowhere. A series of engraved granite markers radiate like the spokes of a wheel, chronicling the world's natural, scientific, and artistic history. It was not his intent, but if alien life were to land in that spot, Istel would have offered them a pretty good—if eccentric—impression of who we are as a species.

We met new friends at the Gila Mountain RV Resort. Sharon spent her evenings at the local casino. Judy hosted a nightly happy hour at the tiki bar she built at her site. John apologized that the hot tub was closed for repairs. I mentioned that I wasn't too interested in sitting in a hot tub during a pandemic and John explained that COVID-19 was not a problem in Arizona because of all the UV light in the desert. The statistics I saw didn't seem to support his assessment.

Karen and I spent January 6, 2021, in our trailer, watching the insurrection on a laptop, not sure how the others in the RV park would respond to the violence we saw on our screen. We felt cautious and vulnerable, yet determined to find connections.

61

Journey to the border

We worked our way along our country's southern border, getting close to the line as we explored from Yuma west toward Calexico and then relocated farther east to Sonoita, near Nogales.

We listened to audiobooks as we traveled. We chose titles to help us understand the history and politics of an area. *The Death of Josseline* by Margaret Regan contained essays about the border, including the story of Josseline, a 14-year-old immigrant from El Salvador who died in 2008 on her journey across the border to be reunited with family. She fell ill in the desert and was left behind by her group just north of the line.

It felt ominous to stand next to the wall. To look through the slats and wonder if I might see someone on the other side. To know that I could cross at a checkpoint as I wished, but someone who lived south of the line could not do the same. Signs on the border wall said to stay back 100 feet, but I wanted a better picture. I approached a border patrol agent in an SUV to ask if I could go closer, and he said, "Do what you want. Those signs aren't meant for you."

At times I could see a half dozen or more border patrol vehicles from where I stood, observing the frontier. Some of them moved out of sight when they saw me photographing. One female agent waved and mugged for the camera. As I walked by her vehicle she laughed and said, "Sorry, you get a little stir-crazy out here on the long shifts."

The character of the wall changed, from bollard posts to steel plating to wire mesh topped with concertina wire. It stretched out to the horizon and beyond.

Random border checks were set up along the highways. They were not always staffed but even when they were, I was never stopped. They just waved me through.

Gary Paul Nabhan is an ecumenical Franciscan brother who does cross-cultural collaborations for environmental and social justice. He is known as a pioneer in the local food movement and has led the effort to save heirloom seeds. An Arab American, he has a great love for arid environments and lives in the desert overlooking the Santa Cruz River Valley near Patagonia, Arizona. The Santa Cruz is a binational river near the United States–Mexico border and supports a rich diversity of plants and animals as well as human cultural life.

The most radical thing we can do is to listen to one another. Let our hearts be touched by people who we once perceived as the other. When we listen, love emerges and that is transformed into compassion for people unlike ourselves. We find that they're more like us in values than we originally imagined, though they may talk, dance, and sing differently than we do.

One of the great academic discoveries of the last 20 years was right before our eyes all along. The places with the richest diversity of wildlife and plants on this planet often are the places where there's also the highest cultural and linguistic diversity. Where there's the greatest human upheavals, it's almost a perfect match of where we have the highest number of endangered species. Where we lack cultures who have long tenure on the land and understand the dynamics of the plants and animals around them.

Indigenous cultures have learned from their mistakes and encoded stewardship messages in all their stories and songs and prayers. The question for me is, how do we support the Indigenous caretakers who are still paying attention to what my friend calls the original operating instructions for caring for this continent?

I'm not Native American, but they respect my Arab roots. They find it fascinating to deal with someone from another desert culture. We found common ground, what Wallace Stegner calls "the angle of repose," where we lean into each other. That's what we all need to find with people who grew up differently than us. We know we're losing a lot of that [knowledge], and it's not going to be top down solutions that take care of all of it. We need to have cultural caretakers in place that are respected by federal and state agencies, by international treaties, and other mechanisms for doing the work that they and their ancestors have always done.

"I have such respect for people who are meeting daunting challenges with humor, love, and determination rather than giving up. We have to buoy each other up so that the whole world floats to a higher level."

—Gary Nabhan

Tony Sedgwick is president of the board of directors for the Santa Fe Ranch Foundation, a working cattle ranch near Nogales, Arizona, located just a few miles north of the U.S. border with Mexico. With a background in international business law, Tony says that in his lifetime the policies and economics of the borderlands have shifted away from development and infrastructure and toward fear and protectionism.

9/11 caused a wave of fear and isolationism in the United States. That wave rippled out and crashed on us here on the border. Americans [thought] that Mexico had become an unsafe place. America turned inward.

The Bible says a nation is judged by how it treats its widows and orphans. And the dudes that were writing that stuff were desert people. They understood that to be a widow or an orphan in a desert community is death. Family is all that matters in a desert community because you take care of each other, and if you don't have family, you're screwed.

How do we take care of the people who are screwed? That's how we're judged. We're not judged by God, a white guy with a beard. We're judged by the consequences to our own society.

One of the things that we suffer from in this overpopulated world is a sense of helplessness. We have a sense that we can't change things, that we can't make life better. And that is absolute bullshit. We can not only make our lives better, we can make the lives of those around us better. It takes a little effort. It takes some concern. The average American spends four hours a day watching television. If you just give up one of those hours to help people around you, you will make a difference.

Do something for your neighbor. Do something for a person that cannot give back. This is what our country stands for. Just by turning and helping the person next to you, that will change us. That's who we have always been as Americans.

"Happiness is awesome. In our country we have enshrined its pursuit in our constitution. It's right there with life and liberty. It's a big deal. And happiness comes from sharing. Happiness comes from caring. It comes from reaching out your hand."
—Tony Sedgwick

> "I don't want to be rescued at the hands of the police from the job that I'm consenting to do. I would argue that sex work is not the problem and never has been. The problem is misogyny, the patriarchy, capitalism, and domestic violence."
>
> —Natalie Brewster Nguyen

Natalie Brewster Nguyen is an artist, mother, social justice advocate, business owner, writer, and a sex worker who lives in Tucson, Arizona. She works to organize for safety and basic human rights for sex workers who suffer violence and theft of services, but cannot go to the police for protection for fear of being arrested.

I don't believe that punishment is an effective teaching tool. As a dominatrix that uses punishment in my work, I am slowly working on a book called *Blue Whale: Parenting Hacks from a Dominatrix* to [explore] punishment.

Punishment is not an effective way to parent. The words blue whale come directly from BDSM culture. When you have a negotiated BDSM scene, you have something called a safe word. And a safe word means we can be in roles and the person who's being punished can be like, "No, no, please don't hurt me. Oh my God. Stop." You're allowed to say that, and I'm not going to stop because that's part of our role play. But if you say our safe word—which could be fuzzy purple kittens or whatever it is—then I know that you need me to stop the scene. It's an out-of-context word that communicates something immediately. That's a negotiation around consent that happens with just about every interaction. We agree on it ahead of time. These are our limits.

So I took that ideology directly into parenting and co-created a safe word for my kids, which ended up being blue whale. We've used the safe word idea in our family since they were tiny. And it's used in both directions: the parents can use it or the kids can use it, and they still do to this day. They're teenagers now, and it's been one of the most effective parenting tools I've ever had.

They respect it. So it's not like any time you're putting any pressure on them, they're tossing out blue whale. They use it with each other in ways that's really heartening to see. It's a way of them being able to wrestle, tickle, push each other's boundaries, and then know that there's this way to say stop. This is our way of creating a consent boundary.

"The relationship between enforcement and migrants is eternal. As long as we've had written documentation, people have been doing two things: forming borders and moving."
—Christopher Montoya

Christopher Montoya was a border patrol agent in Arizona for 21 years until he retired in 2017. He wrote a controversial op-ed piece for the *Arizona Daily Star* in December 2018 refuting narratives that "characterize the U.S.–Mexico border as a 'very dangerous' place for law enforcement." As a graduate student at the University of Arizona, he researched statistics and data from local, state, and federal agencies, and found that "border patrol agents enjoy one of the safest law enforcement jobs in America." Chris supported that assessment with his own personal experience, saying that although he encountered and apprehended migrants on a daily basis, he was never assaulted during his 21 years of service.

We were on the border at night, walking right along the border in Douglas [Arizona] and all of a sudden rocks are flying over the fence. Big rocks. At your head. So what do you do? You have choices. You can run to the fence and start shooting into Mexico, you can stand there and get hit in the face with a rock, or you can back up.

It was common practice. Our senior agents at the station said, "If you take two steps back, you're going to be fine." It's true that throwing rocks at agents has hurt agents before. It's rare, but it's happened. My approach to discerning this idea of a violent border is looking at the hard evidence. And the evidence [says] that it's exceedingly rare. But [when] my op-ed came out, people were pissed off. They didn't like what I said. And I get it.

Data and statistics, you can't refute them, but they under-represent somebody's lived experience. It's subjective. If I tell a border patrol agent [who got hit by a rock] the results of my study, he's going to tell me I'm full of shit. If I tell a person at the university, I'm going to get a standing ovation. That's where I'm trying to live—in that gray area—because that's the hardest place to live in the world.

I talked to one migrant and he said, "I'm going to Bakersfield and picking whatever you guys won't do for that wage." We've got these huge corporations in central California that will knowingly hire illegals. In a purely capitalist endeavor, that's what you want, cheap labor. I don't fault the capitalist or the migrant. It's an exchange. They're both complicit. It's a symbiotic relationship.

[But] when there's a raid on the farm—say the owner is at home, he's playing golf, whatever—he's fine. It's the poor illegal that's going to get deported. So that's part of the hypocrisy that you have to at least think about. It's a paradox, right? It's extremely complicated. It's human stuff. It boils down to economics.

> "Domestic violence is not about being female or male. It's not about sex. It's about power and control."
> —Blanca Acosta

Blanca Acosta is executive director for Circles of Peace, a restorative justice organization in Nogales, Arizona, that offers mediation and healing for domestic violence offenders and their victims. While the traditional criminal justice model seeks to punish crimes, the restorative justice model asks what harm has been created by a crime and seeks to repair that harm.

A lot of victims decide to stay with the offender. Those victims, when we interviewed them, said, "I don't want to leave him. I just want the violence to stop." There's a lot of things we can mention about why the victim stays but, in the end, it's her decision. When you're in the circle, you're offering a safe space for victims to talk about how they feel and the harm caused to them. And that's the beauty of the circle. That's the beauty of restorative justice.

You have to become more resilient and become the person that can control your own life instead of giving that power [away] to another person. I'm in control of who I am instead. That's how we empower victims during the circle. [Don't] let what happened to you change who you are, but use it in a way that you can become resilient.

We bring three distinct, important pieces into the circle: the crime that has been committed, the person who committed the crime, and the victim. And then we bring the community into the circle. The community member is a trained person who is able to express how the crime—even if it was inside a home—is affecting the whole community and how it's affecting the children who live in the house.

The crime is there. We are not changing that, but how can we restore that individual to believe in themselves and be placed back into the community with a different perception, with a different perspective, and with a different behavior? That, to me, is restorative. Yes, you're gonna be accountable for what you did, and I hope that you can ask for that forgiveness and make real changes in your life.

Sebastian Quinac immigrated from Guatemala in his 20s to flee the civil war and threats to his life. After spending time in California and New York, he settled in Tucson, Arizona, where he has lived for the past two decades. Sebastian is now a U.S. citizen and works with the Guatemalan consulate to help migrant families navigate the American immigration system. While he is happy with the life he has built in this country, he also carries the sorrow that much of his family remains and suffers in Guatemala.

I've been working with the Guatemalan consulate [to help] families, because they did not know what to do when they had a piece of paper from the border patrol. Sitting with individuals, calling their families, helping them understand what the paper says, especially when they have their appointment for a hearing. A lot of families, especially the Mayan from Guatemala, don't speak Spanish. They understood that here is your paper, now you are okay. And they thought, "Well, okay, already we are legal. We don't have to go to court."

Besides helping to understand their rights and their responsibility to go to court, I also tell them what to do and what they shouldn't do. We call their family to let them know they are with border patrol and what will happen with them.

When they are told by ICE, "You cannot come in five years," a lot of them [thought], "I finished my five years in Guatemala, I'm here again." They did not understand that after staying five years in their country, they have to go to the U.S. embassy to get the visa. No one explained to them that process.

The [Guatemalan] minister of exterior [created] different kinds of booklets, and videos to educate the community about how dangerous it is to cross the border. But when I interview my people at the border, some of them say, "I want to come back. If I die in the desert, that's fine for me. It's better to die there than be kidnapped, tortured, and killed in my village."

> "One of my friends said, 'If you go back to Guatemala, I'm sure you will be killed. If you stay here, you will educate the gringos to tell them what's going on in your country.' So I stayed. I learned English. And any time I see migrants cross and cry, with blisters on their feet, I feel I need to be with them because I know the journey."
>
> —Sebastian Quinac

01.19.2021: Journey across the border

The day didn't go quite the way I had planned. India Aubry of Voices from the Border agreed to take me into Nogales, Sonora, Mexico to interview Pancho, a street nurse she worked with who cares for migrants waiting south of the border for their asylum hearings to gain entry into the United States.

Our plan was to meet Pancho at one of the migrant shelters to see his work and meet with some of the travelers.

We drove through the Mariposa crossing on the west side of town, and it took a little longer than expected. The immigration official lingered as he looked through my camera gear. I heard India say the word journalist. The man called over a colleague. Then another. They talked amongst themselves. They said we needed a permit. With some broad hand gestures and my woeful Spanish, we thought we understood where to get the permit, but somehow wound up on a toll road heading straight south instead.

India talked with Pancho on a bad cell connection. We couldn't get there from here. I drove on until we reached a toll booth where we could turn around, head back to the United States, and regroup. It was the shortest trip to Mexico I had ever made, but we had burned up almost two hours of our afternoon. We were running out of time to visit the migrant shelter, but I still wanted the interview.

Pancho suggested we try the DeConcini crossing and he would park just a block away from the gate in his ambulance. We could sit inside, masked, and be out of the dusty wind. We walked across the border this time. No inspection of the camera bag. No permit required. We sat in Pancho's ambulance, parked next to the wall, talking about his work with people who longed to get to the other side.

As we finished the interview and stepped out of the vehicle, a crowd marched down the street toward us. They held signs. They chanted. Pancho

70

explained it was a migrant protest. We hadn't made it to the shelter, but the migrants had made it to us.

"Can we go look?" I asked.

"You are free here," Pancho replied. "They want you to see them. They want you to take their pictures."

It was Tuesday, January 19, the day before Joe Biden's inauguration, and the migrants wanted to send a message. They held signs announcing how many days they had been waiting for an asylum hearing to enter the United States. 320 days. 409 days. 425. 511. 706 days and still waiting.

We followed the protesters down the road and along the border wall. Pancho knew several of the migrants in the protest and we had a few moments to talk, to hear their stories, to take their portraits.

The wall on the American side was blank, raw metal. Dark rusted slats jutting toward the sky, concertina wire circling the tops. Stark and functional. Institutional. On the southern side, the rigid lines were softened by art. Graffiti. Protest messages. Wooden crosses leaned against the metal. Sculptures challenged the foreboding structure and the institutions that had built it.

"Our dream of justice," one message read, "No wall can stop it."

It all unfolded quickly, and then it was time to go. India and I walked back to the gate. The return line was short, but slow. A woman with her young daughter pleaded for entry, but she was told they had the wrong papers. There were tears. Distress and confusion. I thought about my own (much smaller) challenge at the Mariposa crossing, trying to navigate a system I didn't know, through a language I didn't understand. The little bit of this woman's story I could gather, her husband was in the United States. She had visited before. She had always used these papers but for some reason today, they didn't seem to work.

We held up our passports and passed through the turnstile with a wave and a nod. The woman and her daughter did not.

We went to the U.S. side of the wall, opposite of where the ambulance had parked, to look for Pancho and say a last farewell, but he had gone. Our crossing had taken too long. And then, as we stood there, a teenage boy approached the wall and called through to the other side. A teenage girl appeared and they both pressed up to the wire grate between the posts to visit. It was casual. Familiar.

"Girlfriend?" I asked. "Sister?"

"Cousin," the boy replied.

"Can I take a few pictures of your visit?" I asked and held up my camera at the same time.

"Sure."

I gave them my email and told them if they sent me a message I would share the image.

Each face a story. A human. A drama in the midst of unfolding. What a difference a human line drawn on the ground can make. What a disparity the geography of your birth can impose.

"One of our goals is that they have human dignity. Not to let them lose their hope."
—Francisco Olachea "Pancho" Martin

Francisco Olachea "Pancho" Martin returned to school when he was 48 and graduated with a nursing degree when he was 54. He is a street nurse in Nogales, Sonora, Mexico, and works with Voices from the Border to support migrants with medical needs as they wait for their asylum hearings on the Mexican side of our southern border.

When I started [working] with the migrants, there was so much discrimination. Even the authorities here, they used to tell me, "You shouldn't be doing that." And I said, "Well, why aren't you doing it? You don't want me to do it, but you don't want to do it either."

What's the point? You just don't like these people? That's fine. I don't mind. So, I said, "Okay, I'll [become a nurse] as fast as I can, no matter how long it takes." It took four years to graduate.

Every time I heard somebody say something negative, I said, "Look, I got my horse [blinders] on. I can only see forward." We don't wait. We're just changing their moment. I mean, I made it and I had all the odds against me.

No matter how big the trouble is, just try to find a solution to a problem and you'll have peace. You grieve the problem, you yell at the problem, then you accept you have a problem. Then you find the solution to the problem, and you work on it until you solve it. That's the best peace.

Juanita Molina is executive director for Border Action Network in Tucson, Arizona. Throughout her career she has advocated for LGBTQ+ communities and offered support to people with HIV/AIDS and terminal cancer, as well as people who are experiencing domestic abuse and sexual assault. Her current role allows her to work for the rights of immigrants and, while she often is responsible for holding immigration enforcement agencies and government officials accountable, she also serves as a bridge between activists and the law enforcement community.

People look at [Border Action Network] as radical because we talk about the issues. We're working directly with affected communities. People see us as radical because we participate in radical acceptance. Sometimes in society, you want to have innocent victims. You want a victim to be a certain kind of person. We're here to protect everyone's rights.

There was a group of kids running marijuana across the border. One of the kids was trying to evade border patrol and border patrol shot him eight times in the back. This young man fell off the border wall and he died. Everything about that whole process—the crime scene, the way that his body was treated—lacked dignity, respect, and process. People say, "You're accompanying the family of a known drug dealer." We get a lot of flack and a lot of hate mail and sometimes threats around it. The reality is, that was a poor process.

We like to blame the victim. If we can assign some level of blame, then it creates a different little pocket of information for us. "She was raped because she wore that dress." Or "she went out late at night." Or "she didn't know her husband well enough before she married him."

There is a high incidence of death in migration, because of all the vulnerable factors of malnutrition, extreme weather conditions, physical movement, all of these different things. These situations are so extreme, people can't imagine. I've heard a thousand times talking to thousands of migrants through the years: "I'd rather die trying."

We will stand with people throughout, whatever their identity is. People aren't perfect. But that does not shape their validity in this world, their worth in this world, their contribution to this world.

> "There are so many people that we [choose] not to see, and the migrant community that comes through this part of the world is one that is not seen."
>
> —Juanita Molina

01.28.2021: At the wall on the day construction stopped

The Biden administration had just stopped construction of the wall. It was a political lightning rod and just a matter of time before the new administration halted it.

I'd been trying to figure out where the construction activity was and, finally, one of my leads panned out with a phone call from an activist. I scribbled directions on the back of an envelope. The landscape east of Nogales was rugged. A web of gravel paths and dirt trails followed along the wall, some of them navigable and others washed out.

Karen and I worked our way east, made a few wrong turns and finally followed a path that looked like it had seen heavy equipment recently. We crested a ridge and could see the wall, and then the place where it changed from a 30-foot steel barrier to a 5-strand barbed wire fence.

One lone contractor stood watch over the idled equipment. "What's up?" he asked as we pulled up. "Just taking a look," I replied. "We live up north and have seen so much in the headlines about it. Just wanted to see it for ourselves." "Alright, watch your step," he said and waved us on.

The wall stretched to the western horizon. To the east, bulldozers had opened a broad gash through the desert. Piles of construction materials lined the road. Nobody else was around.

I stood next to the barbed wire fence and stretched my arm across it into Mexico. I took photos of the surreal scene and tried to wrap my mind around the historical significance of this moment in this place.

Suddenly the man who waved us past pulled up in his truck. "That's a pretty nice camera," he said, and I prepared to get kicked out or at least hassled. "Artist," I said, and shrugged. That word is less worrisome than journalist to most.

But he just wanted to talk. Eventually, he drove off and again we were alone at the frontier. It was getting late. It was a rough drive back to town and we wanted to navigate it before nightfall. We stood for a little longer under the big sky. A historic location on a historic day. All alone.

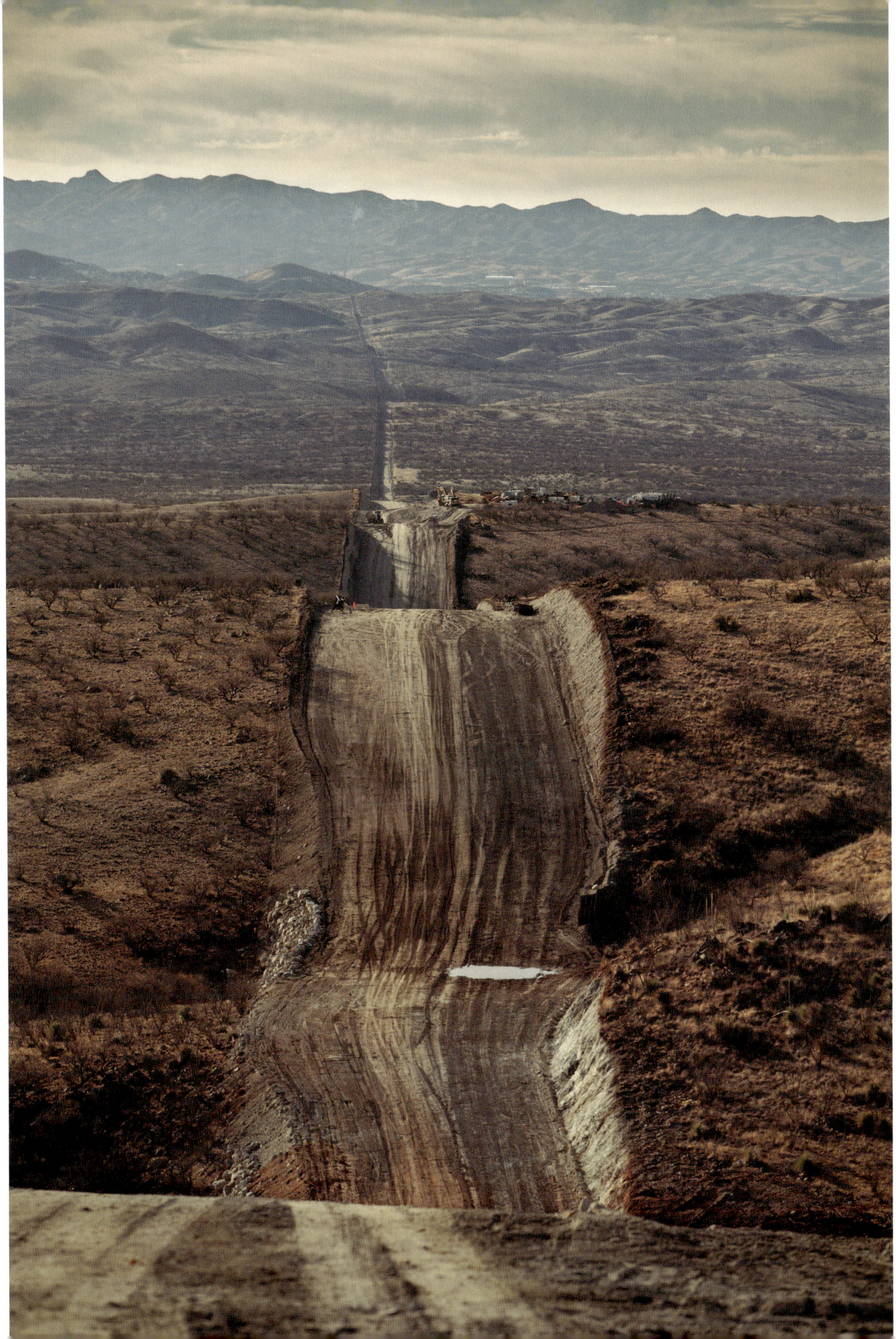

Alvaro Enciso has been placing crosses in the Sonoran Desert for seven years to mark the sites where migrants have died on their journey into the United States. He says his goal is to make the invisible visible, to honor the lives lost, and to draw attention to the policies that lead to unnecessary deaths. A Colombian immigrant who came to the United States in the 1960s, Alvaro finds that his art project connects him to his own migration and heritage. He has found that the experience of going weekly into the desert and honoring the dead has increased his sense of compassion and connected him more deeply to his own humanity.

I came looking for the American dream, like everybody else. An opportunity to be somebody. To find a future that looks a little bit brighter than back home. For years, I wanted to connect in some way with my roots. Because despite all the time that I've been here, I'm still a Hispanic man and people always remind me of that. They don't want me to forget that I'm a pseudo gringo. And somehow you get this idea that you are an outsider and that you don't belong here, even though I've spent most of my life here.

I wanted to find a way to connect with my own migration, to be one of them. I started hiking to the sites where a body had been found. I went to stand

> "The Sonoran Desert is beautiful. People come from all over the world to photograph it, to spend time there, to hike, but this beautiful landscape has a secret. Inside this lovely land, people are dying every day. People are being arrested. People are being treated badly. And no one seems to know that."
> —Alvaro Enciso

there and see if there was anything there, a vestige of what happened, the suffering and the disappointment and the failure. I will go sometimes by myself and just go flat on the ground, hoping to find some epiphany or some sort of revelation.

The cross connects a lot of things. It's a symbol of death, finality. The Catholics appropriated the cross from the Roman empire. The Romans used to make crosses to kill people. Common criminals, enemies of the empire, false prophets. They hang them for three or four days without any water under the sun until they died. Which is exactly what is happening here.

So the cross [made] sense, but I didn't want to be seen as some kind of Christian fanatic putting crosses out there. So I decided that this cross didn't have any Christianity in it. It was nothing more than a geometric equation. The vertical line means that you're still alive. The horizontal line means that you're dead. And where those two lines meet, that's where the tragedy took place. The story of David and Goliath. In this case, Goliath always wins, because the poor person from Mexico or from Guatemala cannot compete with all the technology and all the hate, so he or she always loses at that encounter.

"Meet us in Amado," he said. "By the big cow horns. You'll see."

Karen and I left our campground before the sun came up to meet Alvaro. It had snowed the night before and the roads were slow and icy.

Alvaro has a map marking the location of more than 3,000 sites where migrants' remains have been found in the Sonoran Desert. Through the years, he has placed nearly 1,000 crosses at those sites to commemorate the lives lost.

Until that day, I had known the name of precisely one immigrant who had died in the desert. Josseline Jamileth Hernandez Quinteros, a 14-year-old girl from El Salvador who was the subject of *The Death of Josseline*, a book we had just finished.

Alvaro puts up crosses in the desert every Tuesday. When he invited us to join him, I asked, "Where will you be going?" and he replied, "We are going to put up a cross for a little girl named Josseline."

We met at the giant cow horns, as planned: Alvaro, a few Tucson Samaritans, and a PhD student who was documenting the sites of migrant deaths.

As we drove out toward the small town of Arivaca, we stopped at an intersection to meet one more Samaritan. Two border patrol vehicles were parked by the side of the road, with two migrants in the back of the truck.

"There were twelve," the border patrol explained. "They scattered when they saw us, but these two gave up." They were cold. They had slept outside in the snow, on the ground, the night before. I made eye contact and gave a nod. I had nothing else to offer but a moment of humanity.

It was late January when Josseline died on her journey and the temperature had dropped to near freezing. The night these two migrant men had just experienced had been even colder.

"Probably some people died last night," Alvaro said.

The roads were too slick that day to travel the rugged route to Cedar Canyon where Josseline's body had been found. So we visited three sites that were closer to a navigable road.

The process was simple and quiet. Identify the location with GPS coordinates. Dig a small hole. Dump a bit of concrete mix and water into the hole and stand the cross up straight. Pack in some dirt. Pile rocks at the base. And then Alvaro took a picture to document it.

One of the Samaritans sprinkled sage at the base of the cross. Others looked out across the forbidding landscape, lost in thought. I took photos and stood quietly, bearing witness to a simple gesture of humanity.

"They die of cold in the winter," Alvaro said, "and they die of heat in the summer."

I was trying to imagine what would push me to take such an immense risk when Alvaro added, "They died trying."

Karen and I stayed another week. We met the small group again and drove the rugged tracks back toward Cedar Canyon.

The Samaritans stashed plastic gallon jugs of water along the trail and we walked back to the wash where Josseline's body was found. She died trying to get to her mother in Los Angeles. Had she lived, she would have been the same age as our son, Jordan.

As the border wall was built in some of the urban centers, it pushed migration routes farther into the wilderness and into more deadly conditions. "They used the desert as a weapon," Alvaro explained. "They thought the harsh terrain would be a deterrent, but they didn't consider the determination of desperate people."

We stood under the vast desert sky. Quiet. There was nothing remarkable about that particular corner of wilderness. But it was the spot where Josseline's journey had ended thirteen years ago, a young girl alone in the desert, on her way to meet her mom. Josseline Jamileth Hernandez Quinteros was the one name I knew who had been lost in the human story that unfolds every day along the border. It felt important to be there.

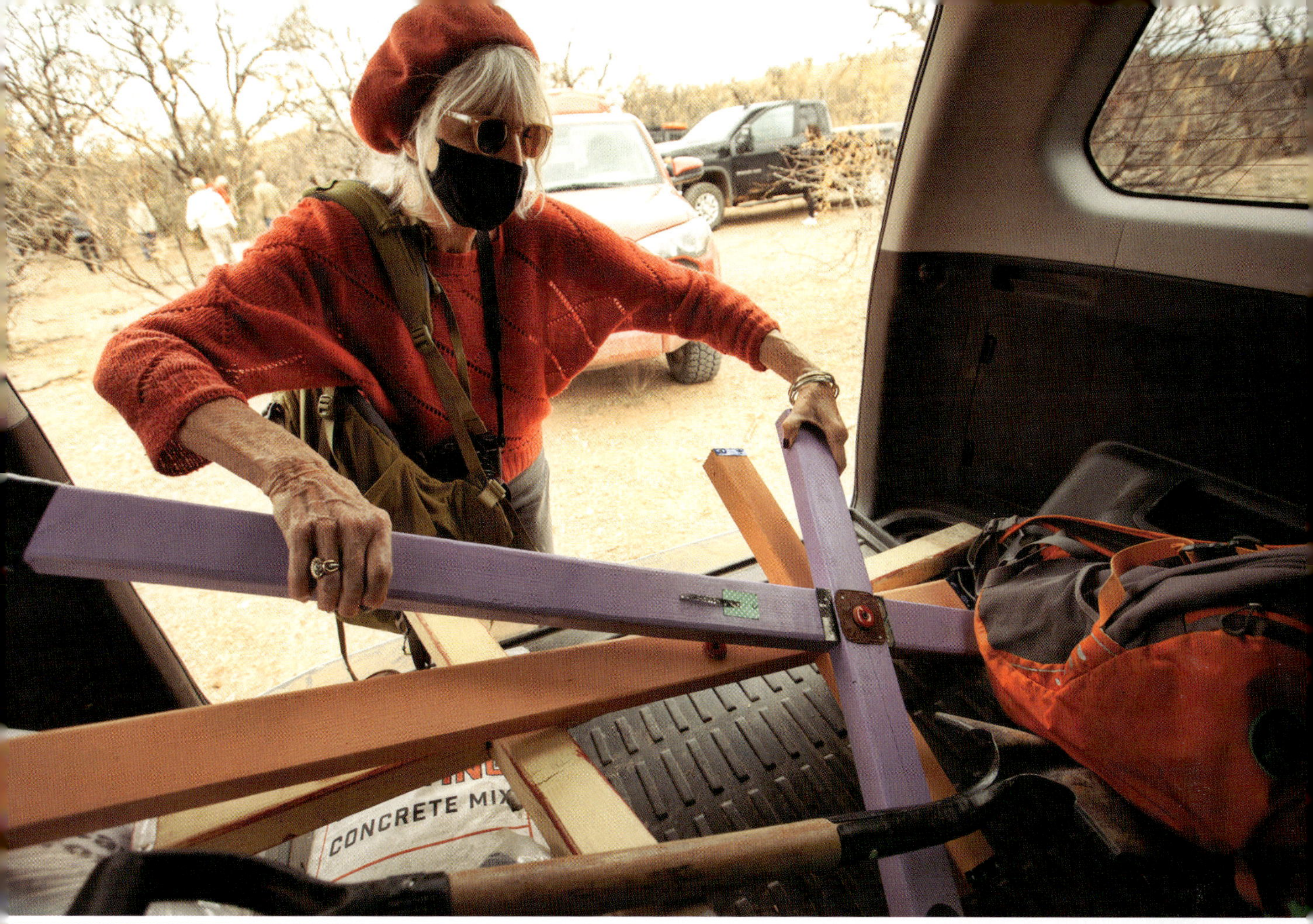
CONCRETE MIX

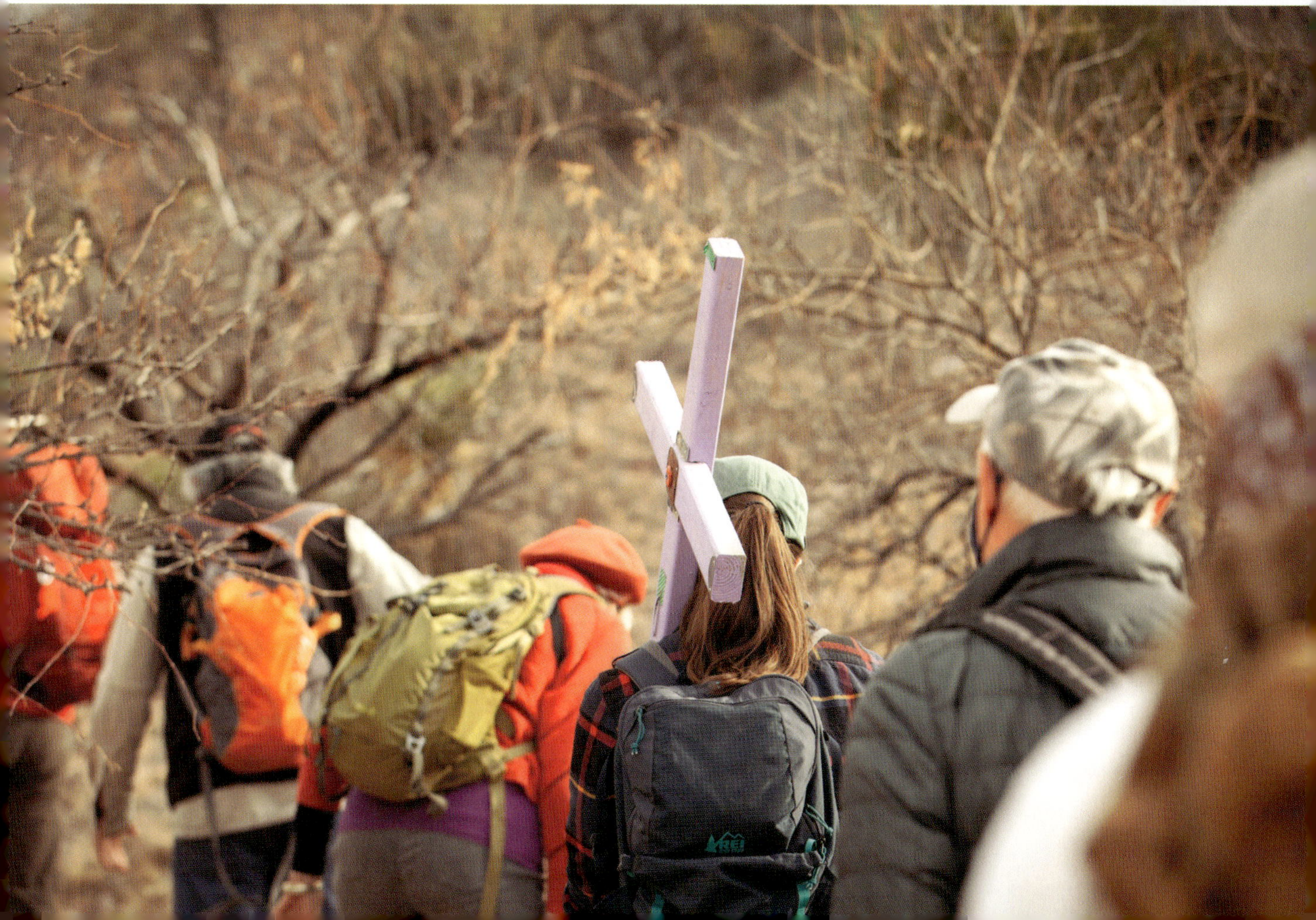

Hard to leave a place

Our pace was slow but our schedule still kept us moving. It was time to leave the border, but after just a few weeks, I felt bound to this place. I'd fallen in love with the landscape. The people. The immediacy of the issues and the tangible need.

We'd only just scratched the surface and our work was incomplete. I could get lost in this borderland forever and never exhaust the stories and complexities of immigration. But if I did that—if I lingered too long—other stories would go untold.

And so with some clarity, I could see the developing rhythm that would haunt me for the remainder of our journey. Arrive at a new location. Fall in love quickly. Leave too soon. Mourn the loss of it. Repeat.

There is a cost to caring. But perhaps the cost is even greater if you don't care at all.

We spent a week in Sedona. Red rock and crystals. Hiking with friends. When it was time to head across Texas on our way to Louisiana, the Lone Star State experienced an epic ice storm that disrupted the power grid and shut down travel. It shut down everything. We called ahead to find a campsite in central Texas and they all said the same thing. "Don't come." So we found a home at the El Paso Roadrunner RV Park. It was really just a gravel lot beside the freeway, down the road from the Walmart, but they had power and we booked the last site available.

We were eager to move on, but the universe had other plans.

02.17.2021: El Paso memorial

On August 3, 2019, a gunman targeted Latinos and immigrants in an El Paso Walmart, killing 23 people. An inscription at the memorial and monument in the parking lot says this:

"Grand Candella
Dedicated to the people of El Paso, may this memorial stand as a solemn tribute to those who lost their lives on August 3, 2019, be a beacon of hope for the survivors, and a lasting reminder to all of the enduring strength, resiliency, and love that unites El Paso.

Envisioned by the Cielo Vista Walmart associates and inspired by the significance of candles, the memorial is comprised of 22 individually lit perforated aluminum arcs bound together to form a 'Grand Candella.' Standing 30 feet tall and radiating a nightly glow, the light transcends borders and connects our hearts as one community."

I've visited too many of these memorials. Each one individually is a tragedy. Collectively, they are an indictment of who we have become.

Journey to Louisiana

After almost a week, we moved toward Louisiana with uncertainty. Texas was still reeling from the storm. Many gas stations were closed. There was a tenuous promise of interview connections at our next stop, but not much more. We weighed our options. We considered our alternatives. "Let's go, and believe that things will work out."

We made reservations at a campground called Swampman RV Paradise in Dulac, Louisiana. Promising. If you take a distant view of Louisiana, most of what's south and west of New Orleans looks like water. But zoom in a little and you'll find a lattice of low-lying land. Bridges, canals, levees, islands, bayous, and houses on stilts.

Swampman had been a site for FEMA trailers after Hurricane Katrina devastated the area in 2005. Some of those trailers were still there, still occupied by people who were never able to rebuild.

Louisiana has been ravaged by a dozen hurricanes since Katrina. Even before things are completely rebuilt and cleaned up from one storm, another storm hits. There were signs of it everywhere. Debris in the water, insulation snagged in tree branches, twisted metal pole sheds, blue tarps over rooftops.

Our arrival in Dulac coincided with the peak of black gnat season. They swarmed. They bit. They snuck in through screens. It would take a little time and effort to fall in love with the bayou. But our campsite was right on the water. Shrimp boats lined the channel. And we were ready to try.

Joey (the Swampman, I think) was kind and accommodating. His dad, Joe, dropped off frozen shrimp to use as bait for fishing in the bayou. Joey had a warm smile. Joe liked to talk. And against all expectations, Swampman RV Paradise had the best Wi-Fi we had encountered since selling our house. We paid in advance and planned to stay for three weeks.

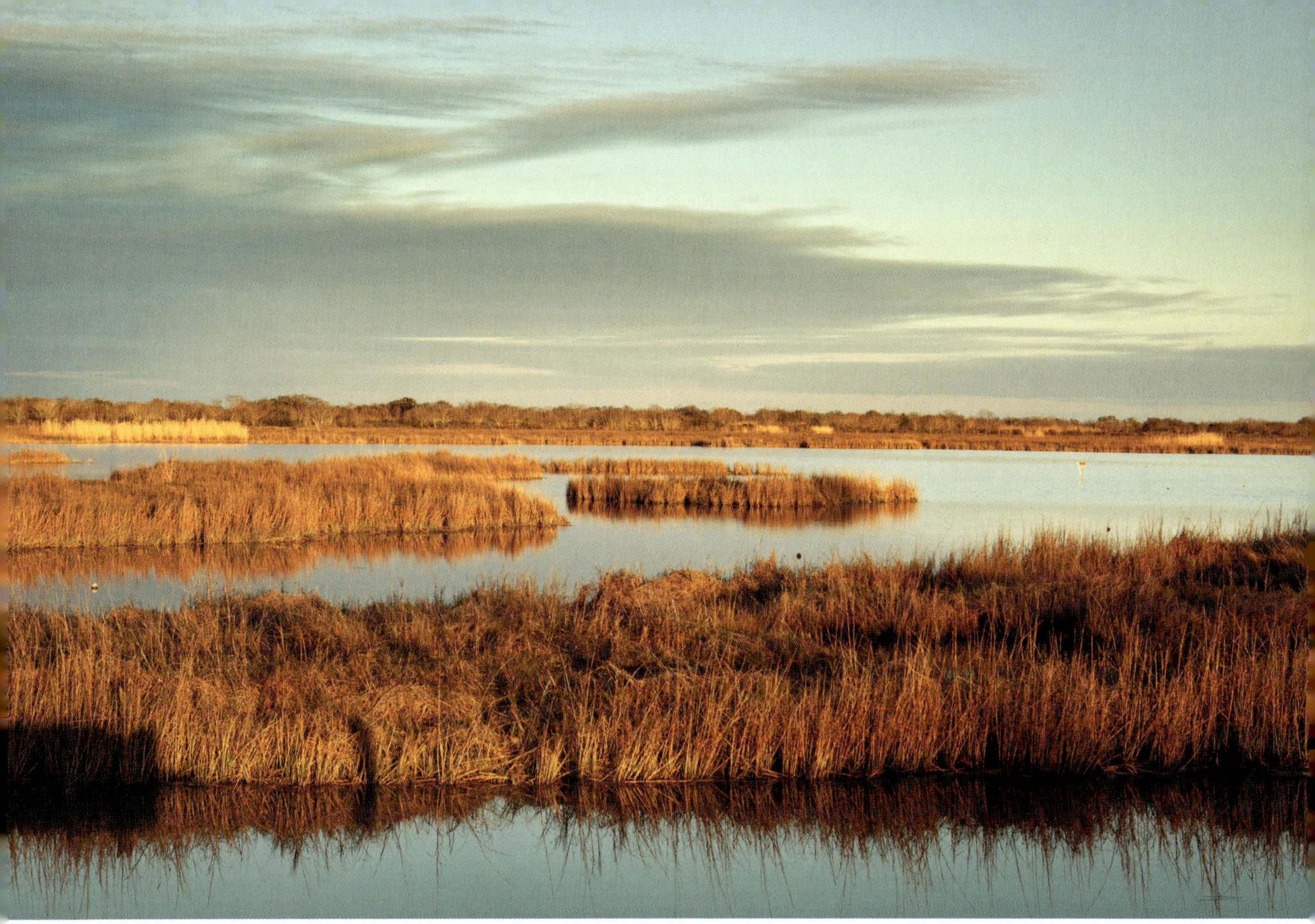

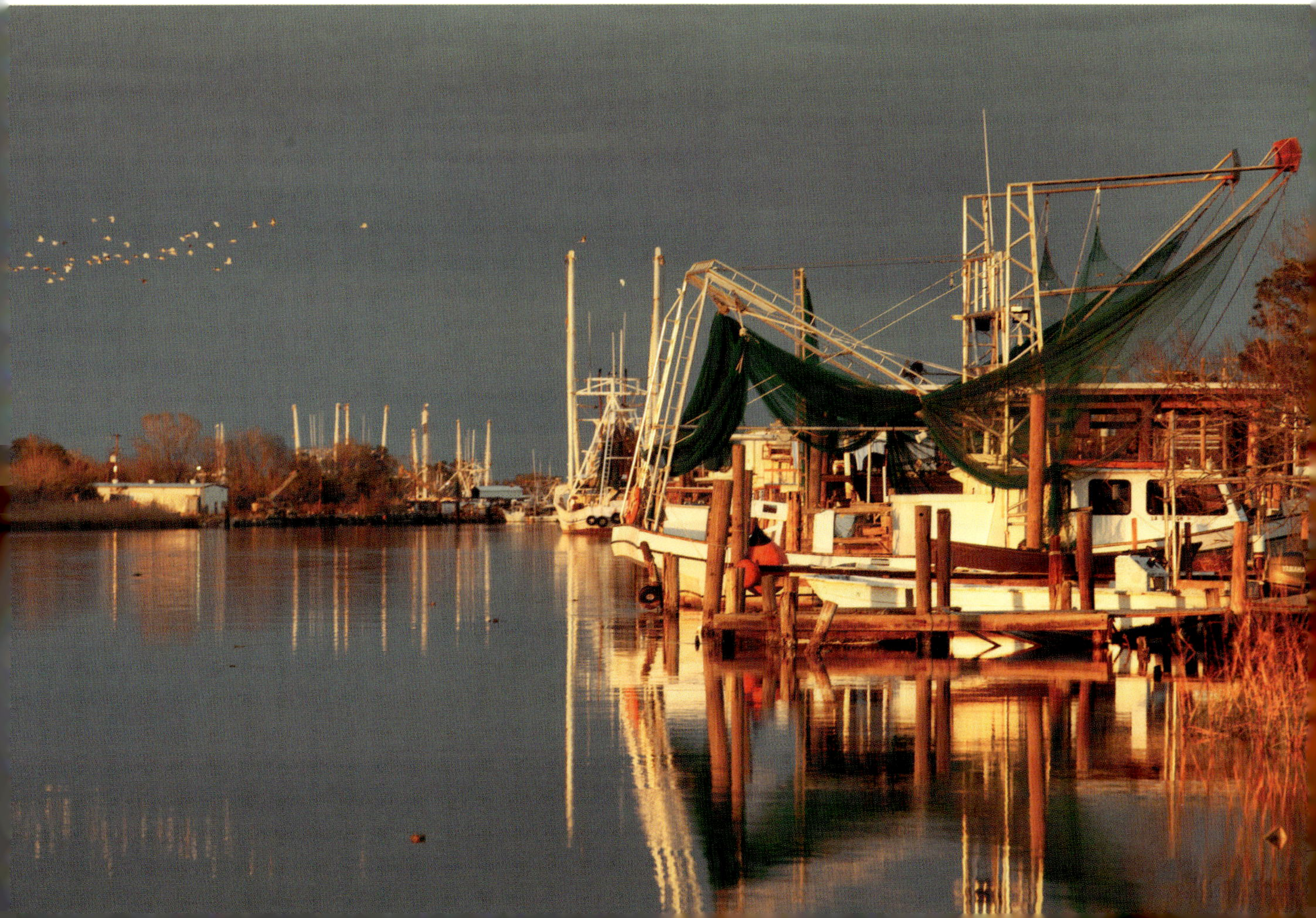

Journey into the bayou

The watery land south of New Orleans was originally inhabited by several Indigenous tribes who were joined by others when they fled forced relocation during the Trail of Tears in the 1830s, leading to a diverse mix of cultures today, including Houma, Choctaw, Chitimacha, Biloxi, and others.

Historically, most tribes lived lightly on the land, and as storms and floods inundated and reshaped the delta and the bayous, the tribes would relocate and adapt to the shifting landscape. That resilience and flexibility was restricted as colonial and European notions of land ownership were imposed on the delta. Parcels were sold, owned, and fixed on the register. As individuals developed that land, they also wanted to protect it.

So when the Mississippi River flood of 1927 rolled through and left massive destruction of personal property in its wake, the European settlers said, "Never again!" and a system of levees and flood gates were developed to tame the river.

It worked. The regular cycles of flooding ended and along with it, the natural rhythms of the river. However, the floods had also brought nourishing silt. The floods wiped out land in some places but built it up in others.

About that same time, oil was discovered in the Gulf and the technology quickly developed to extract it with off-shore platforms. In the process, 10,000 miles of pipeline canals and shipping channels were dug through the marshlands and estuaries that had previously served as a buffer to the biggest storms and absorbed some of their fury before they reached the mainland.

It turns out that was an ecological miscalculation and it has led to one of the largest environmental disasters of our history. The new channels let in the saltwater from the Gulf and that saltwater intrusion killed off native vegetation. The plants died, the roots let go of the fragile soil, and the next time a storm came ashore, the land simply washed away.

Humans doubled down on engineering. More levees, more floodgates. The buildings that couldn't be walled in by that infrastructure were raised up on stilts. But some simple truths remain: the land is sinking and much of it is below sea level. The storms are getting bigger. The floods are more punishing. A new disaster batters the coast before recovery from the previous one is complete.

Chief Albert Naquin, who I interviewed, has resigned himself to telling his people to leave. Just get out. They are fighting a losing battle.

But with the loss of homes comes the loss of culture. The loss of connection. Some members, he said, were afraid that if they left their lands, rich white folks would build expensive fishing camps in their place and only then get the protection of levees. It's a fear that is rooted in experience.

The floodgates can be closed to protect communities when a hurricane or a storm surge from high winds approaches. But when the floodgates are closed, the fleets of fishing boats can't come and go. Last year, some floodgates were closed for a total of 100 days. It saved homes but devastated the local fishing economy.

There are plans to divert some natural river flow to again deliver fresh water and silt to the bayous and help reduce some of the land loss. But for generations now, shrimpers and oyster fishers have been relying on the brackish waters of the altered landscape. Pump in more fresh water to support natural cycles and you might restore the land, but you also risk pushing those fishers another 100 miles offshore to find their catch. That turns into extra time and requires extra money for fuel in an industry that often lives a tenuous existence as it is.

Tribes have established culture camps to try to preserve traditional ways. They discuss how to help people stay. And even as many people leave, others are still arriving. Immigrants from Vietnam, Honduras, and other coastal cultures find something familiar in the landscape.

Plans are in place to rebuild barrier islands. To install locks with the floodgates that would allow fishing boats to pass even when the gates are closed. There are grants available for more fuel-efficient boat engines to offset the movement of fisheries farther offshore. Talk of building schools on floating barges that can be pushed up the bayou when storms threaten. Raise more structures on stilts. But it all feels like a losing battle.

As one person put it, "We are the first of the climate refugees."

"I've been in exile before," Richie Blink told me. "I headed north after Katrina and I found about a week of sympathy. After that, I was just another person in line at the gas station. People didn't want us there."

His meaning was clear: This is a problem for all of us. We're going to have to figure this out, or y'all are going to have to make room for us when we come live in your backyard.

Chief Shirell Parfait-Dardar is chief of the Grand Caillou/Dulac Band of Biloxi-Chitimacha-Choctaw in Terrebonne Parish, Louisiana. She has spent decades helping her community fight for federal recognition of their tribe and finding resilient solutions to the political and environmental challenges that have seen their traditional lands literally wash away into the Gulf of Mexico.

If you speak to our elders, they'll tell you we've always been here. Drive around and you'll see all the dead trees. They used to be live oaks and now they're just skeletons. It's only a matter of time before they sink away into the waters. As the land washes away, the saltwater intrusion kills the plants that are holding all of the soils together. And as we lose land, that opens us up to more flooding. You can't keep small livestock, because the water stays for days. You can't plant directly in the ground because our waters are so polluted. Once those waters come over, you're polluting your garden.

All of our practices have been altered due to environmental changes. It's happening so rapidly, we've become known as the adapting tribes. That's all we've done since the diversions of the Mississippi and especially since the extractive practices with oil and gas. Our lands have been ravaged.

We're used to flooding. We know hurricanes. That water's coming up and the land is sinking. It's not easy and, if you can't get help from the outside, then you need to look within. Down in these areas, this is mostly family. Even those that are not relatives, once they've been here a few months, they're family. We take care of each other. It's who we are. It's our identity.

No matter where you live, you are gonna meet challenges. In the west, you're gonna be dealing with earthquakes. Up north, you have blizzards. In the mid-section, tornadoes. We deal with flooding, but it doesn't change who we are. If anything, it makes us stronger, because through the storms and damage to homes, we come back, we come together, and we help each other.

I was still working to see the beauty in the bayou. We talked about the storms and the economic challenges and the environmental change. I asked Chief Shirell why she chose to remain in such a difficult landscape and she said, "If I really had to sum it up, this is love. I don't think I've ever felt so much love in my life except here." And that made sense to me. It's pretty hard to move away from love.

"I'm gonna love the crap outta you. So that's my call to those who are seeking leadership positions. If you can't lead with love, get out of the way."
—**Chief Shirell Parfait-Dardar**

> "I decided to go into journalism because there's not a lot of faces that look like mine on our local and national television. I want to be one of the first people to say, it's okay to be proud of who you are."
>
> —Baley Champagne

Baley Champagne is a journalism student and an activist in Houma, Louisiana. She is Navajo, Choctaw, Houma, and Apache. In 2019 she successfully lobbied the governor's office to have the state of Louisiana officially recognize Indigenous People's Day.

Louisiana was sold off at a very inexpensive price in the Louisiana Purchase. Ever since then, our voices didn't matter. The proclamation for Indigenous People's Day pretty much informs us that we've made contributions and are still here, and gets the citizens to recognize that as well.

Social media has been bringing people together that would never have been together before. So we're able to see this movement happen across the nation. People are listening more. We can do a lot more work when we have a lot more allies.

Columbus Day has always been an erasure for our identity and our existence on these lands. Indigenous People's Day is Indigenous people coming out and celebrating that we've been here for 20,000-plus years and we were never lost. Indigenous People's Day is advocating for our existence.

Chief Albert P. Naquin is the Traditional Chief of the Isle de Jean Charles Band of Biloxi-Chitimacha-Choctaw Indians. He is a Vietnam War veteran and he has worked with other tribes across the country to explore the importance of preserving culture and tradition. His tribe's traditional lands are increasingly flooded and washed away during storms, and he is trying to help his people find a path forward.

We have 702 members. We have 15 families left on the island and the rest have moved to temporary housing. I moved off the island in '75. Hurricane Carmen came in and got us out. We had a little boy and Hurricane Carmen come and put eleven inches of water in our house.

I'm a strong advocate of getting off the island, because since then, I haven't lost a piece of furniture or an appliance due to hurricanes. So it works. And I didn't have to go far. Get off the island because people have to help you all the time. And I do it for the people, but if you get off the island, then you won't have to worry about it.

I know a lot of people say, if we get off the island, the rich people is going to get there. And it might happen. Because since some people are going off the island, they put in a big old rock barrier, and they cemented it. And they got some fishing piers out there. So I don't know, maybe they're planning on putting sport fishermen out there and give 'em the land. Sell 'em the land. And have some nice million-dollar camps in there where we were. But they wouldn't take care of us.

But the thing is, why suffer for whatever they do? They say I'm giving up the island, but I'm not giving up the island. I'm just trying to reclaim [my] life by making myself better.

If I would've stayed over there, keep on having repairs and repairs and repairs every two, three years, you know, you can't get ahead. So we're not on the island now.

I take a beating for that, but that's okay. I think I'm right. If I would have stayed on the island, I'd still be poor.

"I was 24 and then, the next thing you know, I'm 74. You know, we were talking about the old people [and] now we are the old people. Time goes fast. Just help your brother along the way. Just get along with your brother. I mean, everybody's a brother."

—Chief Albert P. Naquin

Journey to the mouth of the Mississippi

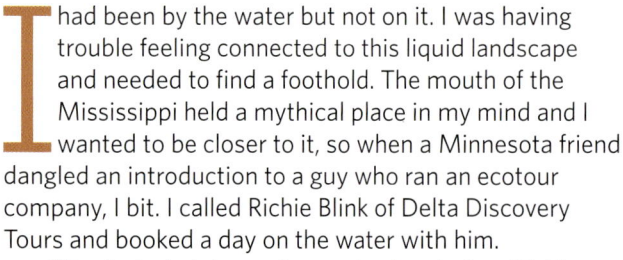

I had been by the water but not on it. I was having trouble feeling connected to this liquid landscape and needed to find a foothold. The mouth of the Mississippi held a mythical place in my mind and I wanted to be closer to it, so when a Minnesota friend dangled an introduction to a guy who ran an ecotour company, I bit. I called Richie Blink of Delta Discovery Tours and booked a day on the water with him.

We started at dawn at a marina located, as Richie said, "100 miles down a dead-end road." Richie navigated the maze of channels and backwaters in his 22-foot traditional Louisiana fishing boat like he had grown up there, because he had. He explained the ecology, the industry, and the culture.

We crossed the muddy channel of the Mississippi in the roiling wake behind a thousand-foot container ship. We wound our way south toward the crowfoot, where the single channel of the river branches out into several as it empties into the Gulf of Mexico. We stopped for lunch at CrawGators Bar & Grill and talked over a basket of brisket and fries about how land and life were changing.

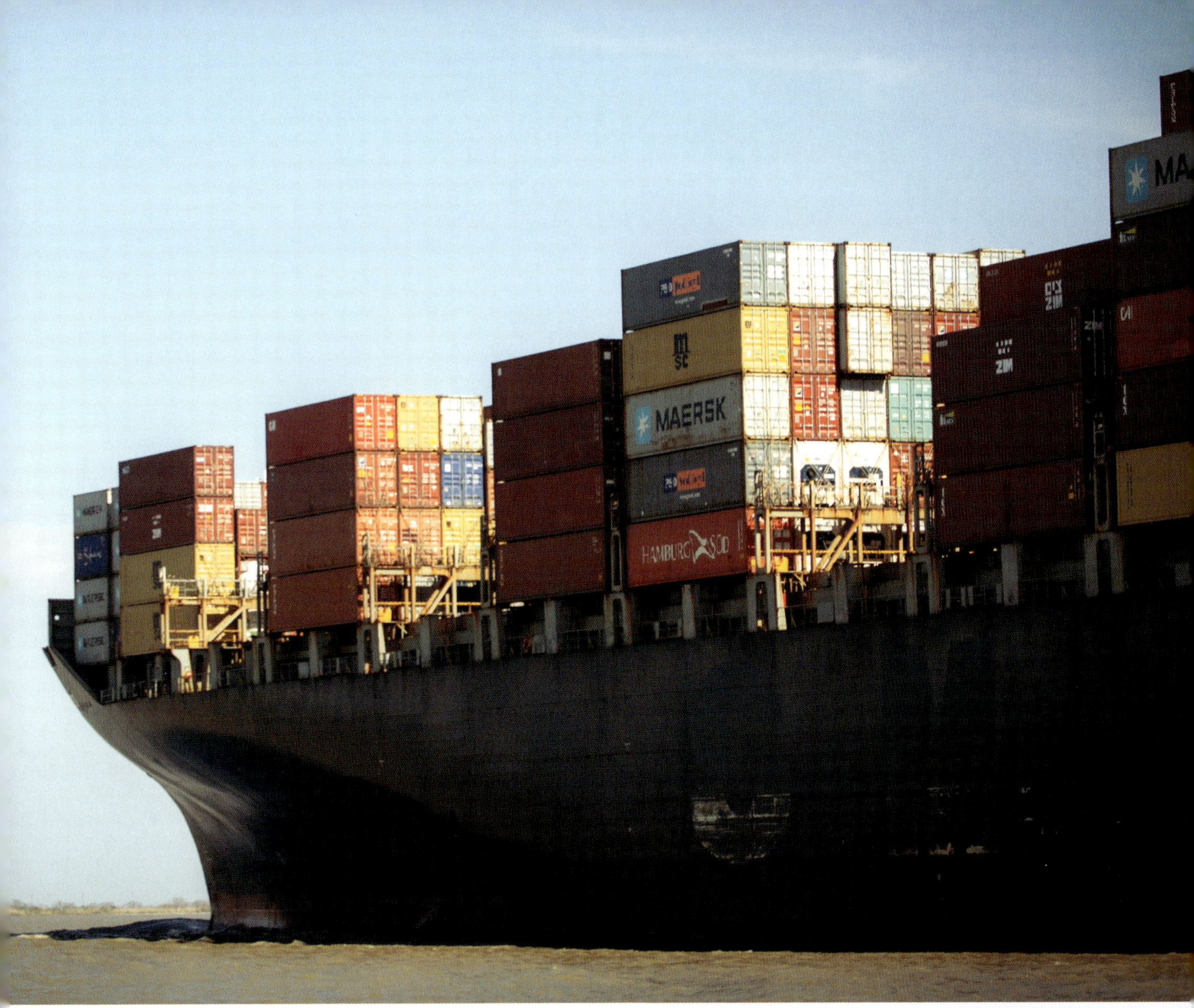
MAERSK
HAMBURG SÜD
ZIM

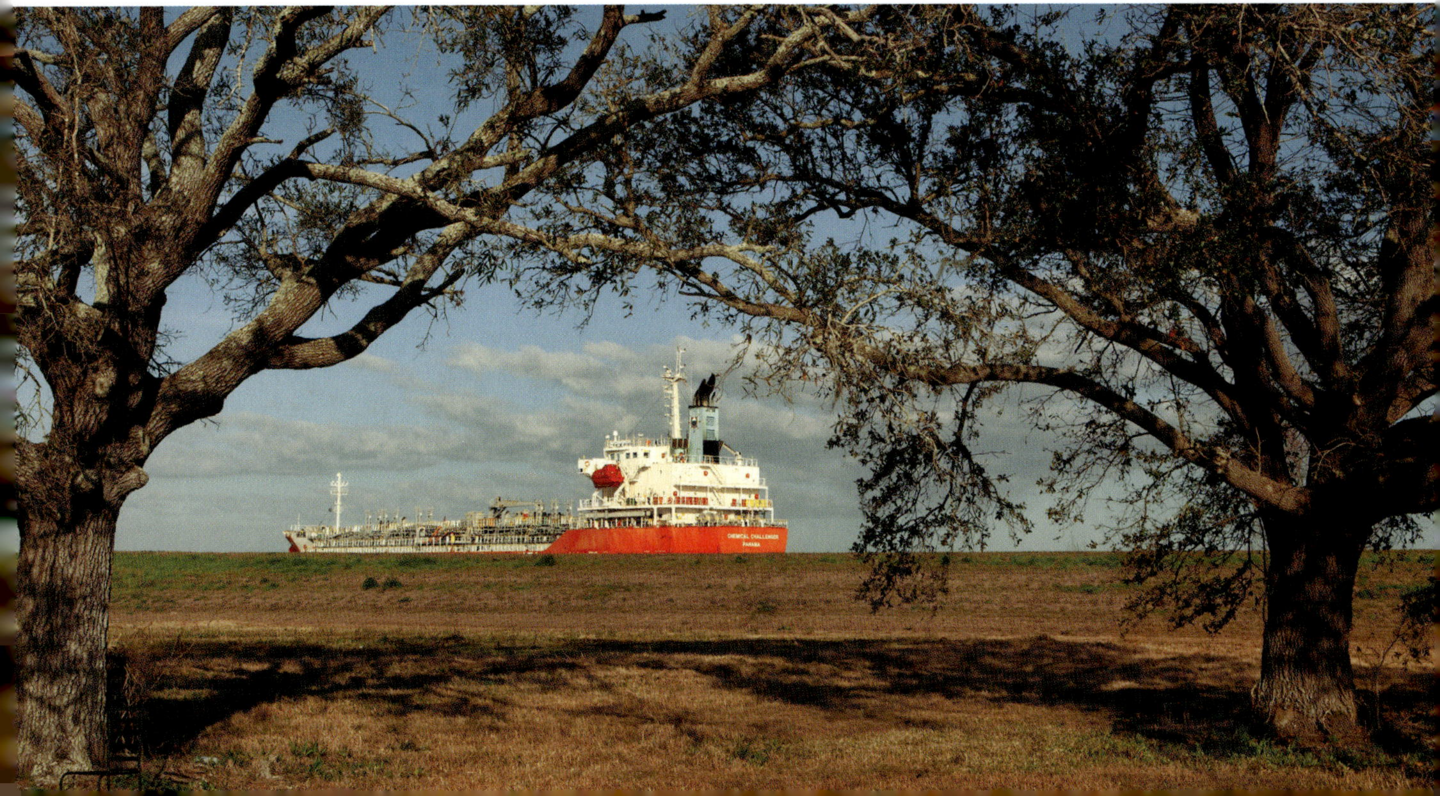

Richie Blink grew up in Empire, Louisiana, in a family of commercial fishermen. He worked for the oil and gas industry as a deckhand on an offshore crew boat and on dedicated oil spill cleanup boats. He has led efforts to plant trees to stabilize coastal shorelines and serves as the District 8 Representative for the Plaquemines Parish Council. In 2015 he started an ecotourism company called Delta Discovery Tours to share his love for the Mississippi River delta and to help educate others about the environmental challenges they face. He said, "I've had to shift my line of thinking from 'I'm gonna be the guy that saves my town' to 'how do we get the things that I love about this place—the culture, the memories—outta here in our pocket?'"

Every drop of water that falls within the levees has to be mechanically pumped out. Twelve years ago, the local government had $50 million in oil and gas revenue to help subsidize our ferry service and take care of our flood control system. We had $4 million in oil and gas revenue last year. A lot of people were very unhappy.

Residents don't realize how much it costs to maintain civilization in a place on the edge like this. But a lot of communities around America are very much like this one. There are things just around the corner or unseen. Folks don't realize just how vulnerable they are to issues like climate change.

Efficiencies in extraction have caused the reduction of oil and gas revenue here. We have barges, cranes, tugboats, and docks to drill for oil. In West Texas, you just need a pickup truck. Fracking increased the productivity of wells in places like Texas and Oklahoma. The cost to lift oil there is like $8 a barrel, whereas here it's $35 or $36. Companies chose to do business elsewhere.

It's incredible how much ingenuity goes into getting oil and gas out of the ground. We could do that with renewables and we're on the cusp of it. There's three or four families that control the shipyards and could call and get a line of credit from Wall Street by lunchtime tomorrow to retrofit the vessels needed to install offshore wind or tidal energy collection. Everybody here needs to realize that we can pivot and it's gonna create a lot of jobs.

The guys that work on the platforms don't care if they're climbing a wind turbine or oil and gas platform as long as they're making $60,000 or $70,000 a year working seven days on and seven days off, and they go home to their family safely at the end of their hitch. They're fine with whatever. It's the capital that makes it hard to pivot.

"Some of the folks that live in town have not accepted that it has a shelf life that may be within their own lifetime."
—Richie Blink

Journey to New Orleans

The idea of taking a vacation when you live on the road feels a little unnecessary and extravagant. But it was good to get out of the trailer once in a while. We booked a night in a hotel in New Orleans. As soon as we confirmed the reservation and bought tickets to hear live music, we found a homemade flier tucked under our truck's windshield wiper announcing a shrimp boil at the Swampman for that same night. Dammit. Double booked. But we were committed to a date night in the city, so we went ahead with our plans.

The Uber driver who delivered us to the French Quarter wondered out loud if the pandemic was over. "Look at all these people," he marveled. "Did they not get the memo?" We wore our masks. We wandered through Jackson Square, uncertain about our decision to mingle with the masses. We had brunch in the shady courtyard of Cafe Amelie and paused to listen to street bands as we wandered the neighborhood, feeding dollar bills into their hungry tip jars. We ordered a bag of beignets at Cafe Du Monde, the ample powdered sugar dusting our shirts as evidence of the snack, and we listened to music on a hotel patio until the crowds got too big and felt too close.

"If it weren't for New Orleans, America would just be a bunch of free people who are bored to death."

—Chris Rose, *One Dead in Attic*

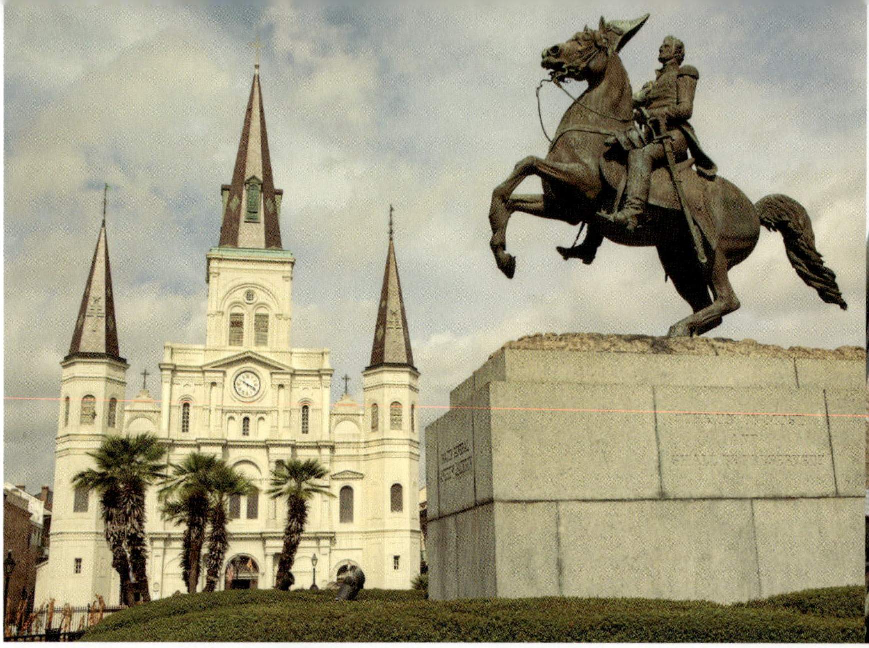

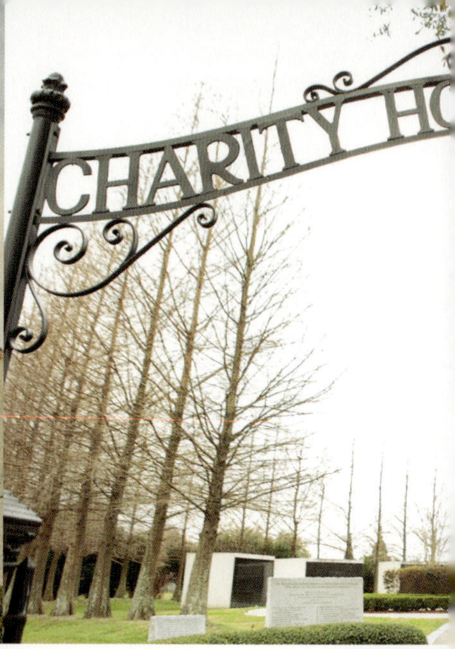

CHARITY HO

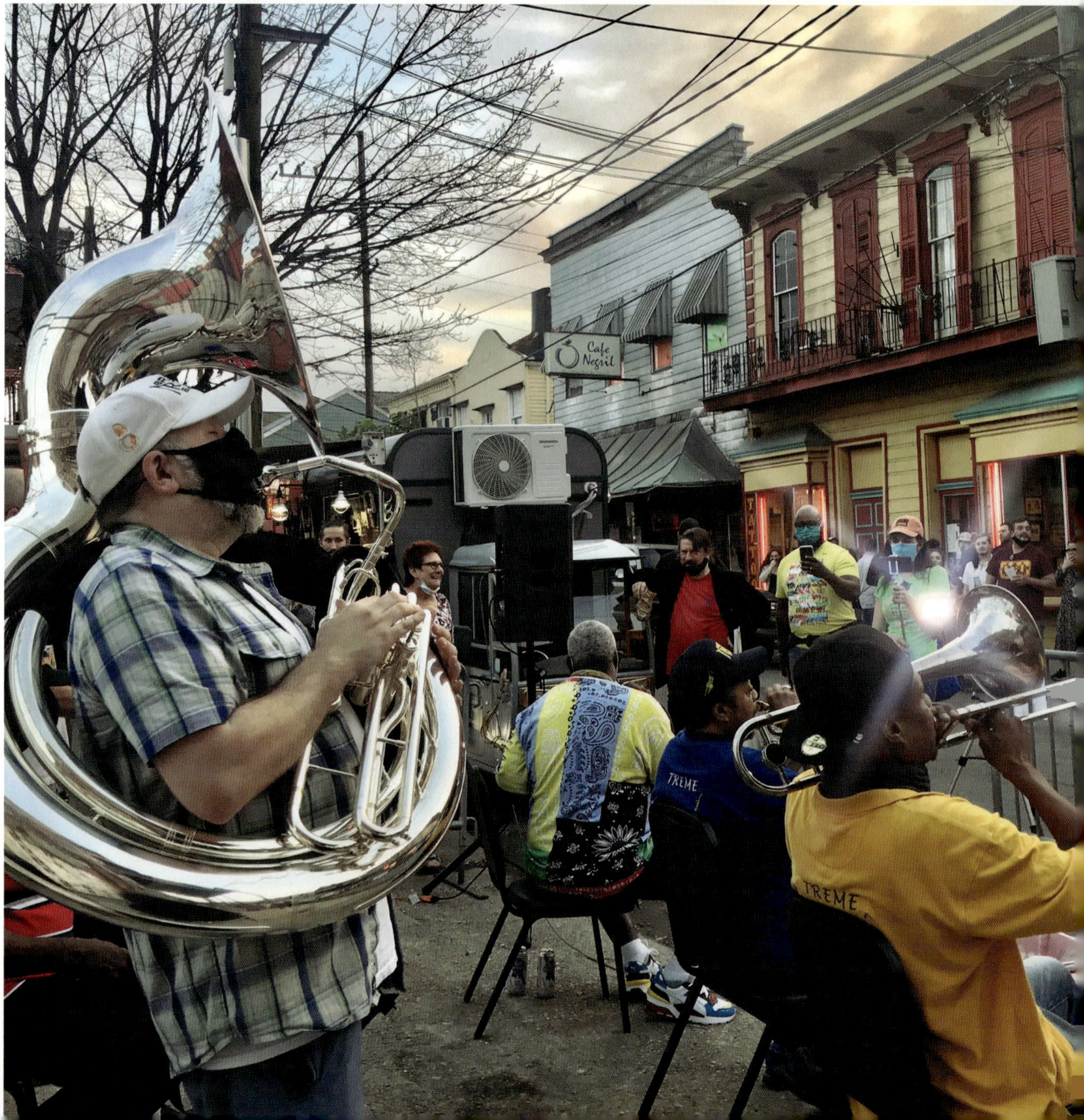

Cafe Negril
TREME
TREME

17TH STREET CANAL FLOODWALL

On August 29, 2005, a federal floodwall atop a levee on the 17th Street Canal, the largest and most important drainage Canal for the city, gave way here causing flooding that killed hundreds. This breach was one of 50 ruptures in the Federal Flood Protection System that occurred that day. In 2008, the US District Court, Eastern District of Louisiana placed responsibility for this floodwall's collapse squarely on the US Army Corps of Engineers; however, the agency is protected from financial liability in the Flood Control Act of 1928.

SPONSORED BY LEVEES.ORG

Will Snowden received a law degree from Seton Hall Law School in New Jersey and worked as a public defender in New Orleans. Through his work in the justice system, he became concerned with weaknesses in the jury system that led to a lack of diversity in jury members and, ultimately, to unjust outcomes. In response, Will established the Juror Project, whose mission is to "change the makeup of juries to better represent the American population and the communities most commonly accused." The Juror Project facilitates community and public education about jury eligibility, the jury selection process, and the power jurors hold in America's criminal justice system.

Our criminal legal system was originally designed—at least in theory—to rehabilitate. To return people to our communities to be productive citizens and not fall back into the behaviors that led them to have contact with the criminal legal system in the first place. I think that has been a huge farce. Our prison system has been purely punitive.

We want to set people up for success, but the logic is absent from being able to seamlessly reintegrate back into our communities. Ultimately when you deny people those opportunities, you're narrowing the lane of their on-ramp to success. You're making [crime] more enticing. If somebody has to provide for their family and they can't get jobs, it makes sense when they resort to unfavorable means.

So the idea of restoring jury rights to people [who have] felony convictions is in the larger conversation of, after the person has served time, they should be able to come back and be part of our community.

> "Louisiana has been the prisoner capital of the world for decades. If incarceration worked, we'd be the safest place in the country."
> —Will Snowden

We have to ask ourselves, "Are prisons the right intervention to change the behavior that we're concerned about?" I would argue that incarceration as an intervention to address trauma, to address poverty, is never going to work. There's a gut response. When somebody commits an incident of violence, we have been conditioned to think that person needs to be punished. It's a human response when a loved one has been harmed by another individual, there should be accountability. But the community has not been part of the conversation of what accountability looks like in this country.

If trust has been broken within that community, there have to be consequences as designed by that community. That leans into conversations of restorative justice circles, and alternative ways to address harm, where the survivor of the crime can be part of the conversation to design what that person needs to do to repent for the harms that they've committed. Studies show how much more impactful these restorative justice circles are than somebody doing a ten-year bid at Angola. We have to wean ourselves off this addiction of incarceration.

Through the years, I have had conversations about prison reform, the death penalty, and restorative justice, but I had never really considered jury selection. I have never served on a jury, but I would welcome the experience. I've heard people talk about avoiding jury duty but, like taxes, it is a part of our civic duty. After George Floyd was killed, there were so many conversations about defunding the police. I tend to lean toward reform over revolution. I'm not saying I'm right, it's just how I'm wired. What an interesting time to sit in conversation with someone like Will.

03.20.2021: Journey back home

Our youngest child is an artist. Grey was getting ready for their college senior art exhibit so we headed back north. These return trips were always full.

Minneapolis was preparing for the trial of Derek Chauvin and the three other police officers who were involved in George Floyd's death. The jury selection was broadcast on Minnesota Public Radio and I listened with a new interest and appreciation after my conversation with Will in New Orleans.

I revisited George Floyd Square. I walked around the courthouse where the trial would take place and photographed the fencing and barricades that had been installed in anticipation for more unrest.

We gathered our mail from the city and found a postcard of origami peace cranes from a photographer friend who was encouraging us on.

I made time for two interviews.

We visited friends in the country to photograph and live in their new Airbnb rental. We settled into a comfortable rhythm with Wade and Heidi of work during the day and communal meals at night. Movies in their barn, helping to gather the chickens at night, boiling maple sap in their creekside sugar shack as spring worked its magic and the landscape came alive again.

We burned brush at our own farm, clearing the stumps and boughs that remained from our Christmastime harvest.

We were living life on the road, but we were still connected to home. No matter how far you go, you never really sever that cord, I suppose. The great mirage of travel is that you can leave all your worries behind, but the truth is you carry your baggage with you.

We were six months into a journey that we had planned to last a year, but it felt like we were just getting started. We recognized that a year would pass too quickly, so we decided to remove the backstop. We knew our nomadic life was not indefinite, but it needed to last longer than a year. How long? We weren't sure. We agreed that we would continue until it felt like we were done and we hoped we would arrive at that point at roughly the same time.

PANDEMIC POSTCARD
by Mike Hazard

I HAVE
DO YOU HEAR US
JUSTICE FOR GEORGE FLOYD

DO NOT ENTER
AUTHORIZED PERSONNEL ONLY

> "Graffiti is the voice of people. We have a need to speak, we have a need to be seen, and graffiti opens the door for that. When you don't ask for permission, you get people's raw voice, for better or for worse."
>
> —Peyton Scott Russell

Peyton Scott Russell is a Minneapolis graffiti artist and street artist who has worked in that culture and creative space for more than three decades. He painted a 12' x 12' black and white portrait of George Floyd and installed it on a bus stop at the intersection of 38th Street and Chicago Avenue, where police killed Floyd on May 25, 2020. It is an iconic example of the street art that became prevalent in Minneapolis and around the world in response to Floyd's death.

When you ask for permission, you start thinking about, "Okay, is what I'm saying accepted?" and "What do people want to hear?" You might change your tone a bit. You start putting different parameters around it when you're in a box, when you go down that sanctioned path. And then the people who give you permission can start saying, "Can you take that out? Can you do less of that, more of this?" And you start opening Pandora's box, taking away your own expression.

You have to wait for approval. Maybe you're not even going to be able to do it. That's where I find what's really beautiful about this whole graffiti, non-sanctioned kind of thing. You get this raw reaction, this raw expression of someone, and it's not always pleasant. Sometimes, we need to actually say the things that we want to say. When I'm out there painting, the most nervous thing I'm up against is, what happens tomorrow when the work is exposed to the world.

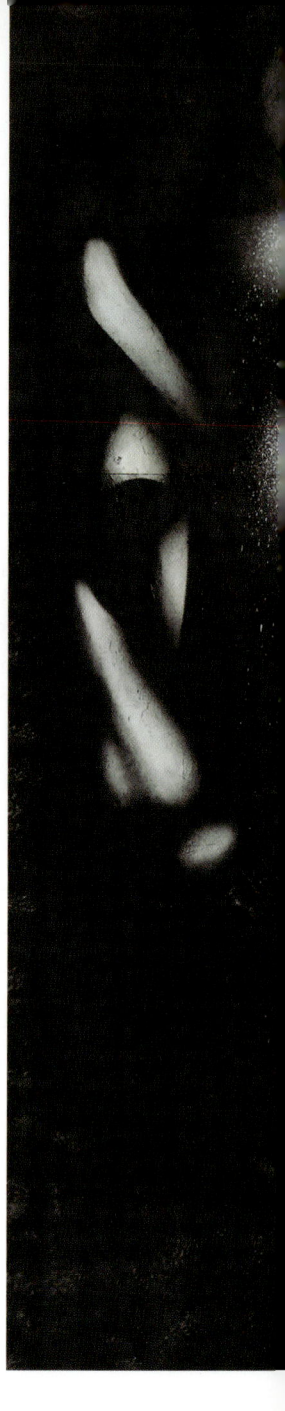

I created [that portrait] during the curfew. I originally wanted to go out and protest physically. I wanted to be out in the trenches. I was angry. Obviously, I'm older. I've got kids and I had mentors calming me down and they were like, "Don't forget, you have a stronger voice than trying to go out there physically. Maybe you should think about doing something that way."

For a moment, I had forgotten about that, because I was so angry. I just had this knee-jerk reaction, like, I got to do something.

Don't let people dictate what you're going to do, but also, how can you have the highest impact of what you're trying to say? The idea was for me to put his face out there, to say, "Okay, look what you did to this guy." That's the whole thing in graffiti. You're forced to see what we do. You paint this stuff in the vandalism format, you trespass, you paint it on a wall or a train. Boom, in your face, you gotta deal with it. There it is, for better or worse.

After spending so much time at George Floyd Square I found it gratifying to meet this artist who had made such an iconic piece of art. Peyton was my age. He was finding his own artistic voice in this difficult season, responding in his own unique way to the events of the day. It felt like we shared a common journey that was unfolding in familiar ways. I loved the notion that graffiti art is meant to be in your face so you can't ignore it.

Jillian Peterson teaches criminology and criminal justice at Hamline University in St. Paul, Minnesota. She cofounded the Violence Project with author and sociologist James Densley, and they have compiled the world's most comprehensive mass shooter database in order to better understand the phenomenon and attempt to prevent future tragedies. The Violence Project uses the same definition of mass shooting as the FBI, which is: "four or more people killed in a public space, not family members, not gang related, and not in the course of committing another felony."

This is a male phenomenon. [Mass shooters are] 98 percent male. I could teach an entire class about why in terms of biology and socialization. I think it's men who are disenfranchised, who feel like they haven't gotten what they're owed, who are hopeless, who are actively suicidal. Nobody goes in with an escape plan. This is meant to be their final act. There's a performative element of wanting people to see how much pain they were in.

The history of America is a history of violence, but there's also this piece of individualism and [the] American dream. If I work hard, I get what I deserve. These are individuals who are angry that life hasn't played out how they expected it to.

I developed this saying: 'The worse the crime, the worse the story,' and it is always true. There is always a story you could follow along. Not that it excused [the crime], but it made some sense. Evil babies aren't born into the world to do horrible things. People are a product of what they've been through. And when you go through horrific things, you end up in a horrific place.

We tend to respond to difficult things with a punitive view, as opposed to a reformative view. How do we shift that culture? As I approach this topic, it's about asking deep questions and listening deeply. It's a delicate balance and I don't want to offend victims. I don't want to cause more harm in telling these stories, but I think we have to tell them.

We're trying to think about the pathway to violence. Where are the off-ramps and how do we think about helping people get off that track? Preventing violence is really just about human connection and we're all very capable of that.

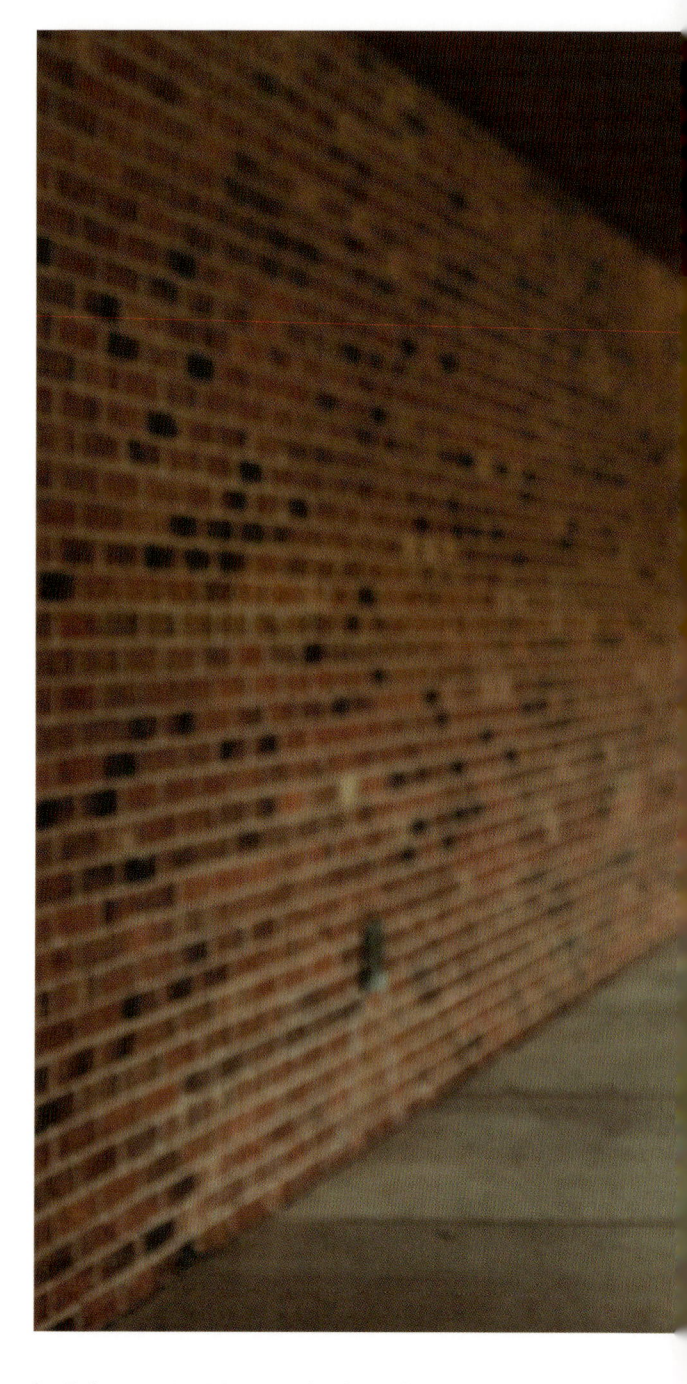

On February 17, 2021, we had just been at the memorial to the 2019 mass shooting in El Paso. On March 16, 2021, eight people were killed at massage parlors in Atlanta. March 22, 2021, ten people were killed at a grocery store in Boulder. We all felt the weight of this violence. We all wondered why. But it's not enough to just ask why. I wanted to talk with someone who was doing the research and crunching the numbers. There had to be a path forward.

"We realized that we knew very little about who mass shooters are. I don't think you can prevent something from happening until you deeply understand why it's happening."
—Jillian Peterson

04.04.2021 : Journey to Memphis

Who is our Dr. King today?
Where do we find our moral leadership?

Last week I stood outside the Hennepin County Government Center at the start of the Derek Chauvin trial. It was mid-morning when I got there, and although there had been a vigil earlier in the day, things were quiet when I arrived. Just a couple dozen people holding signs. Drivers honked to show their support as they passed by and the media was staged a block away waiting for a story to unfold.

Then Karen and I headed south again.

This morning we joined friends at an outdoor Easter service in Oxford, Mississippi. I hadn't been to a church service in more than a year, and even though we were in an unfamiliar congregation in a town that wasn't our home, it was good to gather with people. Outside. At a distance. And celebrate something familiar together.

When a phone alert reminded me that it was also the anniversary of Dr. Martin Luther King's assassination in 1968, I decided to drive the hour to Memphis, to the Lorraine Motel where it happened. Just to stand in that sacred spot for a reflective moment. I wanted to entertain a connection that was forming in my mind between the Easter story, the Civil Rights Movement, and the recent unrest in Minneapolis.

I'm not comparing Jesus to MLK to George Floyd. That's not the connection I want to make. But there's a thread I'm pulling at that runs through these stories and it weaves through truth and power.

Power has trouble seeing the truth. Or saying the truth. Power protects itself. Power can justify outrageous acts as it defends the indefensible. Even as the rest of the world can see the plain and simple truth, power will deny it.

These are slippery times. People will cloud the water and try to convince you it was never clear to begin with. You may question what you have always known to be true. But your heart knows the truth. Listen to what it whispers in the quiet moments. Carefully cultivate the still places where it can be heard.

We have been here before. Look with clear eyes. Listen with an open heart. Seek the truth. And when you find it, hold on like your soul depends on it.

Because it just might.

108

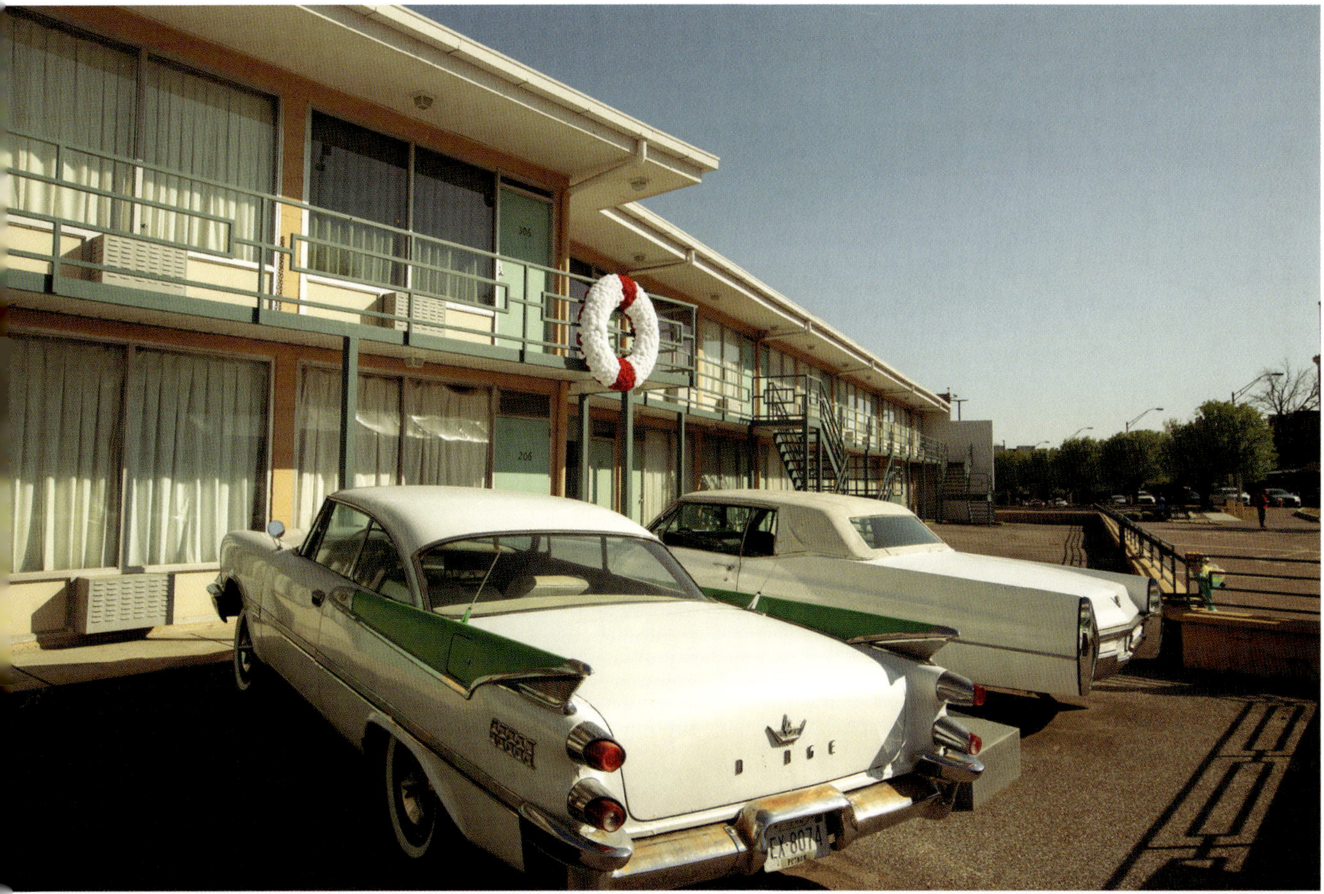

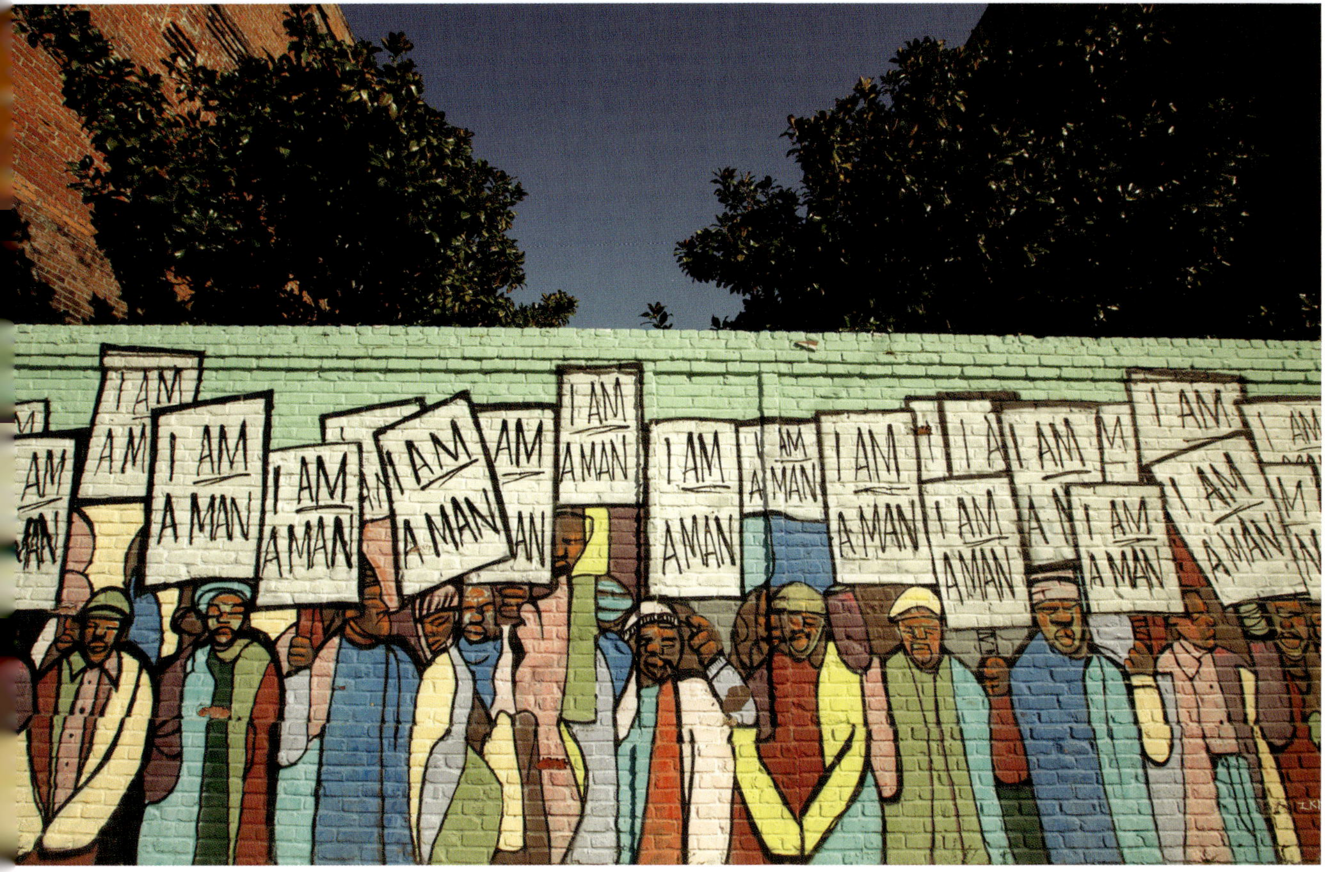
I AM
A MAN

Journey to Mississippi

A friend who lost his child unexpectedly explained to me that at first—in his grief—he felt like he was trying to chase the setting sun. He tried to stay in the light even as the darkness fell around him. He knew it was never going to work. The light receded at a pace much faster than he could travel. But he kept trying. And he kept failing. And as the darkness overtook him, he realized that the only way back to the light was to turn toward the darkness and move through it. It was the fastest way, and then the light would come again.

We resist the darkness. We turn away from it. But that doesn't mean it isn't there. We do it in our personal lives and we've done it as a society. We can find a path forward. We can get back to the light. But only if we are willing to face our difficult history and walk through it. There is pain in that process, but there is beauty, hope, and potential as well.

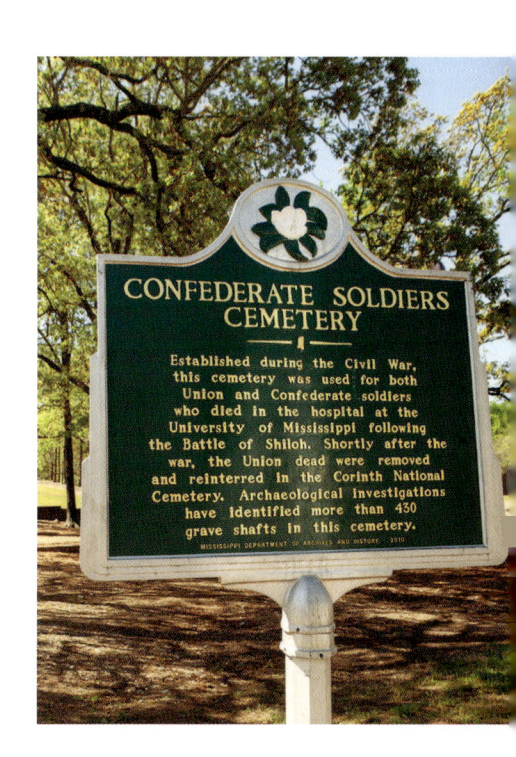

"I'm drawn to places that are complicated, but beautiful. Places that hold a little bit of the heaviness of the history of Mississippi. Part of my calling is to do healing work to lift some of that heaviness so we can move into the future."
—Lydia Koltai

Lydia Koltai is a mother, civil rights activist, and herbalist in Oxford, Mississippi. She is active in a local movement to remove a Confederate monument from the lawn of the Lafayette County courthouse. Lydia said when she was younger, she always wanted to leave Mississippi because of the weight of its history, but she also knew that she wanted to return one day to help make it better.

Truth and reconciliation are really at the center of the healing we're trying to do. You can't reconcile—you can't get to healing—without telling the truth, telling the stories, exposing the wound, letting it breathe. And in Mississippi, people are uncomfortable with that history. For good reason. And there's a real desire to say, "Let's leave that in the past." There's a lot of shame, I think, for white people, that they don't want to be connected to it, they don't want to have to think about it. The grief and the sense of responsibility is a lot to carry.

You can't reconcile until there's been some tangible way of saying that this was harmful. It's not enough to erect the markers or to have the ceremony. There also needs to be actual repair work. How that looks can be a conversation between people who are in relationship, but it's an essential element. And that's part of what people are afraid of.

There's a sense of scarcity, of, "What am I going to have to give up to heal something that I didn't do?" Those are all feelings that I can understand on a logical level. But I also feel like sometimes you have to pay for things that weren't healed, weren't taken care of in the moment. The impact is ongoing and it doesn't get smaller by you not looking at it and not tending to it.

Reparations. Repair. Restoring. I would even say transformative justice. We need to transform relationships and the ways we're interacting, that we're being in community together. That starts with recognizing and acknowledging the history, moving away from this mythology that America is some grand experiment of democracy that's always been pushing forward for everyone's betterment.

There's a piece of truth in that, but that's not the whole truth. We need to examine who's been left out of that experiment and why and how, and what needs to be transformed so that we can live up to what I think is a beautiful vision of what we could be, but we're not.

"Come to the conversation curious and open to understanding the other's point of view. I have a shirt that says, 'More curious, less furious.'"
—Graham Bodie

Graham Bodie is chief listening officer of Listen First Project and also a professor of integrated media communications at the University of Mississippi in Oxford. He conducts research on how people show up for one another during distressing times. I've gotten to know Graham as a coalition partner with the Listen First Project, which convenes hundreds of organizations nationwide that focus on using dialogue to heal the social fabric of America.

When we share what we're going through, most people don't know how to handle that. They give advice. They say, "Oh, listen to what happened to me." They think that's helpful. But what is more helpful is to allow that person space to share their story, ask them insightful questions about why [they] feel that way, and how it fits into how they see the world.

We have very superficial conversations with most people we interact with daily. That's okay, but imagine you're the person at the grocery checkout line and all you have all day long is superficial conversations. Then you get home and you have another superficial conversation with your spouse. At some point, you're going to break.

If that's true for our personal relationships, how much truer for society in general? [Imagine] a hundred thousand people, all [with] no one who listens to them. You see the problem. You see that fractured family times a hundred thousand. Imagine that times 300 million, and you can see why we're in some of the places that we're in in this country.

Whatever the ideology is, the phrases you use to describe this work matters. If you say diversity and inclusion, that's a blue flag. Even though most people can agree on the principle of diversity and inclusion whether you're red, white, blue, or purple. But that terminology, because it's been used primarily by the left, can absolutely wave the blue flag. Therefore, everybody waving the red flag says, "Oh, I know what this is about. I don't want anything to do with that."

The same thing on the other end of the spectrum, where you talk about freedom and patriotism, which is waving the red flag. Even though you'll have blue people who love freedom and love this country, they will turn away from those words because of the societal baggage that's attached to it.

I'm not sure when human rights, civil rights, and voting rights became blue issues. Why are those things blue? All people should have the right to vote unencumbered by circumstance, situation, skin color, and income.

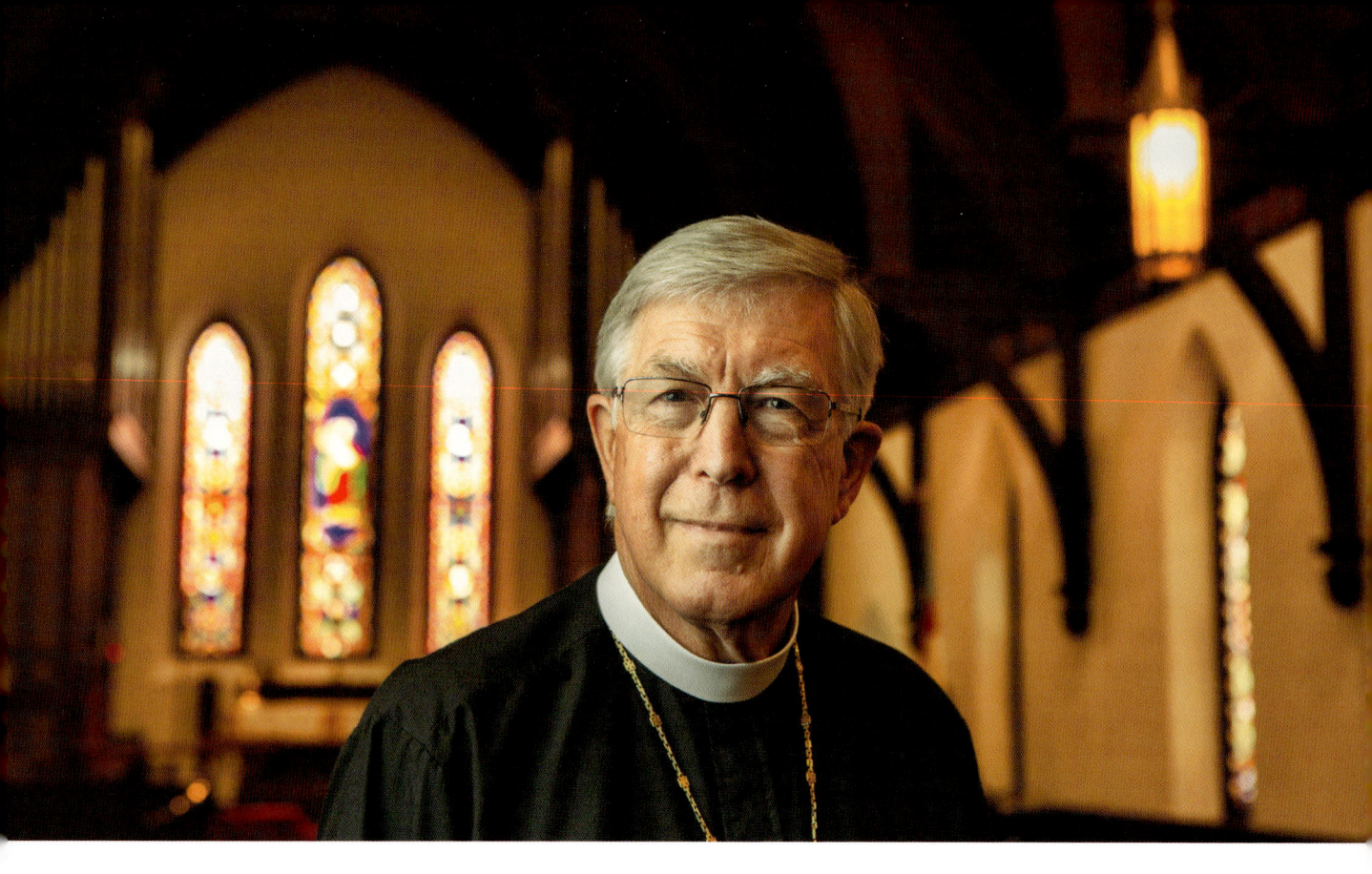

"Can we take [our] history and find ways to bless the good and redeem the bad?"
—Duncan Gray

Duncan Gray is a retired Episcopal priest and was the ninth bishop of the Episcopal Diocese of Mississippi. I met him at St. Peter's Episcopal Church in Oxford, Mississippi, where he was rector, like his father before him. His father served from 1957 to 1965 during the turbulent era when James Meredith was the first Black man who was allowed admission into the University of Mississippi.

St. Peter's organized itself in 1851. The church building was completed just prior to the Civil War in 1860. Its first service was just prior to Mississippi's secession and, according to Duncan, "has a history of being an enlightened community during some pretty difficult times in Mississippi."

My father was involved in trying to keep a lid on the anger around the integration [of the University of Mississippi] and providing some leadership when the university was in great turmoil. In 1962 James Meredith entered the university. The efforts through the courts preceded that by a year or so. All during that time, my dad preached about the need to open the doors and allow this man to enter. As [the case] worked through the court system, his sermons became more pointed. I remember vividly his sermon on the Sunday before Meredith officially entered, and the riots that took place Sunday evening. I remember the sermon following the riots. Half the congregation left.

He was a kind and gentle man and part of the reason the church held together was he never quit loving the folks who hated him. One of his mottos—more than a motto, I mean, he lived it—was, "If you hate those who hate you, they've won." And he refused to go that route.

So he would be prophetic in his ministry and then go make a call on the folks who got upset. That was the model I grew up with.

I remember him shaking his head over what somebody had done and saying words to the effect of, "But Duncan, God loves them and I do, too." So crosses were burned in our front yard and threatening phone calls were part of our common life. We were taught how to respond to the threats.

One time, somebody called and said some terrible things to my mother and threatened to kill each one of us children, by name, and Dad said something to the effect of, "He's got a lot of problems, but he's probably got children of his own." And, you know, he humanized all of these folks that I would [have been] tempted as an adolescent to demonize. And that stayed with me forever.

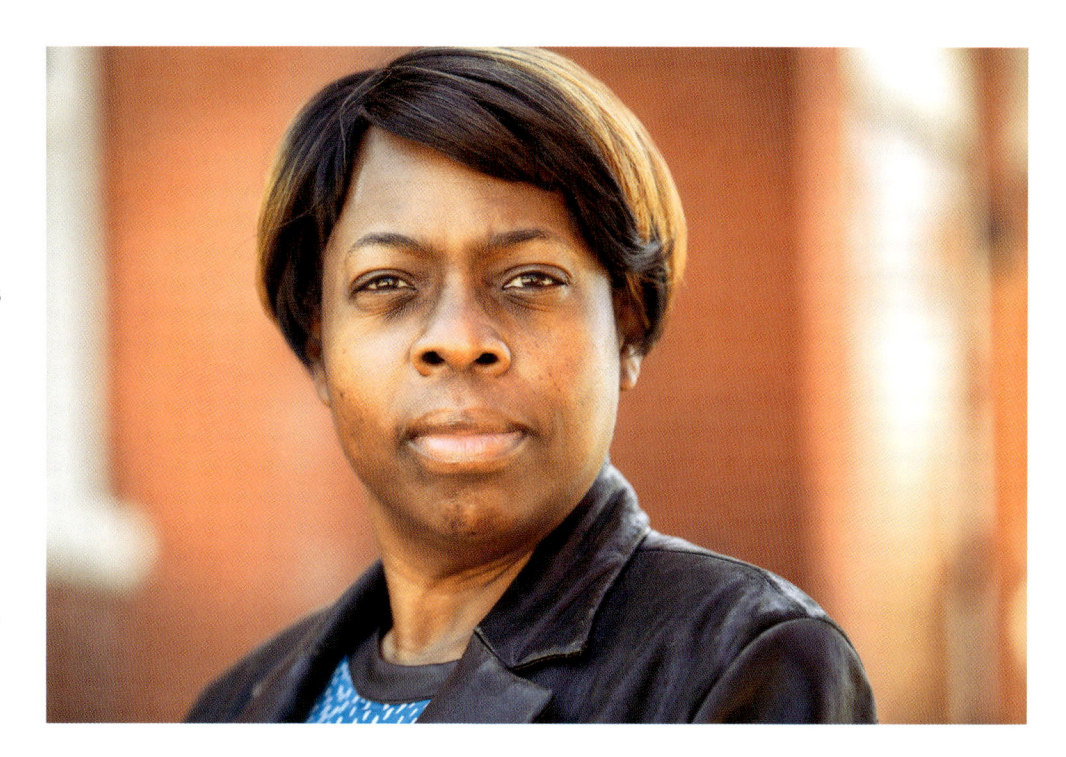

Rhondalyn Peairs is a graduate student at the University of Mississippi in Oxford. She gives tours of Oxford that call out the history of race and inequality in the city and in our country as a whole.

"People get confused about what Mississippi is. If you're a Black person and you say you're from Mississippi, everybody thinks that you ought to hate where you come from."
—**Rhondalyn Peairs**

I fully believe in reparations. I believe if you owe somebody something, you owe them something and you need to find some way to make amends. An apology's not going to do it. Race is America's boogeyman. We say we're the greatest nation. We say we're the wealthiest nation that's ever existed on the face of the earth. That's true. However, we know that the wealth has not been equally distributed. And we know that the wealth came on the backs of stolen land and stolen labor. And that's just the truth. And in a place where truth is supposed to be spoken, I think people get caught up not understanding that you don't have to own somebody to have benefited from your privilege of being white.

There were people that never owned an enslaved human being that profited off their labor, that benefited. The people that built the ships, the people that had jobs in the textile industry, because my ancestors' labor was being used to create cotton. There are tons of people who have benefited and continue to benefit today from people who are poor or women or whatever marginalized group you wanna identify. [People who have been] pushed to the margins for you to get more than you need.

I think probably one of the most stark and frank things I've heard about the wealth gap was from Kim Janey, who became the first woman and the first Black person to become the mayor of Boston. And it is kind of strange because white people have been a minority in Boston for years. It is 45 percent white. Why are there always white men that are either Irish American or Italian American that are mayor? That's not normal. It's not representative.

But, [Janey] said recently that the median net worth of a Black family in the Boston area is $8. And the median net worth of a white family in Boston is $250,000. Very stark difference. And that's why reparations are needed.

I think some people are starting to wake up to the point that our world is unequal and it's really unequal and there's really still a lot of hate and bias around.

The reason why our society is the wealthiest is because you didn't pay for labor for years. Not just the Black people, but poor Irish immigrants, children. You didn't pay for any of the labor to build this country. You stole the land. That's why you are ahead. So something's got to happen to equalize these things.

April Grayson was born and raised in Mississippi. She left after college, but returned ten years later to tell stories through oral history and documentary films about the Civil Rights Movement and the history of race in Mississippi. April is the director of Community and Capacity Building at the Alluvial Collective, formerly the William Winter Institute for Racial Reconciliation, an organization that works to hold space for difficult conversations.

Mississippi has been the epicenter around the history of slavery, the Civil War, and the potential for our country to fracture permanently. [It] certainly has fractured in ways that have not been fully healed. It's been the site of so much trauma, but also of resistance, activism, and all the things that carry us forward.

The stories of Mississippi resonate so deeply because I understand the language so deeply, both from the point of view of white families that have problematic histories and the ways that some white southerners have been fighting for the right thing. I grew up in a predominantly Black community where I witnessed the stories of people who were impacted, but also the stories of [how] they resisted and found strength. They're beautiful, inspiring stories.

Our history often doesn't allow us to avoid the subject in ways that other parts of the country can. Wrestling with it is complicated. My middle name is spelled L-E-A, because my parents wanted to feminize it. I was named after my paternal great grandfather: Ryan Lee Grayson. Ryan Lee Grayson was the son of a Confederate soldier, and he was named for Robert E. Lee, the Confederate general. I heard a lot about that history. My great-great-grandfather was imprisoned in one of the camps on the Great Lakes and had to walk back to Mississippi after the war.

I carry the name of Robert E. Lee in my own name. I think about that a lot. There are all these people before me, and I always wonder, who am I like? Whose qualities do I have? I think about that conversation with my great-great-grandfather. Would I feel completely alienated from him? Could we have a good conversation about this?

I would want him to know that I think that whole thing was a travesty that we're still paying for today. But I don't hold any personal hatred toward him. How much could we have that conversation without somebody getting really upset? The war [ended in 1865.] We're still fighting that same war.

> "Our work is built around the notion that when we slow down, take some breaths, and are open to hearing each other's stories, we can build a relationship that enables us to wrestle better with the hard stuff."
>
> —April Grayson

> "You try to be just and teach your children and model that behavior, and then you don't see it done in public by those we trust."
> —Afton Thomas

Afton Thomas is Associate Director for Programs at the Center for the Study of Southern Culture at the University of Mississippi in Oxford. Afton describes Oxford as "the progressive south," and believes in the importance of continuing to share stories of the past so we can live better today and in the future. At the time of this interview, Afton's involvement and voice in the community had led her to run for local office.

I can kind of compartmentalize. That's maybe not always the healthiest. I'm not bragging about it. I know that—if I sit still—my heart is sad, it's worn out. Being in the pandemic, and with the deaths of George Floyd and Brionna Taylor . . . it's still hard. It's not something you get over. I feel like it's getting harder to not talk about those things.

You feel it at every turn, trying to figure out what you can do. This is not a novel idea. My parents, my grandparents and their parents . . . things happened around them and they tried to figure out what they could do.

I find beauty in that. I think that more and more people are trying to figure out what they can do. Just because I'm not in a position of [power] doesn't mean that I don't have individual power. Just having conversations is doing something.

We need to stretch those boundaries, broaden that lens. It is important that we know things outside of our bubble, outside of our religion, outside of our race, our culture, so that we are building understanding for people.

My husband and I have two children [and we are] not sliding them into any box. I am Black and he is white, and they are no more one or the other. They are their own, and they have to work out that identity for themselves. We talk openly with them about how people are going to maybe read you a certain way and you will learn how to pick your battles.

Each time you tell a story, some things hit you a little differently, resonate with you a little differently. The hope is that little tiny thing that I do is moving that conversation forward. Amplifying, lifting up, and also hoping that people latch on to some nugget of history and how it applies today. Things aren't happening out of thin air. We need that constant reminder.

I received my first COVID-19 vaccine at a drive-through clinic in Mississippi. I was eager to get it because I felt vulnerable being on the road. No side effects and a small degree of comfort as we kept moving through the country.

It was a quiet drive from Oxford to Sumner, Mississippi. Karen was busy at the trailer and I drove the 70 miles by myself. I don't think I said more than a few words all day. Mostly, I read signs, and the signs said a lot.

A sign in front of the Tallahatchie County Courthouse reads:

Emmett Till Murder Trial
In August 1955 the body of Emmett Till, a 14-year-old black youth from Chicago, was found in the Tallahatchie River. On September 23, in a five-day trial held in this courthouse, an all-white jury acquitted two white men, Roy Bryant and W. W. Milam, of the murder. Both later confessed to the murder in a magazine interview. Till's murder, coupled with the trial and acquittal of these two men, drew international attention and galvanized the Civil Rights Movement in Mississippi and the nation.
—Mississippi Department
of Archives and History, 2007

Because of double jeopardy, the men couldn't be tried again, even though they had both confessed publicly.

On another corner of the courthouse, a Confederate statue stands with a soldier on top, a Confederate flag underneath, and below that, an inscription that reads:

For truth dies not and by her light they raise the flag whose starry folds have never trailed; and by the low tents of the deathless dead they lift the cause that never yet has failed.
—Virginia F. Boyle
("Poet Laureate of the Confederacy")

The largest words at the base of the statue read simply, "Our Heroes."

Inside the courthouse there are no signs, but walking up the stairs, I found the door to the courtroom open, so I wandered in to see the room where the trial had taken place. I was alone, but not nearly as alone as Emmett Till's mother must have felt watching the court hearings proceed.

Twelve miles to the south in Glendora is the Emmett Till Historic Intrepid Center, housed in an old cotton gin, once owned by J. W. Milam, one of the men who confessed to the murder after the trial.

A sign just down the road from the cotton gin and museum reads:

Milam's House
This site was the home of J. W. Milam, who along with his half-brother, Roy Bryant, murdered 14-year-old Emmett Till on August 28, 1955.

The two men confessed to journalist William Bradford Huie, during which Milam claimed he and his brother initially beat Till in the barn behind the house. Milam forced several of his black employees to wash out the bloody truck, which had been used to carry Till's body to the Tallahatchie River. He also later admitted to burning Till's clothes in the backyard.

Just a short drive from Glendora will bring you to the site where Emmett Till's body was found. The first sign directing you to the site is riddled with bullet holes. It reads:

River Site
On August 31, 1955, Emmett Till's body was found 2.6 miles to the southeast. Fishermen discovered

the body on a piece of land adjacent to the Tallahatchie River, where it had been dumped, presumably as a warning to the black community. A cotton gin fan had been tied around Till's neck with barbed wire. Till's uncle, Moses Wright, identified the swollen and mutilated body only because he recognized a ring Emmett wore on his finger. The FBI later confirmed the identity through DNA testing.

And if you drive those 2.6 miles down a gravel road, you will come to the river site itself. When I visited two years ago, that sign had been removed, because it, too, had been shot and vandalized. This time a new, bulletproof sign stood in its place and it read:

Graball Landing
Emmett Till's body may have been removed from the river at this site. Cleared by enslaved persons in 1840, Graball began as a prominent steamboat landing. Although an 1894 tornado eliminated all visible evidence of inhabitation, it left a clearing in the otherwise impenetrable vegetation that provided access to the river.

Some historians suggest that the body was recovered a few miles downstream from Graball at Fish Lake Landing near Pecan Point. But from the trial to present, there has never been a consensus on precisely where the body was recovered. Fish Lake Landing is no longer connected to the river.

Since the Emmett Till Memorial Commission first commemorated Graball Landing in 2008, it has become a nationally recognized memory site. Signs erected here have been stolen, thrown in the river, replaced, shot, removed, replaced, and shot again. The history of vandalism and activism centered on this site led ETMC founder Jerome Little to observe that Graball Landing was both a beacon of racial progress and a trenchant reminder of the progress yet to be made.

From this last sign, it's a short walk down to the river bank. And at the end of the muddy trail, I left my own sign. Small, humble, and impermanent, my peace sign scratched into the muddy banks with a short stick would melt away with the next rain, but our need to remember the difficult history will not leave so quickly.

Like so many, I was relieved when Derek Chauvin was found guilty for the murder of George Floyd. But I worry about the temptation to pat ourselves on the back and say, "There, we did it," without actually finishing the work.

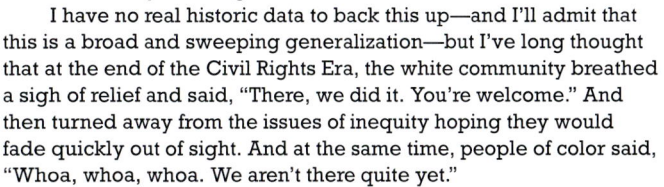

I have no real historic data to back this up—and I'll admit that this is a broad and sweeping generalization—but I've long thought that at the end of the Civil Rights Era, the white community breathed a sigh of relief and said, "There, we did it. You're welcome." And then turned away from the issues of inequity hoping they would fade quickly out of sight. And at the same time, people of color said, "Whoa, whoa, whoa. We aren't there quite yet."

And that's where we've been stuck ever since, the divides growing, the wounds festering.

There are some promising signs of progress. Signs of the times. It has all come at a high cost. But maybe—just maybe—we find ourselves with the rare opportunity to finish the work this time.

Confederate Monuments

IN MEMORY OF
THE PATRIOTISM OF THE
CONFEDERATE SOLDIERS
OF LAFAYETTE COUNTY,
MISSISSIPPI.
———
THEY GAVE THEIR LIVES
IN A JUST AND HOLY CAUSE.

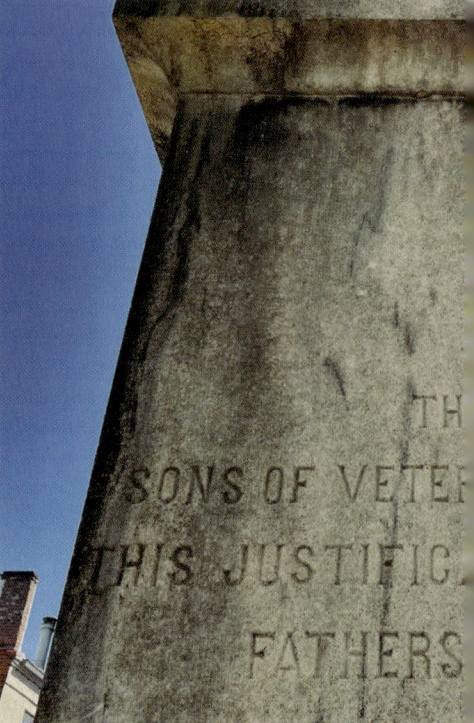

It was more awkward than I had imagined—as a white guy—to stand in the middle of a busy intersection and take a photograph of a Confederate statue. It was the reason we had come to Oxford, Mississippi, to have conversations about monuments and race. But somehow, the moment I raised my camera, I felt conspicuous.

It's the same feeling I had when I pulled my pickup into a driveway near Coeur d'Alene, Idaho, and stepped out to ask the woman feeding her chickens if she knew the way to the former site of the Aryan Nation compound.

The same sense I had when I took pictures of the bullet holes in the sign pointing to the site where Emmett Till's body was found on the banks of the Tallahatchie River after he was lynched.

I don't like to be misunderstood, and there was every chance in each of those situations that people might look at me and misinterpret why I was there. But you can't wear a sign that announces your intentions and you can't control how others perceive you. There was work to do.

Oxford, Mississippi, is home to two large Confederate statues. One is located in front of the county courthouse in the middle of the town square. When you enter Oxford from the south on Lamar Boulevard, it's the first and most notable thing that greets you as you arrive at the center of town. If you walk into the county's halls of justice, you enter under the shadow of that statue.

The other monument is on the campus of the University of Mississippi. That one had been located at the heart of the university until 2019 when it was moved to a less prominent site, near a historic Confederate cemetery on campus.

The statue on the courthouse lawn remains in place. There were calls to relocate it as a part of a national movement after police officers killed George Floyd in Minneapolis. The county board of supervisors—five white men—voted unanimously to leave it in place.

Like most stories, this one is complicated. There is some thought that the city actually owns the land under the county courthouse statue. If that's the case, the more diverse city leadership would be more likely to relocate it. The same county board who voted to keep the Confederate statue has also agreed to install a marker on the courthouse grounds commemorating the seven documented victims of lynching in the county.

The university's monument was moved to the edge of the Confederate cemetery, but the new location was within clear view of the football team's practice field and some of the Black players and their allies refused to practice under its gaze. So now the university has erected a large green tarp to hide the statue from that view.

In 2020 Mississippi became the final state in the union to officially remove Confederate imagery from their flag. So, on some level, Mississippi has acknowledged its difficult history and the pain and discomfort these items convey, but symbols and iconography remain here in large and small ways.

Courthouse studio

"What does this statue mean to you?"

> We have an opportunity to move beyond division and brokenness to reimagine a new symbol for our community.

> Hypocrisy. We declare that all men are created equal yet these symbols deny my humanity. A Just & Holy Cause? When will America be America?

> "A Just and Holy Cause." Those words alone should be enough to tear down the statue and never look back.

> The statue makes me sad because it is a reminder that I was 47 years old before I realized the pain it causes others. It is time we (white southerners) move on.

I recognize that outsiders aren't always welcome in discussions around local issues, so it was with a sense of humility that I requested a permit to set up a studio on the courthouse lawn with the help of the William Winter Institute for Racial Reconciliation.

We were there to listen. And learn. For two days, we set up our lighting a few feet away from the Confederate monument and asked people, "What does this statue mean to you?"

The Winter Institute shared news of the studio sessions in their circles. I asked my connections at the university to share the news in their networks as well. A few random people walking by asked what we were doing and chose to participate.

In the end, 36 people answered our question and had their photo taken. One man said the statue didn't bother him. The other 35 people said it should be relocated. People who wanted the statue to stay also showed up and some even talked with me. Calmly. But none of them wanted their photo taken and attached to their words. The series is powerful, but it would be more complete with the opposing viewpoint as well.

I'd like to try again, though there wasn't time on this trip. Maybe we could promote it differently. One person commented that those who want the statue to stay in place don't need to voice their opinion because currently their perspective and the status quo have the ear of the county leadership. There is science that suggests conservative voices don't feel welcome in conversations about social justice and perhaps people felt they wouldn't be treated fairly in our process.

Our process is rooted in welcoming all voices, but sometimes that wide net does not gather the broad range of perspectives we would hope. Sometimes there are still voices that go unheard.

It's interesting to note that out of the 36 participants, nobody suggested destroying the statue. They said relocate it. Put it somewhere else. Just not at the center of our town.

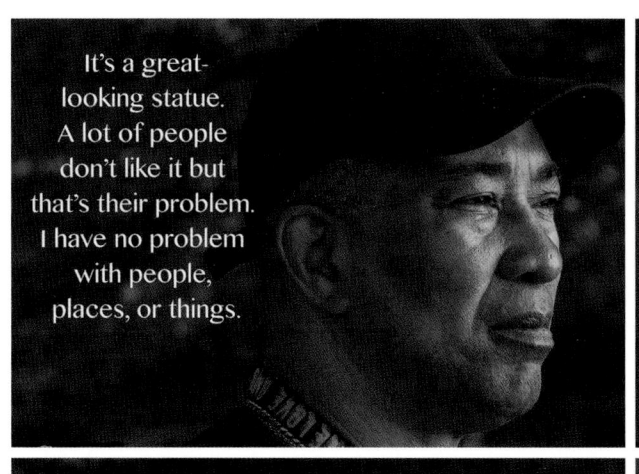

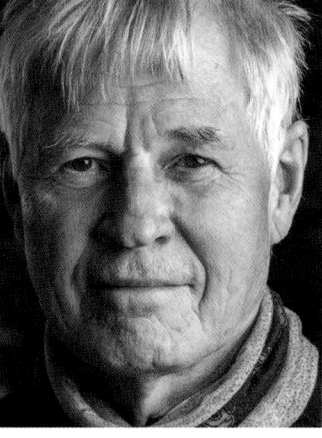

It's a great-looking statue. A lot of people don't like it but that's their problem. I have no problem with people, places, or things.	 The statue was placed here during an era of extreme domestic racial terrorism. It's time for that era to be over. Love your neighbor.
 A people were so engulfed in their hate for others, while mourning their fallen loved ones and their cause, they immortalized a lie.	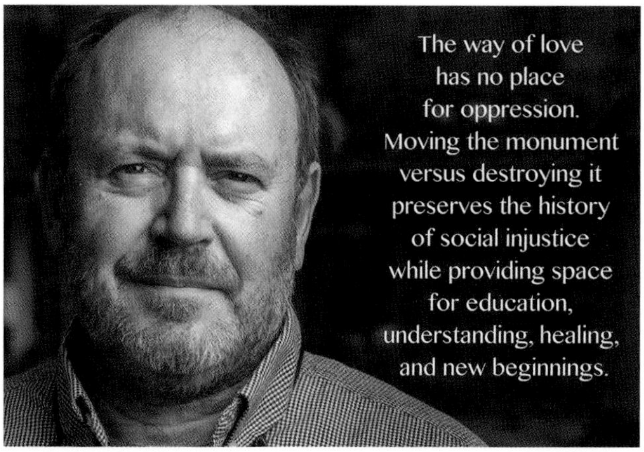 The way of love has no place for oppression. Moving the monument versus destroying it preserves the history of social injustice while providing space for education, understanding, healing, and new beginnings.
 The statue is the ultimate irony- a celebration of defeat, a tribute to "Patriots" who betrayed their country. It should be replaced with public art!	 This statue symbolizes a belief in white supremacy and either a disregard for, or a celebration of, the negative impact it has on others.
This statue now is a divisive symbol that the ruling class erected in 1907 to recontextualize the war.	 This statue honors and was established and defended by my ancestors. It is opposed by me. It will be removed by my children.

Journey to Columbus

Two hours south and east of Oxford, Mississippi, the County Board of Supervisors in Lowndes County in Columbus, Mississippi, voted to become the first city in the state to remove the Confederate monument from in front of their county courthouse. Theirs was going across town to Friendship Cemetery, where there are gravesites for both Union and Confederate soldiers.

Shortly after George Floyd was killed in Minneapolis, there was a motion before the board to move the monument, but it failed in a 2–3 vote along racial lines. Some difficult rhetoric followed, along with a change in board leadership, and after much community input, a new vote was held on July 6, 2020, and this time, the decision to move the statue was unanimous.

When we arrived in Columbus, the footings had already been poured at the new location and on May 22, 2021, the statue was removed from in front of the courthouse and loaded onto a truck to be reassembled later at its new home.

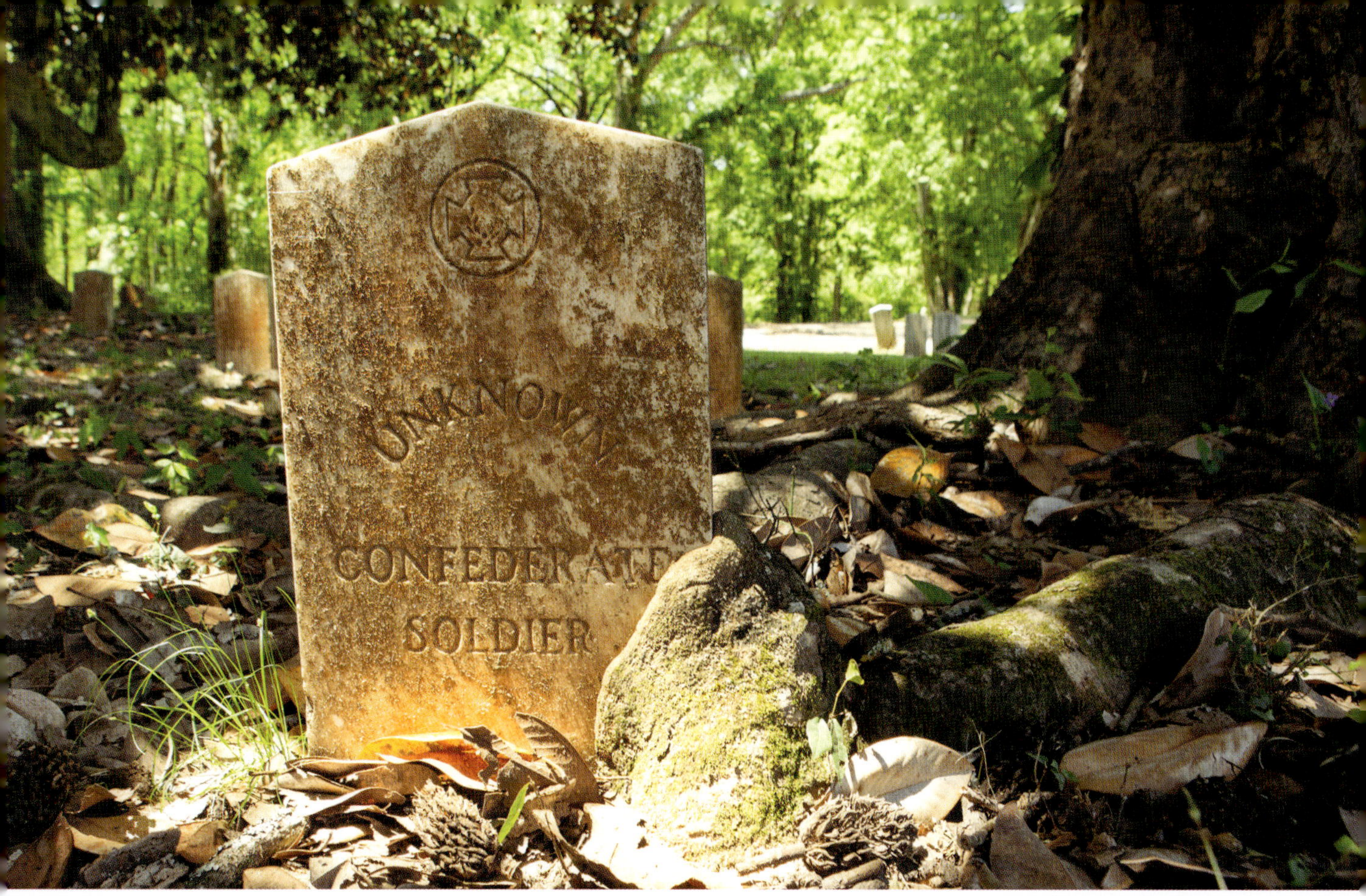
UNKNOWN
CONFEDERATE
SOLDIER

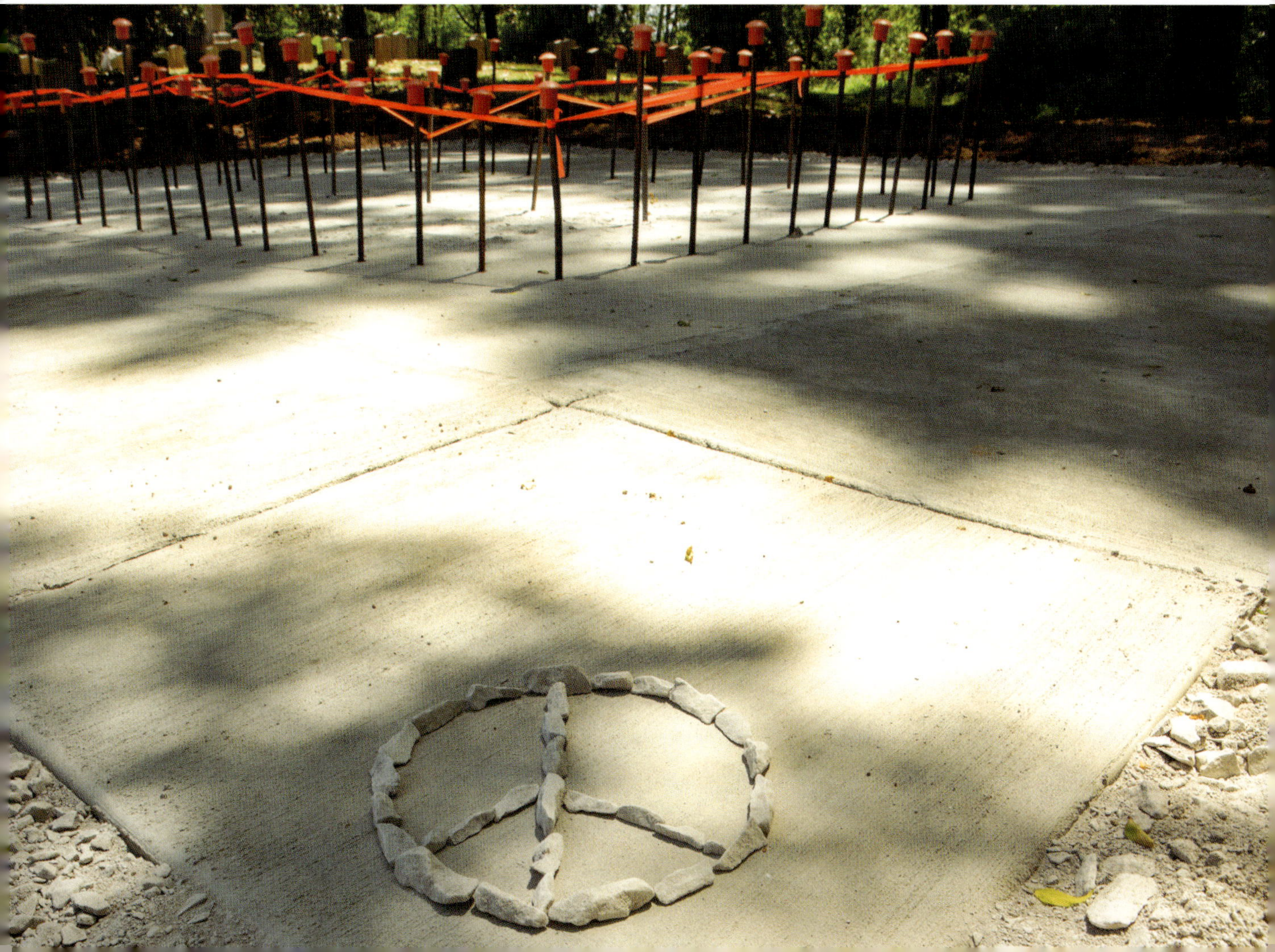

> "Generally speaking, in Mississippi, courthouses have two features in common. One of them is a clock tower, the other is a Confederate memorial or monument. And they both tell you what time it is."
> —Slim Smith

Slim Smith is a newspaper columnist for *The Commercial Dispatch*, the daily newspaper in Columbus, Mississippi, and a community institution since 1922.

The thing you need to know about Mississippi is time moves, but it moves very slowly. It would be unfair to define the South simply in terms of race, but it would be equally unfair not to give it the portion it deserves. To my mind, if you go through Mississippi, we memorialize what we venerate.

My seven-time grandfather was a slave owner in South Carolina. My four-time grandfather died fighting for the Confederacy in the Battle of Lovejoy's Station outside Atlanta in 1864. My story is probably similar to a lot of southerners. We have ancestors who fought for the Confederacy, so you get resistance removing those monuments. Things get personalized. "Those were my ancestors and they fought bravely and they didn't own slaves."

In my mind, it's just a bad way to look at it. Look, I would much rather redeem my family's history than celebrate it. You know, I'm not proud that my seven-time grandfather was a slave owner or that my four-time grandfather fought for the Confederacy. They were products of their time, but basic questions of humanity aren't subject to that sort of rationalization. If it's wrong to hold another human being now, it was wrong to hold another human being 300 years ago. Those are universal truths. But you get wrapped up in all that.

You hear people say, "Well, you're removing history. You're removing our heritage." But I've never understood that argument. History is what happened, right? Heritage is what we tell ourselves about what happened. And so the history is ugly. It is. And the heritage may be even worse, because you're trying to sanitize something that's not worthy of that treatment.

It's disingenuous to say that you moved beyond where you were in the 1860s if you still continue to have those symbols. Symbols are important. I mean, how much does McDonald's spend on [its] logo? How important is that? Those are things that we instantly recognize and that's marketing. Well, we're doing marketing, too, with those statues. Whether we realize it or not. And so what are we advertising? Who are we really? And how far have we really come?

Leroy Brooks has served on the Lowndes County Board of Supervisors for 37 years. He was the first African American elected to the position in this county. He says he was called to the position as an advocate for equality and justice because, as a boy, he grew up seeing a world that left certain people out of the process.

Prior to graduating from high school, I had never been out of Mississippi. I had been in an integrated environment because my mom had work. My father had worked on a farm. As a matter of fact, at one time, my father, my grandfather and my brother all worked on the farm hauling hay for the same guy. So I grew up in this environment that was integrated, but it was segregated.

And the thing that I saw real early as a kid was that the people that my mom worked for, they had two kids and one was a boy, two years younger than myself. And we played together, grew up roaming out in the woods and fishing. And I always said, "Yes, ma'am" to his mom, but he always said "yea" to my mom.

But the most interesting thing was when my mom would go to the house to do what she did—which was cook and clean up—she could not go through the front door of the house. She had to go to the back to go into the house. But once she was in there, she was all over the house.

I started noticing these little things. And I didn't understand the full implications of them until I got older. Here I was a kid growing up, working on these farms, picking cotton, hauling hay, and being around whites and watching the kind of things that they say.

I remember when Dr. King got assassinated, I heard these white men say, "Well, you know, we've got a reason to celebrate. We're going to go have a party."

But the other thing that I reflected back on, the people that my mom worked for, the man was a justice court judge. And so all the highway patrolmen, they would come up for court cases and tickets and they were all huge. I never saw Black highway patrol. I remember my oldest sister being shaken. My dad was rushing her to the hospital and he got stopped by one of these highway patrol. And he looked in the car and he says, "N*****, why are you going so fast?"

And so I just remembered all these things in my mind. I used to say to my mom, "When I get old enough, I'm going to take care of you. I'm going to look out for you." So I joined the Air Force with the

> "God is the center of my life. My family is the essence of my life. And community is the purpose of my life. So that's how I characterize myself as I go about doing what I do."
> —Leroy Brooks

intent of getting out of Mississippi, never to come back again. It was going to be my ticket. I had had high school ROTC, so I understood it. I joined the Air force, not knowing what I wanted to do. I just wanted to join. And, of course, I ended up being a law enforcement specialist and I, and I loved it. I got to meet people from all over the country and I got to meet whites that had never been around Blacks.

I spent a couple of years in Wichita, Kansas. And then went over to England for a couple of years. And life was a little different, but I'm still meeting people. And now I'm coming back home on leave, and I'm seeing a different perspective. I'm getting an understanding of the dynamics that I grew up in. And I felt this calling to come back.

And I thought how important that was for my kids to be around their grandparents and extended family, and how important it was for me, as a boy, going to those fishing holes and just a simple way of life. But at the same time, I was contemplating, if they're going to be here, there's gotta be some catalyst for change. And I understood the dynamics of change could not just be from a political perspective, but to share with people some sense of hope.

04.20.21: George Floyd verdict

Emily Liner grew up in Mississippi. She went to college at Georgetown University and stayed to work in politics in Washington, D.C., until she started feeling the pull to return home. While her home state has a history of "brain drain," she sees the opportunity to use her entrepreneurial skills to make Mississippi better for those who want to come home, as well as those who want to stay.

We are so divided as a country. We are physically divided, we are geographically divided, and we so rarely encounter people who are different from us. We are starting to segregate ourselves from people who don't have the same values as we do. We are seeking communities of people who share our values [but] in trying to achieve one goal, we're actually making another goal harder to reach.

A lot of people boil this down to red state, blue state. I came from a red state—Mississippi—and lived in Washington D.C., which if it were a state would be the bluest blue. I worked for a company based in San Francisco, again, very dark, dark blue. And I started to realize that the conversations I had with people about politics were more difficult outside of Washington, D.C., than they were inside.

Everyone who goes to Washington, D.C.—regardless of their political beliefs—is an optimist and wants to make the world a better place and they see Washington as the vehicle to make that happen. Because we're in the bubble of the capital campus,

"There's an economic imperative to cultural change. How do we create a place that is going to be more inviting and more welcoming so that people will want to come home?"
—Emily Liner

you're always running into different people. You befriend people who have different political beliefs because you're sitting next to each other in the cafeteria or because you have the same commute in the morning, or your kids go to the same schools, or you go to the same farmer's market. And so I had great relationships with people across the political spectrum when I lived in Washington, D.C., but when I would come home to Mississippi, I always felt like I was having to defend my liberal politics to my conservative friends and family. And when I went to San Francisco, I always felt like I had to defend my more moderate sensibilities with the progressives in that community.

And I realized that when we think that Washington is broken, Washington is just a reflection of our communities around the country. We elect our representatives, we decide who gets to go there. So if Washington is broken, it's because of the choices that we made and who we sent there.

Chuck Yarborough grew up on the Mississippi Gulf Coast in an area that his family inhabited for nine generations. He teaches history at the Mississippi School for Mathematics and Science in Columbus, and says he fell in love with history by hearing the stories of people who were directly involved in that history. Each year his students are assigned to research the story of a local person from Columbus, write a script, and recount the story in a local cemetery in a project he calls *Tales from the Crypt*.

"Rarely do you succeed when you tell people what to think. You succeed when you show people something that forces them to think."
—Chuck Yarborough

Each student would pick the name of somebody buried in [the cemetery]. I required that students use primary documents and, as they write a research paper, explain the context of a person's existence. So it's not just a biography, but a story [that] connects [someone] with the larger story of the nation.

[The students] became intimately familiar with their research subjects. Scripts developed that explored, in some pretty amazing ways, race, gender, religion, poverty. Stephanie's research subject was a guy who had two children by two different slave women. He was a slave holder. He was long dead, but he had two mixed-race children, and left all of his belongings to them in his will. Yet legally, they were kept in trusteeship to a white guy and both children had to sue in order to inherit their own stuff.

So Stephanie decided she was going to portray a mixed-race child who appeared to be white because she's kind of a dark-complected white kid. In the middle of this script, she says, "I didn't know if, when my father looked into my eyes, he saw his daughter or he saw the brutes we were said to be." And then she talks about race and white supremacy in the late 19th century. Powerful stuff. And it was transformative to audiences.

The big fault with history is we assume history to be one thing. Most people study history not to get it right, but to get it wrong. To reaffirm their position or some belief system they have or some status quo. And our students are trying to get at the truth as they see it being revealed.

Twenty-five years ago, the story would have been all about the slaveholder's perspective, because that's what's in the documents. But those documents are an incomplete version of our history. We're trying to figure out ways to give voice to the people who are absent from those documents.

Journey to Montgomery

My heart is heavy. It's the news. It's the trial in our hometown for the death of George Floyd. It's Daunte Wright. It's Atlanta. Kenosha. Indianapolis. It's gathering stories under the shadow of a Confederate statue. It's visiting lynching sites.

But it's more than that.

It's how quickly each event is spun and re-spun, then spun again. It's how animosity instantly takes root in the space compassion should claim. It's how tragedies are weaponized and turned on the victims. It's comments in news feeds that start out toxic and grow more venomous from there.

Given the weight of the days, it might be tempting to just seek escape. But while escape feels good for a moment, it does little to address the issue. I am reminded of the mourning process. The importance of going through each step in its time. Sitting with the grief. Honestly reckoning with the struggle and creating space for lament.

On one difficult day I was quick to tears and a little self-conscious about it. The kind soul I was with simply said, "We call that watering the garden."

We protect ourselves from discomfort and, in the process, we deny ourselves the opportunity to process our grief and develop the understanding of how to forge that pain into new strength.

So today, we headed to Montgomery. I knew it would be a heavy day. We visited the Equal Justice Initiative's Legacy Museum. We walked through the sacred grounds of the Peace and Justice Memorial, otherwise known as the Lynching Memorial. We stood beside the stop where Rosa Parks climbed on board a bus and refused to move to the back. She later explained, "The only tired I was was tired of giving in."

"History, despite its wrenching pain, cannot be unlived, but if faced with courage, need not be lived again."
— Maya Angelou

133

I HAVE
A DREAM

AVE THEIR LIVES

me injustice
e the right
ll Americans

REEB

ZZO

DR. MARTIN L.
KING JR.

Journey to Selma

In Selma we stopped at Brown Chapel, where marchers organized for their effort to secure voting rights during the Civil Rights Movement. We crossed the Edmund Pettus Bridge where on March 7, 1965, peaceful protesters were met with brutal police force to turn them back. We drove the historic route from Selma to Montgomery, following the same path that marchers traveled on their 5-day journey to the state Capitol.

It is difficult history. It is tragic history. It is true history. And we need to honestly face it if we are going to fully understand who we are today.

My heart is heavy, and so it should be. There is much to mourn in this season. But it's also springtime. So grieve if you must, but remember to also plant your seeds. When grief overwhelms you and leads to tears, know that you are watering your garden. And, in time, something new and beautiful is going to grow.

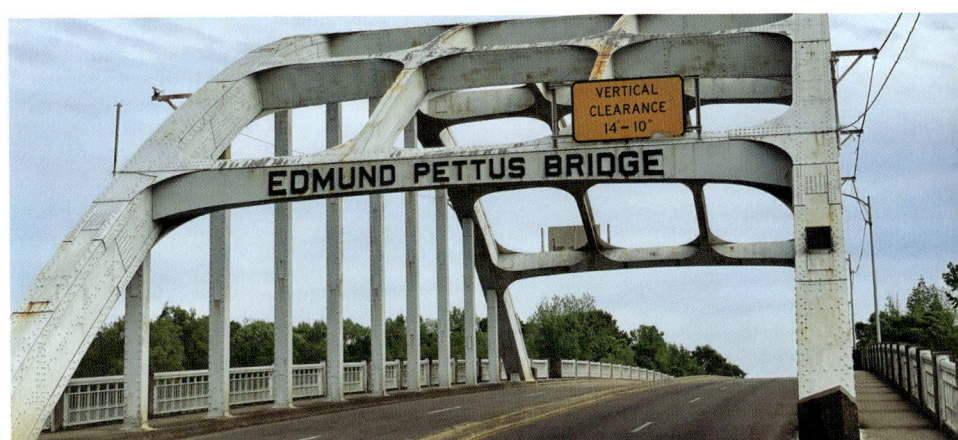

"They tried to bury us, but they didn't know we were seeds."

—from Greek poet, Dinos Christianopoulos and often used in the Indigenous People's Movement in Mexico.

"Whether it be the pandemic or whether it be the headwinds, there are hard times, but you understand that it's temporary. You understand that around the bend, we're going to be okay."
—Neal Moore

Neal Moore is a journalist, adventurer, and expatriate. I met him by chance in a coffee shop in Columbus, Mississippi, and we found time the next day to do an interview. He was in the midst of a two-year adventure, paddling 7,500 miles across the United States in an effort to remember the beauty of this country and the people who live in it. The journey brought him from Astoria, Oregon, to the foot of the Statue of Liberty.

The idea was to paddle the year leading into national elections and then the full year after, no matter how it would have turned out. What would we look like as a nation the year after national elections?

What I'm looking for is that common thread, from coast to coast. What I'm really looking for is the common humanity, and I've seen it. I've seen it with individuals. I've seen it with families. I've seen it with communities.

I'm generally up an hour before first light. I put all of my worldly belongings into my canoe and I push off. In that exact moment, it's just pure perfection.

In many cases on this journey, I'm risking my life. I'm putting myself completely out there and there's a strange phenomenon that takes place, when it's touch and go. When you realize that you're in a situation that can absolutely end your life, it's when you feel like you really live. You have to focus. You cannot freak out and you have to see your way through.

And so whenever you have tribulation—be it the loss of loved ones, be it nature's temporary fury—you have to soldier through. And by making your way through the hard times, on the flip side of that—when you make the safe harbor, when the sun comes out bright and beautiful—then it's all the sweeter because you've earned it.

I think our greatest strength is empathy. When you stop and take away these labels that we like to identify ourselves by. When you strip all of that away, what we're left with is something beautiful. It's something I think that we can all connect to and if we let ourselves, we can all love in a positive way. That is our common humanity. That is the natural desire to help, to have empathy for our brothers and sisters. And I think from coast to coast, when you're looking for it, you see it. And when you do see it, it strengthens your belief in mankind.

I really wanted nothing more than a couple days off. We'd been running hard. We'd navigated some emotional issues. I was way behind on downloading and editing stories and my plan was to pick up a latte at the local coffee shop and hunker down at our campsite on the Tombigbee River to get caught up.

But in the coffee shop, I met Neal and he told me a little bit about his journey. I really wanted that day off, but sometimes something else lands in your lap and you don't get to choose.

Water Protectors

This journey was never a straight line. It was time to head north again. Grey, our art student, was graduating from college and even though COVID-19 kept spectators out of the arena as graduates walked the stage, we parked in the lot outside and watched a livestream of the ceremony on our laptop.

Karen had plans to see friends in the Twin Cities. I had arranged to spend time at the Water Protectors camp in Palisade, Minnesota, where an Indigenous women-led movement was protesting the Line 3 pipeline. We had recently spent time near the mouth of the Mississippi, now it was time to get close to the river's source.

Early in the summer of 2016, I was on my way to photograph a magazine assignment in North Dakota and as I drove across the state, I tuned into a local radio station to listen to reports of the Standing Rock protests that were then gaining traction. I heard the protesters described as dangerous troublemakers, malcontents, squatters. I don't remember hearing any of the protesters get any air time. People talked about them, but rarely with them or to them.

The same thing was true about the Water Protectors. Much of the rhetoric was negative, just like it was with the George Floyd protestors. In Minneapolis, what I saw at the intersection of 38th Street and Chicago Avenue did not square up with the narratives I heard from critics. I wanted to spend time with the Water Protectors and hear their stories for myself.

I had a week. The first day I showed up without my gear, just to say hello. Trust was tough to find and I understood the reasons why. Take a look at the history and it's not hard to figure out. People who looked like me had made plenty of promises and then failed to follow through. Someone once said you can make progress at the speed of trust and I had to invest some time to earn that trust. I had to slow down and work on building relationships before we could begin the work. Actually, building relationships was the work.

I can be impatient when I have something I want to accomplish. I had to slow down to the pace of muddy spring trails, the smell of campfire, the sound of drum circles drifting through the chorus of spring peepers from the surrounding wetlands. I slowed down to the pace of the camp, warmed by the sun and cooled by the breeze. And slowly, a space opened for connection and conversation.

It was time for my second COVID-19 vaccine and I was able to get on the schedule at a community clinic set up in a church in McGregor, Minnesota. This time, I experienced side effects: fever, chills, exhaustion. I spent the day in bed and then got back to work.

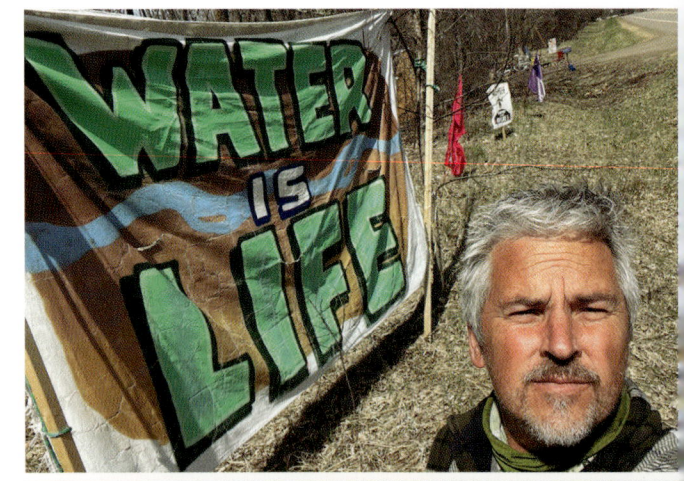

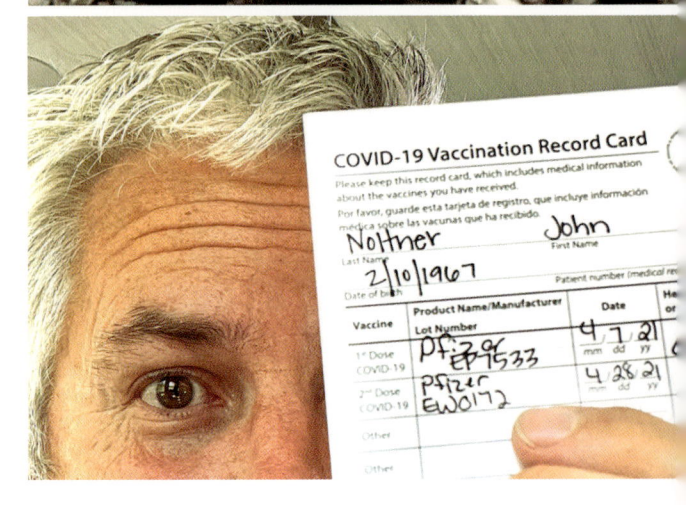

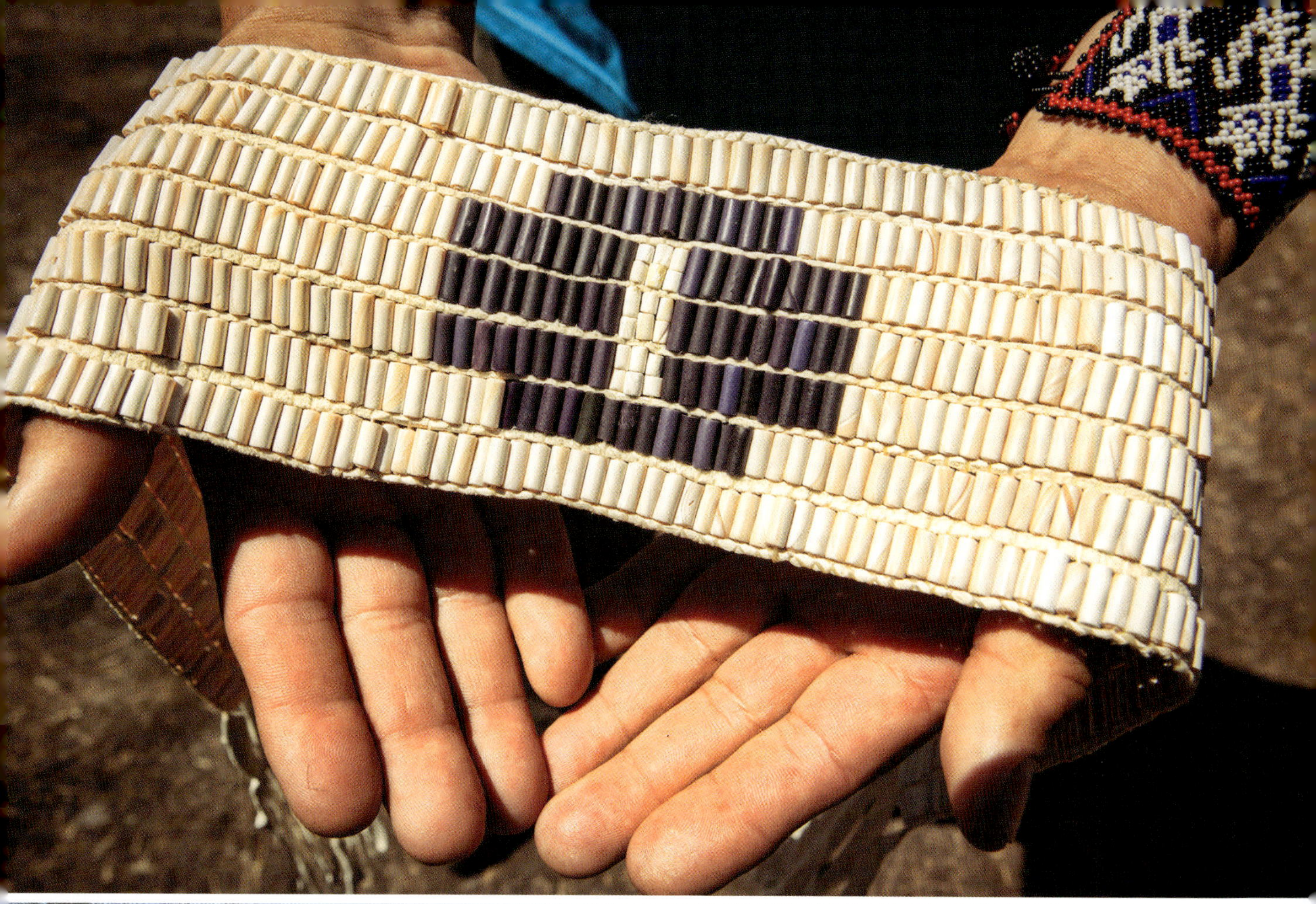

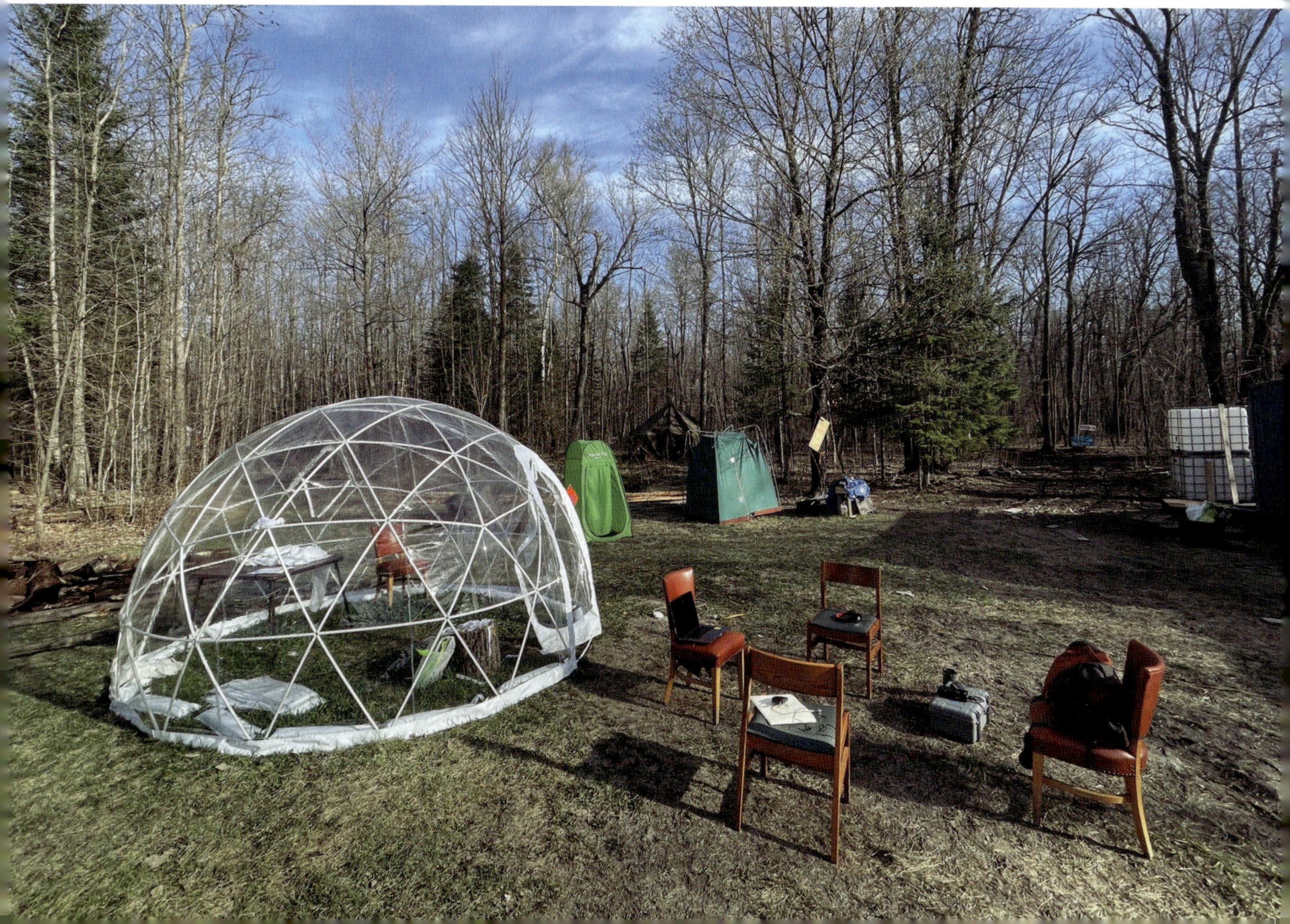

Over the course of several days, I asked the Water Protectors,

"What has brought you here?"

In the good humor that circulated around the ever-present campfire, there was broad consensus that Gus, the camp dog, should have a voice in the project as well. So, together, the community crafted his message and added it to the mix.

In light of the impending demise of global civilization it is incumbent upon our generation to effectuate radical change to reorient social structures and banish the capitalistic hegemony. Also, bacon.

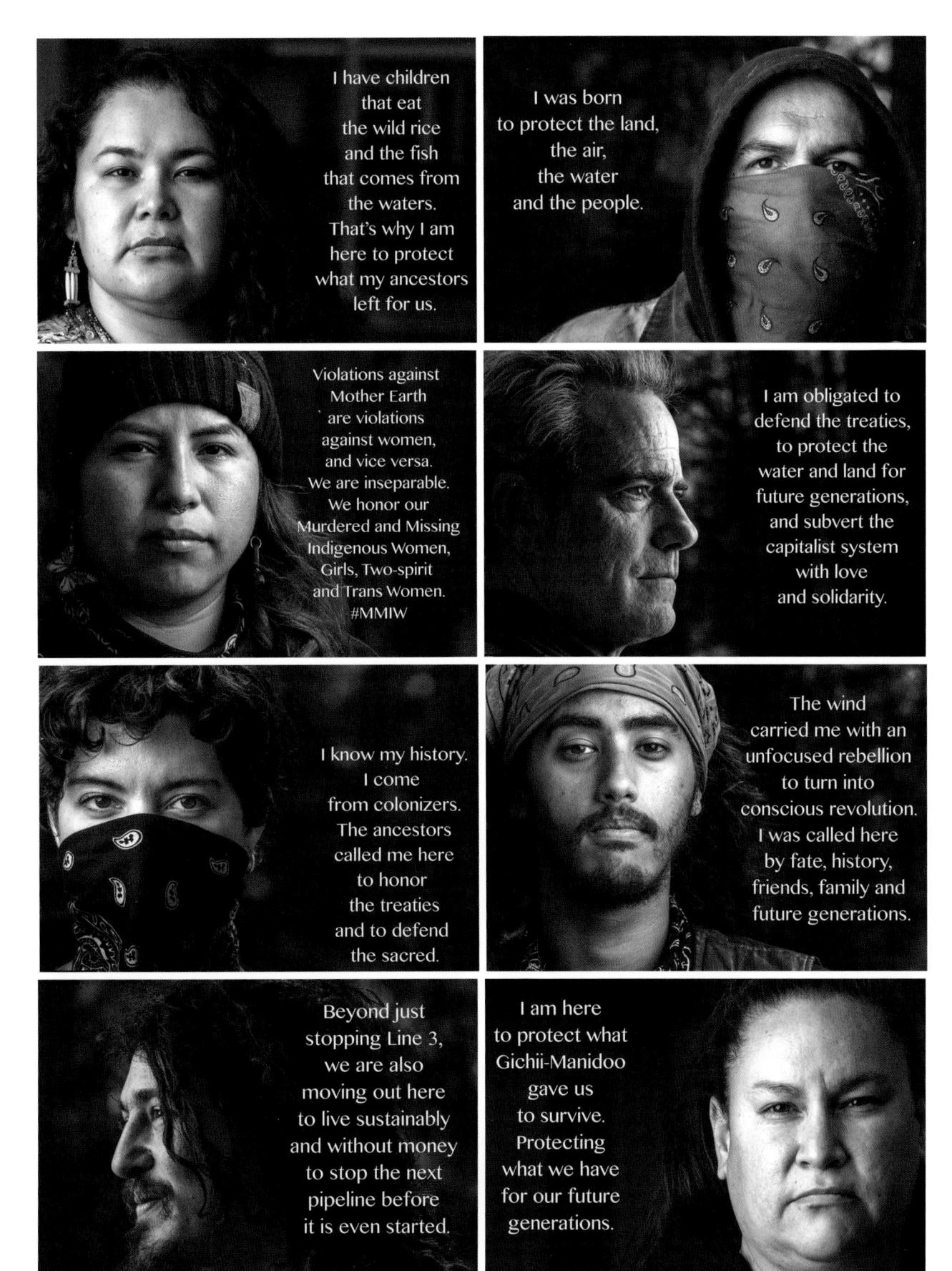

Water Protector studio

I have children that eat the wild rice and the fish that comes from the waters. That's why I am here to protect what my ancestors left for us.

I was born to protect the land, the air, the water and the people.

Violations against Mother Earth are violations against women, and vice versa. We are inseparable. We honor our Murdered and Missing Indigenous Women, Girls, Two-spirit and Trans Women. #MMIW

I am obligated to defend the treaties, to protect the water and land for future generations, and subvert the capitalist system with love and solidarity.

I know my history. I come from colonizers. The ancestors called me here to honor the treaties and to defend the sacred.

The wind carried me with an unfocused rebellion to turn into conscious revolution. I was called here by fate, history, friends, family and future generations.

Beyond just stopping Line 3, we are also moving out here to live sustainably and without money to stop the next pipeline before it is even started.

I am here to protect what Gichii-Manidoo gave us to survive. Protecting what we have for our future generations.

Tania Aubid is an Anishinaabe woman who is involved in the Water Protector movement that resists construction of the Line 3 pipeline in northern Minnesota. She says she is driven to care for the natural resources so they are available for her children, and her children's children, seven generations into the future, so that they have a place where they can feel safe and happy and exercise their inherent rights.

The face paint is because of the ceremony that I have been through. It's a ceremony for me to be able to come out and speak about the truths of our people, to be able to speak up for the voices that can't speak.

I am an original person from these lands. My family has been here for over 15,000 years. Harvesting is in the treaties that have been signed by the federal government, protecting my inherent rights to hunt, fish, and gather here, to be able to stand strong in the community and to be able to protect the things that I have for future generations. Just like what my ancestors have protected for me.

The settlers of these lands have invaded like parasites. [They] have done destruction by poisoning our resources and poisoning the people in [many] ways. You know, they wanted their pristine lands, and then they pushed us all into the swamps. And now that the swamps have resources for them to exploit, they want to push us out over here, too. Through the logging companies, through the pipelines, through the mining—they want to exploit the resources that we've been sent here to protect.

We've fought so long and so hard, and the Indian people are so tired right now. We need non-native allies to step up and help protect the Anishinaabe people so that they get more rested.

In our traditions, there's this spirit being called a Windigo. And that Windigo is never satisfied with whatever it takes, whatever it eats. It just keeps going after more and it kills and destroys whatever is in its way. So, to me, all those people that came from abroad and immigrated over this way, they had that mentality of always wanting more. Nothing was ever satisfying to them. That's kind of like the Windigo spirit that I see.

"I can't trust the process. The process doesn't work.
If you get along, these are the toys and trinkets that you'll be able
to have, but if you don't get along, you'll be denied all that."
—Tania Aubid

> "There are very few opportunities to come together and do something selfless and beautiful and loving and compassionate and respectful with humility. This is it, right here."
> —Joe Hill

Joe Hill is from the Seneca Nation near Buffalo, New York. Originally located near Rochester, the Seneca Nation was pushed westward after the Revolutionary War in retaliation for their neutrality in the war and in order to open up the land for European settlement. Joe traveled to northern Minnesota to a Water Protectors camp north of Palisade to protest an oil pipeline that will cross the Mississippi River and many others. He spent the winter there living in a yurt, and said he had come to support an Indigenous women–led movement, to live simply, and to exercise his obligations under the Great Law of Peace.

Over a thousand years ago, my people were having a hell of a hard time. Strife, killing, and the Peacemaker brought us a new way to live together and principles we call the Great Law of Peace. That is the model for the United States constitution.

Our agreements [were on] wampum belts. The purple is the quahog shell. The white, a whelk shell, and our most solemn agreements were made into these belts. We would say that every now and then, we've got to polish these up and we would take them out and read them. As we read them, we would tell the story contained in them. That's how we remembered our histories. It was the mnemonic device which triggered that memory.

The museums in New York State took our belts, said they were for safekeeping and kept them for a hundred years. Those institutions are nothing more than trophy cases. They were never going to understand what these meant without the oral tradition that goes along with them. Maybe they thought we would forget. And as we forgot, we would lose our way. We weren't supposed to be around anymore.

Being [in Minnesota] has taught me how little I really need. In the winter, I needed warm gear. I need food. We have learned how to care for each other here because in the severe cold, when there was only a handful of us here, we did whatever it took to keep each other warm and fed.

That's a beautiful thing. That's love. That's what brought me here. Love of Mother Earth and love of my people. Not just the Seneca, but all Indigenous people. We're still here. We haven't gone anywhere. They have tried so hard [to remove us] and we're still here.

Noemi Aidee Tungui Aguilar comes from the Purépecha people of Michoacán, Mexico. She is an activist and an educator, on a journey to celebrate a culture that was nearly wiped out through colonialism. I met Noemi at a Water Protectors camp near Palisade, Minnesota, where she went by the camp name Luna. She traveled there from her home in California to protest the construction of the Line 3 pipeline and to continue her advocacy for Murdered and Missing Indigenous Women (MMIW).

I've reconnected with my roots, going from assimilating for so many years to actually going back to my homeland to experience the music, food, and culture, and to have a sense of pride for my Indigenous roots. Indigenous culture is beautiful. That wasn't taught to us. What was taught to us in school was that Indigenous people were no more. That Indigenous people were extinct.

I'm glad that I still have my grandmother. She still speaks the language. They actually brought her to the schools to teach the teachers so they could teach the kids. And the culture is being preserved. Our culture was about to be gone because we were almost wiped out through colonialism.

I would love to see more spaces for people to heal. I would like to see an intergenerational movement where there is respect among people. I would ask our elders to share their wisdom with us because there's so much that they have been through. Our young people need to know those stories, to have that wisdom passed on to them so that they can move forward with all this knowledge that exists.

I would like Indigenous women to see their inner warrior strength. I would like to see all of our communities talking about this epidemic of murdered and missing Indigenous women, girls, two spirits, and all of our relatives. And I would like people to recognize that our voices are powerful along with our actions. We need to put down our egos to do this work because it's going to take all of us and we can't rise if we don't all rise.

> "I would like patriarchy to fall and for us to continue unlearning colonial systems and to relearn our roots because they are within us. We are medicine and we need to tap into our inner ancestral wisdom that we carry with us."
>
> —Noemi Aidee Tungui Aguilar

> "So I carry all these things for my family. And now I'm the top of my family. I have my mother on her side, but on my father's side, that's it. My grandpa's gone, my father's gone. There's nobody else. So I gotta carry it all for my sons. Gotta be strong, you know."
>
> —Harvey Goodsky Jr.

Harvey Goodsky Jr. lives in McGregor, Minnesota. As a member of the Sucker Fish Clan, he carries the responsibility of being the shepherd of the land. His priority is to keep that teaching and learning alive through his own seven children and their future generations.

I just gotta keep doing my ceremonies. I don't know how many Anishinaabe are still doing ceremonies, so our culture's dying out. I can talk more English to you than Anishinaabe and that's bad being an Anishinaabe. I should be able to know my language, but I don't, because I was teased about being Anishinaabe in school. The reason why I have short hair is because the white boys would pull my hair out. I would have chunks of hair missing because it would all be on the playground. I've gone through a lot of racism in my life.

My kids are my priority. To teach them the right way so that they know they're good. They're my world. I will try my best to make sure that they get to be normal human beings. To be able to hunt, fish, and gather, to be able to feed themselves. To be able to survive in this world.

There's a lot of pain and trauma in the world. We have a lot of people that don't understand each other because we don't talk to each other. [There is a feeling] of hopelessness. The feeling of there's not gonna be any change, or any change that's gonna be made is not gonna be good.

That comes from the history of what our people have gone through because our traumas live through our DNA. Ancestrally, we go through these traumas that our parents, grandparents, great grandparents, they've all lived through.

There's not much infrastructure here. Here. There's the feeling of not having a place to say it's your own. Our ancestral homelands are right over there and it's called a National Wildlife Refuge. That's where we're originally from and we got moved east. They made a couple dams, they flooded us out. We came this way just like they did the Sioux when they wanted to put infrastructure there on the reservations.

We're getting boxed in each and every day compared to the original way that we used to live. These treaties that my ancestors signed and agreed to ensured that I had a right to hunt, fish, and gather among these lands. That's a binding law between two governments. That's real deal stuff. And nobody takes that seriously.

I used to gather berries, but who can find a wild berry patch? It's been so long since I have seen one. I used to go berry picking with my grandma, but none are even available.

And that means I'm never gonna be able to take my kids out berry picking naturally like my ancestors used to. I'm luckily able to go out wild ricing and teach my kids how to wild rice. Are their kids gonna be able to wild rice? And are those kids' kids' kids gonna be able to wild rice? Are they gonna be able to do the same things that we do, that's in our treaties?

What happens when the hunting, fishing, and gathering no longer exist for us? What are we? What's left? Indigenous people are only 1.78 percent in the country. There's not that many of us. And we used to be the shepherds of this land. We used to take care of it.

Shanai Matteson moved home to Palisade, Minnesota, with her two children during the pandemic to be closer to family and to be a caretaker at the Welcome Water Protectors Center, a part of the movement led by Indigenous women to resist the Line 3 oil pipeline near the spot where it would cross underneath the Mississippi River. Although she is not Anishinaabe herself, she is there in support of the 1855 treaty and the rights it grants to the local tribes.

Chaos produces a lot of creativity, too. Sometimes it's the spark of the individuals who are in a space together realizing their own potential. That is what makes it possible for a movement to flourish or for a community to really adhere and do something incredible.

We've all been called here. This is an incredible spot to be. It's so inspiring to be right on the river and to be able to watch the way it changes and all the things that are alive around us. We have this incredible opportunity to learn from that and to learn from each other. What we're starting here isn't going to go away as soon as the pipeline is stopped or done.

I tell people when they come here, even for a short period of time, that they see what we're doing here and they take a little piece of that home. And they put that to work in their community. So we're showing people what's possible and how you do it. Not that we have all the answers, but we're learning a lot of things.

Empire is this centralized controlling clamping down on the people that has moved across the world. We're living inside of it. But so is the movement

"A lot of the conflicts that we're having in our society are about questions of who and what belongs."

—Shanai Matteson

of people and the resistance, people's desire for liberation.

People know deep down what really keeps them safe and what really makes them experience joy. What really matters is not something that a company can give you. Money doesn't actually do that and it never has. But we keep believing in that. Like if we just had a little bit more, we would have what we needed to be safe and happy and content.

And we know that that's not how it works. But when you're in a community of people and you're like, okay, well now we gotta go chop wood, because we need to have this fire to be warm so we can stand around it. And now we're sharing our stories and we're opening up about the things that are hurting us and we're working through conflicts and we're growing food and we're listening to the frogs. You start to realize that what you actually need is all around you.

We've been told from the time that we're born that we're supposed to be climbing up this ladder and trying to achieve these other things. Once people see that and they experience that little spark of what it means to be in a community, then they want more of that.

Randell Sam is a member of the Mille Lacs Band of Ojibwe. I met Randell while spending time with the Water Protectors near Palisade, Minnesota. Randell shared some of his struggles with alcohol and drug addiction. After years of using, he found the true meaning behind his Anishinabe name, which is "I Am The Walking Light." Randell is now sober and plays an important role in the recovery movement in his community, fighting the opioid epidemic. He found his life's calling, saying that he is "recovering loudly so addicts don't have to die quietly."

I faced death three times. I flatlined three times. A lot of people from my community are fighting the same fight. We all had to bottom out to find our purpose here on earth. My family, 90 percent of them are active addicts, so I had to make the sacrifice of stepping aside from them to be able to live today. Other addicts saved me in the beginning. It was people I've never met before, just showing up, knocking at my door, saying, "Hey, we're here to help."

It took me a while. My pride wouldn't allow me to accept that help. But these guys just kept showing up every day, picking me up at night, taking me out, doing fun things. [They] were so happy to be sober and clean and in recovery.

I just kept going. I kept pushing because I had to do something if I wanted to live. In native culture, there's no word for hell. If you don't go to the happy hunting grounds, they say your spirit stays here and just wanders. So, when I'm around my community today, when I see people that are lost, sick, or whatever, I don't shame them because I know what it's like to be doing that. That was me a few years ago.

It takes somebody like me, who has been in that hole, who knows how to jump in that hole, [to] help pull them out. I lived my life thinking this was normal. Drink for a while, party for a while, go to jail, heal up, get out, and do it again. That's how I lived my life for 35 years. I never went to treatment because I always just went and did my jail time. I never asked for treatment, because I wasn't gonna accept it anyway. And I'll tell you something. When you start to believe in yourself, you raise your bar a little bit.

I know myself. Inside every addict—everybody out there struggling—there's a little voice in their head that says, "There's a better way. There's a better way to live."

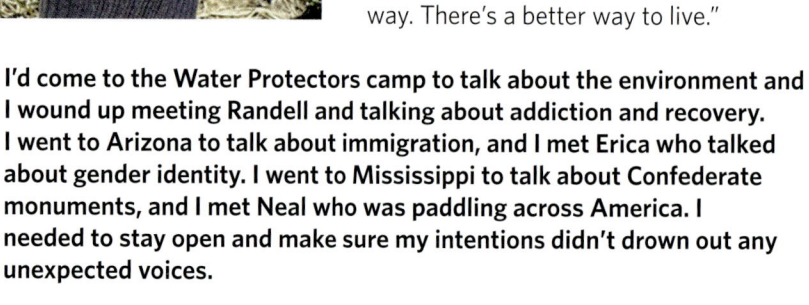

I'd come to the Water Protectors camp to talk about the environment and I wound up meeting Randell and talking about addiction and recovery. I went to Arizona to talk about immigration, and I met Erica who talked about gender identity. I went to Mississippi to talk about Confederate monuments, and I met Neal who was paddling across America. I needed to stay open and make sure my intentions didn't drown out any unexpected voices.

148

"Everybody has their rock bottom. Some might not be as bad as mine, some may be worse, but everybody's rock bottom is when they decide to stop digging."
—Randell Sam

Journey on the river

These stories are threads that weave through the fabric of our land. These waters flow from here to there. We are connected in more ways than we recognize. Certainly in more ways than we acknowledge.

I drove away, listening to drum circle music on Pandora. I don't pay for Pandora, so I get ads, and the first ad on the stream was from Enbridge, the company putting the pipeline in place. The ad talked about how they cared for the environment and how the Indigenous communities supported the pipeline and the jobs it would create. Money will buy you a platform, I thought. Or maybe they had met different people than I had.

I've been around a lot of water lately.

In the Louisiana bayou, where sometimes there's too much water and humans have tried to tame its power and flow. A thousand miles to the north, near the headwaters of that same river, I spent time with the Water Protectors. And now on to Bayfield, Wisconsin, perched on the edge of the greatest freshwater lake on Earth (as measured by surface area, for the statisticians in the crowd), where people are working in various ways to preserve the resource that holds 10 percent of the world's fresh surface water.

The stories are all connected. The world is smaller than you might imagine.

Lake Superior is vast, so it's easy to perceive it as invincible. But its size is what makes it vulnerable. With 2,726 miles of shoreline, it draws from an enormous watershed and is governed by the rules of multiple states and two different nations.

We once thought the great clouds of passenger pigeons were too large to become extinct. Until they did. Thunderous herds of bison were wiped out for sport—or to deprive Indigenous people of their food for survival.

You could fill a page with stats. Lake Superior covers 31,700 square miles. The deepest point is 1,333 feet deep. The largest wave measured was 31 feet tall. If you spread out all the water in the lake, it would cover the entire landmass of North and South America with a foot of water.

You can talk about the stats. The science. The history. The ecology. The policy. Those things are important. But when you go out on the lake, you can feel it. The experience is visceral when you float on the surface and watch the first light fall across the red rock cliffs. Look out at the horizon and you'll see nothing but blue water. You can hear the gentle lap of the boat's wake bounce off the rocky shore and see the ripples of the sandy bottom through 20 feet of crystal clear water. It saturates your soul and nourishes your spirit.

There are things that can't be measured in dollars and cents. Power and whimsy and wild abandon can't be put on a spreadsheet—and they are some of our most precious things.

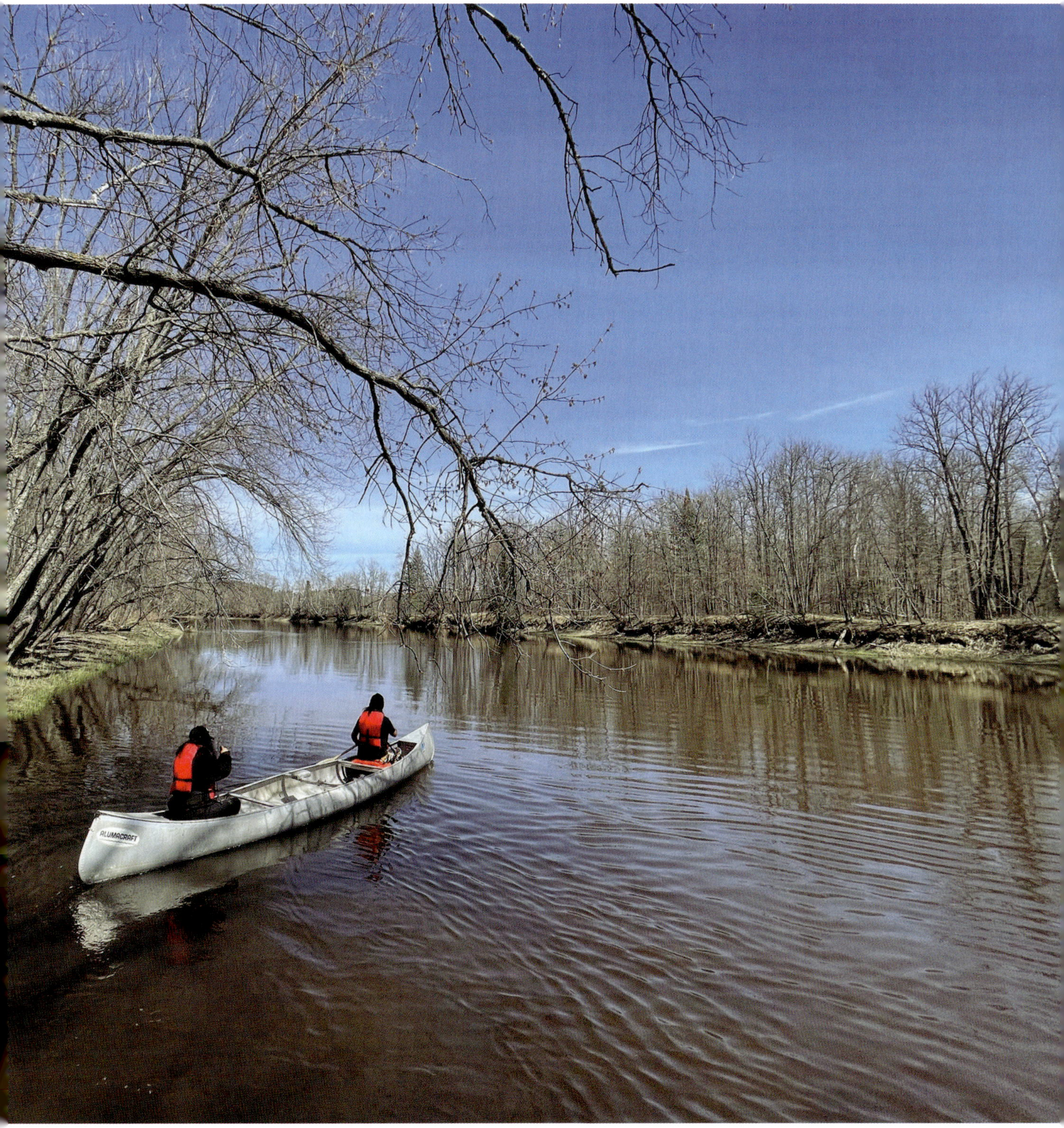
ALUMACRAFT

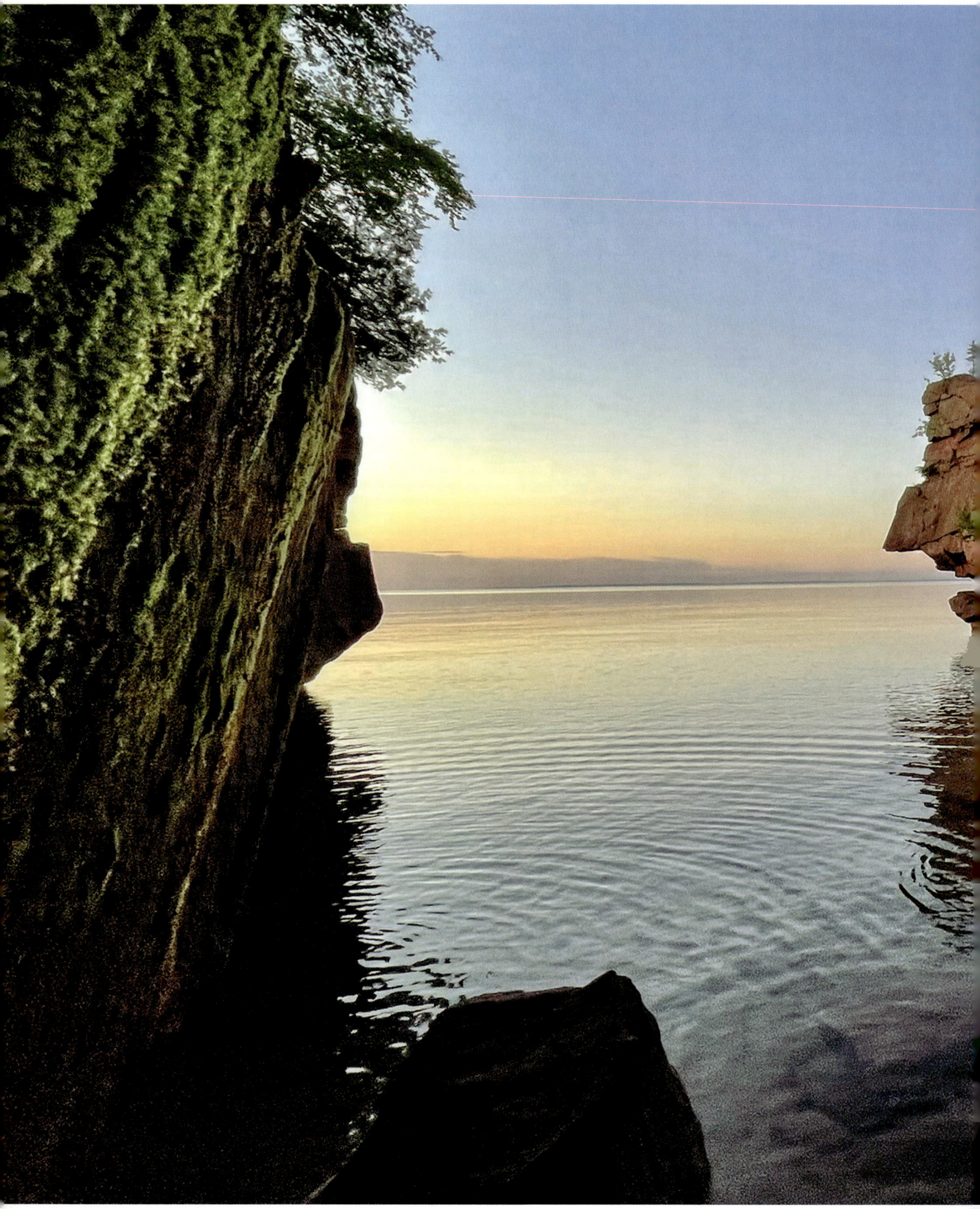

Journey to the Apostle Islands

Bazile Panek is a student at Northern Michigan University, majoring in Native American studies. He is an enrolled member of the Red Cliff Band of Lake Superior Chippewa in Red Cliff, Wisconsin. Bazile sees both burden and opportunity studying in a white-dominated institution. He feels a responsibility to advocate for Indigenous students at college to honor the sacrifices made by his elders who created the space he lives in today, but also to embrace the opportunity to educate others on the things he loves about his culture.

I'm conducting academic research on decolonizing entrepreneurship by Anishinaabe people and how traditional values can be integrated into entrepreneurship. When we think of entrepreneurship and business, we think of money, we think of capitalism, we think of white people. There are ways that we can decolonize entrepreneurship to integrate our traditional values and perspectives on leadership and business.

[We can] create more equitable frameworks within businesses that value all voices. Like the voices of the elders or the youth and what they think would help them. Integrating their voices and what they want is decolonizing. Caring for your community is decolonizing, because that doesn't happen a lot in western culture.

With the idea of humility and care for community, the aggression of negotiation or getting the cheapest prices possible can hopefully be eliminated. Paying your suppliers as much as possible or getting your product directly from other Indigenous people is how we can eliminate that aggression or extraction. Making sure everybody is paid well within the spectrum.

I joined a business student organization where it was required that you wear a fancy suit and tie and dress shoes. I had never worn that before because for native people, business attire is ribbon shirts, beaded medallions, beaded earrings, and moccasins. Being required to wear a suit and tie was odd for me. I didn't feel as confident. I took a step back, I didn't speak as much. Instead of a tie, I put on a beaded medallion along with the suit. It was kind of a decolonized tie, if you will. Wearing that beaded medallion with my suit made me feel more confident. I was more willing to speak in a meeting or put myself out there.

My advice to others is be proud of who you are as an Indigenous person. The ancestors have gone through a lot and created this space for all of us. So be proud of who you are, recognize those ancestors, and do things that will be a benefit to our future generations.

The decision about how to shape the portrait is usually a collaborative process. After our interview, Bazile wanted to return home to retrieve the beaded necklace that his father had given him for his high school graduation, and then he suggested we drive out to Raspberry Bay on the Red Cliff Reservation for the portrait. I trusted the process enough to believe that we could make something work and, as usual, I was not disappointed.

"Ever since colonization in 1492, things have been hard for native people. It's hard to even exist sometimes. So the power and the resiliency is especially tangible in native people today and you can see that within them."
—**Bazile Panek**

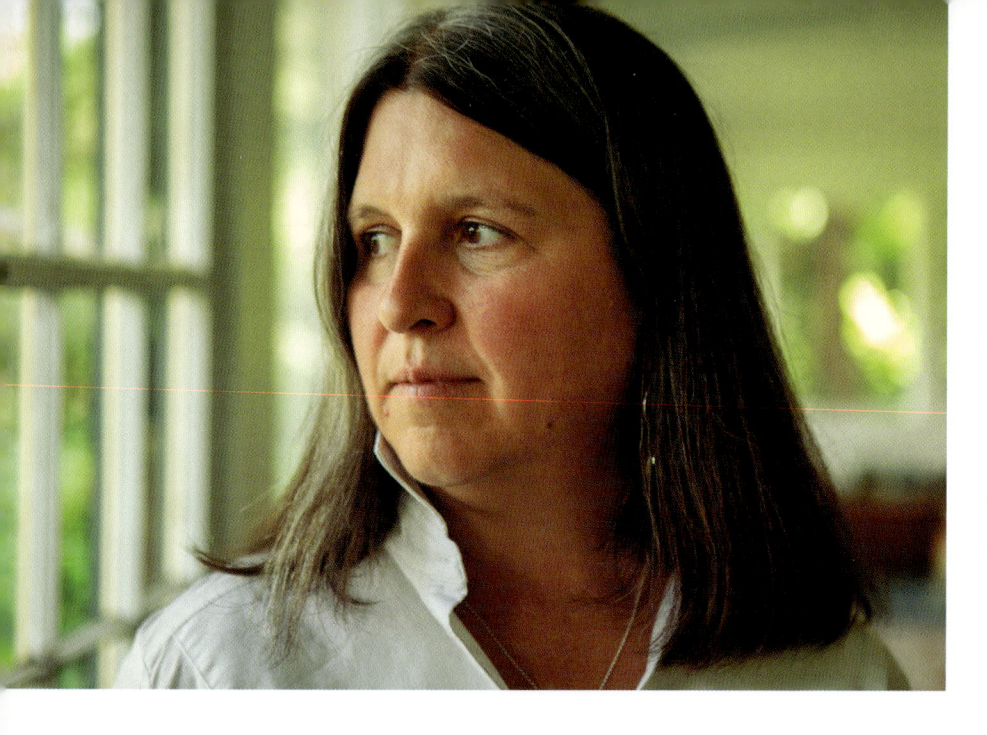

> "When you show up with tools, that implies that you have agency, that you have the confidence to do something, that you are willing to do the work."
>
> —Mary Dougherty

Mary Dougherty lives in Bayfield, Wisconsin, on the shores of Lake Superior. As she says, just about as far north as you can go in the state without getting wet. She has worked as an activist and is the author of *Life in a Northern Town: Cooking, Eating, and Other Adventures along Lake Superior.*

When you look at watershed—about clean water and how important it is—it helps to go upstream from that question and figure out what's happening on land. What does it look like for the people that live in the places that ring the watershed? Do they have access to good jobs? Do they have access to housing? What's transportation look like?

Clean water doesn't happen on its own. It happens from the sustainability and the health of the folks on the land that surrounds that water. I don't think you can take out one thing without talking about the whole watershed.

We have something undiscovered and very special here in Bayfield. We want to be a community of people that live here full time and that have the heartbeat that all communities have, but we're only 400 people. And so how do we welcome and balance—find peace with—the tourists that come up here? I want them to fall in love. Like I fell in love with this place. Because you protect what you love.

But then, how do you create balance? You don't want to love it to death. We live in a space where people don't have access to what we have access to every day, and people are hungry for what this looks like. It's quaint. It's beautiful. It's relatively quiet. We don't have any stop lights.

There has to be symbiosis and working together. Porous boundaries. Because if anything gets out of whack, it throws everything else out of whack.

The question always is, do you want to be right? Or do you want to win? And what does the win look like? Being right is very much ego-based and finding a winning solution for everything requires a little surrender of ego and taking a more expansive view of whatever issue you're grappling with.

I went out to Standing Rock and there was this Native American guy next to us at the campsite. We were hanging out with him by his fire and this young kid came and asked him if he could take some of his embers to start his fire, two [sites] down. But this young man didn't show up with a shovel. And this guy with us said, "Well, where the hell's your shovel?"

You don't show up and you don't take from people that have their fire burning. You have to show up with a tool or something to make it. We're not here just to take, take, take. I'll share my embers with you, if that's what you want, but you gotta show up with a shovel. You gotta show up with the tool to make it happen.

Think like a watershed. What I mean by that is, realize that we are all sharing the work. Watersheds operate to feed one common source, but some people are Class 4 rapids. Some people are intermittent streams. Some people are wetlands. Some people are creeks. Watersheds don't judge. They don't say the Class 4 rapids are more effective than the wetland people. There is balance in a watershed.

Someone from Ontario has a whole different understanding of this lake than I do in the Apostle Islands, but we're both living on that same lake. And so, if we think like nature, that would help us see the divides are just a mirage that's been put in our midst to keep us scrapping. And that scrapping is not serving the work of getting to that common body of water.

> "The forests of Northern Wisconsin were considered so vast that we could never deplete them. And in a very short time, we did. And to say that somehow we can't mess up Lake Superior because it's so big, well, that's ridiculous."
>
> —Mike Radke

Mike Radtke retired as the operations manager for the Madeline Island Ferry Line in Bayfield, Wisconsin. He started there as a captain and, over 32 years, he has made the 20-minute, 2.5 mile journey between the mainland and the island thousands of times.

Historically, the channel for the ferry route has frozen over during the winter and an ice road is maintained for island residents and visitors to drive across. But over recent decades, weather patterns have changed and for several years the channel has not frozen and ferry service has continued year-round.

There's no normal anymore. I started in April of 1989 and you could almost set your calendar that the freeze up would happen sometime around the first or second week of January. There would be a shutdown and it wouldn't start to break up until late March or early April. People just came to expect it and plan for it.

I believe 1998 was the year of our first year-round season. We didn't shut down at all. We operated continuously that year. And that was a shock. And since then, we've had six year-round seasons. Prior to that, there'd never been a year-round season in the history of our company.

So the first one was shocking. The second one was an eye-opener, and then the rest [told us] things are clearly not what they used to be. And even in those years when we've been shut, we've had shorter freeze ups than in the past. So we've seen the evidence, at least in our area, of climate change.

I think sometimes people think of peace as meaning "no conflict." And I don't see it that way. I think that it's rather how we navigate the world in such a way that we avoid harm, and we accept that there will be challenges and that we will experience the world differently than other people. We will have conflict, but we're striving to do no harm. The Hippocratic oath, in a sense. You know, how are we going to avoid harming the planet?

A peaceful act is to not harm the planet and the creatures that live here as much as that's possible. And the same with your fellow human beings. You limit your harm. None of us are perfect and we will harm in some ways. And you hope that maybe there can be some restitution in some way for the harm that you do. So I see it as limiting the harm. Or if you do harm, how do you correct that?

Sandy Gokee is Anishinaabe—Bear Clan—and lives in Ashland, Wisconsin. Her Ojibwe name, Wenipashtaabe, means "she carries a light load."

A mother and an activist, she is concerned about the invisibility of Indigenous people and how imbalanced life has become between human and nonhuman beings. Sandy seeks to educate others on her community's cultures, beliefs, and treaties, so that they can heal and restore harmony and balance in their way of life.

"One of our values is bravery. And people tend to think bravery is not being afraid. On the contrary, bravery is doing the right thing even though you're afraid."

—Sandy Gokee

Indigenous people are invisible. You come imposing your ideals on us and then taking our land, and what are we supposed to do?

We didn't lose our languages, we didn't lose our culture. They were stolen. When we want to reclaim who we are, we've got to understand that the things that were taken from us were taken deliberately and purposefully. And we've got to reclaim those things with the same level of diligence and purpose.

I told my little boy that it's okay to be angry. It's normal. But what we do with that anger is what's important. We can choose to be destructive with it—we feel powerful with anger—but does that help anything? Is that helping solve the reason for your anger? Or we can choose to be creative with our anger.

We've survived genocide and we're angry. It's important to be angry, because if this stuff doesn't piss you off, then you ain't paying attention. Well, what are we gonna do about it? Are we gonna pout? Are we gonna wreck things? Or are we gonna use that anger to motivate and create something better? What we do with that anger is the important part.

White culture benefits from the genocide of our people. If your feelings get hurt over that, then you need to look at what has happened to us at the hands of white people and for the benefit of white people. And understand that if you're really trying to be an ally, don't let hurt feelings stop you from doing the right thing.

We've had more than our feelings hurt. We continue trucking on because we don't have a choice to step out of this. And if, as an ally, you choose to step out, then you've never really been an ally. You are looking to do it for other reasons. So if you want to be an ally, step in and be willing to stand with us. Meet us where we're at, not where you want us to be.

*"Lake Superior is my inner sanctuary.
I find so much peace and inspiration from this body of water.
I let nature heal me from the stress of the other part
of the real world that seems to be overwhelming us."*
—Bob Jauch

Bob Jauch is a retired state senator from Poplar, Wisconsin. He served his district for 32 years but retired in 2015 citing concerns over increasing polarization in the political process and his belief that he could no longer be effective in that climate.

In the nineties, people just didn't understand tribal sovereignty and couldn't accept the importance of tribal sovereignty and the relationship to treaties and long-term history of the Native Americans. People resented the results of those treaties. As a lawmaker, I respected the facts and tried to tell the facts. I stood right in the middle of that controversy without any apologies to remind people that treaties matter.

First of all, we ought to respect sovereignty. Just as we respect the sovereignty of foreign lands, we should respect the sovereignty of these tribes, because that's what was created back when the land was stolen from them. It was what was agreed to. And, therefore, the United States couldn't make a case in trying to establish a treaty with a foreign land if we weren't keeping our word with our own people.

And so it was very basic. It was in the treaties that they could spear and gather in the ceded territory. This was, in fact, land that was set aside for them or rights that were set aside for them. It was very controversial. It went on for several years and, eventually, their rights were upheld by the courts. And some very positive agreements were reached. It was actually healthy for the lakes of northern Wisconsin, because more fish hatcheries and rearing ponds were funded. And we were going to end up replenishing more fish and strengthening the resource and protecting it after the controversy than before.

It was one of those cases where your goal is not to be politically popular, but to be right. Not to be righteous, but to try to do the right thing to solve problems.

Lori Schneider has climbed the tallest mountain on all seven continents, a feat she accomplished after being diagnosed with multiple sclerosis. It took her 16 years to reach the final summit, which was Everest, the world's tallest peak at 29,032 feet. When she reached the summit, the clouds had rolled in and she had no view. She used a satellite phone to call home and share the news, but nobody picked up. She realized that the real victory was inside her and in the fact that she did not give up. Now that she has reached her goal, she uses her experience to encourage and empower others to reach theirs.

I'm not a climber by nature, I just happen to be determined. What I love about climbing is that you walk for hours every day and you're really by yourself. There may be other people, but you walk with your own thoughts and you have to learn to find calmness in yourself. If your mind is filled with, "Do I have a blister on my big toe?" Or, "How do I pee with ten men hooked to a safety line?" I'm not going to be able to keep going. Things can overwhelm you, or you can just let go. My strategy has always been to let go. It's a meditation, really. A walking meditation. A step is a step. It's just how many steps you put together.

When you climb in Africa, the guides say, "Poli poli." Slowly, slowly. And that's what you do. You walk slowly, slowly. On Everest, the summit is at 29,032 feet and the lack of oxygen makes you walk incredibly slow. You'll take a step and then seven to ten breaths, then another step and seven to ten breaths. You go this way for hours. The pace slows down to a crawl. You're so exhausted. You wonder if you're ever going to get there.

Life gives you so many obstacles. A little over a year ago, I was diagnosed with cancer. Two days ago, I finished the last of my chemotherapy pills. I was lucky. I was cancer-free very early on in the treatments.

I realized that you don't just get one thing in life. It's not about climbing an obstacle, because we've all got them. Finding peace is finding space within myself that recognizes how resilient we can be and feeling okay with the next obstacle that will come along. I've realized that an illness isn't the worst thing that's going to happen to somebody. There are lots of mountains that are much more difficult to face. Depression and grief after a loss. Those are hard, horrible things, but you have to choose happiness. And I chose happiness, dammit. I chose it again.

> "When that official diagnosis came, I was just afraid. I ran away from my whole life. But it was the running away that helped me find myself, finally. Yes, it defined me. But it defined me as somebody who wasn't afraid to try."
> —Lori Schneider

Kristen Sandstrom is a self-professed word geek. She is an avid reader, writer, and seller of books. I interviewed Kristin in Bayfield, Wisconsin, where she shared this story about her grandma: "This is a story I told at my grandmother's funeral and it has absolutely shaped who I am. My grandparents had a cabin on Madeline Island when I was growing up. There were these big boulders in the water that we would climb up and jump off. I was climbing up on the rock and I fell and smashed my knee. My knee started bleeding. I started bawling. My grandmother swims over, she looks at my knee and goes, 'Oh, it's not that bad. Stop crying. Sometimes you just have to say, "Goddamn it!" and move on.' At eight years old, my grandmother said that to me. Not everything's going to kill you. Sometimes you just need to say, 'Goddamn it!' and move on."

> "I don't use the word victim, I always use the word survivor. That's very important for me."
> —Kristen Sandstrom

When I was 16, I took a trip to Belfast, Northern Ireland. I was raped behind a nightclub and my body turned it off. Within 24 hours of the event—in my mind—it didn't happen.

Fast forward 10 years, I'm having nightmares. My mind was finally strong enough to deal with it. Nightmares, nervous breakdown, lost my corporate job. I ran away to [Lake Superior]. I needed to be here, and the healing began. Eventually, I realized, oh, this is real. This actually happened to me. I finally came out to my family, [told them] what happened, and [admitted that] I wasn't quite sure how to deal with it.

Lots of therapy. I [blogged] very briefly about my experience and a friend messaged me saying, "I grew up in Belfast. There's no statute of limitations in the United Kingdom for rape." I said, "Why are you telling me this?" He goes, "Because I think you should be counted."

The next day, I Googled Belfast Police Department, filled out a form, and, within 48 hours, a detective got back to me. One of the first things she said was, "We believe you. It's been a really long time but we want to do what we can to help you."

I literally wanted to be counted. Flash forward to July 2019, my phone rings. It's the detective in Belfast saying, "First, are you with somebody?" I said, "Yes." She goes, "I want you to know that we feel we have finally exercised all of our resources and we have decided to shelve the case." They don't close cases over there, they just sort of put it on a back burner.

Again, the waterworks came and then peace. It was this sense of, oh my God, okay, it's done. I am planning to go to Belfast in November. My mom's going to come with me and I'm going to go to the nightclub. I want to have my own sense of closure. I don't like the word regret, because I don't think I actually have any regrets in life. But it does make me sad that I had to wait as long as I did to be able to process it.

I didn't know this is where Kristin's conversation was going to lead. She dropped a hint about a particularly difficult time in her life and I simply asked, "Do you want to say more about that?" And she did.

The big lake

My friend Jeff Rennicke is the executive director of the Friends of the Apostle Islands National Lakeshore. He has a boat named Little Dipper, which he regularly pilots out onto the open waters in the pre-dawn hours to chase the morning light.

Jeff is a writer by trade but he is also a remarkable photographer. And, as he says, photography can do two things: It can help you see new things. And it can help you see old things in new ways.

We had the chance to do that together. We boarded his 16-foot C-Dory at about 4:00 a.m. and motored across a smooth lake to see what we could see.

It's good to feel small.

"The lake is the boss," Jeff likes to say.

"And you are the captain," I replied. I am not a nautical man. I was along for the ride.

Jeff Rennicke is a writer, photographer, and a storyteller in Bayfield, Wisconsin. He spent 20 years as a freelance writer and traveled to six continents, wrote nine books, and hundreds of magazine articles for publications like *National Geographic Traveler*, *Sierra*, *Backpacker*, and *Canoe*, among others. His home is just a few blocks from Lake Superior and he is executive director at Friends of the Apostle Islands National Lakeshore. He often begins his day before sunrise, motoring out on Lake Superior in his 16-foot C-Dory, seeking a glimpse of the beauty the lake has to offer.

There's a true privilege in bouncing across the world telling stories. I loved it. But there's also a cost. Edward Abbey once said, "To be everywhere at once is to be nowhere forever." And I was beginning to feel that way. I had just returned from someplace that, prior to the trip, I couldn't have found on a map. I still wasn't quite sure the right pronunciation of it. And I was completely jet lagged. I walked down to the lake early in the morning as everybody else was asleep. I'm looking out at this incredible beauty. And I thought to myself, "How many miles do I need to travel before I begin to see the beauty right in my own backyard?" It seemed ridiculous because all I was doing, in this beautiful place, was leaving.

Then the phone rang. It was my editor. A story I had written had won something called the Lowell Thomas Travel Journalism Award. And in appreciation, he said, "We'd like you to go anywhere you want to go for your next story." I said, "Could I just stay home?" At first he thought that meant I didn't want to write anymore. I said, "No, I live in this incredibly beautiful landscape. All I'm ever doing is leaving. I would like to see [if I] can bring the same poetic sensibility, the same depth of attention, to my own backyard."

Luckily, he didn't fire me. We rented a sailboat, we sea kayaked the islands, we toured the lighthouses. And I realized, yes, I could find beauty in my home area. So, that was the end of my travel writing career. I decided I don't want to go broad, I'd rather go deep.

My friend and mentor Richard K. Nelson said, "There is more to learn from climbing a single mountain a hundred times than climbing a hundred different mountains." A place that touches your soul is endlessly deep with stories and information. The problem is we skip across the water like a stone rather than letting ourselves sink into one place.

"Pay attention. Things get really interesting below the surface. Wherever you are, there's more going on than a superficial glance will reveal to you."
—Jeff Rennicke

There was that familiar rhythm again. Arrive at a new location. Fall in love quickly. Leave too soon. Mourn the loss of it. Repeat. I could hear the call to sink into one place.

Bayfield had long been familiar. I'd been there many times to photograph for travel magazines. After this week, it felt like home. It was exerting a strong gravitational pull. What if this was the place?

It was a welcome time spent with a good friend. Karen and I were enamored with life on the road, but every good thing comes at a cost. There is joy in traveling a new road, but there is also joy in walking down a familiar lane. We missed the process of sitting with old friends who knew us well. We missed being in community.

But this wasn't our time to stop. There was more country to see. There were more stories to hear. One day we would know which place to call home, and when that happened, we would run to it. But this was not that day. Our home was still on the road.

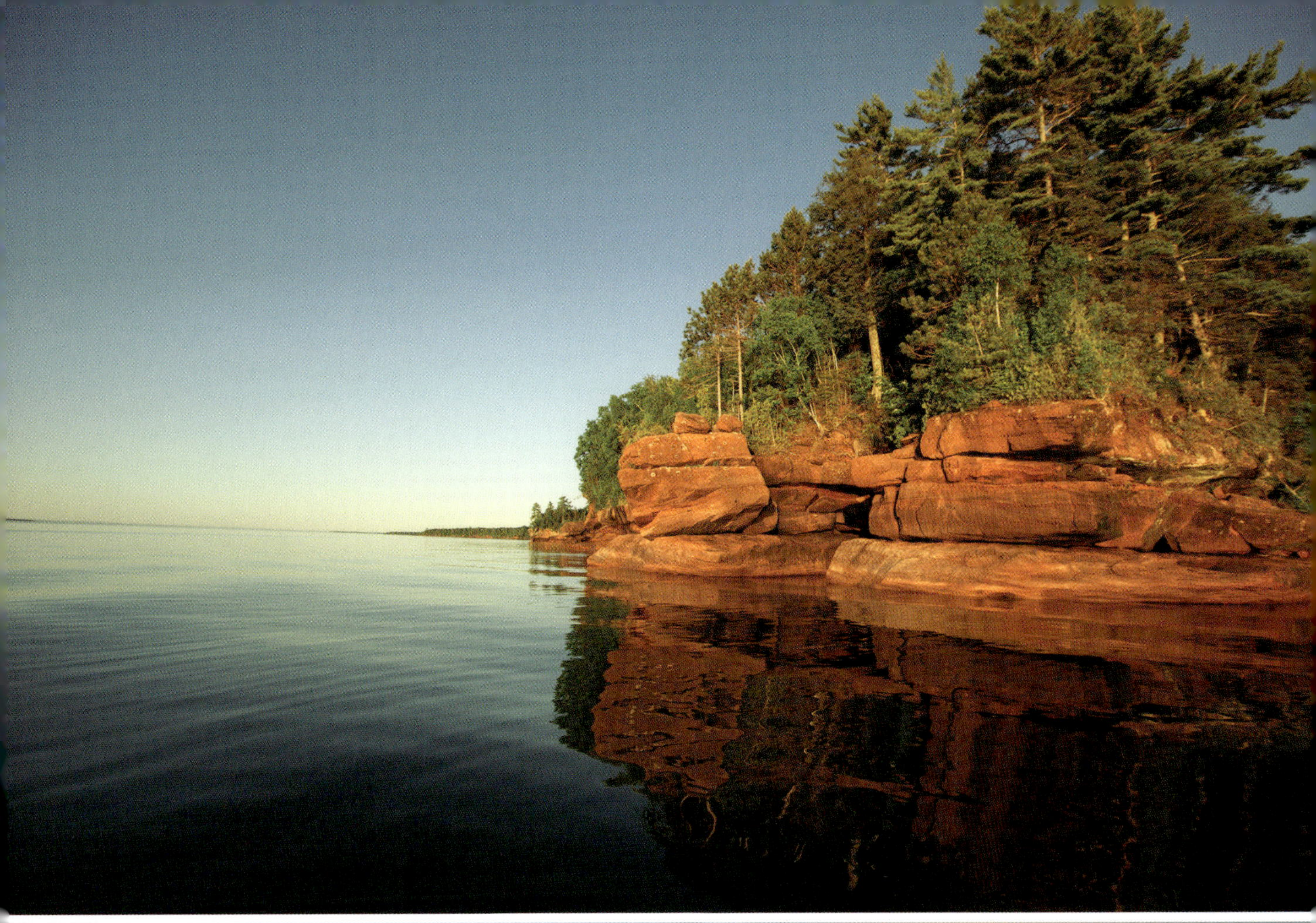

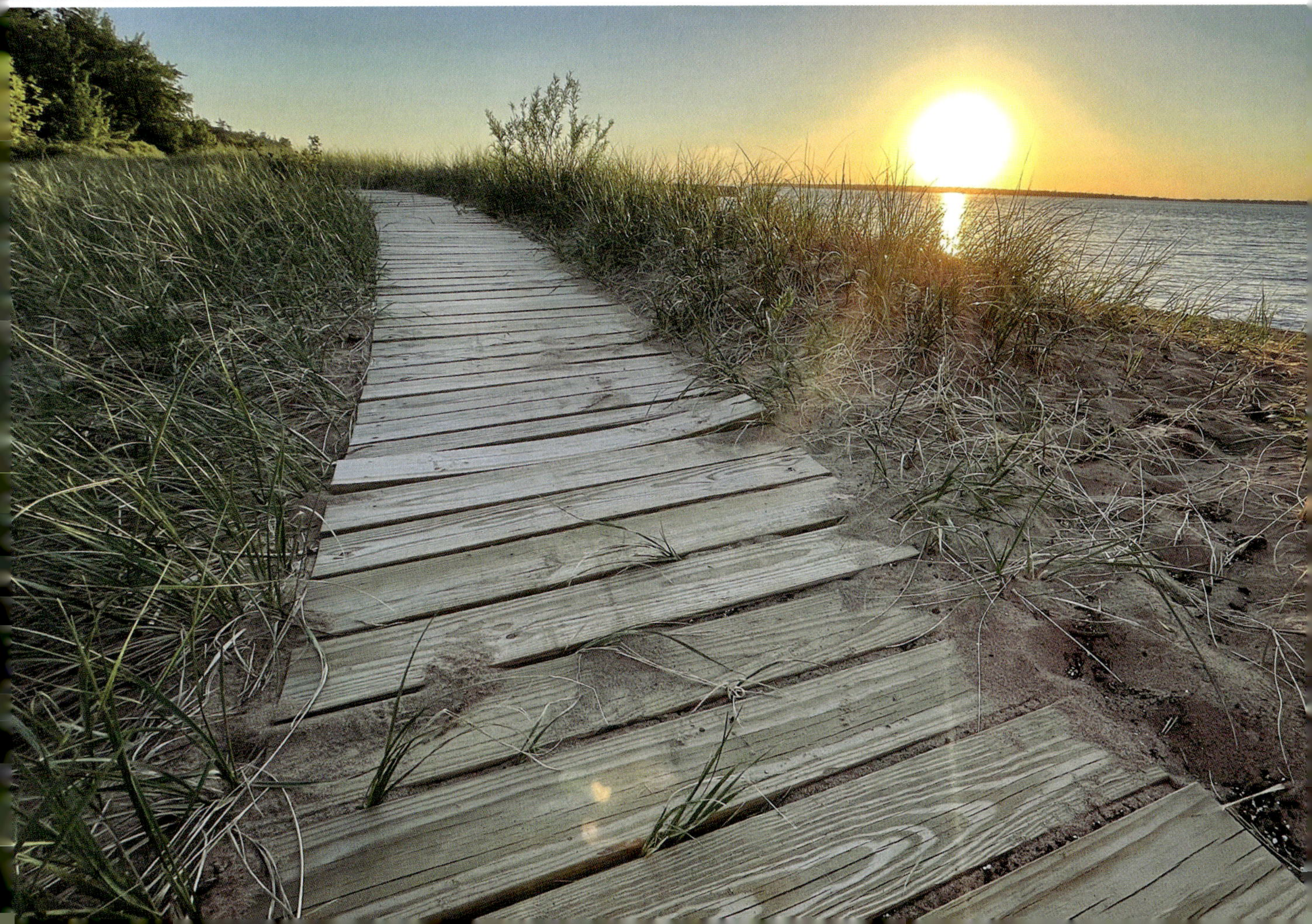

06.17.2021: Journey to California

Our niece Emma was graduating from high school in California and the grandpas and uncles and aunts from the Midwest geared up for a road trip. We agreed to meet in Des Moines, Iowa, and caravan west on I-80. Karen's sister Genie and her husband, Dwain; Grandpa Wally; and Uncle Harry in a rented RV, and us in our truck pulling the camper. We arrived in Ogallala, Nebraska, at sunset the first night and grilled steaks for dinner, a thunderstorm lurking on the horizon.

We left early the next morning and made good time through Denver. The pretty part was just ahead. Dwain was leading and, at the first exit for Vail, he signaled to get off. Gas, I thought. But he slowed down and stopped on the side of the ramp. Hazards on. I pulled over behind him, checked for traffic, and walked up to see what was going on. He'd lost power.

Long story short, the rental RV was not going to make it to California, but we still had to. After spending an afternoon on the side of the road, the RV was towed to a shop. Dwain rented a minivan and we decided we could fit everyone in our trailer when it was bedtime. The literature said our camper could sleep ten. I was skeptical, but surely we could make room for six.

I'm a light sleeper. I know that I snore, but that never wakes me up. If someone else snores, however, there's zero chance that I'll get any sleep. Given the odds in the trailer, I chose to make my bed on the campsite picnic table, under the harsh glow of a sodium vapor street light, because a bad night's sleep is better than no sleep at all.

We made it to California, celebrated Emma's graduation, and started exploring issues of housing insecurity.

168

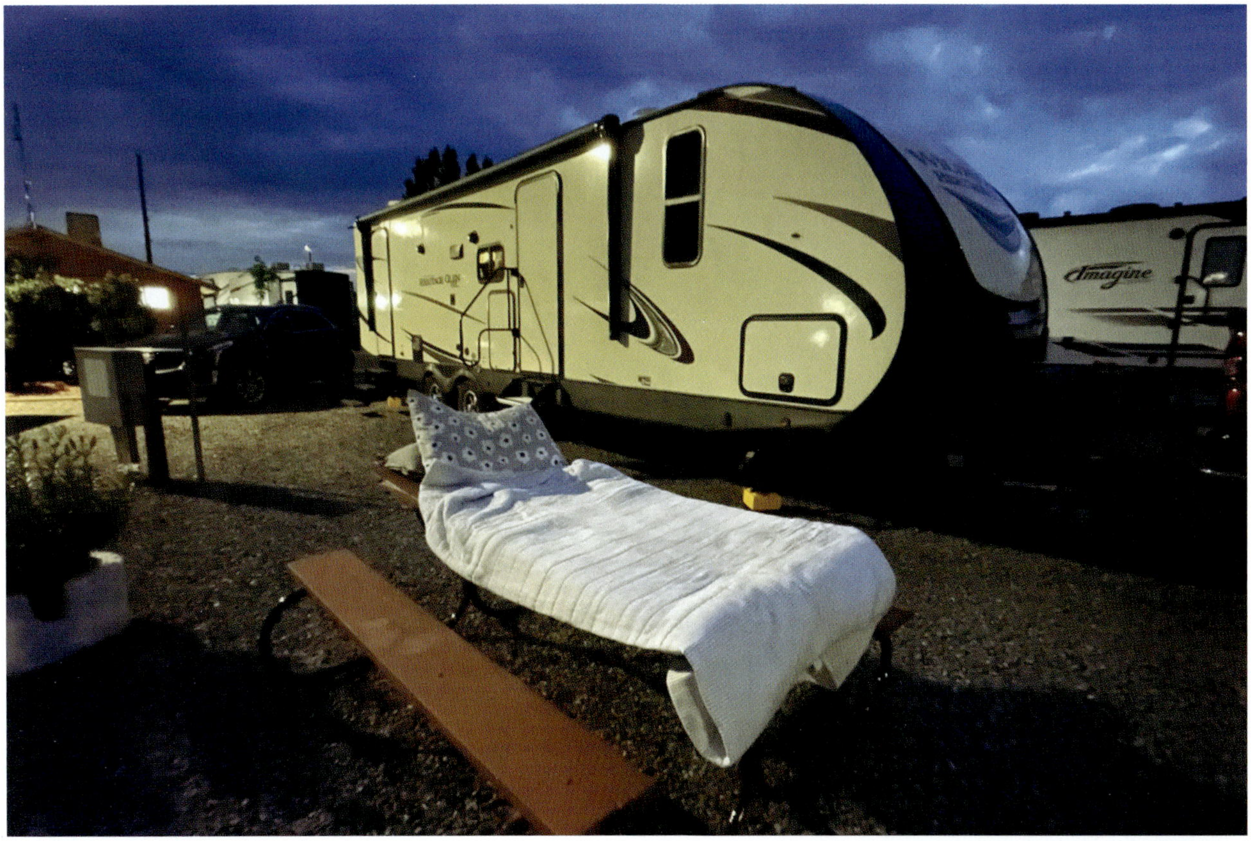
Imagine

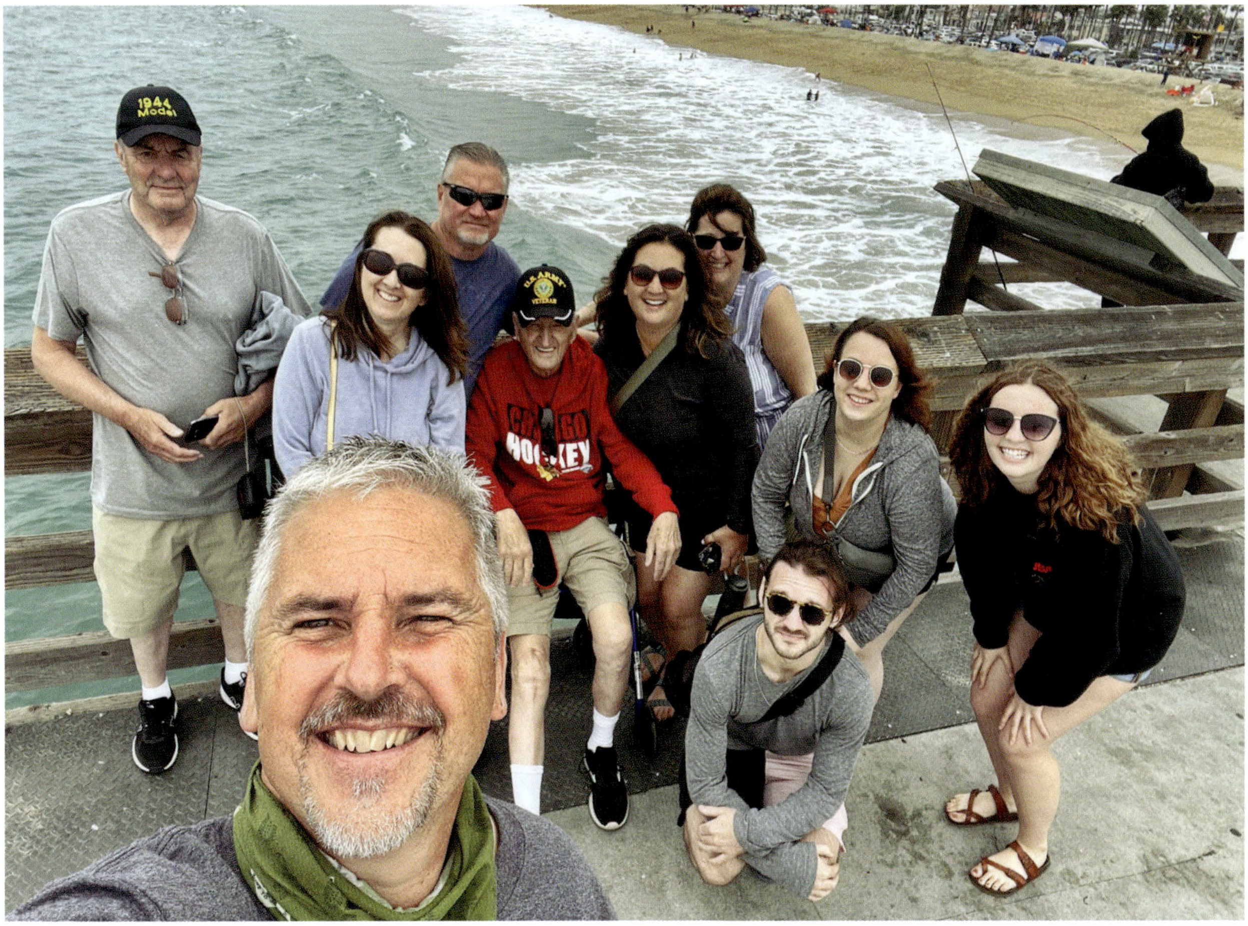
1944
Model

170

Ken Craft is founder of and chief executive officer at Hope of the Valley, a rescue mission in Los Angeles that offers temporary housing solutions and services to transition people into permanent housing. The official Los Angeles County homeless census for 2022 was 69,144, but Ken estimates the number is closer to 80,000. I interviewed Ken at the Alexandria Park Tiny Home site, the largest tiny home community in California. At that location, there are 103 tiny homes, 200 beds, toilets, sinks, laundry facilities, and services. As he says, "Anything and everything that somebody would need to overcome the barriers that are preventing them from being housed are offered right here."

We didn't just wake up one day and wonder where all these people that are homeless came from. Unfortunately, there's been some systemic and systematic decisions that have isolated certain people.

An organization called the Alliance for Human Rights filed a lawsuit against the city of Los Angeles and [the judge] said, "I'm not going to let you enforce your no camping laws until a particular city council district is able to provide beds for 60 percent of the previous year's homeless count." He put the pressure back on the city council and said, "As soon as you hit your 60 percent, you can have your enforcement."

Why 60 percent? Because in Orange County, they found that if you have a park that has 100 homeless people in it, and then right next to it you build 100 tiny homes, and you go back to the park and say, "Listen, we have laws. You can't camp in a park like this. We have provisions for you. We actually have a tiny home for you. And either you take advantage of what we have, or unfortunately, you're going to have to face enforcement."

They found that 20 percent of those people self-resolve. They figure it out, they go live with somebody. They leave the streets. Another 20 percent are just shelter resistant. But 60 percent will actually come inside and they'll access the services that are made available to them. And then, in a humane way, they can say, "Listen, it's not okay for you to be on the streets. We have provisions for you."

We know that this is not the end solution. This is temporary. This is what's known as interim housing or bridge housing. Last month alone, we were able to move 24 people from interim housing into permanent housing, in their own places.

To leave people on the streets while you're building permanent housing is cruel and inhumane. That's like taking somebody that has hypothermia and telling them to wait out in the snow until the doctor could see them. You wouldn't do that.

> "Imagine if there was an earthquake here in Los Angeles and 100,000 people became homeless. I promise you the Red Cross would be here. The National Guard would be here. And within 24 hours, there would be makeshift shelters available so that people would not have to sleep outside. And yet we've been kicking the can down the road for years."
>
> —Ken Craft

171

Skid Row

It's not often that I go out without my camera, but that's what I did on Skid Row in Los Angeles.

"Be careful," my contact at the shelter told me. "Watch out for yourself," said the security guard in the garage as I handed him my keys and walked up the ramp toward the bright light of the street.

They had good reason to show concern. Skid Row consistently ranks in the top three most violent neighborhoods in the country. The other two on that list are right next door. But that's not why I decided to leave my cameras in the truck.

I had been doing interviews in Los Angeles about housing security and homelessness for the past week, and I hadn't yet been on the streets. Not really. I talked to people who ran the shelters. I interviewed folks who lived in the shelters and others who had once been on the streets and had found a path to stable housing. But I did the interviews in the office. In the shelters. I hadn't yet been on the streets myself and it was bothering me.

Los Angeles is ground zero for the housing crisis in America. When they did a census of who was unhoused in 2019, they counted about 65,000 people in the city, but advocates think the number is likely closer to 80,000. Skid Row is roughly 50 city blocks. Depending on who you ask, there are 4,000 to 5,000 people living on the streets just in that neighborhood.

I was stunned when I first drove down South San Pedro Street. I had seen clusters of tents as I passed through the city, but here, the streets were lined with them. Some cobbled together. Others tattered or collapsed, maybe abandoned, but maybe not. I wanted to show the scene in order to tell the story. That's what you do when you're a photographer. But I couldn't figure out how to do it well—with any kind of dignity—so I left the cameras packed away.

But still, I needed to see it for myself, walking down the street, not just through the windshield as I drove by. I've been to the slums of Nairobi. Worked in the shanty towns of Honduras. But I'd never seen anything like this.

People urinate on the street. There are just a handful of public bathrooms for the thousands who populate the area, so what's a person to do? Mental illness and addiction underlie some of the stories of homelessness. It was all on full display during my walk. One woman stood in the middle of the street with her head in her hands. A man shouted at nobody in particular. Another rocked back and forth on his heels as he pulled at his face. It was startling. Heartbreaking. But there was also music and celebration. Singing and dancing. Laughter and art. People braiding hair and stopping to talk with friends.

Workers in vests cleaned the streets. People sat on the ground. In doorways. On broken chairs. The air was thick with the smell of weed. Car fumes. BO.

I only walked a half dozen blocks. There were no chance encounters. No transformative conversations at an intersection waiting for the light to change. Just a sea of humanity trying to make it through another day, with struggles and joys like the rest of us. Different, but the same.

I took two photos with my cell phone on the walk. One of a row of tents that didn't show any people. The other of a wall with street art scrawled across it that said, "It's not how you fell down, it's how you get back up."

The challenge of homelessness is big. But it's not impossible. I met people who are working on effective solutions. Policy changes. Innovative approaches. I heard from people who have turned their lives around. Mostly because someone was there to lend a hand. Lift them up and get them back on track. It seems the thing we need most is simply the will to make a difference.

The first time I drove Skid Row I was overwhelmed. I didn't know the neighborhood. The standard pedestrian/vehicle rules didn't seem to apply. I didn't want to hit someone and a thousand scenes competed for my attention. I turned the wrong way down a one-way street. Something seemed off. A man on the sidewalk saw what was happening and flagged me down. The oncoming traffic noticed my error and stopped short of an intersection so I could sneak out down the next street. Skid Row is haunting and yet, there in the midst of it, people were still looking out for one another in large and small ways.

Its not how you fell down
Its how you get back
UP — WENDELL

Reverend Andy Bales is president and chief executive officer at Union Rescue Mission on Skid Row in Los Angeles. Just east of downtown, Skid Row covers 50 city blocks and has been known since the 1930s for its large concentration of homeless individuals. Some estimates put the homeless population there at 5,000 to 7,000 people.

I worked my whole life to end up on Skid Row and finally made it about 16 years ago. I should have naturally done this kind of work because my dad experienced the devastation of homelessness from age 4 to 17. His parents would pack up and jump on a freight car and move from Iowa to California. When things didn't work out in California, they'd move back to Iowa, and it was kind of back and forth.

Lots of struggles, lots of violence, and an eventual breakup. At 17, my dad helped his mom escape the streets by getting his own apartment and inviting her in. This all should have come naturally to me, but it took a message that I shared with some seventh graders about how we need to care for other human beings.

"When we feed somebody, it's like feeding God himself. When we turn our backs on somebody, it's like turning your back on Jesus himself." I shared that message with students because I didn't think they were treating each other well. They all heard the message once. I heard it six times.

"It should be very apparent to us how we're failing, but I'm not sure what falsehood or lie we're caught up in that we think this is okay."
—Reverend Andy Bales

The next day I was working at a parking ramp and a man who was homeless approached my booth. He knocked on the window. I looked up and here's this bearded man, missing his teeth, dirty coat, a bag of soda cans slung over his shoulder. He asked for my sandwich and I said, "I'm sorry, sir. I need my sandwich." And his face drooped with disappointment. He disappeared into the darkness. I had not practiced what I preached, and I hoped and prayed for another chance.

A few weeks later, I found him on the street and fed him dinner. A few weeks after that, I was asked if I wanted to work at a downtown rescue mission. That was 35 years ago. I really found my passion by failing. I used to look through people who were homeless and not feel any of their pain. But after that episode, I'm haunted by the idea of a person being without a home.

Vincent Turner once lived in a liquor store parking lot in Los Angeles. He put up barriers to keep others out because he was disappointed with himself. When he was ready for a change, he used the one bus token he had in his pocket to go to the Union Rescue Mission on Skid Row. They took him in, he worked through their program, and now that he has graduated, he works there as a maintenance technician and has his own apartment.

I was raised in Compton, California, an area with drugs and alcoholics and gangbangs. And you know, it was my choice. I wasn't forced into it. It came upon me and it was exciting, but I didn't know the ups and downs until I got into the thick of it.

I went to the military after high school, and things didn't turn out too well. It felt like a loss in my life. It kind of depressed me. When I got out of the military, my mother passed away. I was 22. That hit me like a ton of bricks. When your mother's eyes are not on you, you do anything you want. So when she went to heaven, I figured what I got to live for? Who I got to stay straight for? Then I got wild, you know what I mean?

Wherever the gangs or whatever the drugs were, I was there, but it got down to where I was living in a neighborhood parking lot. A liquor store. Everybody that knew me, I could stay in contact with them, but I could keep my distance from them because I felt bad for myself. I didn't like hurting them right in front of their face.

One of my lady friends pulled up. She had a bag of food. She said, "You need to stop. Stop hurting yourself, hurting me." She gave me the food and drove off. Well, that started sticking. I just woke up with a feeling of sorrow and sadness. I knew I had to do something.

You need to help yourself. So this time around, I started clinging to everything that was positive. If you constantly work on one thing, you get more successful at it. Pay your rent, pay your bills, come to

"You got to know if you run your batteries down, you need to get a charger. You don't need to get another dead battery and try to connect."
—Vincent Turner

work. See, I got over that fear that I can't accomplish something in my life, 'cause it's been a period of time that I went further than I've been before and it's still working. You got to stay strong. You got to believe that you have a purpose.

Vincent said it was hard to talk about his addiction. There was a price to revisiting his ghosts, but he chose to do it in the hope that it would help someone else. Every day is a struggle to stay on track, to stay clean. Addiction doesn't ever go away, he said. I hoped the cost wasn't too high for Vincent. I've seen these stories help other people. I've seen them shine a light into the darkness, but I didn't want to create pain. I took Vincent at his word that he wanted to do this. I told him I'd try to do what good I could with it.

07.03.2021: Journey to Corvallis

176

We migrated north. To get out of the city and to find cool ocean breezes as the West Coast roasted under record high temperatures.

The notion of being housed or not was becoming blurry for me. The margins become more visible as they become more familiar. Our fellow mobile, transient, vagabond travelers and neighbors shared much in, but there was a vast range of experiences on the road. From a quarter-million-dollar bus pulling a full-sized pickup with a golf cart in the bed to a 1970s Winnebego held together with bailing wire and duct tape. We crossed paths with people living their retirement dream and others who were one repair away from being destitute.

We walked along the wild and rugged shoreline of Fort Bragg, California, on a foggy evening as we waited for the 3rd of July fireworks display. I suppose you get a little discount if you schedule your Independence Day celebration that way. Like an early-bird sale.

We aimed for a rocky headland jutting into the sea and, as we crested a small rise, we saw a man sitting beside his bike, sheltered from the wind. He was surrounded by several bags and he was finishing a snack.

"Hello," we said.

"You folks ever been here before?" he asked, relaxed and welcoming, and he proceeded to explain the history of the area. He pointed out the easiest path to the tip of the peninsula and highly recommended the view. He told us to watch for two wooden posts, where they used to tie up the ships that carried lumber out of these forests and down the coast to the cities.

His name was Jeff. He had clear blue eyes and an easy smile. He wore a gray beard and a dark, tattered raincoat. "I need a new one," he said, as he took the rubber band off his cuff and the split sleeve hung low. "But look! It gives me wings," he said, spreading his arms wide.

Jeff liked this quiet spot. Out of the wind. Not too many people around. But sometimes he got to visit with folks passing by and share some of his local wisdom. He liked that.

Jeff talked about the United States and the divisions he saw. "You know," he said, "you change a couple letters around and you get the Un-tied States. I'm worried about us."

Me too, I said. Me too.

In the past, he explained, the police told him he couldn't be in that spot after dark, but Jeff pointed out that there was no light above the sign that was not there to explain that rule. He told them, "These are navigable waters. You can't close the coastline. I'm here waiting for my ship to come in."

And he kept coming back.

It's almost Independence Day, I thought, as we said goodbye. And Jeff's about as independent as they come.

God bless America. Here's to a more perfect union.

We camped along a wild and rugged stretch of the Oregon coast. Cape Blanco is the westernmost tip of the state and if you head directly west from there, the next land you hit will be somewhere near the northern islands of Japan. The wind comes in hard and fast with nothing to slow it down for 5,000 miles.

There's a meteorological phenomenon called the marine layer that happens along the coast. When the cool ocean air meets the warm landmass, clouds form. They can sit offshore as a wall, just above the water. But if the wind shifts, it can move over the land and swallow it up.

When you wake in the morning, you might be wrapped in mist, but after a trip to the bathhouse to brush your teeth, it might be sunny again. And, after fixing your morning coffee, the fog could just as well return. Some days, the fog settles in and it never leaves. But even then, if you drive a few miles inland, it's sunny all over again.

It's simple science, but here's the weird part.

Even when you know the sun is shining a few miles away, that fog can still consume you. The damp air will chill you to the core. The wind will beat you up. It is the world you know—the world you are experiencing—and it is hard to imagine anything else.

We do that as humans. I don't see racism in my day to day, so it can't be that bad. What sort of parents would send their kids across the border alone in this dangerous world? I kept my job through the pandemic; it wasn't so terrible.

But that's the weather above your head. Have you looked to see what it's doing elsewhere? We get so consumed in our own marine layer that it is hard to see what is happening inland.

The sun may be shining on you, but is it raining on your neighbor today?

Corvallis studio

"What do you want people to know?"

To all the addicts out there, there is hope. Whatever pain there is in your life, it's not worth it. I've been clean since Mother's Day.

I want to smile more than I frown for the rest of my life. Stay positive. Own your mistakes. Learn from them and always stay you.

We are all; military, civilian; to be Ambassadors of and for our country. When anyone is in peril, we are to assist. Help anyone, for that is the way of life.

We're all going to make it.

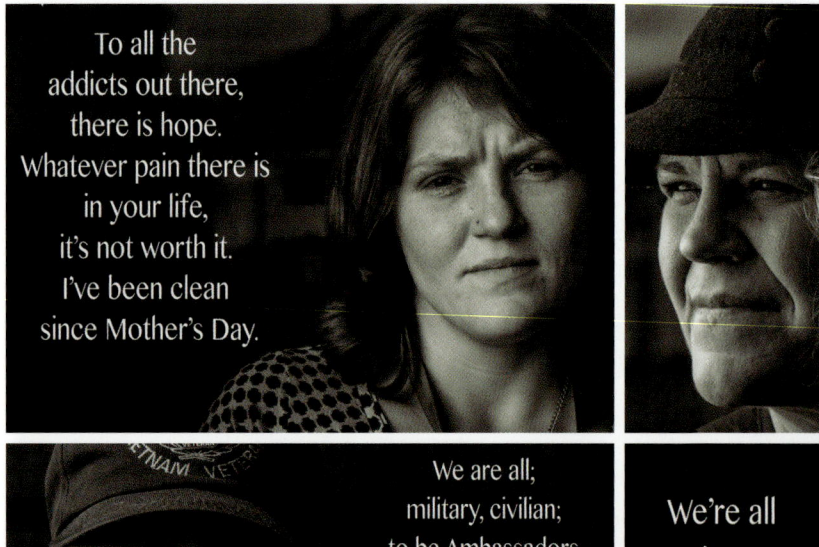

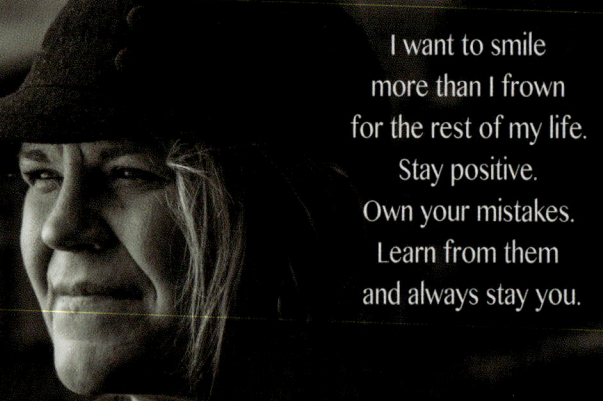

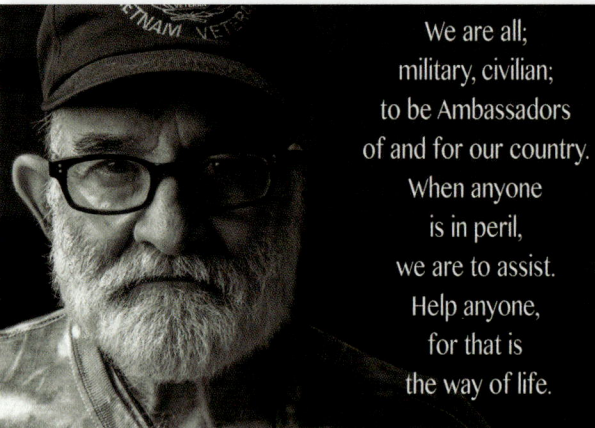

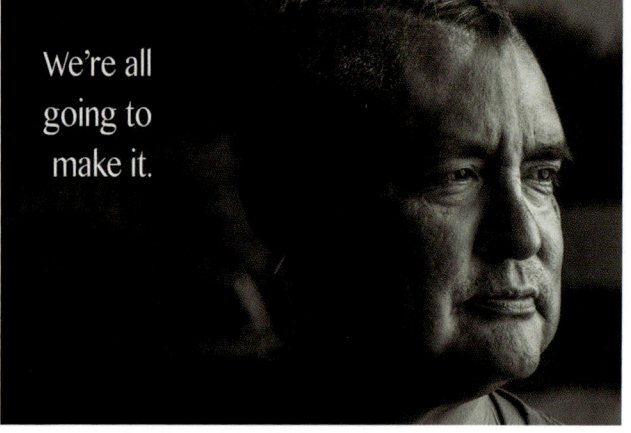

We spent a few days with the Corvallis Daytime Drop-in Center, a community resource hub to help connect people with services and resources around housing security. We set up our studio and asked, "What do you want people to know?" The goal is to craft an answer that is 25 words or less, so that the text fits on the person's portrait. But of course, there is so much more to say than that. So, in between portraits, we hung out and we visited.

Some of the people who shared a story were clients. Some volunteers, others were staff. Sometimes I didn't know which of those boxes a person fit into, but really, it didn't matter.

Marcus had just rolled into town and was trying to figure out where to charge his cell phone. His car was older and he worried about running down its battery.

Amy was getting a wound dressed.

Rene talked about the times she had been harassed to keep moving, while resting from the weight of her pack and the blisters on her feet.

Sandra thanked me for "treating everyone the same." Which made me quite certain that that wasn't always what she experienced.

Randall was excited to share a quote, but didn't want to be identifiable, so we agreed to do the portrait with his hand over his face.

And Calvin announced quite firmly on the first day that there was no chance in hell he was going to be a part of the project. No way, no how. And on the third day, he showed up and said, "Can I still do this?"

Zach said that when the pandemic started, he told everyone in the homeless camp, "We're going to make it." Eventually, he realized that maybe he was trying to convince himself.

180

Bear witness where you can. Build trust established on love and respect. Find humanity in others.	Start with empathy and compassion. Then see where that takes you.
People need to be more human. There are wolves out here. If you see someone struggle, help them out. It could be you.	Remember times that preconceptions were wrong. There are times I have been certain I knew the answer. Then I learned a new truth.
I'm changing my life. I'm starting to love myself again.	When people are tired and worn down, it's hard to move on and see the next steps.
Every single person matters.	You don't know what you don't know. Kindness is free. Say hello to those who look like they walk in a cloud. Their eyes light up.

Kate Adair lives in a women's shelter in Corvallis, Oregon, as she works toward more stable housing. I met Kate at the Corvallis Daytime Drop-in Center, where she shared her journey that led to homelessness. We also talked about her love of singing and her desire to once again have a kitchen for cooking, a bathtub, and a door that locks.

I became homeless two years ago. My boyfriend, we had gotten our HUD voucher. We got a great apartment, a perfect place. Unfortunately, Jason had some mental health issues and he had a psychotic break where he was seeing things that weren't there. Threatening things. So he felt he had to protect me and our home. It all culminated with him [sitting] on the curb in handcuffs. One of our neighbors took a picture with the cops leaning over him and sent it to the homeowners.

We got a 30-day, no-cause eviction notice. That same month, I was in an accident and damaged my foot. So when I got out of the hospital, I was homeless and I have been ever since.

I never thought it would happen to me. I thought that good things happen to good people. We had a little money saved up and Jason and I lived in a fleabag hotel for a month or two. After that, we lived under the overpass bridge. In winter, in the mud. [It was] demoralizing. It wasn't a tent under the overpass. It was blankets.

We'd tried to get help, but he was an alcoholic. He was never violent, but he was loud and that kept us from programs that could have helped us a little more. I wasn't willing to leave him. The idea of him dying under that bridge alone, I couldn't let that happen.

He was a good man. He made me laugh every day and I did the same for him. We were each other's tenuous hold on humanity. On being human. The world might look at us and say, "They must be on drugs." Or, "There's a good reason why they're homeless." In actuality, there isn't a good reason.

People say, "You have income." Okay, I do. I get disability. But what I don't have is two grand in my pocket for first month and deposit. Utilities. And so you want to know why I'm homeless? Well, that's it. That cushion. That little bit of stability. It doesn't exist for 99 percent of us.

> "I'm an intelligent, worthy woman. I might be destitute. I might be homeless. But I'm a lady and I expect to be treated as such."
>
> —Kate Adair

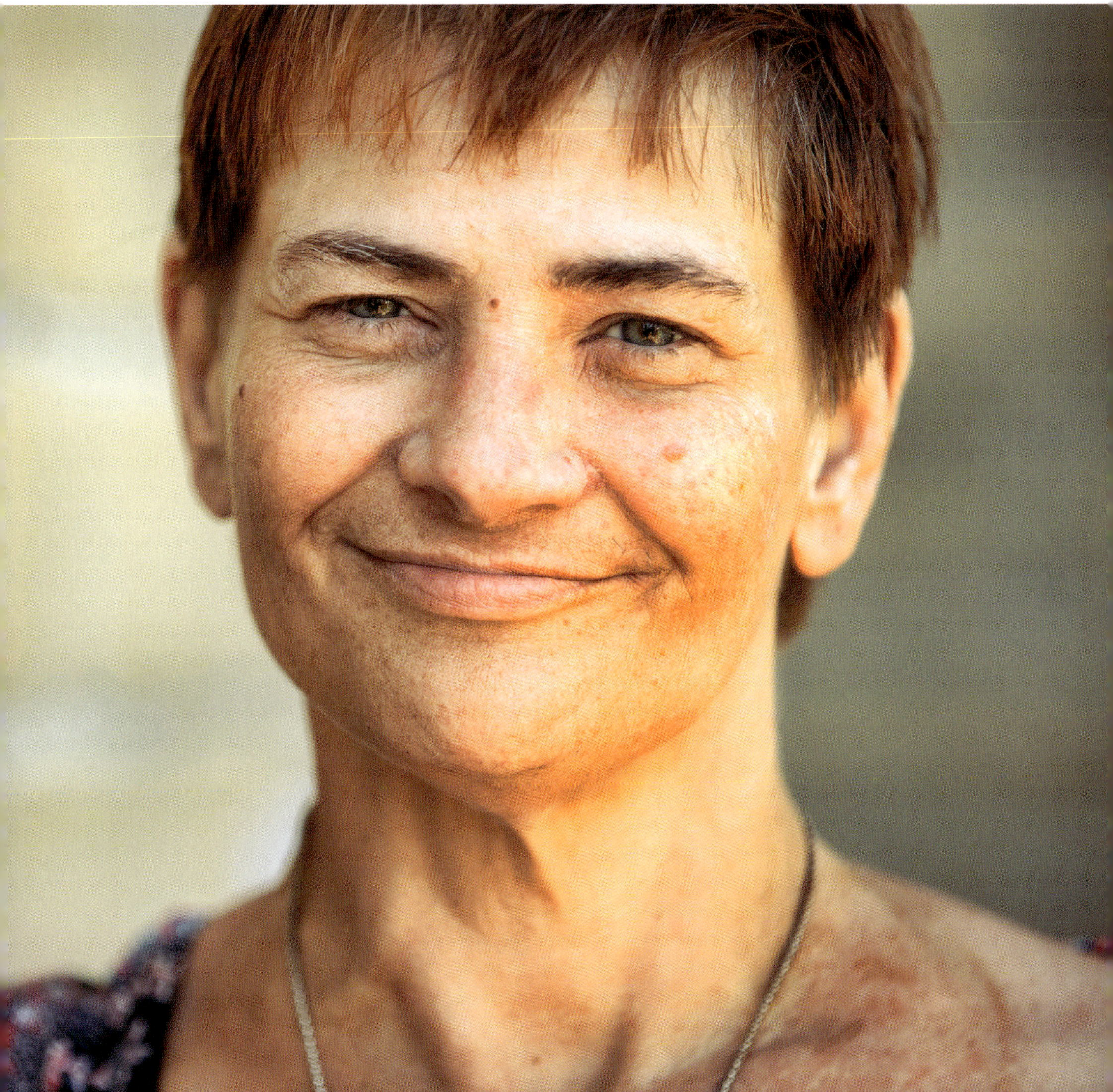

07.13.2021: Journey to Blue River

What happens when everything burns to the ground? Figuratively, and literally.

On September 7, 2020, the Holiday Farm Fire started near Rainbow, Oregon, possibly from downed power lines. It was a windy day during a dry season and in just a few days it consumed more than 173,000 acres in the McKenzie River Valley. It was one of the largest wildfires in Oregon's history. One person died.

The entire town of Blue River, population 850, burned to the ground.

How do you begin to pick up the pieces? Do you stay? How do you remake your future? I am drawn to the stories of people who face hardship head on and choose to do the difficult work of rebuilding.

The fire was named for the Holiday Farm RV Resort, near where the blaze started. The RV park was rebuilding. People were replanting. That's where I found a place to stay.

Sean Davis, a military vet, author, and forest service wildfire fighter lived just north of the fire. A friend of a friend, he agreed to help connect me in the community.

184

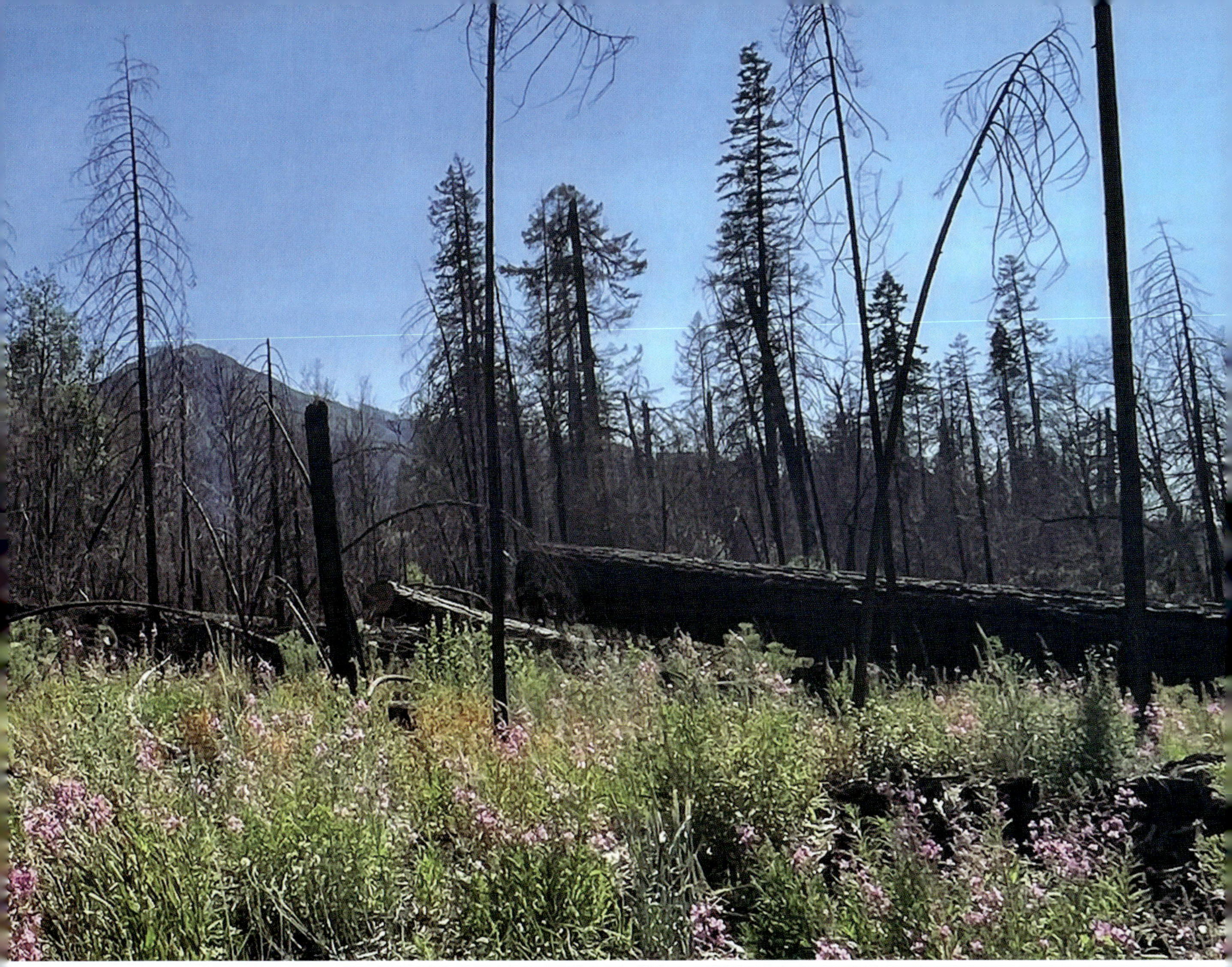

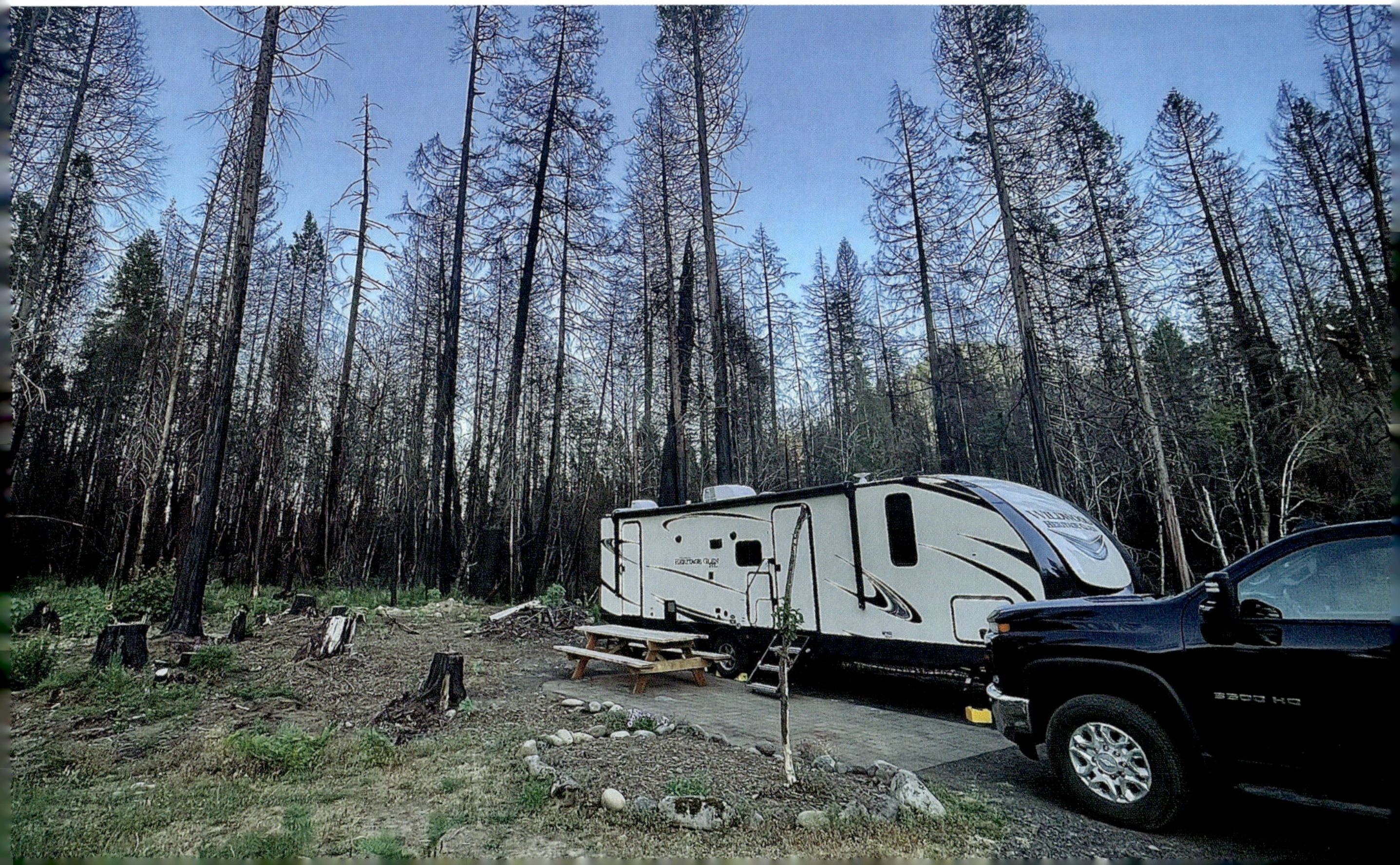

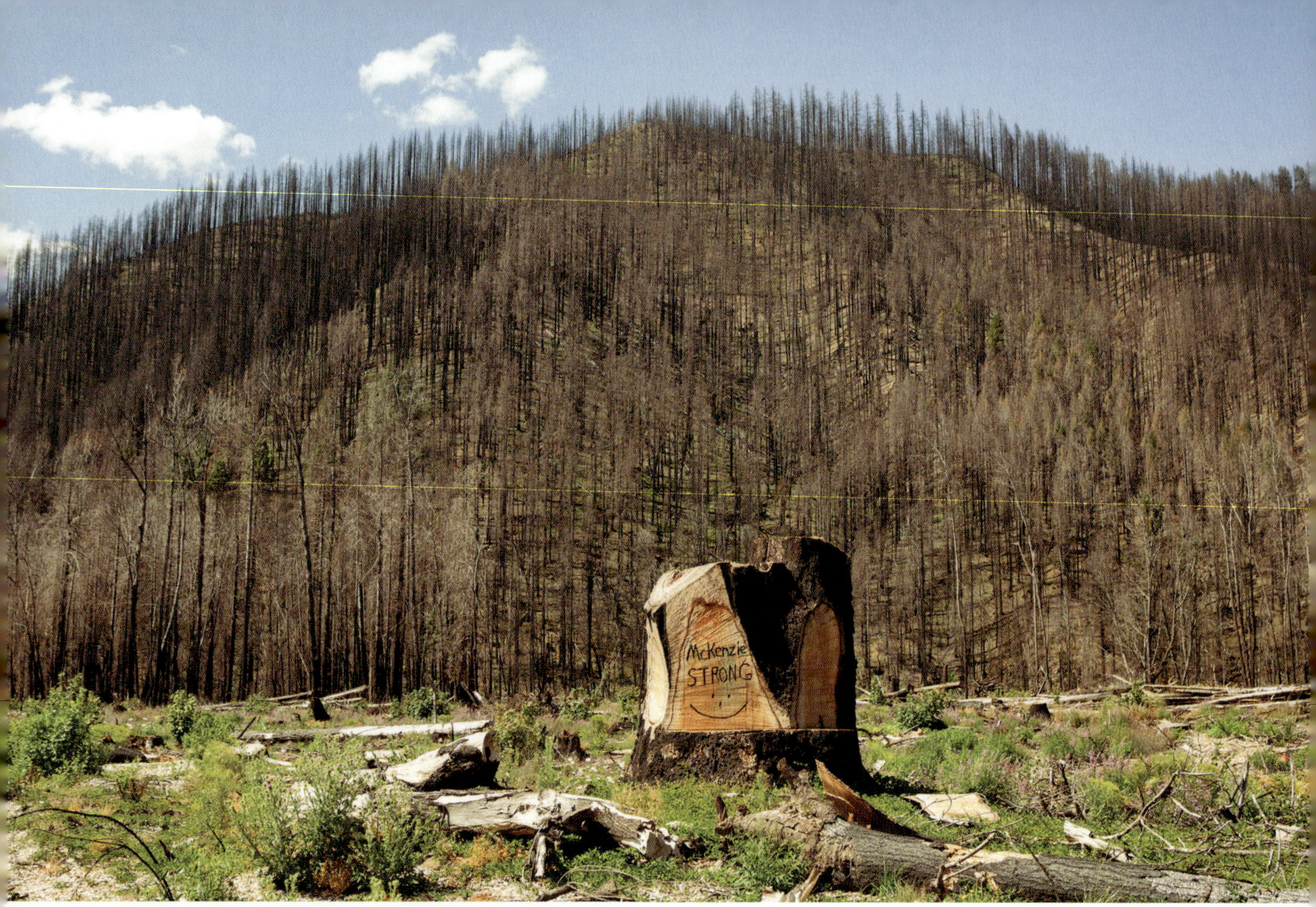
McKenzie
STRONG

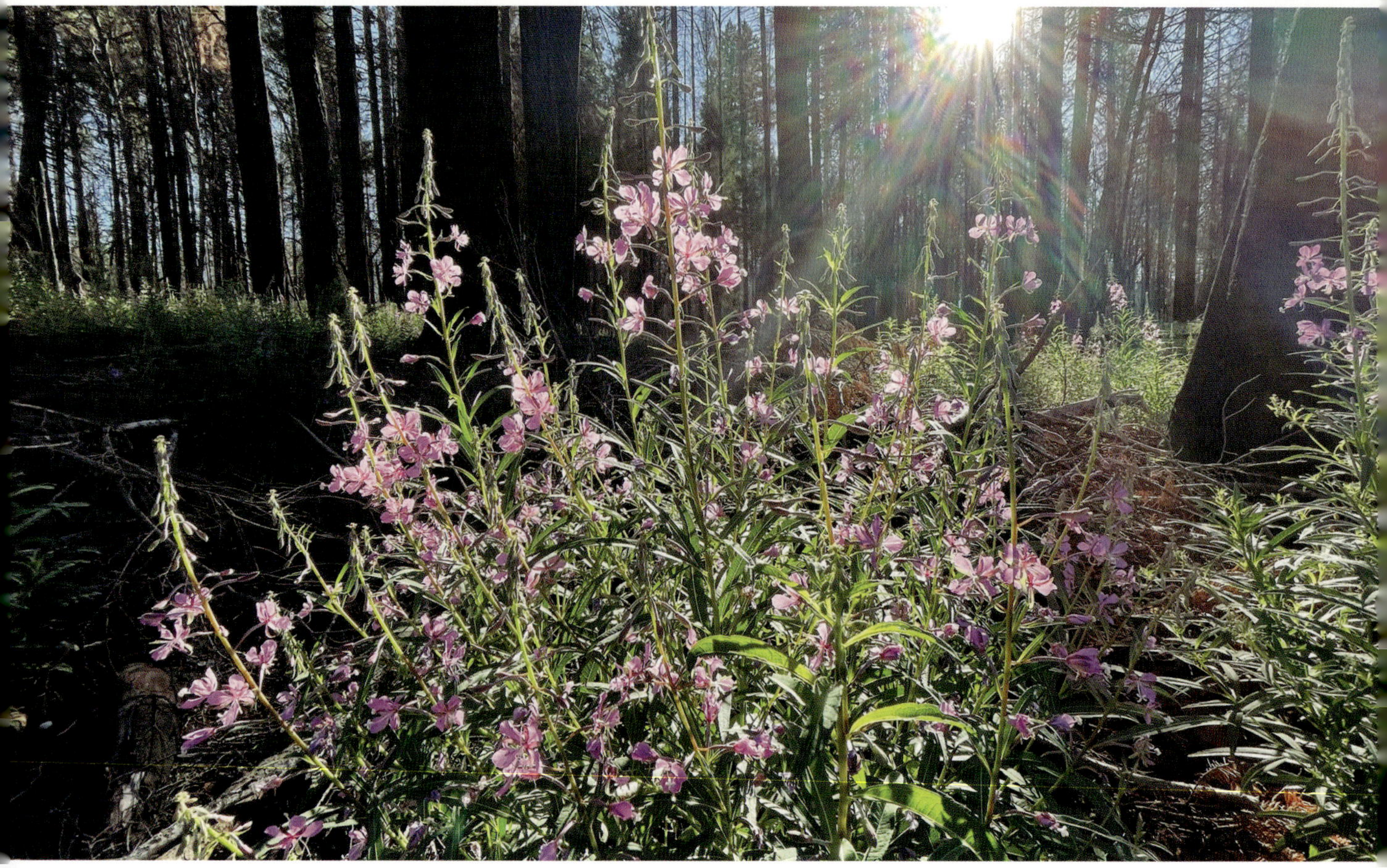

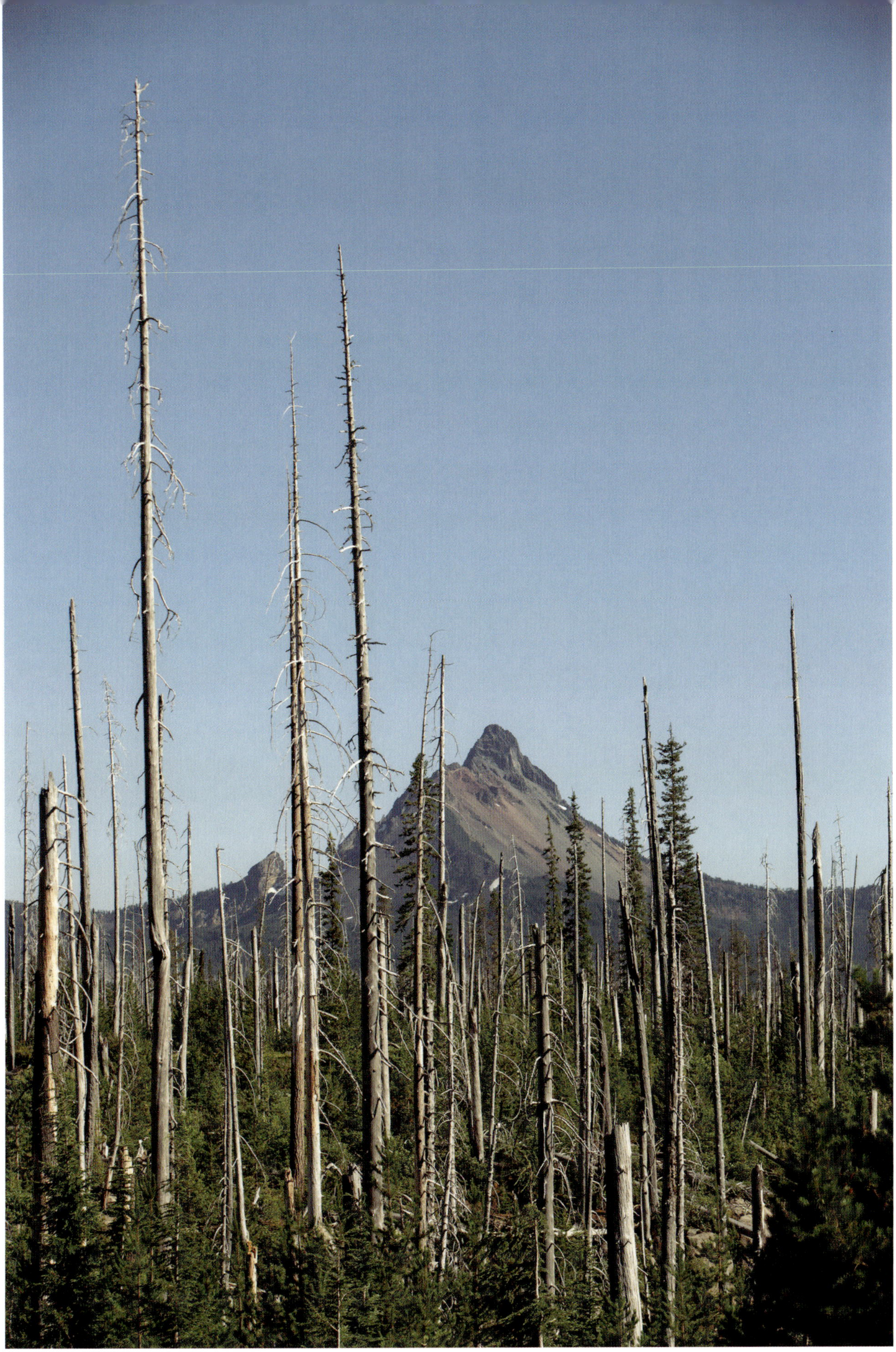

"I'm stronger than I gave myself credit for."
—Donald Dow

Donald Dow was the first person to get a new home in Blue River, Oregon, after the Holiday Farm Fire destroyed the entire community in September 2020. I interviewed Don the day after his new modular home arrived, ten months after his last home burned to the ground. He had to evacuate so quickly that he had to leave without his cat, Socks, but firefighters found Socks unharmed and reunited them two weeks after the fire.

A lot of people lost everything, but we all have hope that it's gonna come back. I had a little one-bedroom, one-bath modular. I put everything I had into that place. It wasn't big, it wasn't fancy, but it was mine. To come back up after the fire and see what's left took a big toll.

I was sound asleep and the state police came down the road and said, "Get out now." I jumped up, threw my boots on, stepped on my front porch, and I was surrounded on three sides by the fire. Getting outta here, I was driving over trees and through flames. It was scary.

Right after the fire, I moved back up in a trailer, living on a generator and hauling in water. I've been one of the first to know what hoops you have to jump through and who to contact to get things done. Hopefully, people will see my [new] house and see that there's hope. We can all come back if we just knuckle down and do it.

Look at us. You come from nothing and you're able to come back. You get help from your neighbors. I've been running the Cascade Relief Team, cleaning the town. We've got volunteers coming in by the hundreds to help.

With that kind of support, how can you not come back? How can you not rebuild? When I first came up here, I'm sitting in my trailer and somebody knocks on my door. Nobody that I know. And they hand me a hundred dollar bill to help with propane or fuel for the generator. Out of the blue. It gives you faith in humanity again.

People were driving down the road with a handful of gift cards and they stopped for whoever they saw. You just never expect that kind of stuff. Everybody has their own life and their own problems. You don't think that they're gonna come all the way up here to help you with your problems.

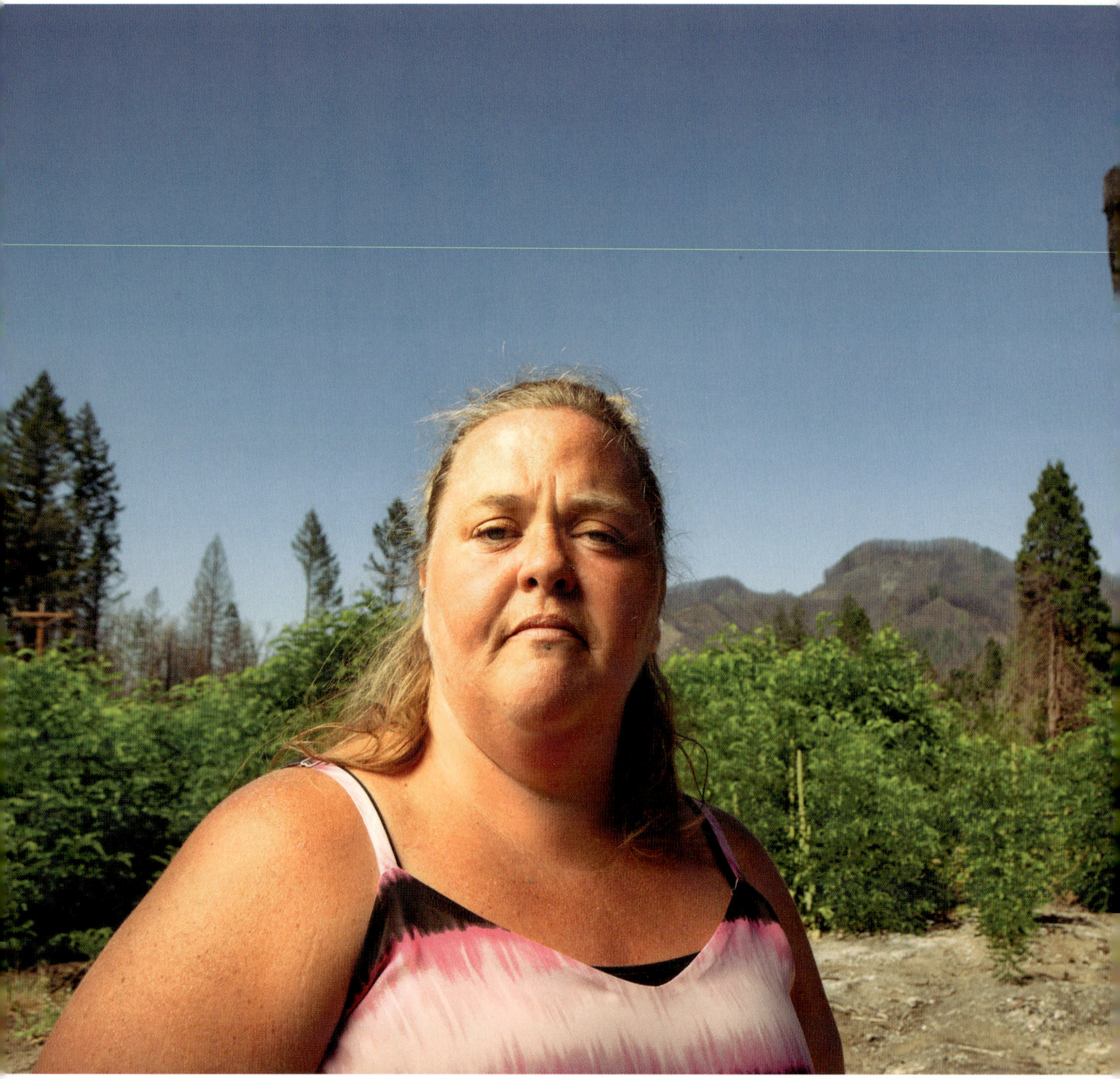

Melanie Stanley lost her home and business in Blue River, Oregon, in the Holiday Farm Fire of 2020. The Meyers General Store and Liquor Shop had been in her family for 29 years. I interviewed her on the cement slab that remained.

My identity is in this place. I've been here for almost 30 years. I can't see myself anywhere else. There have been times in the last ten months that I could tell you that a vacation someplace else would be nice. But this is home. I can't let this place die. Not that I'm the only thing that matters. But I have fought hard with my family and with some very key community members to keep this place alive and this fire wiped us off the map. So I have to help bring it back.

> "I ran back to the house, started grabbing all of our medications and paperwork. And then something told me to grab pictures off the wall."
>
> —**Melanie Stanley**

I worry about gentrification. I worry that people aren't gonna be able to afford to buy some of the properties that have gone up for sale. I'm worried that we're not gonna get enough families, that we're gonna get a lot of people who are gonna just build second homes and not be part of our community. I worry because we lost a lot of generational families because of this fire. We lost a lot of our old timers [who] won't rebuild because they don't have the time or the energy. And I don't blame them. A lot of 'em are in their 80s.

I didn't used to cry as much as I do since the fire. But I worry that we'll never be able to recover. My hope is that we can come back better than we were, even before the fire. Before the fire, like my business, this was doing fine, but overall, Blue River itself was kind of flailing. We had a lot of closed storefronts. We had a lot of stuff that just kind of needed some help. So I'm hoping that we can consider this like a blank canvas and rebuild with some purpose. When we came here 30 years ago, everything was already decided for us as a community. My store was already a grocery store and next door was already built as a gas station. I feel like we have a unique opportunity to rebuild what we want for the next generation and to decide what Blue River's gonna look like for the next 50 years. And so I just hope we get it right.

So that is honestly about the only thing that keeps me going is knowing that I need to help the community. Even though sometimes it's rough. And I hate living in a trailer. I want my house back and it sucks. This all sucks. It just sucks a little less some days.

My mom died in 2000, and my mom was a volunteer extraordinaire. She kind of instilled that in all of us kids. She made it important that we care about community. The fire department building that burned to the ground was named after my mom.

Her name was Pat Stanley. The firefighters that were here saved part of the sign that says her name on it. It's hung at the upper McKenzie fire department. So we will hang it in the new department. She instilled a sense of community from a very young age.

So, I hope that she's proud of everything that we're doing.

Sean Davis is a writer, veteran, and wildland firefighter. He is the author of *Wax Bullet War* and *The Misfit's Manifesto*. Sean says he has been to the apocalypse four times, having served in Haiti after their revolution; in New Orleans after Hurricane Katrina; and in Iraq, where he was blown up by an IED. He moved to McKenzie Bridge, Oregon, to find a quiet life but instead found his fourth apocalypse when in 2020, the Holiday Farm Fire burned 173,000 acres of the idyllic mountain valley where he lived.

My dad was abusive when I was a kid. He blew up all the time, so I was used to bad shit happening. In a way, I guess that helped.

We were [in Iraq] to win hearts and minds. We weren't there as an invading force, although, I would argue, that's what we turned into. Our job was to help people. The problem was that the people we were there to help looked exactly like the people who were shooting at us.

There were no uniforms in these wars. There wasn't an army fighting against us. It was these poor people who had nothing left, and somebody would say, "Hey, if you dig this hole, I'll give you 50 bucks." What do you do if you have a family depending on you? What are you going to do?

So I don't blame them. I'm not mad at anybody. Even the guys that blew me up and killed my buddies. The situation sucks. But it's how it is. There is no evil ideology, just desperate people. There was no mission. There were no WMDs. It was just us sitting there creating our own enemies.

> "I don't like the word peace because it usually comes out of some politician's mouth when they're trying to figure out how to send more people to war."
> —Sean Davis

Somebody would blow us up with an IED and then we'd go out and shoot them. Then all their cousins and brothers and sisters are our enemy. And they'd come at us and we'd shoot them. Then all their brothers and cousins would be pissed off and come at us and we'd shoot them. It was like a fractal, it just kept going. We created a whole nation that hated us because we were trying to protect them to death.

This is my new working theory: There are so many religions and so many different ways to believe. And if you go by this code, then after you die, you go to a really awesome place or a really shitty place. I don't think that you have to wait until you're dead to get there. You can build it now. People put themselves in their own hell. I'm just trying to build a nice place. This is our holy land. It's very literal.

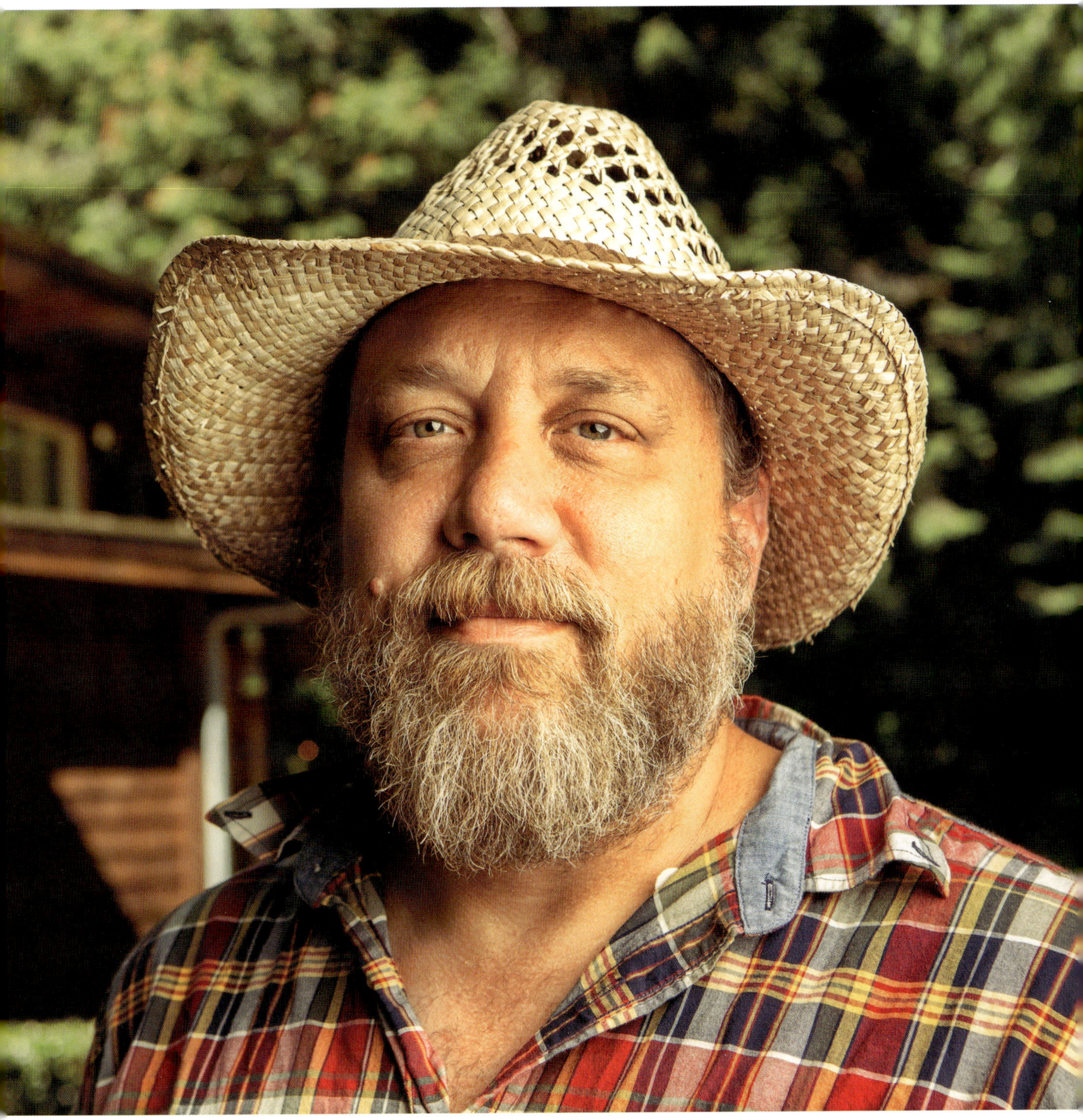

Kelly Britt Davis worked as a fashion stylist in New York City. She worked as a bartender and as a cue card holder for Conan O'Brien's talk show and *Saturday Night Live*, until the city chewed her up and spit her out. She was surrounded by addiction and she became an addict as well. Today Kelly works in healthcare and talks about the need for self care. "You can't always be like superwoman and do it all," she says. "You have to recognize your limitations and how to put boundaries up because you're not doing a service to others if then you're starting to be broken down."

I did a lot of hospice work and I spent time with people in their final days, up to their passing. It's a very powerful thing to experience that moment. It sounds morbid, but it's not. It's beautiful. We're born and we die. We all die.

Their hearing is what goes last and that's something I always tell people. They still hear you. They still know.

I told one guy, "I'm with you, Jack. Don't worry. I'm gonna be with you. Don't worry. Don't worry. I'm gonna make sure you look great."

And then he passed and I had a friend come in and my friend played harmonica for him. And I made sure he had his plaid shirt on. You do certain things. There's something special.

> "We always say that we're human. We feel. We hurt. We cry. We laugh. And that's what you want. That's the gift that you need."
> —Kelly Britt Davis

One woman was in hospice in the saddest nursing facility I've ever worked at. Conditions that nobody should live in. It was a job and I had it and I tried to do everything I could to pick up other people's slack. Treat people with dignity. We dealt with a lot of people who had been living on the streets at the end of their life and they needed skilled nursing.

This woman's wish was to have a passage from the Bible read to her in her last stage. My boss said, "Can you go in there and read to her? This is her wish." The family had called and they were not going to come. But they're really hoping someone can go in there and read her this passage. And I'm like, "Oh, of course, I'll go in."

I open up the Bible. She's this Catholic woman and would she ever think this tiny redhead Jewish girl from Brooklyn is reading her this passage as she passes away? It was one of those moments. It was kind of surreal.

It was unheard of for me to interview two people from the same family. Certainly not four. Maybe I was calling back to Jeff Rennicke's admonition to sink deeply into a place. The Davis family's warm welcome was immediate and genuine. Sean was my guide for the week, but his crew was my family. They fed me, included me around their campfire, shared stories. This, too, was a place I could call home. The tall pines, the swift river, the mountains. But mostly, the people.

Jackie Juniper Davis is 12 years old and lives in McKenzie Bridge, Oregon. She likes to catch snakes and salamanders in her yard. She'd like to work in claymation when she grows up. In late summer of 2020, the Holiday Farm wildfire swept through the valley where she lives and her family had to evacuate. Her house wasn't damaged by the fire, but more than 500 other homes were destroyed.

Jackie was named for her grandfather, Jackie Herman, whom I also interviewed for this book (page 196).

The fire was scary. I was more worried about my friends because they lived closer to where it happened and they drove through the flames. So I was worried if they were gonna get hurt, which they didn't.

My dad just got home. The power went out and we were playing cards. I was really scared because of all the wind and since it was a power outage, so I started packing even though there wasn't a fire warning yet.

"Things can happen and you should always have a backpack ready."
—Jackie Juniper Davis

Then my sister called and said that there is gonna be a fire happening because she was a firefighter at the time.

The wind started getting worse and we packed everything up. I grabbed my whistle and my knife and my bag—clothes—and we got into the car and went down to Al and Angelica's house. They live two houses down from us and we told them to get everything packed, but they already knew. We said that we were gonna all go down to Bend together because Bend was the closest place.

I love to be surrounded by trees. It makes me feel more safe even though it is more fire worry. Living out here just makes me feel more comfortable. I don't know why.

Nothing really happened to our house. So, really, I tried to help others instead of them helping me. There's one of my friends, her house burned down. Also her grandpa's house burned down. All of her stuff was gone, so my dad got a trailer for them. They were really happy about that.

I tried to help them, too. I let her open up to me. Stuff about the fire.

Jackie Herman is a retired hair dresser from Brooklyn, New York. I met Jackie in McKenzie Bridge, Oregon, where he was spending time with his daughter, Kelly, after losing his wife of 59 years.

I'm a peacemaker. I try and make everything fair, like I would like it because people are people. We're all human beings. You love me. I love you. It's cool, man. Honey is better than vinegar, you know? Like I always say, encouragement, not discouragement.

I was so in love with Sheila. I was married at 19. We had our differences. I was out there always, but she just leveled me. Kept me pretty much grounded.

Our first date. I was a football player and it was during football season. So I figured since I was a football hero, I'll take her to a football game. People would recognize me. And then we wound up after that going to get Chinese. Back in those days, you could get a good combination. Fried rice, egg chow mein, dessert, for $1.95. I was a hitter.

> "You wanna have spaghetti? Go ahead. It's cool. I'm gonna have the fish. I just want everyone to get along. Come to my house for dinner. I wanna show you how I live. And then I'm gonna go to your house. You know, get along, man."
>
> —Jackie Herman

I just wanted anything to keep this girl. I knew this was it. And from then on it was history, man. We were in love. I was with my wife until she died. We were an amazing team. Fifty-nine years. We had three beautiful daughters.

My wife wanted to live. I look back and, for some reason, I think it's sort of healing me to see what pain she was in. I mean, she's not here now and it's killing me, but I saw how she was suffering. It was taking her down, you know? And I look at that and say to myself, 'Well, maybe God was right. She didn't want to be in that body no more.'

You know, grief's not gonna go away; you just gotta learn how to handle it. But along with grief, I have a lot of guilt. You know, was I good enough? Did I take care of her good enough?

No one has the tools for that, unless you are trained. My therapist helps me. I'm understanding it more and more that I had to let go. She didn't want to be here.

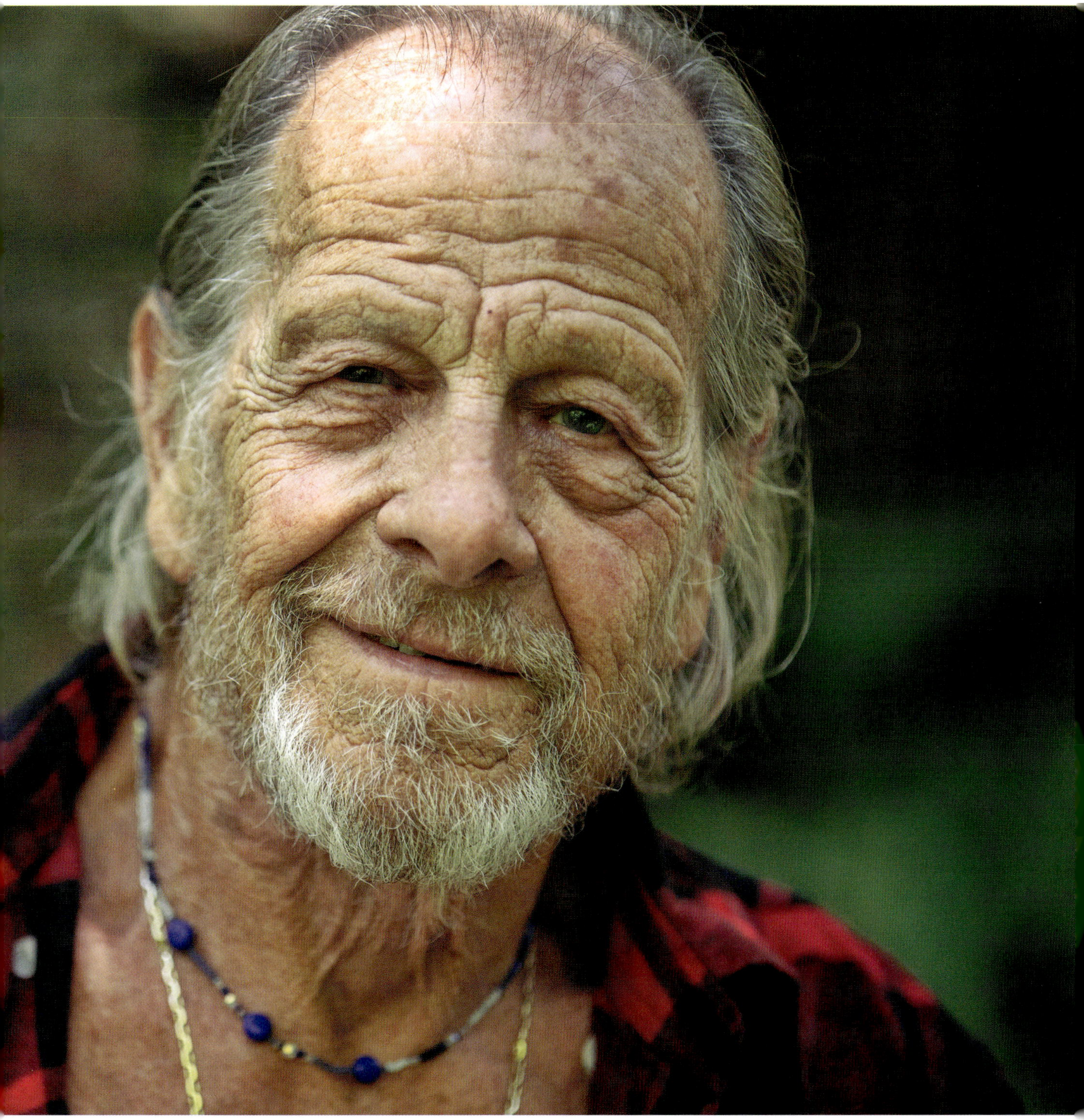

Journey to Portland

We have friends in Portland. Part of the joy of the road was meeting new people. Part was in reconnecting with our far-flung network. Corey and Rebecca offered to host a backyard party for me to talk about *A Peace of My Mind* and the journey we were on. I missed the public programming that had been shut down by the pandemic. This gathering was small and outside, but it fed a hunger. Corey helped prop a TV on a folding table. Rebecca cut flowers from the garden and a neighbor lent a hand to prepare and arrange the food. The evening was accompanied by the sounds of ducks and chickens in the coop beside us.

Ben Young, my high school classmate in Beaver Dam, Wisconsin, now worked in the area. We weren't close friends in high school but we moved in some of the same circles. We were connected on social media and he showed up for the night. At one point, I asked him if he ever went back to Beaver Dam and he said "No. It wasn't always a positive experience for me. It was mostly fond memories but there were some racial and prejudiced incidents that I am still trying to reconcile."

Beaver Dam is overwhelmingly white. Ben is not. Racial slurs and harassment were not uncommon. His family owned a restaurant and shots were fired into the building. I had no idea that was going on when I grew up. I wished I had been a better friend.

Before leaving Blue River, Sean Davis learned we were headed to Portland. He asked, "Would you be interested in interviewing the oldest performing drag queen in the world?" And I said, "Hell, yeah." And that's how I met Darcelle.

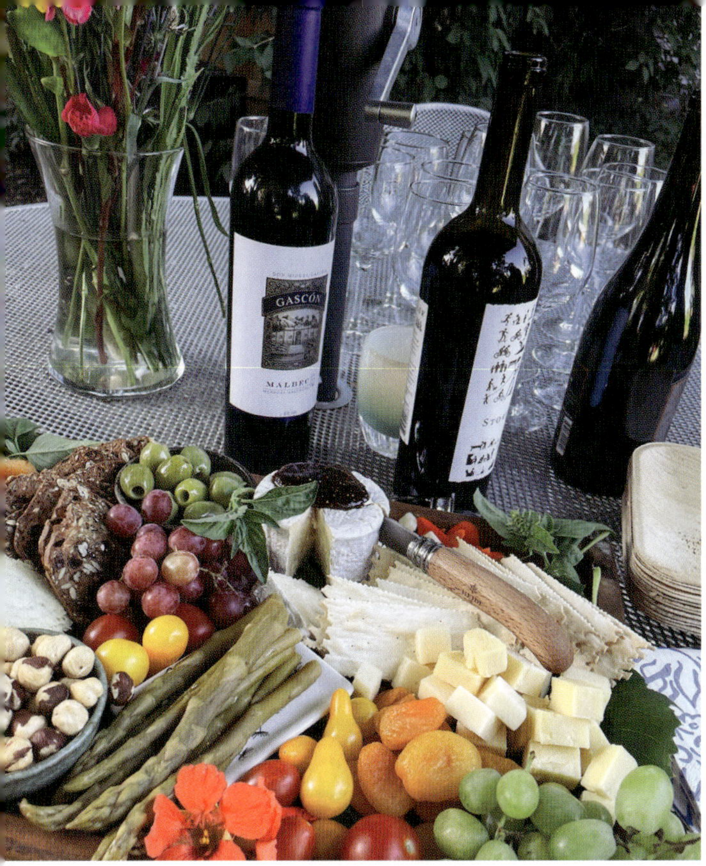
GASCON
MALBEC
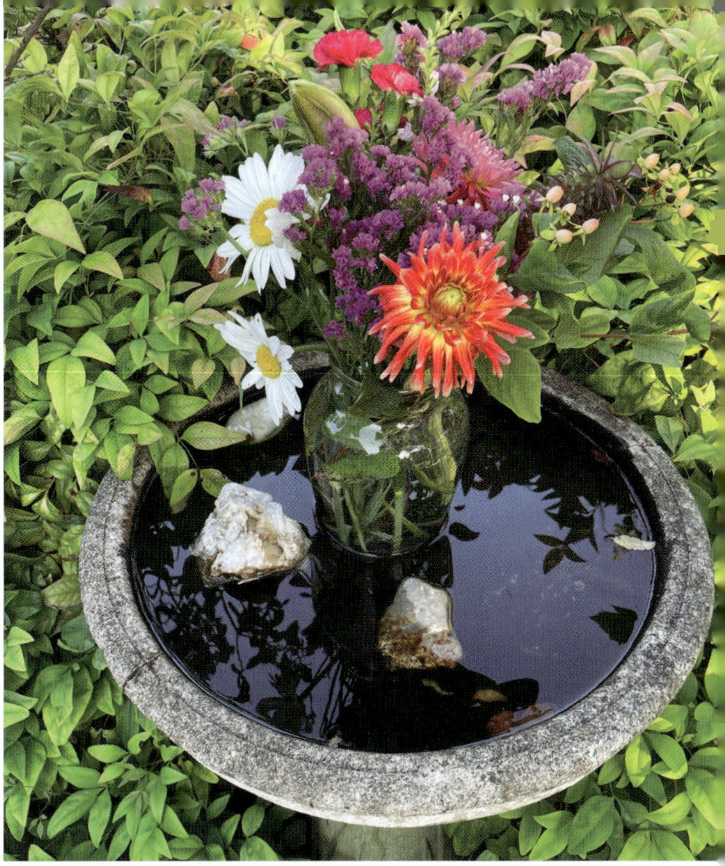
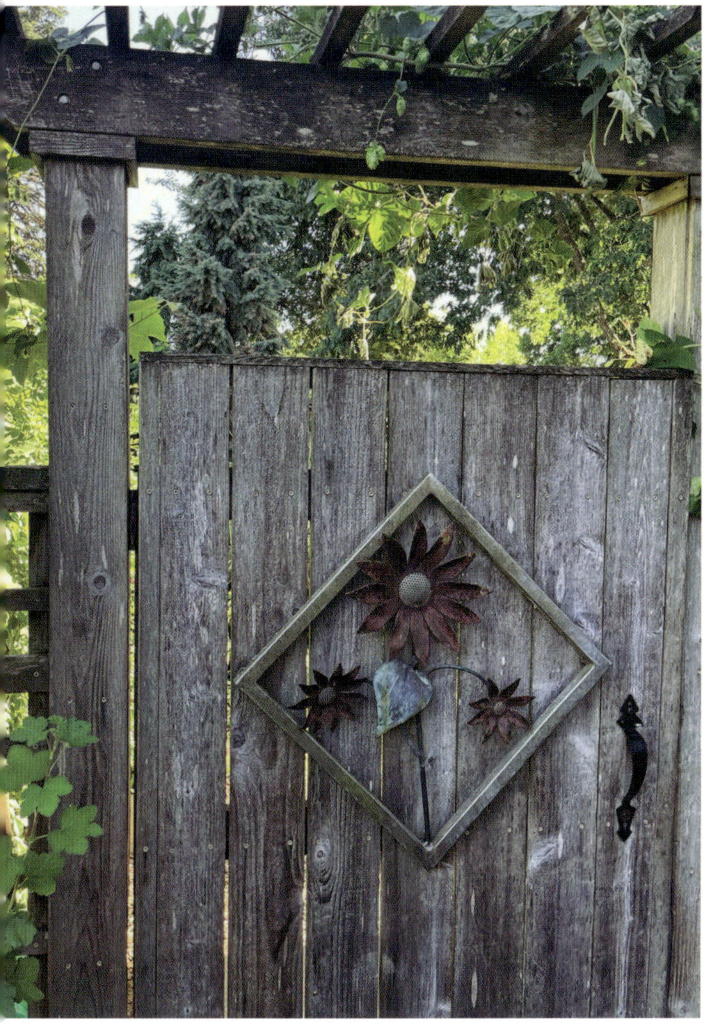
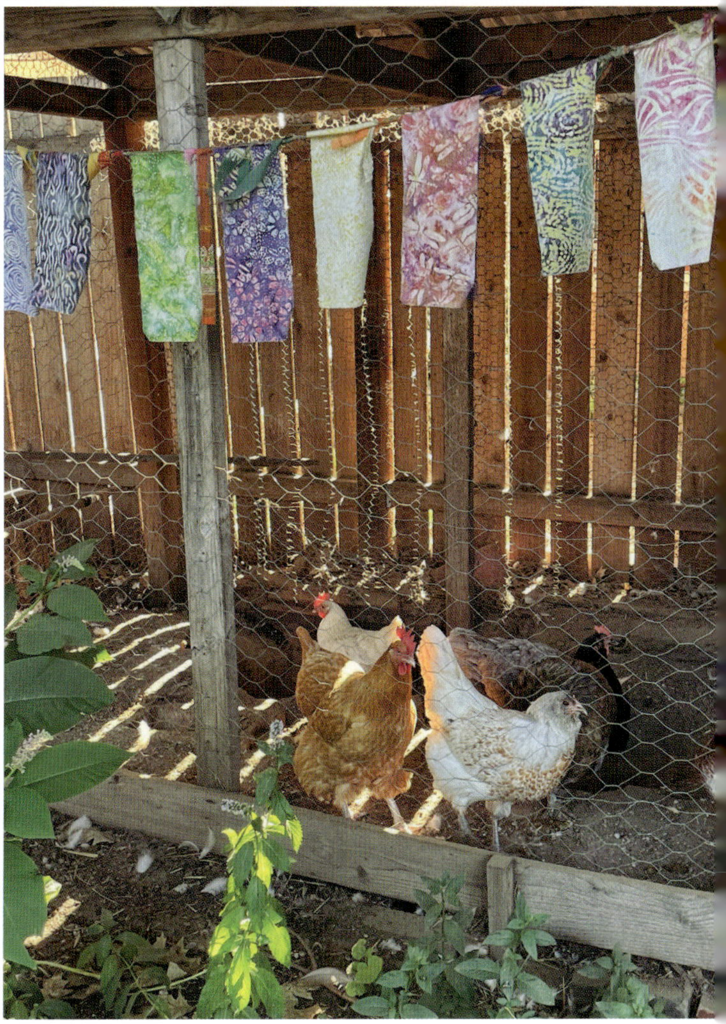

At 92 years old, Darcelle was the oldest working drag queen in the world, and also the owner of Darcelle XV Showplace in Portland, Oregon. Darcelle's entertainment career spanned more than five decades.

I have owned a female impersonator cabaret for 54 years. My partner and I started it in 1967. When I found this little gem, beer was 25 cents a glass and I don't think the toilets had ever been cleaned. It's skid row. It was then.

I love theater. I go to New York as often as I can. We used to go to all the shows. We'd do five shows in four days—come back—it's like charging your batteries for an entertainer. I was in local theater. I always played an attorney or a doctor. So I took my suit off and put on a dress. It's that simple. I don't want to be a woman. I just want to do this. This is my vehicle for entertaining.

[People] came in, and I proved to them that we didn't have two heads. You're here to be entertained, to forget your troubles. People say they feel comfortable. I love my audiences. Every night it's different.

You don't know what you're stepping into. I've heard it all from the stage. Anything that anybody has to say that's negative, I just put 'em in their place. I'm the one with a microphone. I'll take care of it. And smile. See, when you're doing drag—Darcelle especially—can say anything to anybody and it's taken the right way. It's good. I try to get involved with [the audience.]

You never know who you are touching when you work on stage. One night I'm on stage. I'm doing my thing. And a lady at the end of the runway was smiling and she had four ladies with her. I said, "You have some really beautiful bahambas." Breasts.

See, I figured most men don't really say that unless they're talking trash. And I say it with fun. She started to laugh and her friend started to cry. I found out that this was her first night out after a double mastectomy. And I complimented her. Who knew?

I interviewed Darcelle at their home, but we decided to do the portrait at the club. Karen and our friends joined me. I had been to a drag show before, but I asked Darcelle what I was going to see at the performance that night and Darcelle replied, "Joy." Darcelle was not wrong.

Darcelle performed her final show on Wednesday, March 15, 2023, and died of natural causes eight days later on March 23, 2023.

"If you're not happy with your family, with your friends, with your job, where you live, the city you're in, move on. Find the place where it all works for you. Keep looking."
—**Darcelle**

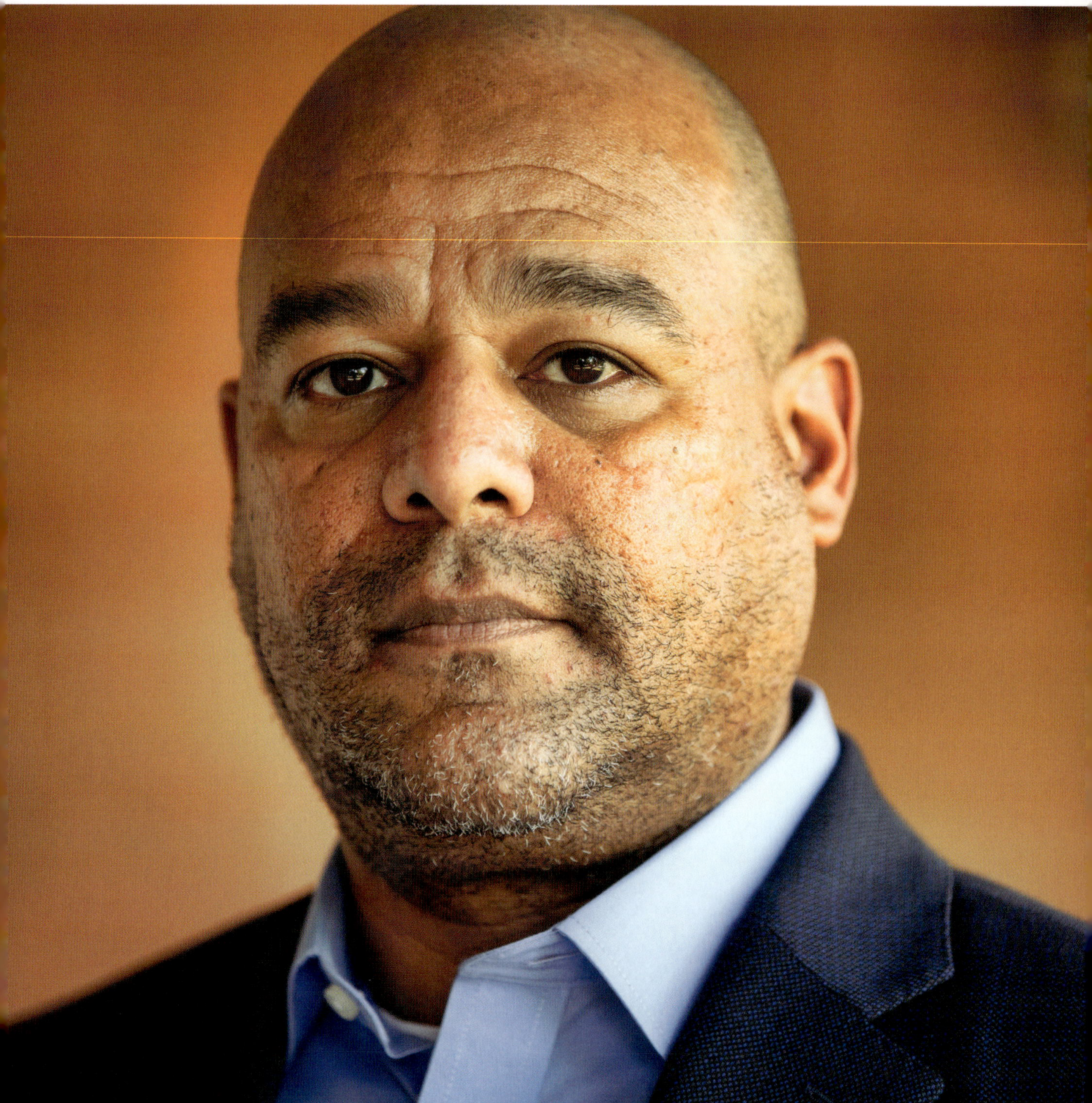

Nathan Sheppard is a lieutenant in the Portland police bureau, and a father. He and his wife of 21 years are Army veterans who were psychological operation specialists. After George Floyd was killed in Minneapolis, Portland experienced 170 consecutive days of unrest. Nathan spoke to me as an individual and not as a representative of the police department. He said, "I will definitely share my thoughts as a member of law enforcement. I think that more members of law enforcement should talk, there should be more conversations. That being said, my thoughts are my own. My ideas are my own. This is Nathan."

As all this unfolds, I ask myself, "Is the end result of what's going on now going to lead to a safer world for my kids, for my son?"

Obviously, as a police officer, I look at what happened with Floyd and it was disgusting. I don't want to say there was any personal shame, because I'm not going to be ashamed of what somebody else has done. But there's definitely a shame for the profession, that there are still people in the world who would do something like that.

I've definitely had to wrestle with that. It hasn't made me want to stop being a police officer, though, because there are still people out there who are begging for help and I think I can give that to them.

America hasn't been perfect for a very long time, but now a lot of people are speaking up and, frankly, putting most of the load on law enforcement. But we didn't create this country. The citizens created the country. The citizens voted.

> "Unfortunately, in the United States, most Black people are put in a box and that box—to people who are not Black—says danger on it."
>
> —Nathan Sheppard

The citizens had a chance to allow me to go to whatever school I wanted to, but it took a Supreme Court decision. The citizens had a long time to allow me to live where I wanted to live, but it took a Supreme Court ruling. My wife—she's white—it wasn't until 1967 that the Supreme Court ruled that, yeah, we should probably allow people to marry who they love.

These were laws. These were lawmakers who were voted in by the people. And I think that so many people in the United States have consciously decided to ignore their role in how things have turned out. Where were you 10 years ago? Where were you 15 years ago? This isn't new. There's frustration for me, personally, that it took so long. But not only that it took so long, that people are still unwilling to own their part in it.

Trust is important. Nathan showed up with his own recorder and wanted to document our conversation. He didn't know me. No doubt, he had seen peoples' comments used out of context. We both expected the interview to address difficult issues of race and policing. I wanted Nathan to feel free to speak openly and I had no problem with his request. As we got set up and ready to start, I noticed his recorder wasn't active and I reminded him to press record.

Journey to Washington state

I've had a life-long love affair with the Pacific Northwest. Since the first time I visited with my parents as a 12-year-old, I have loved the sea, the mountains, the cool weather, and the lush green landscapes. Put them all together and my spiritual home is somewhere in the northwest corner of Washington state.

When our kids were four and six, we took them on their first backpacking trip to the Olympic Peninsula. It was a nine-mile loop. More of a triangle, really. Three miles on a boardwalk through ancient forest and out to the coast, three miles along the rugged beach, and three more miles back through the forest to the trailhead. Now, 20 years later, the kids flew out to meet us so we could hike the same trail again.

Misty coastline, colossal banana slugs, and a campsite beside the water decorated with flotsam gathered by earlier hikers to rival the set of Tom Hanks' *Castaway*.

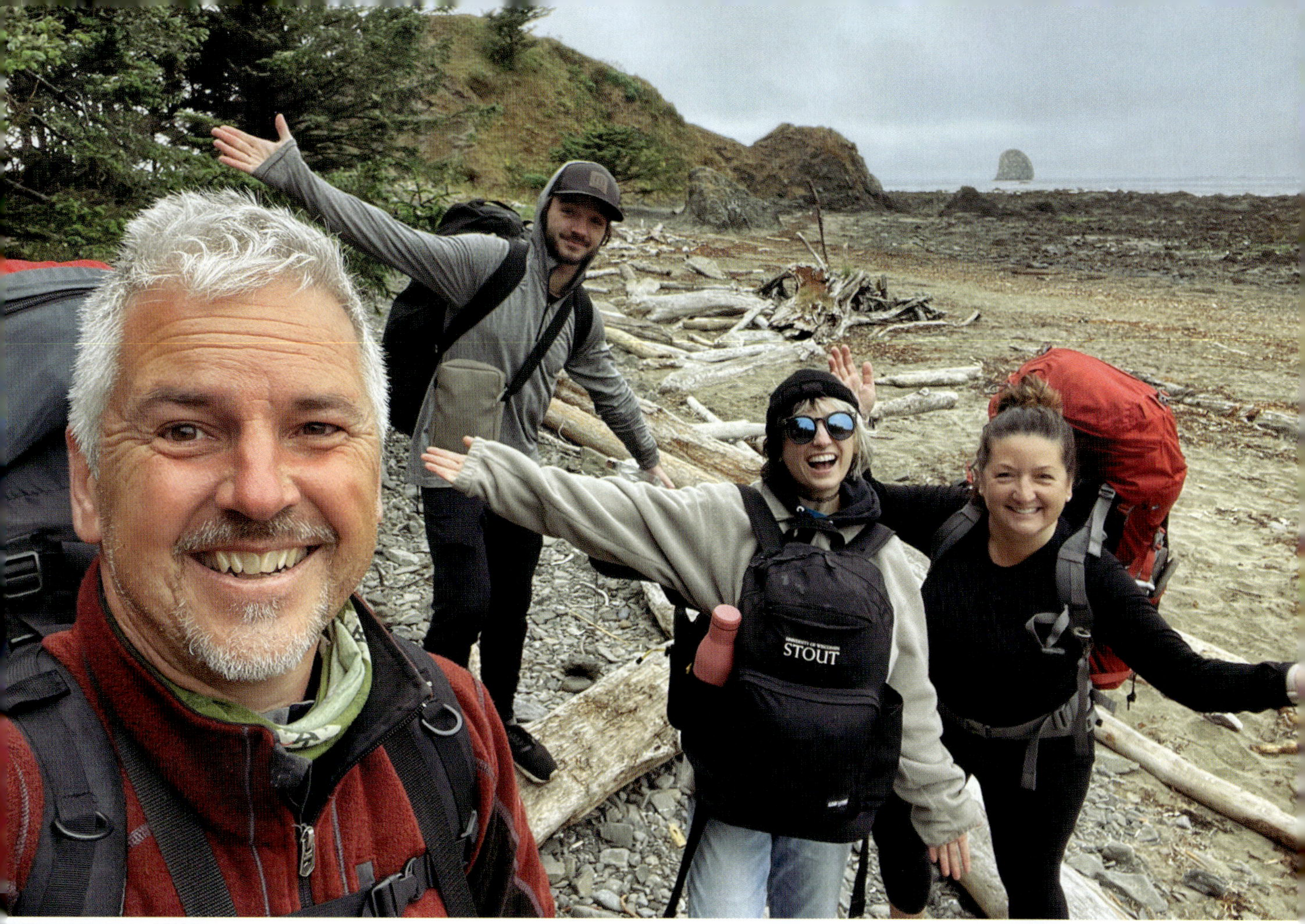
STOUT

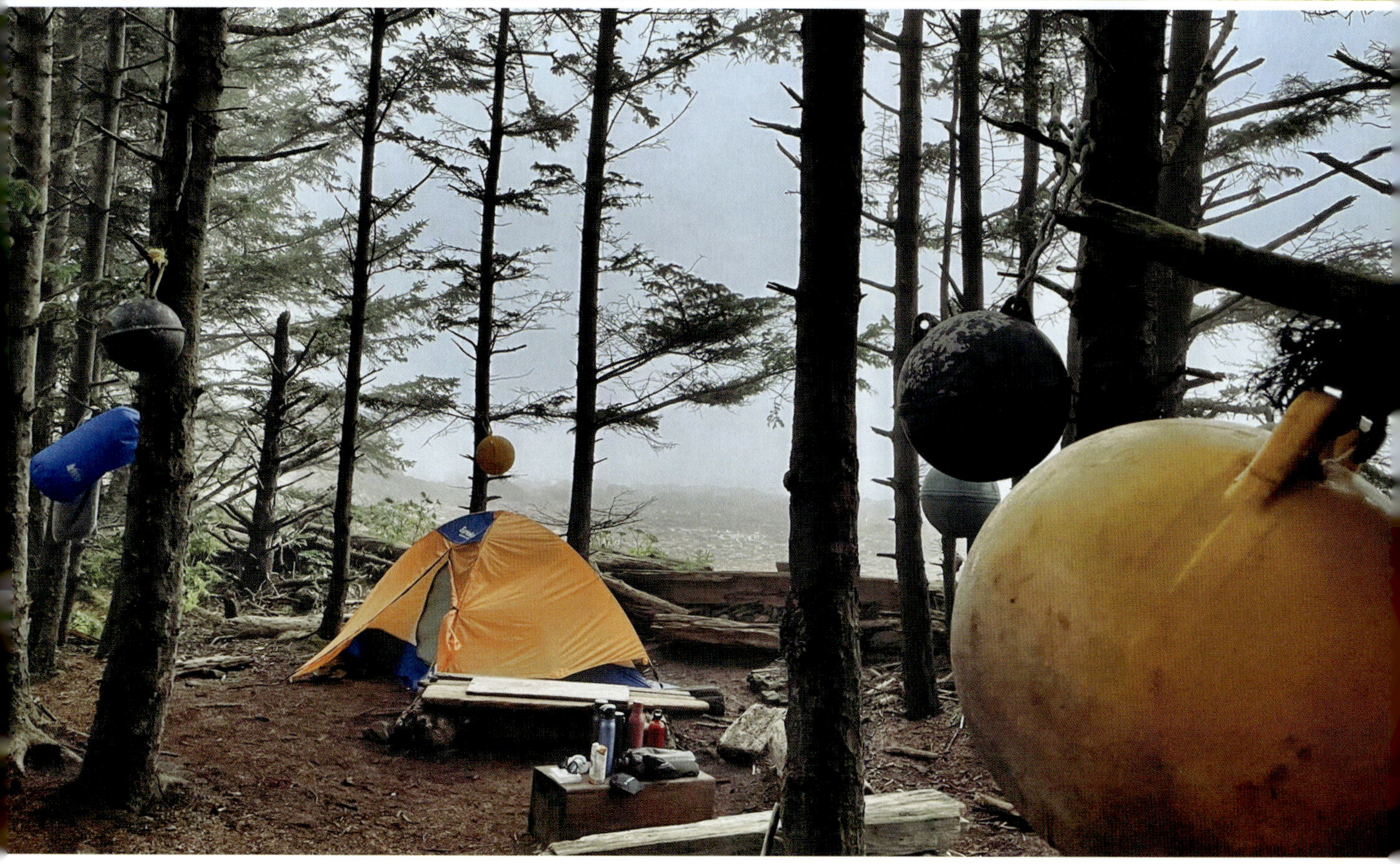

Project Sanctuary studio

"What have you learned?"

Life isn't all giving and receiving. It's listening and humility.

Don't struggle alone.

Love and kindness can overcome fear and anger. Hope and faith can overcome doubt and resentment.

The person you see is rarely the person they are.

Don't hold back love. Our time together is brief, so give love freely and loudly. The ones we care about deserve to know and be loved by you.

It's ok to not be ok. To reach out for help is from a position of strength, not weakness.

I've worked with Project Sanctuary before, a group that tries to help reintegrate soldiers into civilian life after returning from their deployments. As I browsed their schedule of programming for the year, I saw that they would be in Warm Beach, Washington, at the same time we were in the area, so we arranged to gather stories at their retreat. As they worked on trauma and PTSD, we asked an open-ended question, allowing people to interpret it as they wanted. We asked simply, "What have you learned?"

Karen and I were asked not to join one session because it was expected to be a personal and raw experience for the vets. I was disappointed, but I understood. About half way through, Steve walked out and I asked, "How's it going in there?" "It's hard," he replied. "It's supposed to be, right?" I wondered.

"I'm going for a walk," he said and disappeared into his room. I had a flashback to Danny, a student and family friend who died by suicide during his senior year in high school, a month before graduation. When Steve came back, I walked over to him and failed to hold back the tears. "This is my own trauma coming out," I explained. "Because one time not so long ago someone told me they were alright, but they weren't. And now they're gone. Are you alright, Steve? That's all I need to know."

"I'm alright," he said. "I've been there before, but I'm not there now. I'm alright." And he gave me a big hug.

You can do everything right but still fail. This is not weakness, it's life.

A misconception about grief is it resolves. Grief never ends because the relationship with the deceased never ends.

Each of us has within, the ability to answer our own questions, counter challenges, and the potential to consider and change.

Trauma doesn't define you. You may feel lost and alone but you are not broken. If you are alive, hope lives and healing can follow.

You do not get to define what being feminine looks like for me. I am my own woman.

You don't have to understand veteran issues, that's ok. But a little empathy towards veteran issues can help with a better understanding of the veteran community.

I used to have a future, but I can't see it now. I'm still looking for what works for me.

Don't compare our childhoods. We live in different worlds.

Seth Nickell describes himself as a husband, a father, a combat veteran, and a man of God. I interviewed Seth in Stanwood, Washington, at a retreat for Project Sanctuary, a nonprofit that helps reconnect returning soldiers to civilian and family life. Seth had to advocate for himself when he returned from his deployments and struggled with PTSD. He finally got the help he needed and has made a habit of "counting the wins" in his day—no matter how small—to get through the difficult times.

"My turning point was when I started being invested in my own treatment. I had to make the decision that I was worth something."

—Seth Nickell

My combat time was ground shaking. It changed the course of my life. I learned about how strong I can be, how compassionate I can be, and how violent I can be, all in the same breath. It's like learning all sorts of truths about yourself compressed into months instead of over the course of a lifetime.

Seeing the worst of what humanity can do, it doesn't compute. I just had to push it aside at the time because I couldn't deal with it as it was happening and still expect to go on that next mission later in the day.

[Re-entry] was rough. I was obviously elated to be home, but I knew I had issues. Stuff was not making sense. I was acting in ways that were not normal to me and I knew I had what people call PTSD—but I didn't have any idea how bad. I spent all my energy putting on a good face, like everything's great. The boy's all right.

But things started going downhill rapidly. [I was] having flashbacks and intrusive thoughts. I was depressed. I was super angry at nothing. Not able to sleep. And it didn't take very long for me to say, "I need help."

My wife sat down with me one day and I was kind of moody. Just in a bad spot. And she said, "You went overseas to fight, to provide better lives for people." And I was like, "Yeah." And she said, "Including your brothers and sisters that were over there." And I said, "Oh yeah, for sure." And she's like, "And you would put your life on the line to make things better for other people." And I said, "Oh yeah." She said, "Well, when are you gonna start fighting this hard for you?"

That was the ultimate kick in the gut. She was right. Like, when am I going to stop dancing around the thought of being a better person and actually start doing that? And that was my turning point. I had to make the decision that I was worth something.

Bethany Cram lives on a remote island in Puget Sound that has a year-round population of 12. I met her in Stanwood, Washington, at a retreat for Project Sanctuary, an organization that helps veterans "transition to a new normal." Bethany enlisted in the U.S. Army when she was a senior in high school and left for basic training at Fort Leonard Wood, Missouri, two weeks after graduation. Once she completed her Advanced Individual Training, Bethany was deployed to join her unit in Iraq.

"Not every disability is as visible as missing a limb or missing body parts or scars. There are things that affect us internally, beyond what the eye can see."
—Bethany Cram

Veterans are not all angry people that are going to put our hands through walls. I've encountered people who, after finding out that I'm a veteran, treat me differently. It's awkward, because I don't think that anything they've seen me do should warrant them acting like I'm a time bomb. There was a place I worked and I was the only veteran. The people I worked with started actively avoiding me, which made doing my work extremely hard. I found out that they didn't understand PTSD. They didn't understand disabilities and, through their ignorance, they were afraid. I felt sad for them.

Most people would never know by looking at me that I've had eleven or twelve surgeries. You can't see most of my scars. You can't look at me and see what's been hurt under my skin. You can't see the scar tissue, you don't see the wounds. You just see an outline of a mostly normal-looking lady, and they think that I'm fine. I would love to be fine, but I'm not.

It depends on how well I know or don't know the person. If it's a person I don't know very well, I try to make a gentle correction and say, "Hey, not everything is visible." Or if it's a person I know well, I say, "Hey, can we take some time and sit down and talk about that?"

Are you familiar with the spoon theory? We all wake up with so many spoons as units of energy. It costs so many spoons to do a basic task. For some disabled people making dinner, it's gonna cost them five spoons. An able-bodied person, maybe it will cost them two spoons. So depending on where my headspace is for the day or how many spoons I have left, if I know that a conversation is going to cost too many spoons, I'll just unsubscribe and leave it. Because I know that it's not in my best interest and it's not within my current realm of capabilities to do that.

Journey to Everett

Our plan was to stay in Washington state to get caught up on editing. To allow ourselves time with friends. To soak in the dreamy landscape. We house-sat for friends in Everett, north of Seattle. We explored the islands. We paddled kayaks. We hiked up the slopes of Mt. Rainier. Programming was returning to our calendar slowly and with uncertainty. Our bookings were starting to dictate our route and the logistics were getting complicated. We installed an exhibit at the public library in Everett. Another at a church in Tacoma. We flew home for a wedding and then to lead programming in the Midwest at a high school, two colleges, and a church.

When we returned to Washington, we paused again to enjoy the view and then, as the autumn chill settled in, we shifted south toward warmer weather.

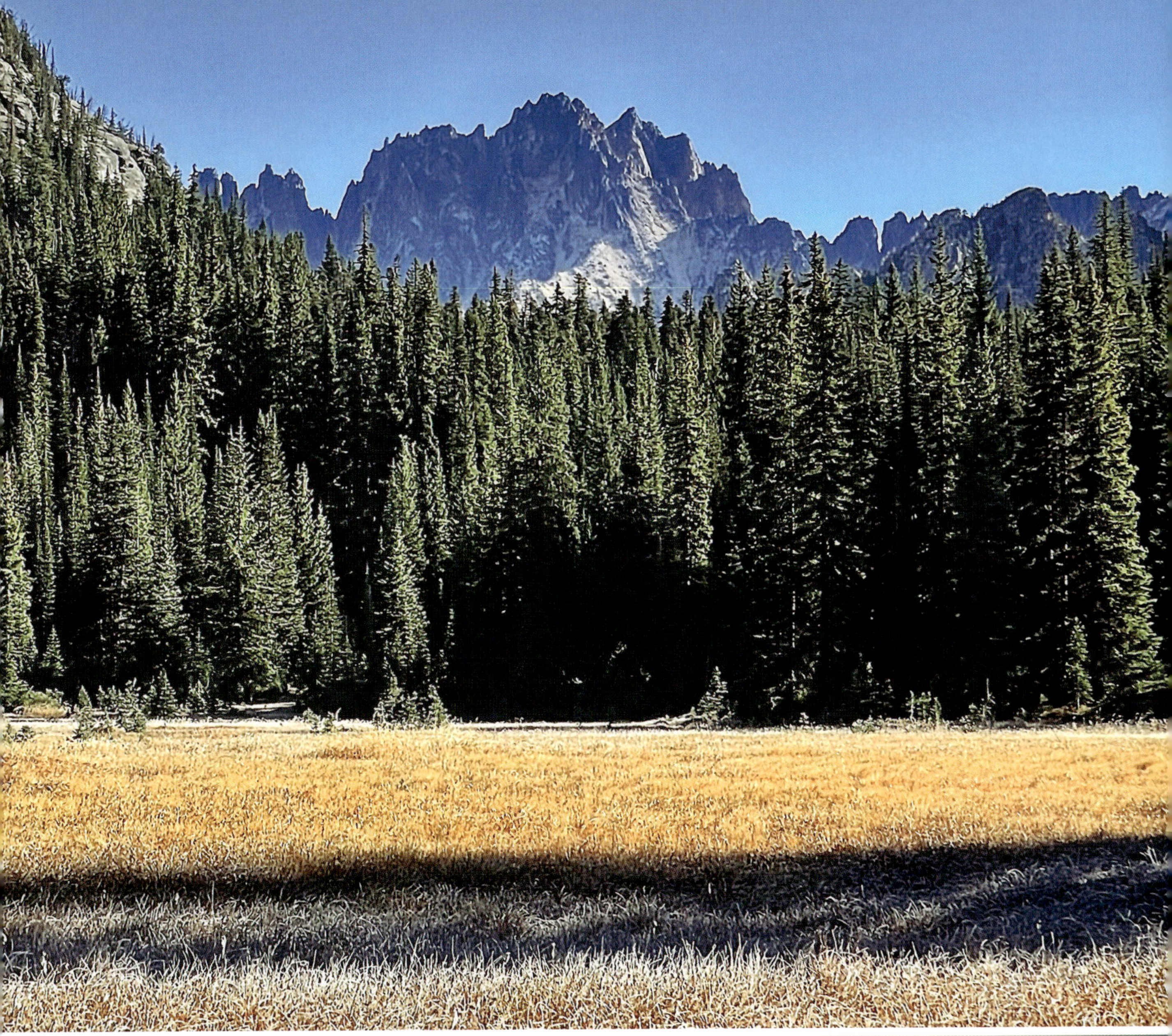

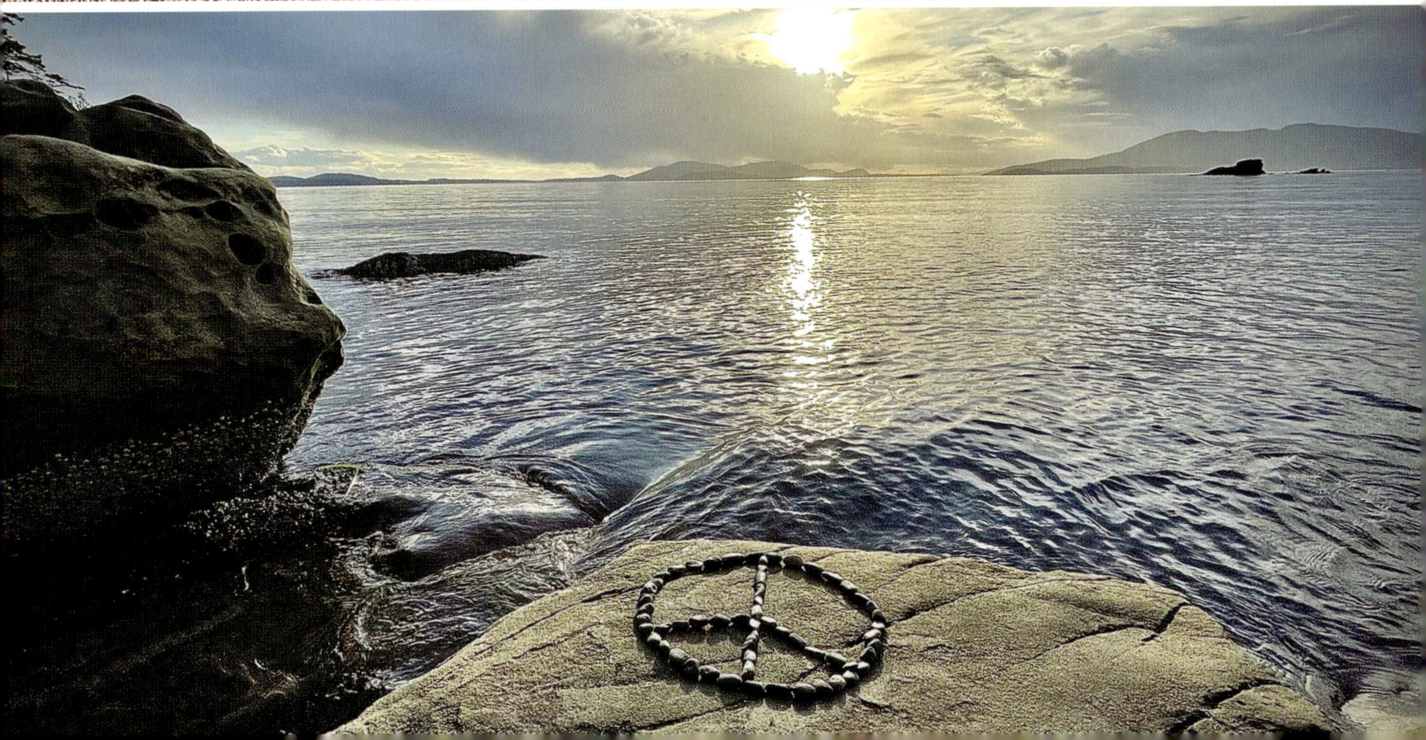

212

213

10.22.2021: Journey south

We charted a course down the West Coast toward California. We weren't in a hurry, but we didn't linger much along the way.

We passed through red blueberry fields and yellow vineyards as the harvest season muted the colors of the Oregon landscape. We slept within view of Mount Hood and Mount St. Helens. We traced the McKenzie River Valley upstream toward Bend and marveled at the thick scent of sage and juniper after a warm rainstorm.

We passed Mount Shasta, which earlier in the summer had been almost completely bare of snow for the first time since 2014, a result of the long drought and low snowpack in the Cascade Range. As we drove by in late October, the mountain wore an encouraging white cap from the summit down to the treeline.

A hundred miles to the south, Shasta Lake was hosting a fishing tournament, but the water levels were well below normal. Spectators stood on the banks where water would have been if the reservoir was full. The boats were far below in the channel, swimming upstream like salmon to spawn as the tournament began.

We aimed for San Francisco and made reservations at a campground north of the city and along the coast near Olema, California. We started hearing reports of a bomb cyclone and a series of atmospheric rivers expected in the area. I'm not sure I knew those meteorological terms at the time, but it didn't sound good. We called ahead to the campground and they said, "We're good. Come on over," but we were nervous to put ourselves in the path of the storm.

Driving south on Interstate 5, we started exploring other options. If we stayed north of the storm, the temperatures would drop below freezing. If we headed west, we would move straight into the strong winds and more than a dozen inches of rain. To the east, we would climb into the mountains and all that rain would turn to snow. Our best option seemed to be straight south, and we found a spot to camp in the San Joaquin Valley near Patterson, California. They still expected rain, but not a dozen inches. They still expected wind, but not enough to flip a camper. The temperatures would drop, but not below freezing.

We waited out the storm and were treated to a rainbow. Facebook posts for the campground near Olema showed an evacuation as their local stream overflowed and campers drove out through 18 inches of floodwater. We'd made a good choice.

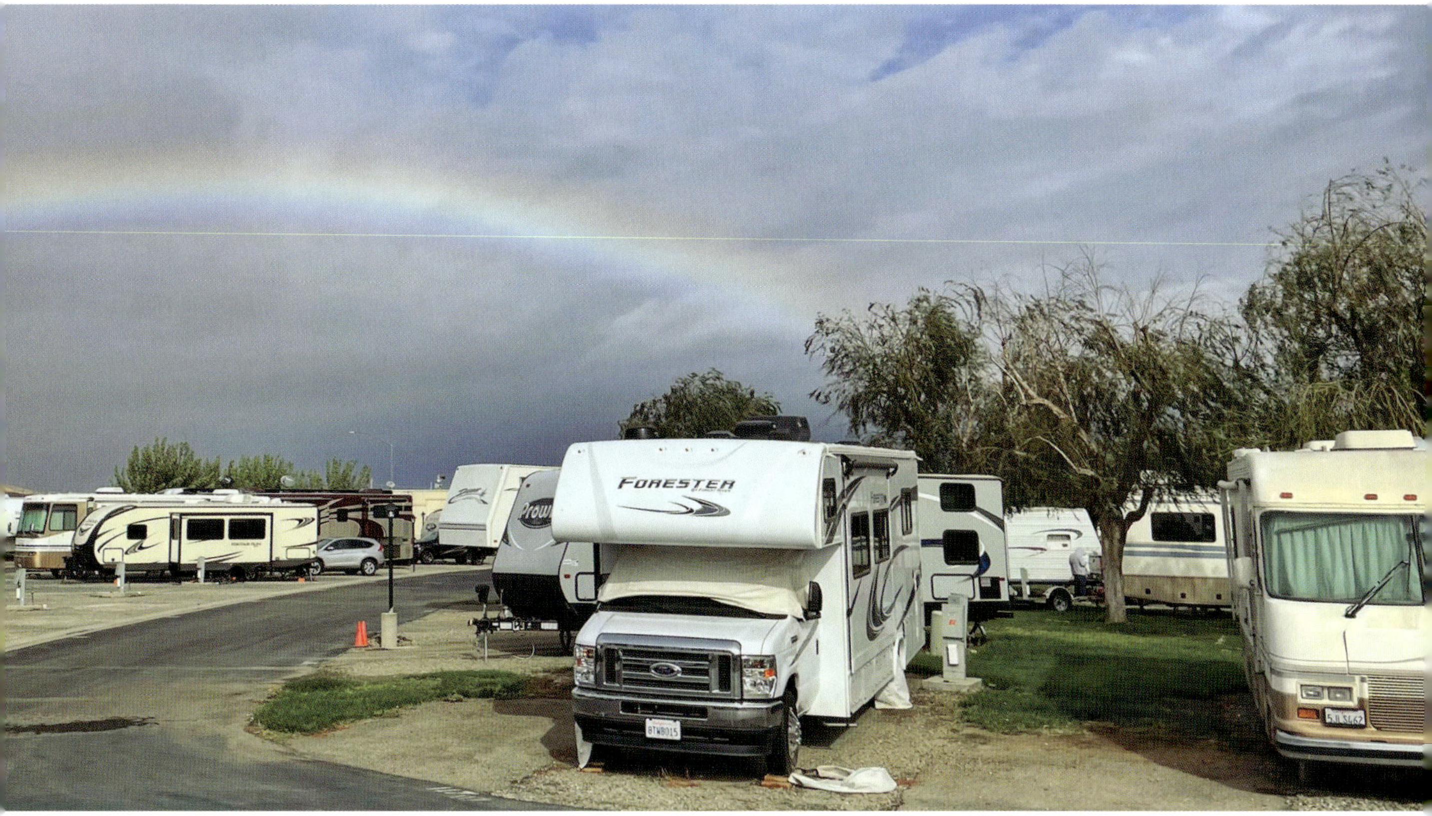
FORESTER

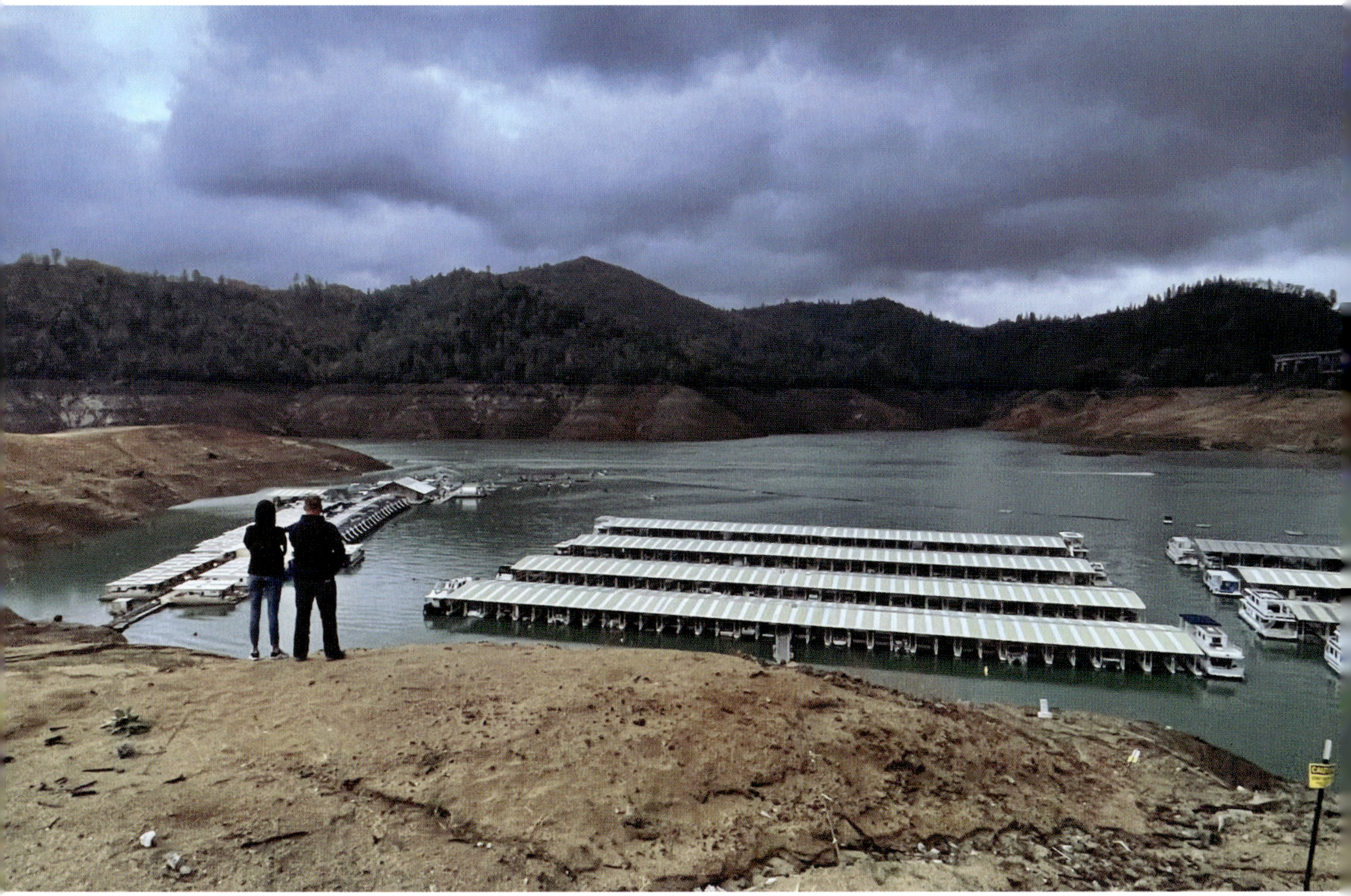

11.01.2021 : Breakdown

We had coordinated with a friend to cross paths at Bon Niche Cellars near Paso Robles, California. Steve was a photographer as well, selling his prints at art fairs and traveling in a small RV. He was spending time at the vineyards to help with their harvest and to take photos for their website. The parking lot had room for a few campers and it was a chance to see an old friend as we relocated toward the southern end of California for winter.

As we pulled in, something sounded odd. Karen got out to guide me into our spot. We'd made a habit of talking on our phones at times like this so we didn't have to shout out the window. "Something doesn't look right," she said. We parked and looked closer. It was bad. Basically the box structure of the camper was sitting on the wheels. I examined the damage and it looked like the suspension had failed. The leaf springs had torn loose from the I-beam of the steel frame. I'm no expert at these things, but something devastating had just happened that would change our plans. A local mechanic crawled underneath and described what he saw as a "catastrophic structural failure."

It was obvious we wouldn't be leaving any time soon. It was certain that our journey had just hit a major hurdle. And it was clear how fortunate we were that our catastrophic structural failure happened at 2 mph as we pulled into the vineyard and not at 70 mph as we went down a busy freeway. It would have been a very different story.

We were lucky to be in a gorgeous setting. We were fortunate to be with friends, old and new. We spent all day sorting out repair details and, at night, we gathered for communal meals and wine as we watched the sun go down over the surrounding hills. We nursed our wounds and laughed. It softened the blow.

FREEDOM ELITE
GRAND CANYON
National Park

WILDWOOD
HERITAGE GLEN
CA165123 • US DOT 2383
80
JOHNBOY'S
TOWING

Problem solving

We were stranded with a perfect storm of bad options. This damage wasn't an insurance claim because we hadn't had an accident. The trailer was under warranty, but the manufacturer didn't feel the same sense of urgency to resolve the issue that we did. During the pandemic, RV sales boomed and most dealers were overwhelmed. They would only service a trailer if you had bought it from them, ignoring the basic nature of RVing, which was to be hundreds, if not thousands, of miles from home when you encountered a problem.

We couldn't even get an appointment for a shop to look at our trailer for three months. We couldn't stay where we were, so we had the broken camper towed to a storage lot, emptied the contents into a separate storage locker, and flew home to sort things out.

Our friends offered an open-ended invitation to stay in their basement. We refused to end the trip on these terms. There would be a path forward, but we couldn't see it yet.

When you are on the road, living in a camper feels like a grand adventure. When your trailer experiences "catastrophic structural failure" and you move into your friends' basement, you start to question some of your life choices.

At first, this new development felt like a bump in the road. As days turned into weeks with no resolution in sight, that bump grew into a mountain.

Uncertainty

We flew back to California over Christmas as the trailer was inspected. Spending the holidays in a very average hotel 1,500 miles from your family is sad. The news we received was worse. The frame manufacturer would repair it, but that would take a few more months. We gathered our truck (which we had left in California when we flew home) and our belongings to drive back to Minnesota, and we learned a quick lesson in macroeconomics.

People were moving out of California because of the cost of living, increased wildfires, traffic, and politics and regulations that rubbed some people the wrong way. As a result of high demand, renting a 5x8 trailer from U-Haul one way from California to Minnesota was priced at $4,500. Mild panic ensued, followed by resourcefulness. If we drove across the line to Yuma, Arizona, the same rental cost $450. It meant a nine-hour round trip to retrieve it, but we chose the time on the road in order to save $4,000 we didn't have.

As we were sorting out the details, someone said to us, "So, you are actually homeless?"

And if you wanted to be quite literal, yes, I suppose that's true.

But not really. We have an address where we get our mail. We have friends with spare bedrooms. We have a family who will always welcome us. And we have money in the bank. We could rent an apartment, buy a home, or even escape to the south of France if we wanted to. That would be a poor financial choice, but we could do it.

In our travels, we have spent time with people who are actually homeless. People who have lived under bridges. Been kicked out of shelters. Run out of options. That's different. It doesn't even compare.

After being on the road for a year, we'd seen a

wide range of marginal living. Stories that are hidden from the suburban day to day. A community of folks I never really knew were out there.

Even in the affluent suburbs of Palo Alto, California, you'll find a trailer park with full-time RVers, braiding their kid's hair at night in front of the campfire, and driving to work in the morning to do construction, or clean your house, or cook your next meal. Housing is expensive in California and paying $75 a night to park your camper is still cheaper than rent in a bad apartment.

Depending on the campground we choose for the night, we might settle in with retirees, millennial adventurers, disabled vets, or folks who are one car repair away from despair.

In Washington state, I met a guy who was driving a motorhome held together with baling twine and duct tape. Vintage 1992 or so.

"This isn't going to last much longer," he said.

"But I forgot to make a million bucks before I was laid off." He's doing the best he can to live the American dream. But I worry it's going to come to an abrupt end for him. There wasn't much of a safety net.

Not everyone who is on the road is "living the dream." Some of them can't afford a home any more. Some of them are teetering on the edge. Some of them still find joy and show up when their neighbors need them. There is community out there, even when the prospects are bleak.

We were doing just fine. In a sense, our dilemma was self-imposed, even if it felt uncertain. But uncertainty is okay. I was humbled by the discomfort and the glimpse into other stories. Wherever we went, we found good people who were willing to help. And that gave me hope.

We are all a little more vulnerable than we believed. And we are all a little more connected than we knew.

Be kind to one another. Life can be hard.

02.05.22: A new home

Karen had been talking about downsizing. We realized we have been traveling with things that we never used and didn't need. Thirty-four-foot trailers don't fit into the most beautiful camping spots and we were often relegated to big gravel lots on the periphery, while smaller campers were tucked into lovely old-growth forests nearby. We'd seen van lifers wake up in the morning and roll immediately while we went through a 20-minute process to pack up and hitch up our trailer.

I was skeptical, but Karen was looking at van ads. Once she started, social media fed her a steady stream of offers, and one of the manufacturers who built camper vans was in Gypsum, Colorado. Dave and Matt Vans had their shop just off our route as we drove from California to Minnesota, so we stopped to take a look. We liked what we saw.

Back in Minnesota, sitting in our friends' basement, we decided to take the leap. We ordered a van. The normal turnaround time was six to eight weeks. COVID-19 had made that much less predictable, because it was hard for Dave and Matt Vans to access the RAM Promasters they worked on, but we hit the timing just right. We placed our order and two weeks later, we got an email announcing that our van was ready.

We flew to Colorado with two duffel bags and two suitcases to pick up the van—which we promptly named Vinny. Vinny Van-Go.

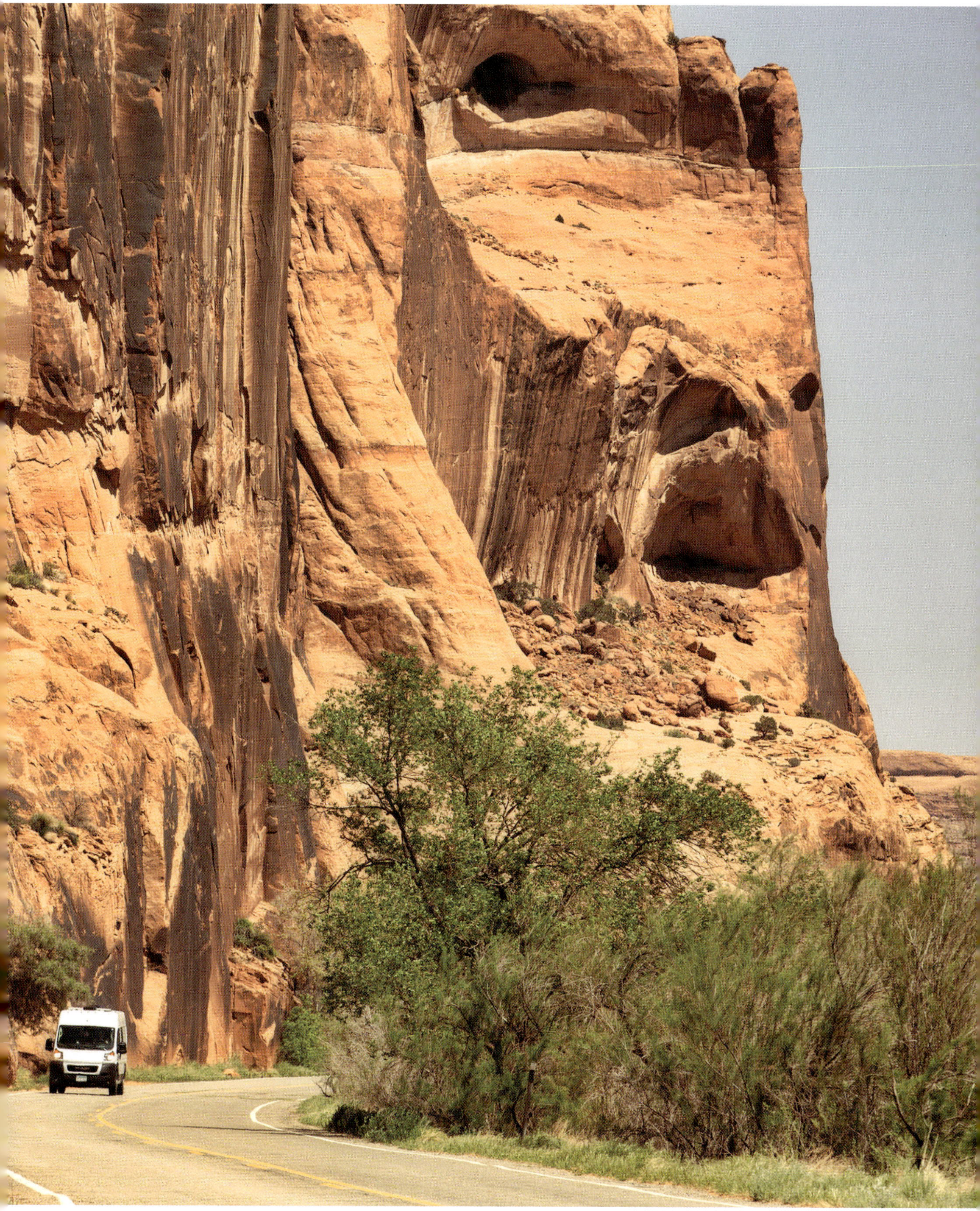

Journey to Moab

We were in and out of our friends' basement as we navigated a busy programming schedule. We traveled to a conference in Kentucky, another in Georgia, a church in Minnesota and led a few virtual engagements. But now we found ourselves with four weeks of open time on our schedule. This sort of lull was going to become increasingly rare as programming continued to ramp up. We decided to give ourselves time to get used to living in even-smaller quarters.

Dave and Matt Vans walked us through the logistics of the van's systems and set us off into the wild. We stopped at the local Target for a few essentials, shopped at a grocery store, and aimed Vinny toward Moab. We were giddy. It was love at first sight. Small was beautiful.

224

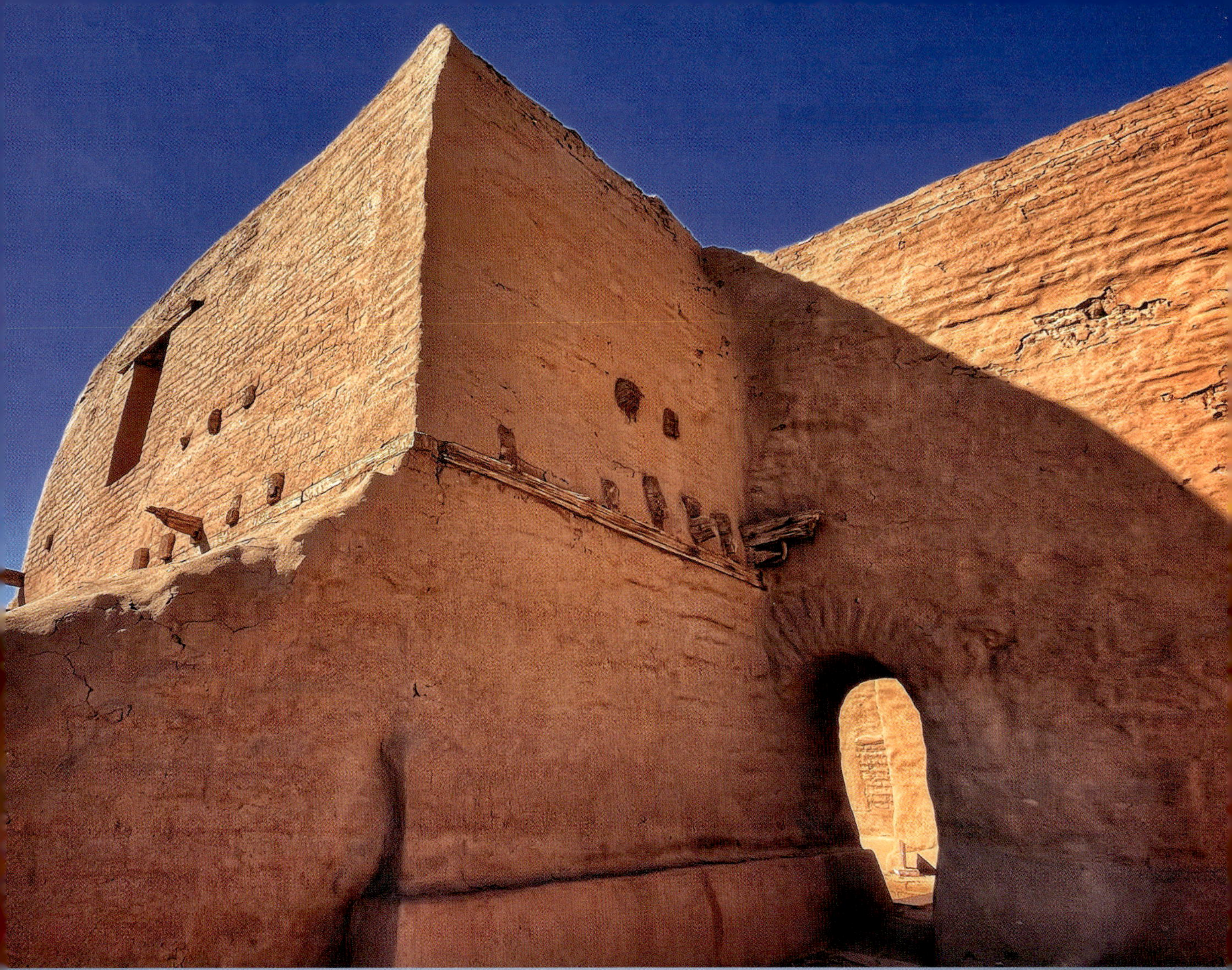

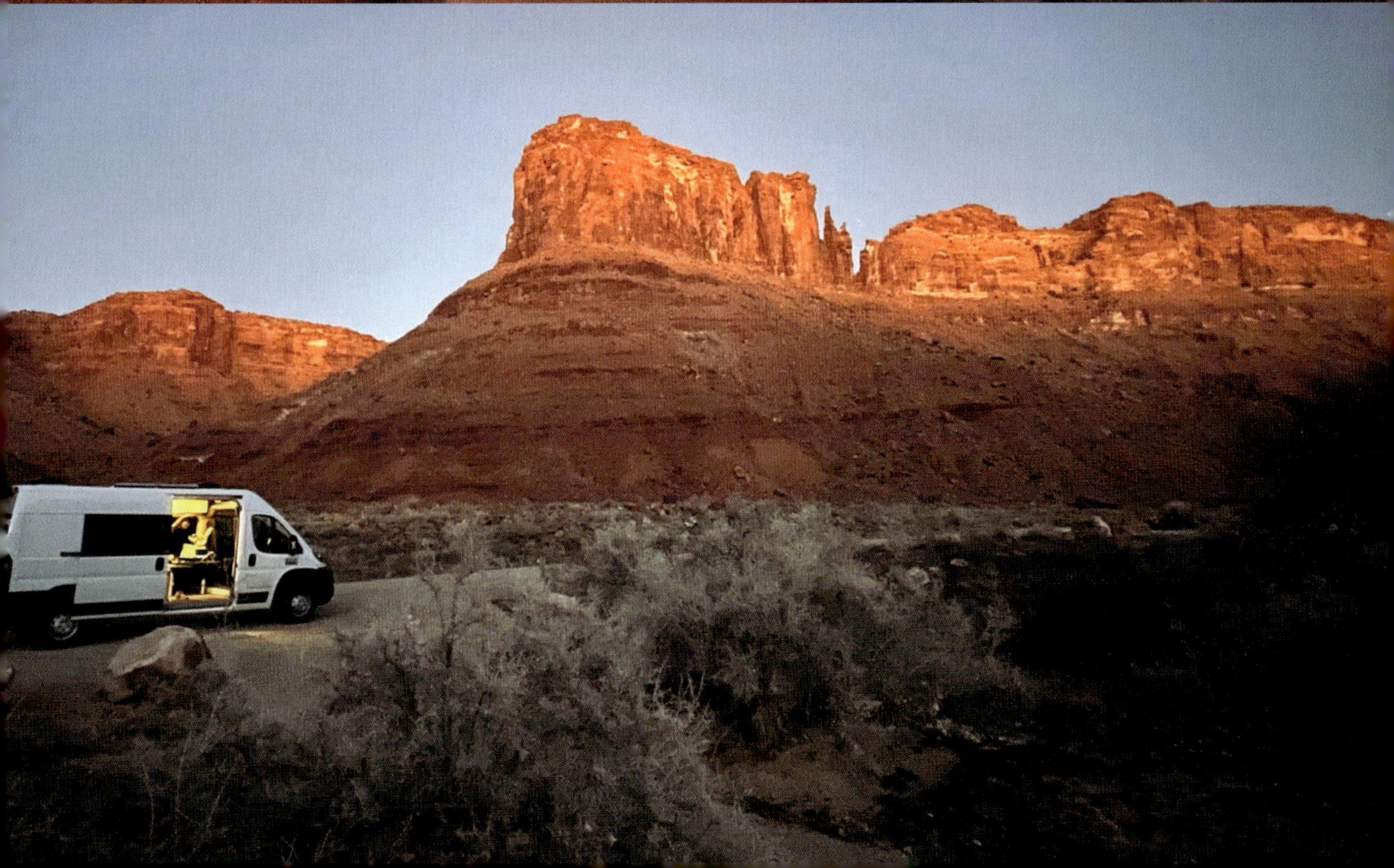

Learning how to live even smaller

Vinny had no oven, no stove, and no shower. Karen and I each had a small cupboard and a suitcase for the clothes we brought along. It was a dramatic downsize, even from living in a trailer, but none of it felt difficult to manage. In fact, less stuff meant less to manage.

We bought a two-burner propane stove for cooking. We had two plates and two bowls. A pot and two fry pans. A small wardrobe meant fewer decisions about what to wear each day. Everything had its spot and there weren't too many spots, so we rarely had to hunt for things.

We stayed at campgrounds with showers, and when we stayed farther off the grid, we had fewer people to impress, so showers were less of a priority. We sometimes drove to a nearby RV park and paid a few dollars to use their shower, even if we didn't stay there. In all my years of traveling, I never used a truck stop shower, but when I finally did, it was just fine.

Vinny had 320 watts of solar panels on the roof, so we didn't need to plug in. We could carry seven gallons of fresh water. We were small and nimble and suddenly very popular. If you want to meet new friends, consider getting yourself a puppy or a van. Everywhere we parked, people came up to peer in the windows. If our door was open, they would start a conversation. One woman in a grocery store parking lot saw our Dave and Matt Vans logo sticker and came over to excitedly announce that she had just ordered herself a Dave and Matt Van.

We'd found a new home and a new community and it was good.

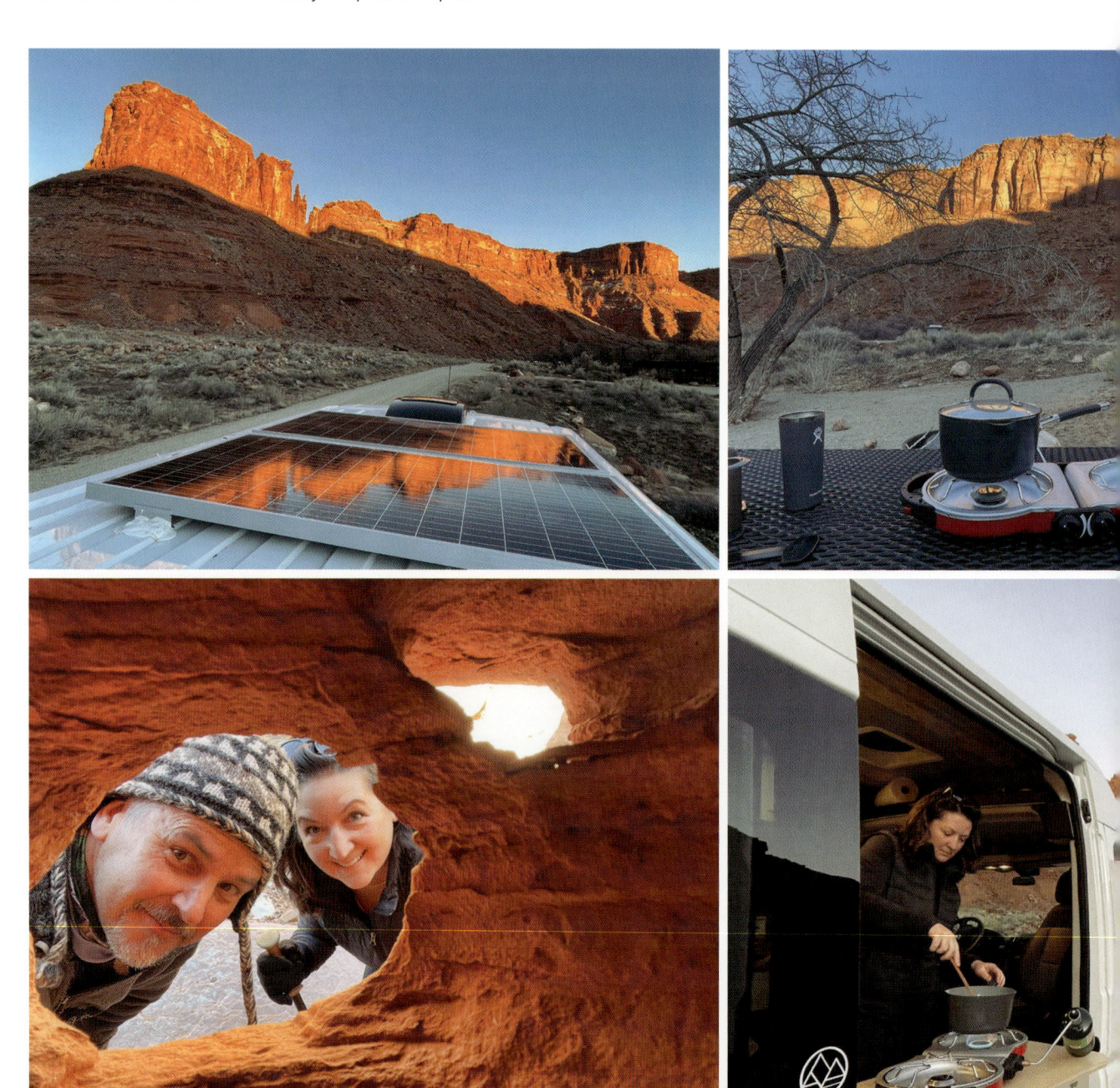

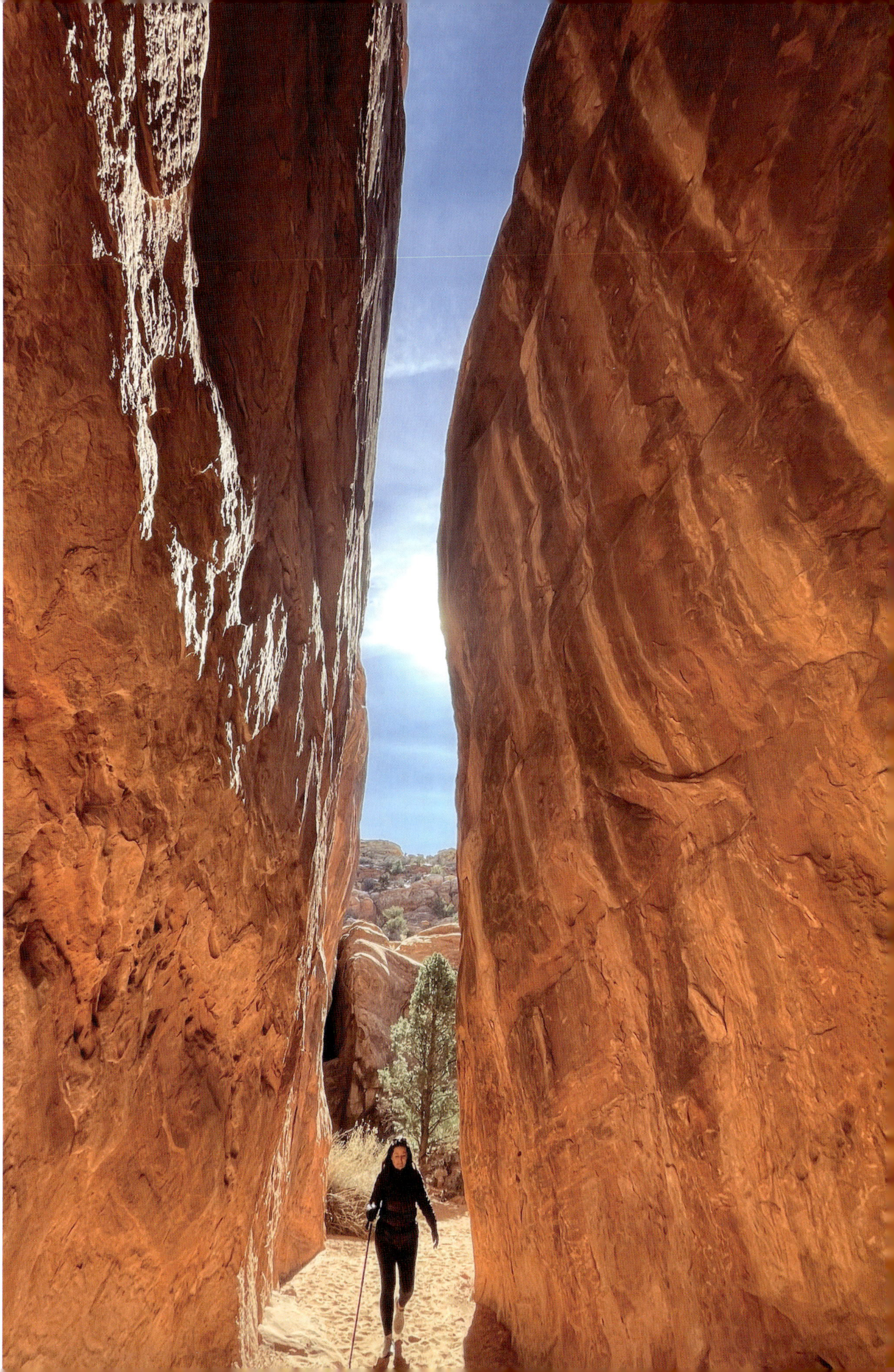
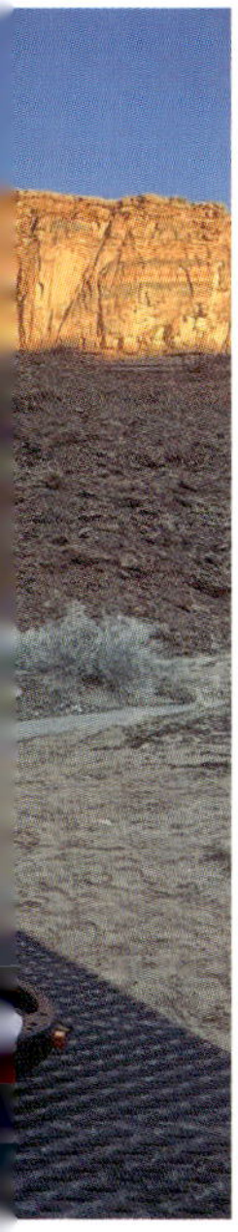
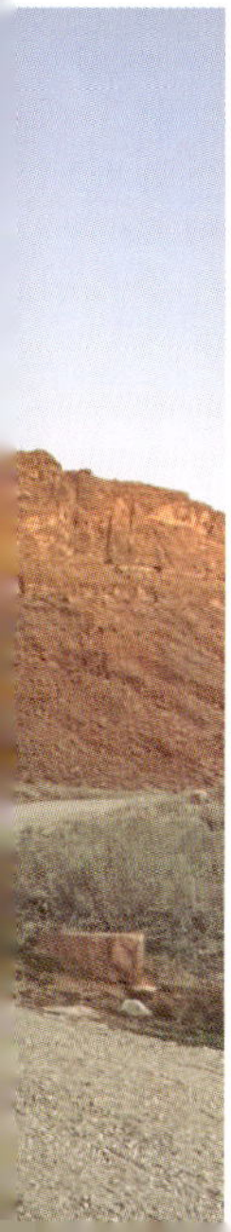

Journey to the Colorado River

We'd been working to line up a series of water scarcity interviews for months, and it's a good thing. Suddenly stories about drought in the Southwest were everywhere in the news. Lake Mead and Lake Powell were at historically low levels. The Colorado River was listed as our nation's most endangered watershed. The original intake pipe to deliver water to Las Vegas was suddenly exposed by lower water levels, as were human remains from past murders that were submerged for decades until lake levels receded.

National and international crews from the New York Times, BBC, and Mother Jones magazine were in the neighborhood. Several of my interviews were immediately preceded or followed by other media outlets. One of my contacts went radio silent for days and I started to worry, but then I saw him quoted in an article for CNN and I realized we were doing our work in the midst of a media frenzy.

Given the timing, it was amazing we were able to get some of the access we did. As always, some of what we had planned fell through and other welcome surprises presented themselves.

Part of this journey was embracing the ability to explore, to allow curiosity to lead us, and to change course when new opportunities presented themselves. Eric Balken in Salt Lake City suggested we talk with Lisa Rutherford in St. George, and so we did. John Weisheit encouraged us to visit Hite Overlook at the upstream end of Lake Powell and we followed his advice. Our ability to say yes guided the way our journey unfolded.

228

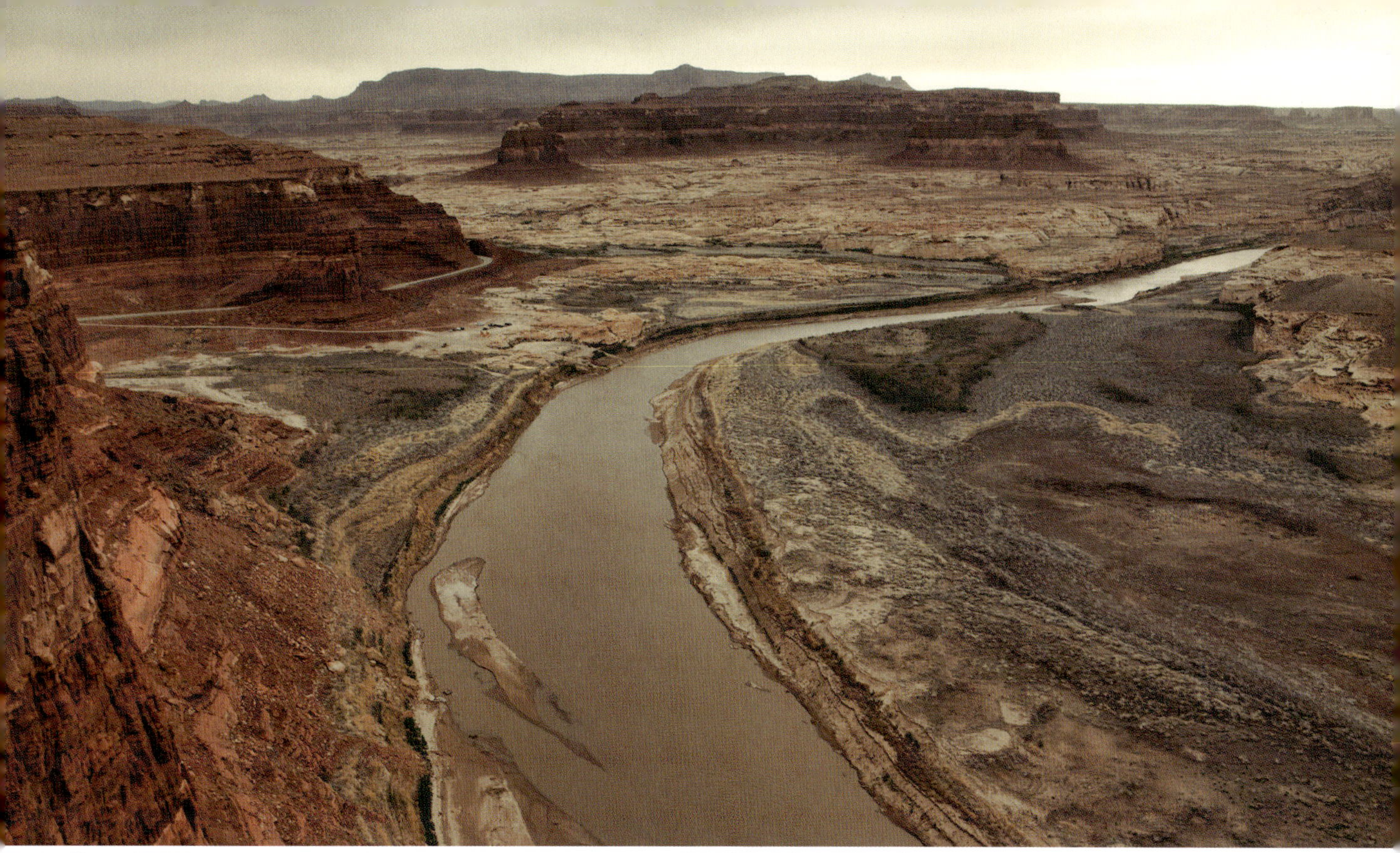

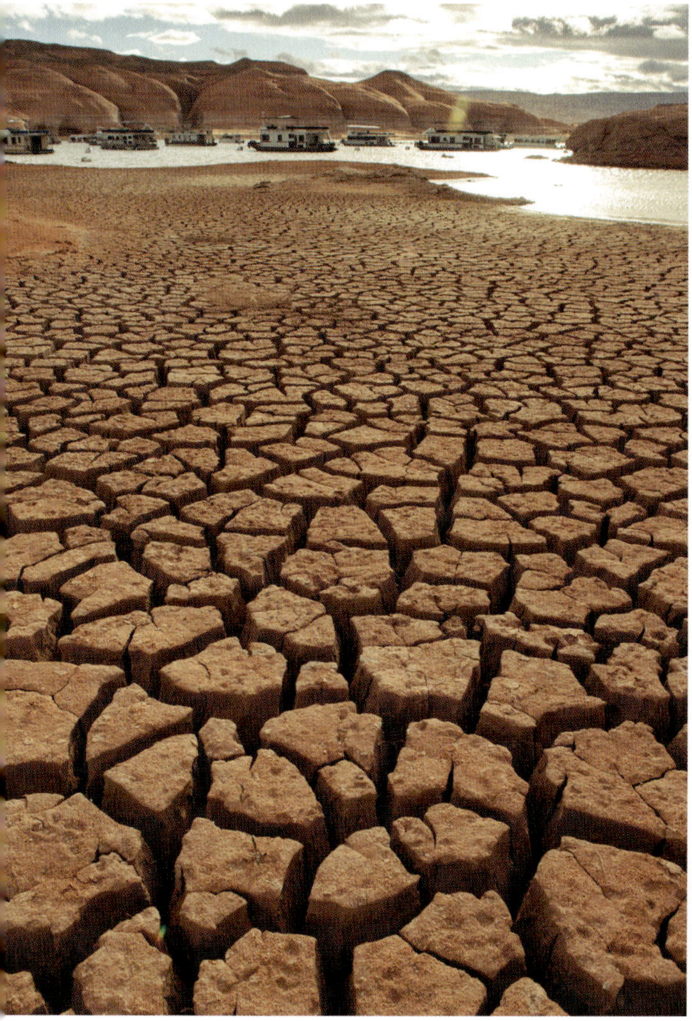

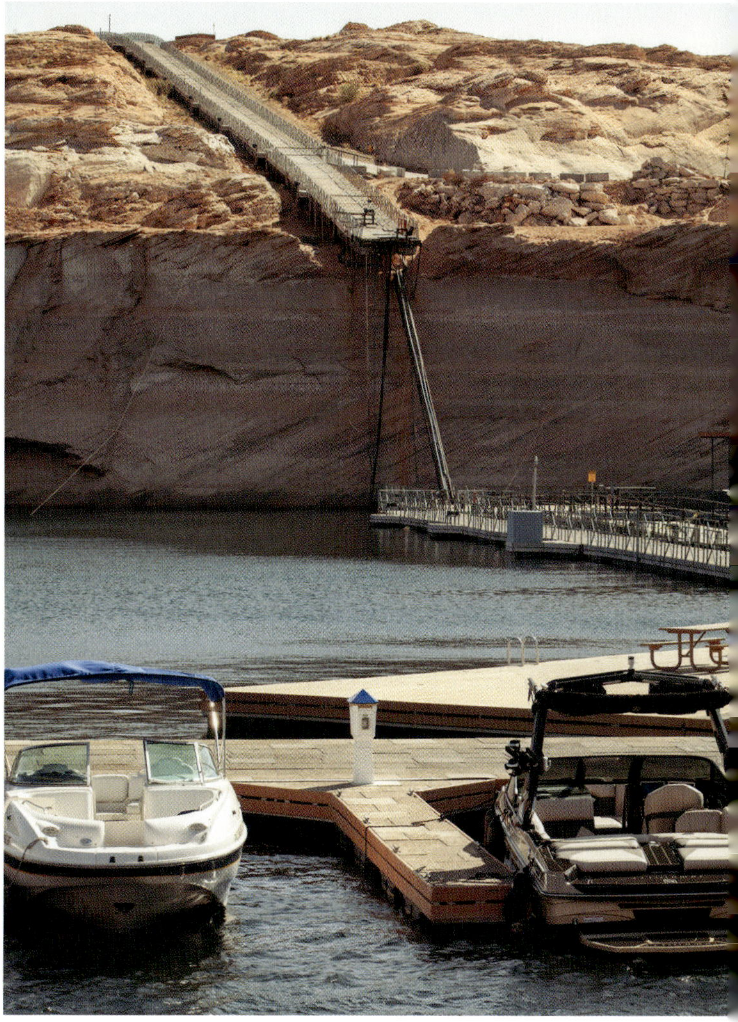

Eric Balken is the executive director for the Glen Canyon Institute, which is dedicated to the restoration of Glen Canyon and a free-flowing Colorado River. Eric grew up and still lives in Salt Lake City, Utah, where he developed an early love for mountains, rivers, and deserts.

Today, if you drained Lake Powell down to deadpool, Lake Mead would still only be 65 percent full. There is not enough water on this river to keep both of those reservoirs full, which means we have to start rethinking Glen Canyon and Glen Canyon Dam.

If we can't fill Lake Mead and Lake Powell, and Lake Powell was this massive environmental mistake, why not fill Mead first and give Glen Canyon a chance to come back?

Glen Canyon is shaped like a martini glass. Most of the storage in Lake Powell is in the top hundred feet of the reservoir. And once it dips down into these levels that we're seeing now, you can see really rapid fluctuations in reservoir elevation. For the park service to try to manage boat ramps and marinas with this wildly fluctuating reservoir, it's sort of a nightmare scenario. So, we need to start thinking about how to phase this reservoir out entirely.

We've been portrayed as people who want to ruin other people's houseboat vacations. But the reality is that this is happening one way or the other. This reservoir, at least the version that we knew in the eighties and nineties, is long gone and all the climate science available suggests it's never gonna fill again.

We need to have a thoughtful and strategic transition from a reservoir-style economy to a national park–style economy. Instead of houseboats and marinas, this would be more like river rafting, hiking, off-road vehicles.

There's going to be a lot of heartache on the Colorado River and a lot of stakeholders are going to have to make sacrifices. Glen Canyon is sort of this one, beautiful silver lining where there's so much opportunity. There's so much hope. And I think the world is starting to wake up to that.

The sooner we start thinking about transitioning to a national park–style economy and treating this landscape differently, the more benefit there will be.

> "Wherever you live, realize that we have to get smarter with water and learn about it and be a part of the solution."
> —Eric Balken

Lisa Rutherford lives in Ivins, Utah, just outside of St. George, a fast-growing metropolitan area on the doorstep of Zion National Park. Lisa spent two decades working for the oil industry in Alaska and is one of the founding board members and current advisers for Conserve Southwest Utah.

We have the cheapest water anywhere in Utah, hence, it's overused. What you don't pay for, you don't value.

We're not gonna stop the growth. That would be a fool's errand. But, how are we going to manage it better?

I think that we need to realize that this planet has given us much and asked very little. And yet, we put demands on it all the time. Give me this. Let me drill here. Let me mine here. Let me build here with little consideration for the creatures that we're building on top of or digging up.

"That's what being a good steward of the earth is all about. Believe that your actions—combined with the actions of millions of people on this planet who are trying to do the right thing in spite of the forces and the headwinds that they face—will help."
—Lisa Rutherford

I know that humans want to enjoy life as much as they can during their brief time on this earth. But do we have to do it in a way that destroys [the planet] at the same time?

There was a debate on NPR the other day. It was renewables versus nuclear and, at the end of the debate, after all the facts were presented on both sides, the renewable debate came out ahead. But the point that really bothered me was that the person who was supporting the nuclear side said that we don't want to tell people not to use energy. People want to use energy and they want to use a lot of energy. And I'm thinking to myself, why don't we want to tell people not to use so much energy?

To me, that's the crux of the matter. Because we waste so much, whether it's turning the air conditioning down to a temperature that requires you to put on a sweater. Or turning the heat up in your house, instead of putting on your sweatshirt to become comfortable.

[There's] the idea that technology is always going to save us. But what I see is that technology is creating many of our problems. All the technology that we have, our computers, our cell phones, that all comes from materials. We can't keep buying the latest and greatest.

[People] need to be more conscious of what they're doing. When I was growing up, every time a TV commercial would come on, the whole family would say, 'We don't need that!' That was our mantra for dealing with the advertising forces that were coming at us.

If you are consuming, give some thought to why you're consuming. Are you doing it to fill some void in your life? If so, figure out what that void is [actually] about and fill it with something else that is not as impactful on this world and its resources.

Izzy Collett is cofounder and owner of Desert Adventures, an outfitter in Boulder City, Nevada, that takes clients on outdoor adventures. With more than 20 years of paddling experience, Izzy calls herself a searcher, always looking for new answers.

We just keep growing. If you look at plant life in the desert, it's sparse, and you think there's nothing there. But the reason it's like that—sparse and scattered—is because those plants are spacing themselves so that they can survive. They're not taking up someone else's water, they're spacing themselves far enough away that all the plants can survive. The west can't support this type of growth that we're having now.

People are trying to sustain big cities by tapping into the water tables of farming communities. It's a complex issue. It's just not as easy as saying, "Don't have golf courses in Vegas."

There's actually a lot of science that goes into golf courses, in the types of grass and preventing evaporation. The fountains also have water-saving strategies to prevent evaporation.

I don't think people understand water consumption. Our guides spend a lot of time [talking] about education and awareness and advocacy for the river and conservation. We're trying to educate people as to, "Hey, this is an issue that affects the whole Western United States."

"Water is a finite resource. It's not an unlimited supply. We're on this little ball in the universe and we only have what we have. If we destroy it, we'll destroy ourselves."
—Izzy Collett

When we do river trips, there are places where we have to carry our water because the water quality is silty. It'll clog up the pump immediately. We think about how we have to carry this huge pail of water up this giant bank. You truly think about your water usage and the quantity that you have available and how you're using it.

I don't think anybody even realizes it. You just turn the faucet on and it's there. People leave the water running while they're brushing their teeth, take showers that are too long, have pools, have grass in the desert. It's little things, but if everyone does it, it truly becomes part of your way of living. So think about what you can do to help and add to a solution rather than contribute to the problem.

Chad Taylor is director of sales and marketing for Lake Mead Mohave Adventures. He grew up on Lake Mead, where his dad was general manager of Callville Bay Marina in the Lake Mead National Recreation Area outside of Las Vegas. Lake Mead is the largest reservoir in the United States, and it is currently at historically low levels as the population in the southwest continues to grow and the region faces ongoing, historic drought conditions.

This lake is doing exactly what it was meant to do. A hundred years ago, they built this big reservoir. 1984 was the last time it was full. It didn't start really declining probably until 1995. It's taken this long to go down 170 feet and we still have another 400 feet to go. Now, does that change some things? Sure. But it's doing exactly what it was supposed to do.

If we ask ourselves what has changed downstream over the last 30 years, I bet if you did those numbers—and I'm not the guy—but if you did, I would think that it's more of a consumption problem than an inflow problem. They're all trying to figure it out right now, which is great. And someone will come up with a solution. I think it'll work itself out. So it's not doomsday for me. It's just, "This too shall pass," as Rod Taylor would say.

[I was a] lake half full guy all the time. And actually, at this point, I'm an overflowing river guy. We're below half full at this point, but we are definitely overflowing as a river. So, the way I look at it is, this lake is beautiful. It's gorgeous. I don't want people to stop recreating because of perception. There's so much water here. There's so much surface area. There's still so much shoreline. There's an enormous amount of space for people to come out and recreate.

"If we've proved anything about humanity, it is that we figure out how to fix our problems. It may take us some time, but we get it done."
—Chad Taylor

For me and my family, it's kind of like Lake Mead is the greatest treasure hunt ever. I have three wedding rings living out here on the beach somewhere and, lately, we're taking the girls out with the [metal detectors] on the beach. I swore to my wife I was going to find them one day. We're able to see things that we haven't been able to see in a hundred years. How often do you get that opportunity?

I don't see a day that I don't do this. I've grown up on lakes. Lakes are my thing. I love them. And I'm just here taking it in day by day.

"The reality is, this is gonna crash. The train is going over the cliff, but I have to have hope. That's what keeps me going, because I believe the human character does have resilience and does have sustainability. It's kind of built into us. We just need to revive it. We need to wake it up."

—John Weisheit

John Weisheit grew up with a love for the Colorado River and has worked as a river guide for more than four decades. In the year 2000, John cofounded Living Rivers, an advocacy group that seeks a path to restoring the ecology of the Southwest, balanced with meeting human needs.

I interviewed John in the cool shade of his backyard boathouse in Moab, Utah, just after he returned from a rafting trip through the Grand Canyon.

There's two ways to recruit. One is through promotion and one is through attraction and we prefer attraction. Promotion is fake to me. It's a con. It's what advertisers do.

So that's why we believe in attraction. When the phone rings, I'm going to answer that person's question. I'm not gonna send them to somebody else. I'm here to help you. That's my job. That's my mission. Let's think about how we can do this. Who are your allies?

This is how you build a constituency. Ten thousand people working on their issues will get a lot more done than one organization that has a $5 million budget. The most powerful person on this planet is the individual. So you need to believe in yourself. And I'm here to encourage you.

You do this all the time. You've made a commitment to your wife, a commitment to your children. Well, you can make a commitment to your community as well. Can you do it all? No, but you can, if you have allies. That's how things get done.

People ask who's the best company to do river trips. And my answer is, 'They're all fine.' There's no such thing as a bad outfitter. It's [all about], what are you going to do to make this trip you're on as enjoyable as it can possibly be? You're gonna meet strangers. Are you gonna be warm and friendly to 'em? Or are you gonna be combative? Are you gonna fill the trip with distractions and things that don't matter?

You can have a bad river trip with the best outfitter in the world, but I would say the best river trip is the river trip you are on now. What are you gonna do to make it the best river trip? Are you gonna contribute? Are you gonna be a part of it?

It's fun being engaged and enjoying people and enjoying problems. I have more friends than I've ever had before. My life is full of phone calls and answering questions from students and reporters. I feel very alive for taking this on. So if you're depressed, be an activist. If people make you unhappy, find a way to bring joy into the system. It's hard work. It takes a lot of patience. But it's worth it.

Bri Hernandez Rosales is a graduate research assistant at the Desert Research Institute in Reno, Nevada. She wrote her graduate thesis on the feasibility of rainwater harvesting for a local tribe. I interviewed Bri two days before she walked the stage to receive a master's degree in hydrologic sciences. Bri's love of rock climbing and the natural environment led her to study water, and her applied research led her to work with underserved populations and communities in arid ecologies to strengthen their right to water security.

I can't talk for every rural or tribal community that's experiencing these things, but from my research, you can see patterns in underserved communities or underrepresented communities that get the brunt of everything. For the past 20 years, the Southwest has been experiencing drought. Recent research mentions how the current drought has been the worst since the year 800.

It's being felt along the Southwest, especially in areas that are considered food deserts: areas that don't have access to good reliable food. One thing will be connected to something else and it just becomes exacerbated. So when it comes to the drought, finding other ways of augmenting or diversifying water portfolios is pretty important, if this help is wanted by the tribal communities or the rural communities. It's important for research to be done with permission, to be able to address questions that need answers right now.

The municipalities and metropolitan areas will feel the extent of this as well, but there are resources in those areas that they can pull from, while a lot of the tribal and rural communities are on their own. [Researchers need to] listen to what is needed from these communities. Being okay with being told what to research, instead of doing it your [own way]. Science for the sake of science

"Communities are trying to thrive, but the climate is changing so rapidly that they don't have time to adapt."
—Bri Hernandez Rosales

is great and we've propelled forward a lot. But I feel like we're at a crossroads where we have to include how this science is going to be applicable or how it's going to benefit all individuals and influence policy.

There's such a big disconnect between policy makers and scientific researchers and the communities that need this to be changed. There is a crisis in our hands right now with drought destroying people's livelihoods and crop production and water quality. I think it's important to have policymakers look at what needs to be done and actually have the facts from the researchers to make decisions that are going to help these communities. We could be doing more.

A water crisis

We spent time at the two largest reservoirs in the nation. We camped beside Lake Powell at Bullfrog Marina with acres of cracked mud flats where water should have been. White, chalky markings high on the sandstone cliffs—the so-called bathtub ring—indicated where the water used to be. Row after row of houseboats in the marina rental fleets had for sale signs in the window, suggesting a lag in tourism to the drought-stricken lake, but who would buy those houseboats as the lake levels dropped lower and lower?

We walked through the inner tunnels of Hoover Dam and felt the hum of the turbines spin. In Las Vegas, we watched the fountains dance at the Bellagio to the delight of crowds. We swam in the palm-ringed, sparkling pool of our RV park. We talked to activists and Indigenous leaders, researchers and water district supervisors, river runners and marina owners. As always, no single person held all the answers, but when you start weaving those stories together, you begin to understand the enormity of the issues, the complexity of the challenges, and the creativity of the people who are working to find solutions.

Standing beside a critical reservoir that is 170 feet below full pool is sobering. Hearing stories of the seven states that make up the Colorado River Basin cooperating and making hard choices for the common good is encouraging.

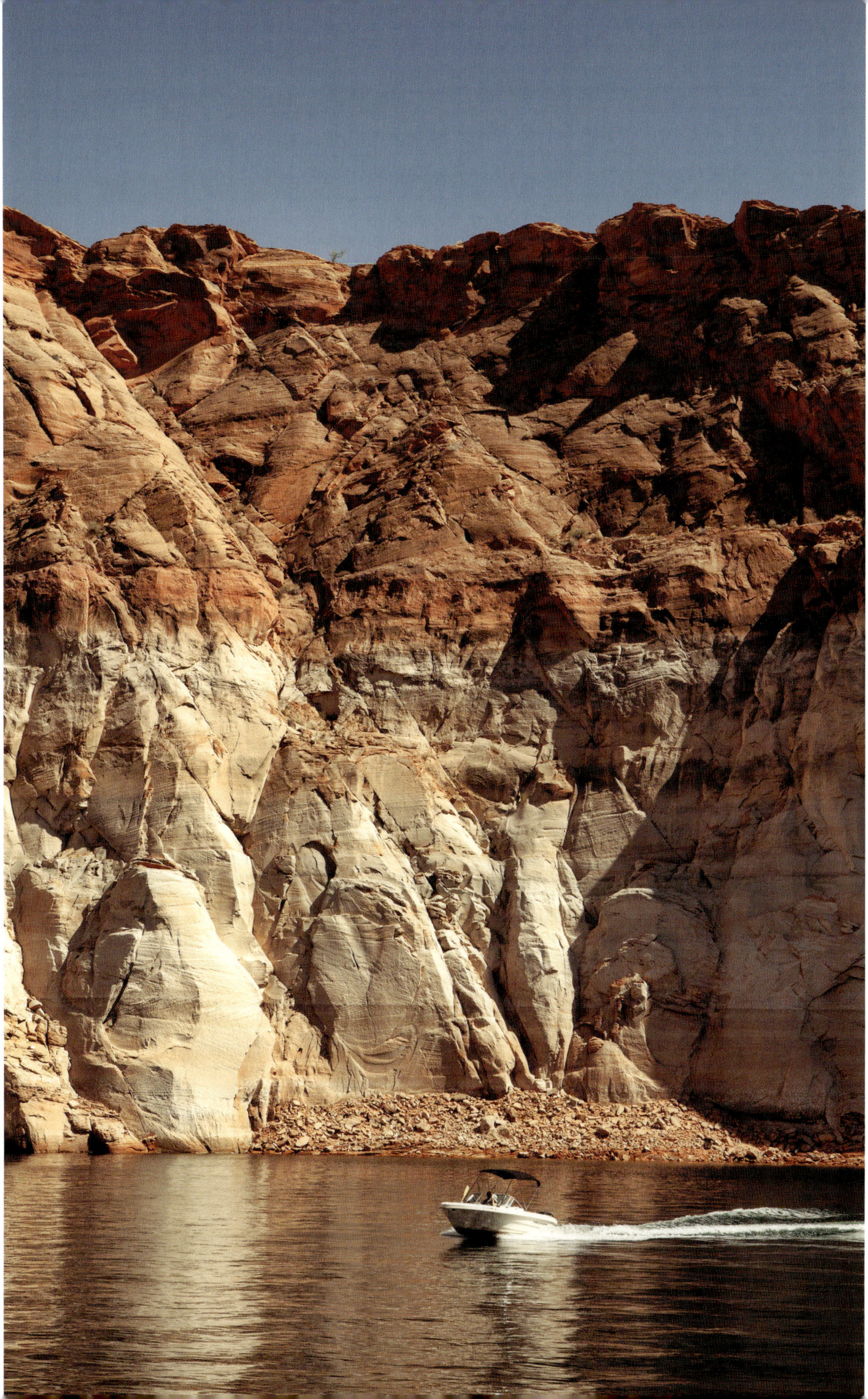

David Arend was named deputy regional director for the Bureau of Reclamation Lower Colorado Basin in December of 2021. His responsibilities include oversight of Lake Mead, the largest reservoir in the United States. I interviewed David at the Hoover Dam near Boulder City, Nevada.

We release water out of Hoover Dam based on the water needs of the irrigation districts and the farmland and the tribal interests down river.

We're approximately 30 percent full right now. And that number is continuing to drop. Also our inflow of the water coming into it is only about 72 percent of average. And so we recalculate. We look at every two feet of change in Lake Mead. We recalculate what our new capacities are.

There is no one solution. There's no way—with the current hydrology conditions—we're not going to conserve our way out of this issue. So there has to be other things. Maybe desalinization is part of the answer. Water reuse is a big part of the answer. That's where you're recycling the water that's been taken out and put it back in. So your consumptive use drops significantly.

Some of the comments that you read say, "California's taking all our water. Arizona's taking all our water." It's not one entity's water. It was decided years and years ago in a compact. 2022 is the hundredth anniversary of the compact that divided up the river, and we're still following that compact today. But we are doing everything we can to make sure that all the water is available.

As the water level dwindles, there's going to be less supply for everybody. So everybody needs to look at what can we do to reuse water? What can we do to save water? Don't just look at it in terms of "It's my water, and I gotta protect my water and the heck with everybody else."

Reclamation used to look at it as the Upper Basin and the Lower Basin. And in the last several years, we've started to look at it in terms of the Colorado River itself, as a whole. It is one flow and whatever affects them upstream, affects us downstream.

The states are well aware of where we're at and they understand that we're all in this together. One of the [state] representatives said, "We're gonna get through this because we have no other choice." It's no longer esoteric. It's no longer somebody thinking, "This could happen." It's happening. We've been in over 20 years of drought now. It's not getting much better. In some cases, [it's] getting worse.

One of the things that gives me hope is the resourcefulness of people themselves. We find a way and come up with an answer. A lot of times we have to wait for it to become a crisis before we respond and we react. But the resourcefulness and the ingenuity of the human race itself is very strong.

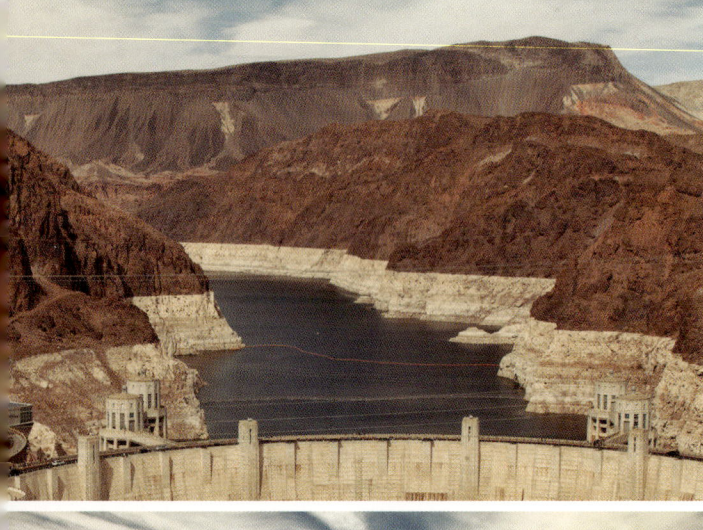

"If the water's not there, it can't flow downstream.
It's pretty simple math. This is 100 percent uncharted territory.
We have never been this low since the filling of the lake.
So every day, it's a new historic low. But we'll find a way.
We have to find a way. We have no other choice."

—David Arend

Colby Pellegrino is deputy general manager of Resources for the Southern Nevada Water Authority in Las Vegas.

Las Vegas is the driest metropolitan area in the United States with an annual rainfall of just four inches. It is one of the fastest-growing metropolitan areas in the nation. And it is a leader in innovative water conservation programs the city has developed to remain viable in an arid landscape.

Water conservation is a journey, not a destination. As we look at our options to meet the needs of a growing community and a diversifying economy, we want to make sure we can control our own destiny. And the way that we can do that with limited resources is through water conservation.

So we really stood up our conservation programs at the turn of the century, and we've just continued to build upon them since then. We have this monster, a three-headed Hydra of conservation programs, where we use code to make the necessary changes for how the community develops in the future. We have incentives and pricing, which we use to influence our existing customers. And then we have a really robust education and outreach component to make people aware of the other two legs of the stool, just to remind people that we live in a desert.

Most people in Las Vegas are transplants. When I was born, 300,000 people lived here. Now, 2.3 million people live here. So the number of people that move here from somewhere else is striking. You have people coming and going all the time from different climates and different regions, and they don't necessarily think when they move in, "I'm in a desert and that should influence my lifestyle."

The water authority was originally created as Southern Nevada's Colorado River use was rapidly growing. Our city's populations were rapidly growing and there wasn't a centralized voice to speak with the other states that shared the river. So the vision for the authority was originally based upon coming together and having one voice for Nevada in these negotiations, instead of having each municipality trying to get a little more from themselves at the expense of the greater good.

The community bought into that approach. That quickly transformed into a way to be uniform in the conservation actions that we take, because where we have seen failure in other communities or disparity in other communities is where you have these different land use governing municipalities right next to one another.

So on one side of the street, you're allowed to do this. And on the other side of the street, you're not. That's not what we thought Vegas needed to be successful. So we've centralized the development of our conservation programs with the authority, as well as our future water resource planning and those go hand in hand, the way we manage our demands has a really huge influence on how we meet the community's future water resource needs.

Forty million people in the United States and

Mexico rely on the river, millions of acres of irrigated agriculture, 29 federally recognized tribes, the largest national park units in the nation, all rely on the waters of the Colorado River. And when we talk about what needs to be done to meet the challenges of the future, the first place that most people go to is to find somebody else to blame for the problem.

We often get asked, "Why isn't this city doing what you are doing? And what do you think about that?" I think that all 40 million people need to do more to conserve water. All of the different users, whether you're a municipality or a farmer or a rancher or a paddle boater—everybody needs to do what they can to save water because of these challenges. We're only seeing the tip of the iceberg in terms of what climate change could throw at us. So being resilient is going to take everyone's collective effort.

"Since 2002 our per capita water use has gone down 49 percent. Our total Colorado River use has dropped over 25 percent. At the same time, we added about 750,000 people to this valley. So, we added three quarters of a million people and we are using significantly less water."

—Colby Pellegrino

241

Nora McDowell is a member of the Fort Mojave Tribe in Mojave Valley, Arizona, and was chair of the tribe for more than 25 years. She's part of the leadership team for the Water and Tribes Initiative and is passionate about protecting all natural and cultural resources along the Colorado River. Through the years, Nora has led efforts and litigation to claim and preserve tribal water rights and to clean up industrial pollution from sacred lands.

These are the traditional homelands of the Mojave people. I was born and raised here. Our people were created and placed here. Our creation story dates way back, and it's oral history has been passed down from generation to generation. Our primary responsibility is to take care of the land that we were given and to protect the water, where all life comes from. Our elders always told us that land without water is nothing.

> "The water, especially. We have to care for it. We have to speak for it."
> —Nora McDowell

I think [there is] a reawakening now of who we are as people. Even though a lot was taken from us, we always managed to survive and rebuild. We've had ethnographers come, trying to tell us about who we are, and we're like, "No, I'll tell you who we are."

At Fort Mojave, they took our children when they were five and six years old and put them in boarding school. They cut their hair. They forbid them to speak their native tongue. They made them little soldiers, and they trained them to be cooks and farmers. Some of the younger girls were taken to California and they were maids until they got old enough and came back home.

My vice chairman went to those schools. He ran away from school and he made it all the way back home. They came right after [him] but the elders hid him away. And then he grew up with all those scars.

The elders didn't want that to happen to us and so they wouldn't teach us the language or anything, so that way we could blend in with the rest of society. Assimilation into that other world.

But it never took away from us who we are as our people. Some of the traditional practices—beadwork and cradleboard making—they're still there and they're part of who we are. But yet the healing part of that, it took a long time.

The focus of our council now is on wellness. We continue to learn from what happened to us. And we're still connected to our history, our culture, and the protection of these sacred site places.

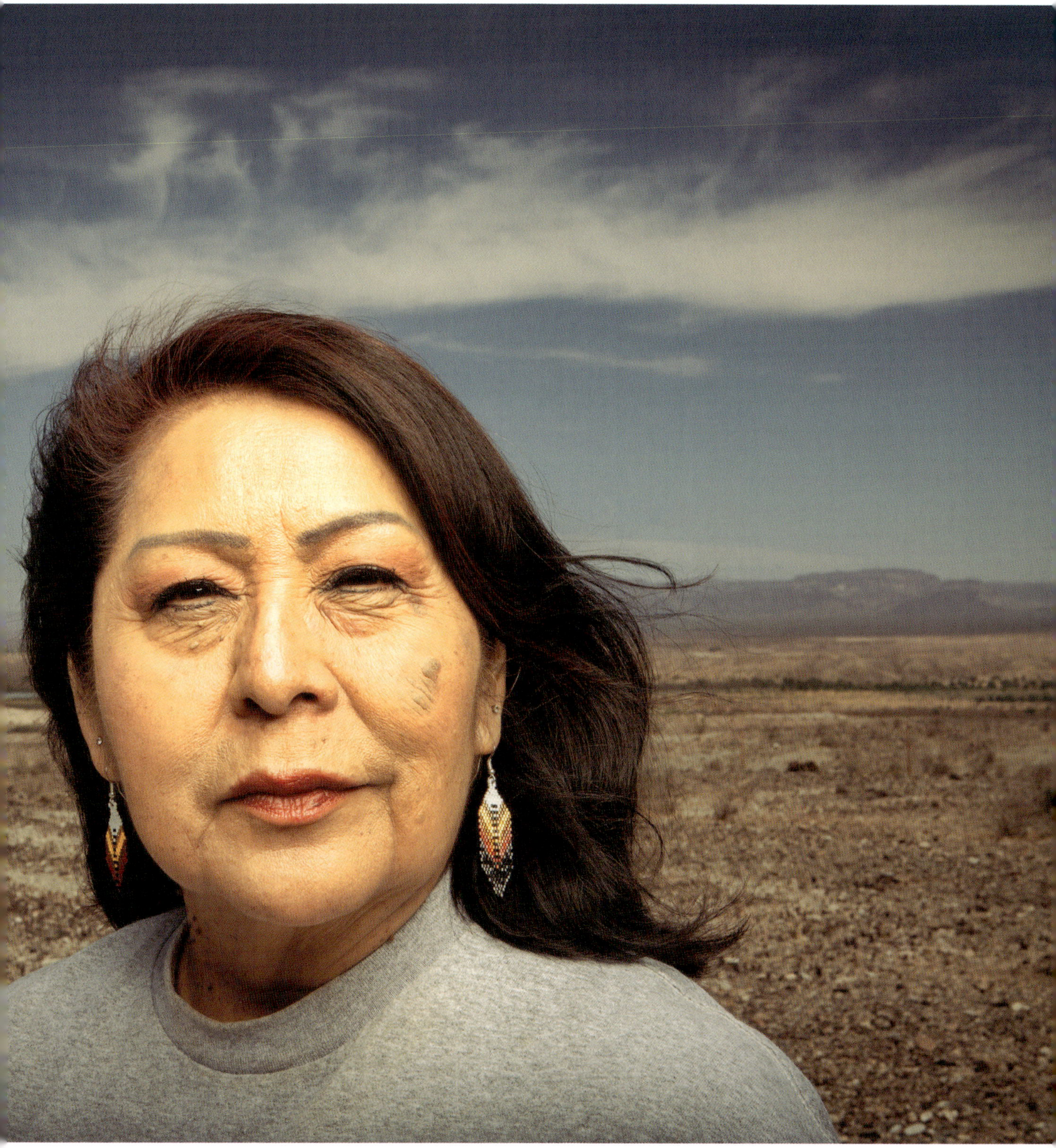

Journey to Minnesota

We returned to the Upper Midwest for programming in Minnesota. We spent time at our farm and with family.

The transition from the arid red rock of the Southwest to the lush green of the Midwest was jarring. In two days, we traveled from a desperate drought to a land of liquid abundance. It's not that people in the Midwest are wasteful, but they don't have to conserve water resources in the same urgent way that people do in the Colorado River watershed. It is a different relationship with water.

Every year, we get a call from Karen's dad, Wally, to remind us that it's the anniversary of the day he was drafted into the U.S. Army. It's an important day for him and so it's an important day for us. Memorial Day is just as significant. And so we made plans to pass through Lake Mills, Wisconsin, on Memorial Day to watch Wally play bugle at the ceremonies.

We were ducking in and out of our old life while we were being welcomed into a new one. We had a sense that we belonged everywhere, and yet we belonged nowhere at all. We weren't ready to be done with this journey, but there was a tug every time we said goodbye. We could start to imagine the day it would be time to stay home.

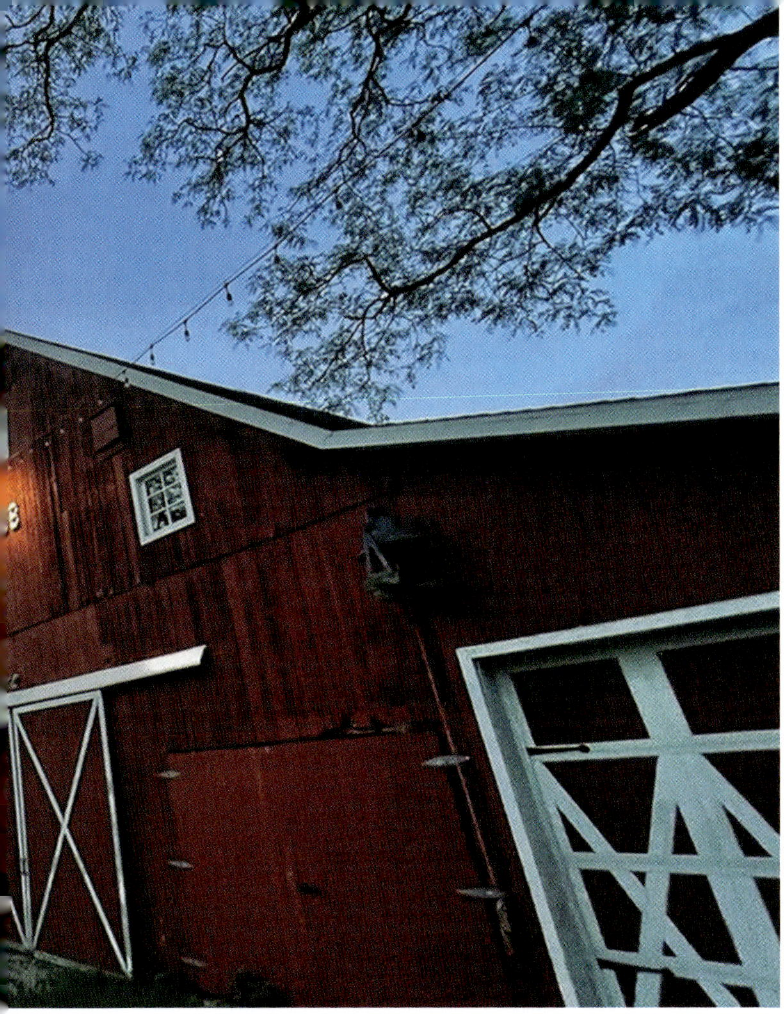

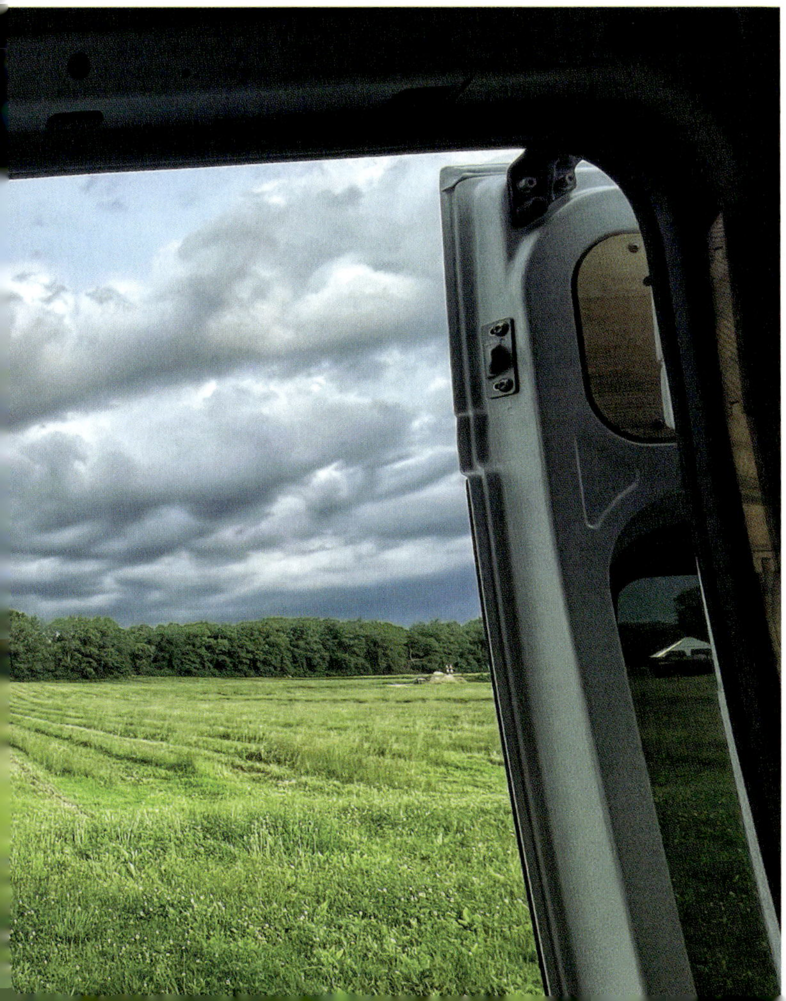

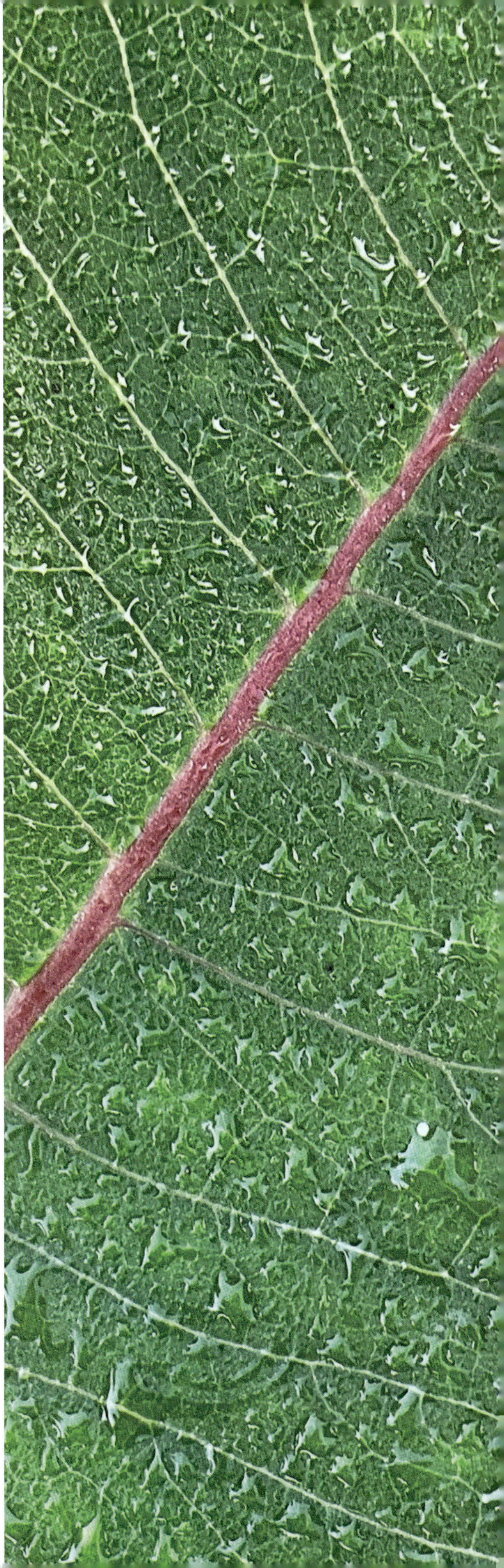

Journey to Nashville and Ashville

We made a slow drive toward the east coast for a summer of stories around faith and justice. We stopped to hear some music in Nashville. Our son, Jordan, designs and programs lighting for music tours. He was traveling with a hip-hop artist and when we saw that Nashville was on his tour, we made it part of ours as well. We were the old folks at the young folks' show and it was fun to see him do his thing.

We visited Franklin, North Carolina, to explore the mountains. Our friends Jen and Greg, who hiked the nearly 2,200-mile Appalachian Trail in 2017, had opened a hostel in Franklin, and invited us to stay while they were out of town.

We returned to Durham, North Carolina, and made our way eventually toward Washington, D.C.

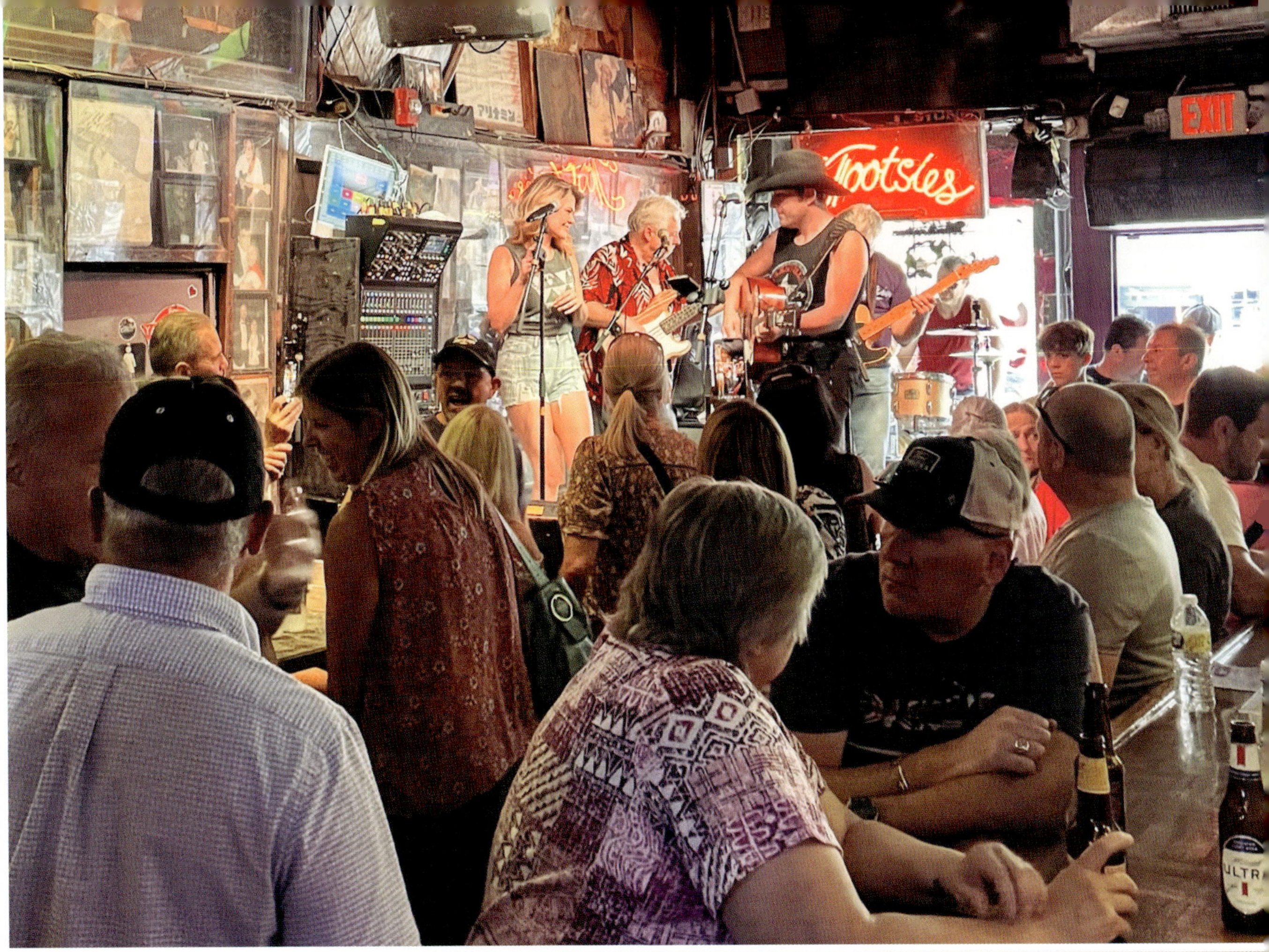
Tootsies
EXIT

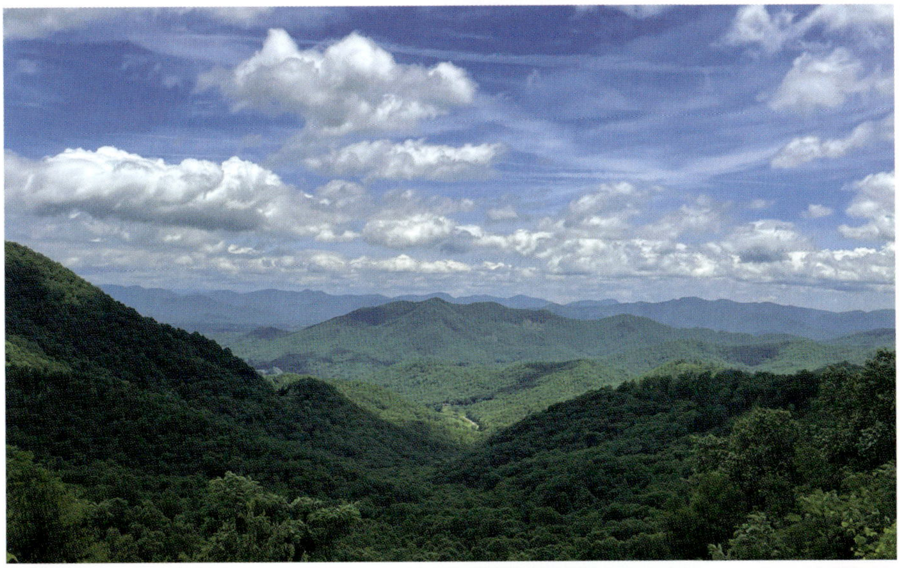

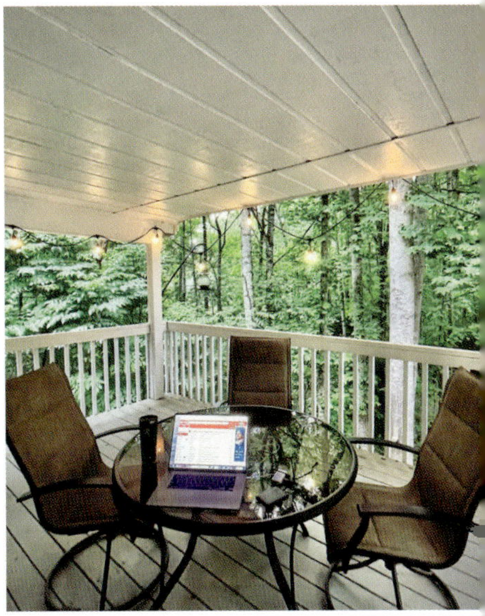

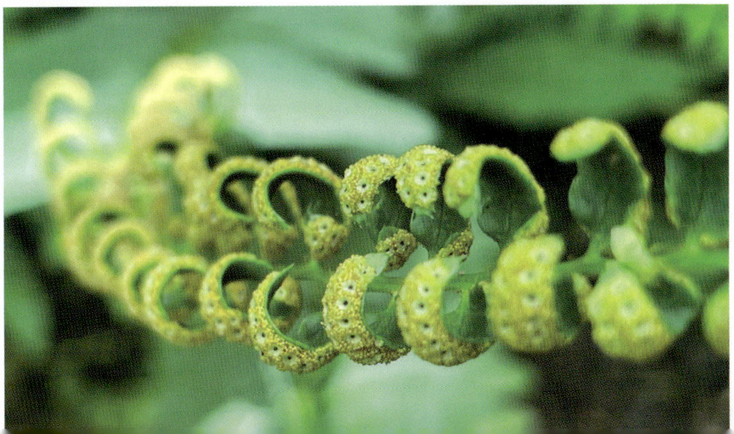

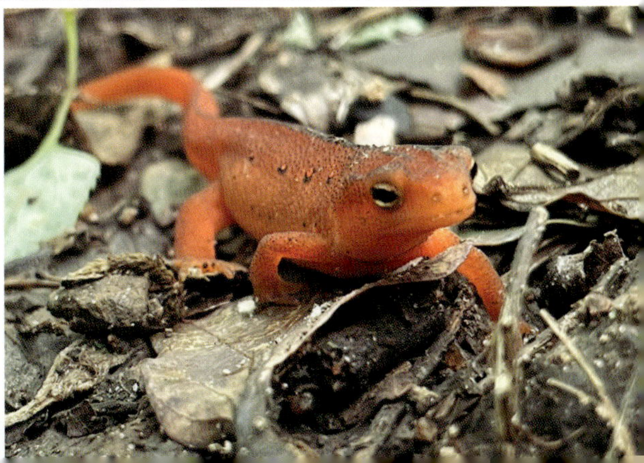

Journey to DC

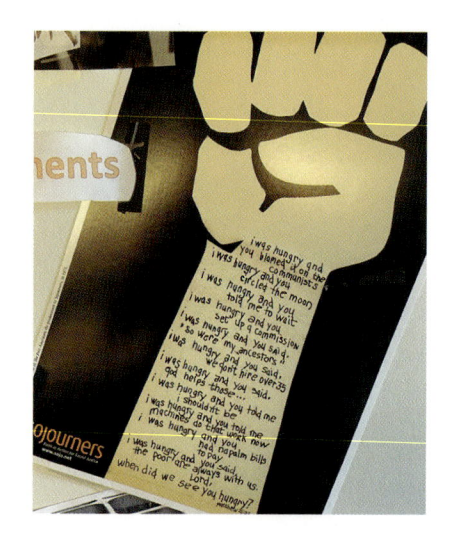

Life in the countryside with Vinny was simple enough, but we had a 10-day stretch in Washington, D.C., and that presented a new kind of challenge. Campgrounds were located too far out of the city and the prospect of a daily commute in D.C. traffic was unpleasant. A hotel would make the stay unaffordable.

I had worked with an organization called Sojourners in the past and they offered to help connect me with people to interview for this series on faith and justice. As we talked, they also said that most of their staff was still working remotely and the office—which was in the Capitol Hill neighborhood and just a few blocks from the Supreme Court—was mostly empty. There was a parking lot in the courtyard behind the office and they thought we could probably park Vinny in the lot and live back there. Sojourners was set up for bicycle commuters and so there were showers at the office. They gave us a key and the Wi-Fi password and let us use their place as our home base.

We were learning quickly that it was easier to stay warm in Vinny during the cold weather and a little more challenging to stay cool in the humid 95 degree heat of Washington, D.C., in June.

In the background of this work, our broken trailer saga continued to unfold. The manufacturer repaired it. We found a buyer who understood its history. He was a mechanic who knew the whole story. He inspected it and made an offer. Karen flew out to California to close the deal, pass off the title, and close the chapter on seven months of stress and uncertainty.

248

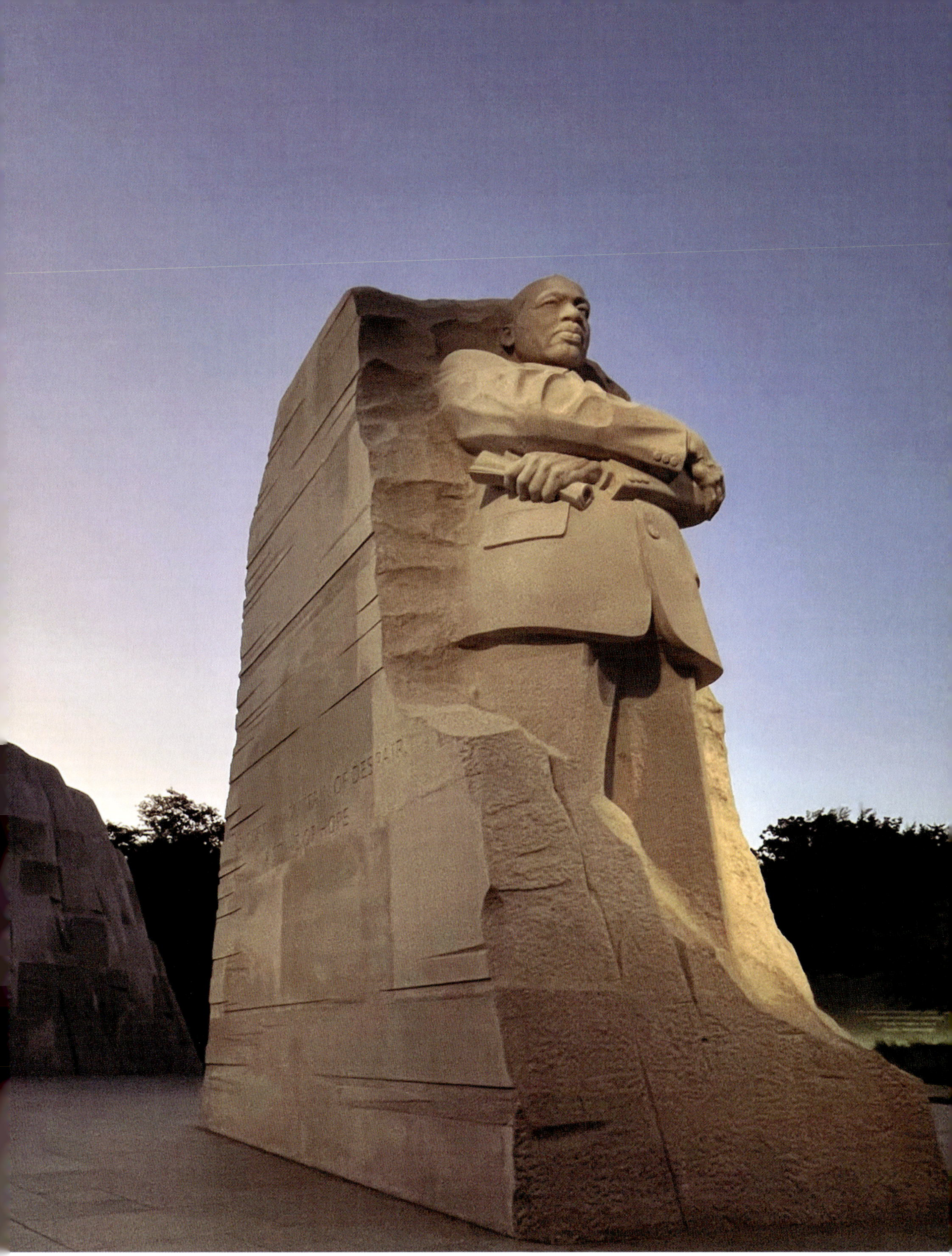

Adam Russell Taylor is president of Sojourners, a faith-based organization exploring the Christian call for social justice. I interviewed Adam at Sojourner's office in Washington, D.C., on the eve of the Poor People's Campaign Moral March on Washington, where I joined Adam and tens of thousands of others in a call for moral revival in America. Adam's mother is Black and his father is white. The couple got married in 1968, a year after interracial marriage was legalized around the country in the Supreme Court case of Loving vs. the State of Virginia.

The strength of our country is not in some kind of conforming uniformity or having to assimilate into one version of America. The strength of our country is in its diversity, and out of that diversity, we become one. We don't have to relinquish the beauty of what makes us different.

I still see this tug of war going on in the soul of our nation between a multiracial, inclusive, just democracy, which I think is in line with Dr. Martin Luther King's vision of a Beloved Community, and this very pernicious, racialized, zero sum America, where white Americans are the true Americans. We're still embroiled in this fear-based struggle.

While, on the one hand, there's been some reckoning and coming to terms with some of that, there's also been a huge backlash. So, in one sense, I'm pretty worried about this counter movement against the Beloved Community. But I also deeply believe that there are enough people of faith, in particular, who believe in that vision rooted both in our best civic values, as well as in our best religious values.

Our lives are shaped by the stories we tell ourselves, the stories we tell of our history, the stories we tell about who we are. And there's been this ongoing struggle of expanding the "we" of America to expand the promises of liberty and justice to all Americans.

You can't overcome or counteract a negative, pernicious narrative without having a more hopeful, inspiring, and unifying narrative. And that's why I still believe that this narrative of the Beloved Community really could be that narrative.We have this opportunity to not only reckon with that past, but to co-create an America that truly lives into its full promise. That's the work that's in front of us. That is the America that I believe most of us want to be part of.

> "One of the things that has been a real weakness is this very superficial understanding that reconciliation is just about forgiveness. That is a part of it, but at its core, reconciliation is about repair."
> —**Adam Russell Taylor**

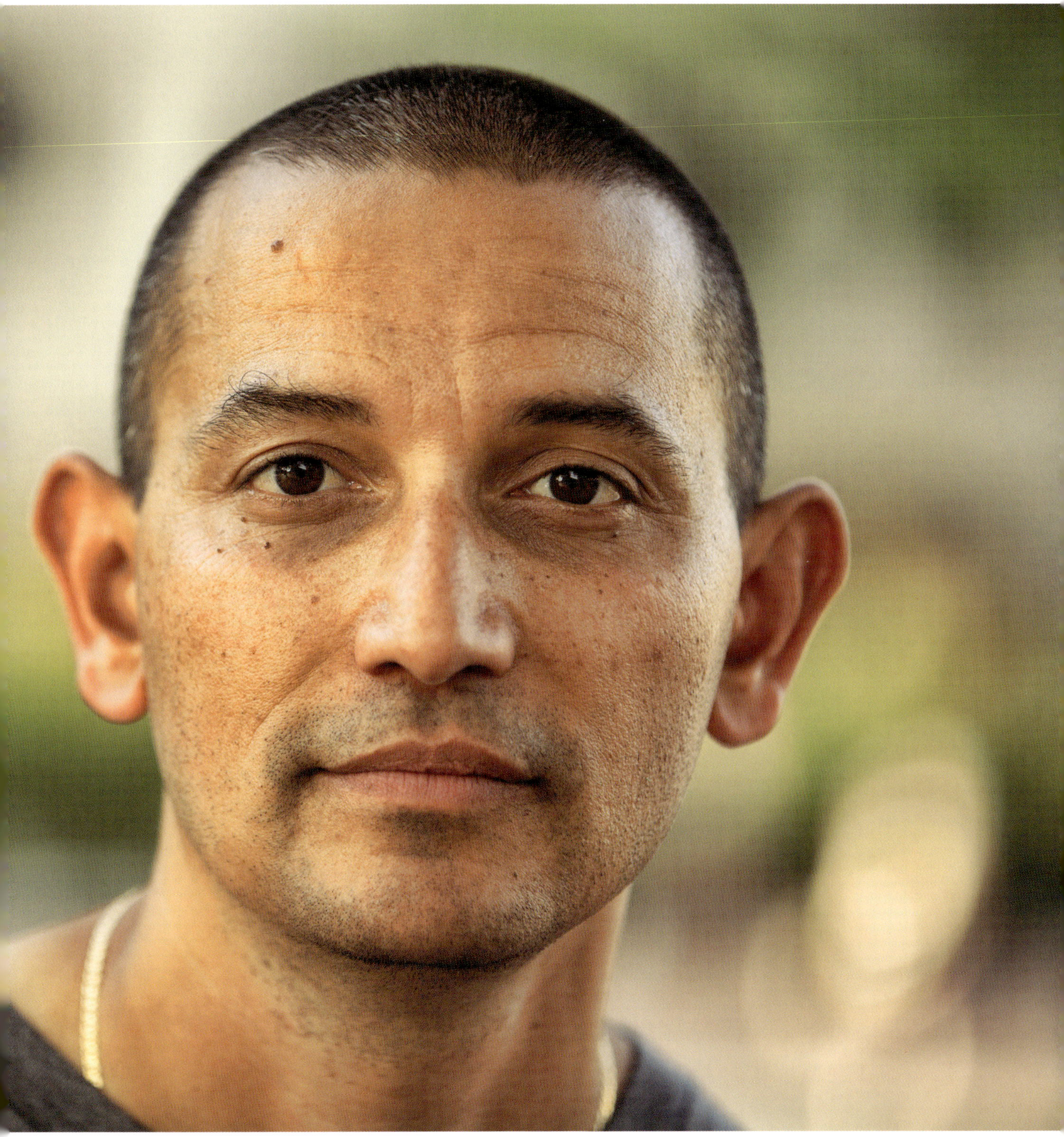

The Poor People's Campaign

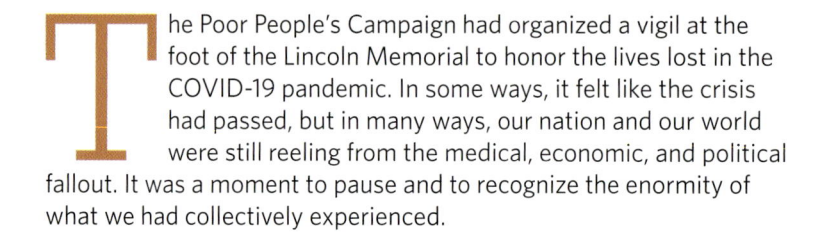

The Poor People's Campaign had organized a vigil at the foot of the Lincoln Memorial to honor the lives lost in the COVID-19 pandemic. In some ways, it felt like the crisis had passed, but in many ways, our nation and our world were still reeling from the medical, economic, and political fallout. It was a moment to pause and to recognize the enormity of what we had collectively experienced.

MEMORIAL WALL

sullivan
Anne Roberts
nda Goen
jørn Türlison
McAllister
Mama DeSi
Paul Bailey
Taylor Kouts
Jim Steinhaus
Sherwood Baker
Luisa Colon
Lucy KraKauskA
Luis Ramos

The Moral March on Washington

> "You can't have the levels of injustice that exist now and think the nation is built on a solid foundation. The issue is not a scarcity of money. It's not a scarcity of ideas. The only issue is a scarcity of moral consciousness. . . ."
>
> —Rev. William Barber

It takes a long time, this pursuit of justice. Sometimes it feels like things move slowly. Sometimes it feels like nothing changes at all.

When I interviewed Rev. DeMett Jenkins in Charleston early in this journey, she spoke about her grandfather, Esau Jenkins, and the civil rights work he did back in the day. DeMett said, "We're dealing with the exact same type of stuff that my grandfather had to deal with. Not a different fight, the same exact one."

Change is slow, but it does happen. We have a long history to prove it. Slavery was abolished. Child labor ended. Women's suffrage became the law of the land. Washington, D.C., is filled with reminders of those changes, as well as the work that remains.

At the National Archives, I stood in line to view the original Emancipation Proclamation, on display for Juneteenth celebrations. But on my walk to the museum, I passed the Supreme Court, where people on both sides of the debate for reproductive choice gathered outside the security fences to await the ruling that would challenge *Roe v. Wade*.

On Saturday I marched with the Poor People's Campaign down Pennsylvania Avenue, along with tens of thousands of others, many of them from faith communities across the country. The movement is an extension of—or a continuation of, perhaps even a revival of—Dr. King's Poor People's Campaign in 1968, which called attention to the issues of poverty.

On some level, it seems absurd that, as a society, we are still talking about the same issues that have gone unresolved for the past 50 years. On the other hand, the work isn't done until the work is done. And those with their eye on the prize need to stick with the movement and see it through. I heard it from so many different directions here in D.C.

At the U.S. Institute of Peace, Lucy Kurtzer-Ellenbogen, the director of the Israeli-Palestinian Conflict Program, gave a lecture and shared a recent poll that indicated trust between Palestinian and Israeli youth was at an all time low. It's discouraging, of course, but it is also—as my friend Ray would call it—an opportunity.

Change doesn't start and end with legislation or with agreements. A signed piece of paper makes a good headline, but it's just a marker. There are years of effort leading up to an agreement to do the community work and shift the societal narrative that will lay the foundation for that agreement. There is education, advocacy, and community organizing that prepares the soil and will eventually offer the political cover for politicians to sign that agreement.

But even then, an agreement is just a seed, and it's up to civil society to make certain it takes root. The people need to be on board. They need to believe it. There needs to be a common vision and a shared commitment to make it work.

So even if peace in the Israeli-Palestinian conflict seems far away at the moment, there is important groundwork going on to build capacity and develop leaders who can usher peace forward when the time is right.

At Sojourners, political director Lauren W. Reliford talked about the small windows of opportunity she is always watching for. It's hard to get things done in D.C., especially these days. But there are rare moments when the stars align, moments when political will, societal attitudes, leadership momentum, and the news cycle all come together and present the opportunity for change.

During the in-between times, you need to do the work of preparing for the opportunities. You have to build capacity. You have to develop relationships. You need to strategize and build momentum and pay attention, so that when the time is right, you can act.

Michael Skoler of Weave: The Social Fabric Project (a part of the Aspen Institute) spoke about letting go of outcomes. It's important to keep your goals and work toward your objectives. But as a simple act of self-preservation, sometimes you need to let go of the outcomes. If you measure your worth and your effectiveness and your success by the headlines you see in the newspaper, you might get discouraged. You might burn out. You might give up.

We move toward justice, because it's the right thing to do. You might never see the results of your efforts in your lifetime. But that doesn't mean it's time to stop trying.

In *Portraits of Peace: Searching for Hope in a Divided America*, I asked Hassan Ikhzaan Saleem about the justice work he does. "I'm not Mahatma Gandhi. I'm not Martin Luther King Jr. or Nelson Mandela," he said. "My parents said to me, 'You might never change the world, and you might never see the change you want to see, but at least you tried. At least you can be accountable.' So that's why I try, and that's the goal. One day, there will be peace. Maybe I'll not live to see it, and maybe my kids won't live to see it, but we tried. That's why we do it again and again."

I'm not a patient person, but I'm recognizing a pattern. Even in the darkest days, it's not hopeless. It's all a part of the process and it is always possible to plant seeds.

As I looked out over the crowds at Saturday's march, I saw seeds. The Poor People's Campaign is reviving a movement. Expanding a movement. Building a movement. They are planting seeds of energized leaders from across the country. Lifting people up and encouraging them to have a voice.

Rev. William Barber is one of the co-chairs of the Poor People's Campaign, and he said this about the work:

"You can't have the levels of injustice that exist now and think the nation is built on a solid foundation. The issue is not a scarcity of money. It's not a scarcity of ideas. The only issue is a scarcity of moral consciousness. And the only way that changes is for us to realize we have work to do. We will do it. We have to do it. Because we refuse to give up on the possibility of America."

"If you're going to take your faith seriously, then you have to go where people are most vulnerable, and those situations are sometimes chaotic. There's no guarantee of safety and that's why we have our faith."
—**Rose Berger**

Rose Berger is senior editor at *Sojourners* magazine, a monthly publication focused on issues of faith and justice. She is a poet and a Catholic peace activist. She's traveled to conflict zones around the world to be in fellowship with faith communities who are working toward peace. I interviewed Rose just days after she returned from an interfaith delegation to Kyiv, Ukraine, where she supported and encouraged the Ukrainian people and prayed for peace with them.

I believe that by responding in one place, you're responding in many places. [I've] been in so many different situations where distance and isolation become weaponized by people who have an interest in gaining power. I think the only way we can mitigate against that is through neighborliness.

Our goal [in traveling to Ukraine] was twofold. It was to show that a religious international interfaith delegation could indeed go to Kyiv, and then to hold public interfaith prayer services for peace.

As I spoke with my wife about whether I would go on this, we kept going back and forth, because it was very inconvenient timing for us, but that seemed a small sacrifice compared to the inconvenient timing of war for the Ukrainians. I realized that they needed people with good experience moving in conflict zones. I had a set of skills, a set of relationships, and a basic working knowledge that would be useful for this first delegation to get people in and out safely.

I kept asking myself, "Is there someone better, more appropriate than me to go?" And there wasn't, so it was time for me to step up and move forward with it. And I was very glad and humbled to be able to do it.

My experience has shown me that things look scarier the farther away they are. There are people who never would come to my neighborhood in Washington, D.C., because they were sure they would be killed instantly. The closer you get to a place and know what the dynamics of the conflict are, then you can make prudent decisions about safety. I don't think you can make prudent decisions about safety from 3,000 miles away.

There are things that you just cannot understand. You cannot give encouragement to people at the level that they need without being there in person. For me, it was important to hold Ukrainians—literally hold them—while they cried. And that's not something you can do over Zoom.

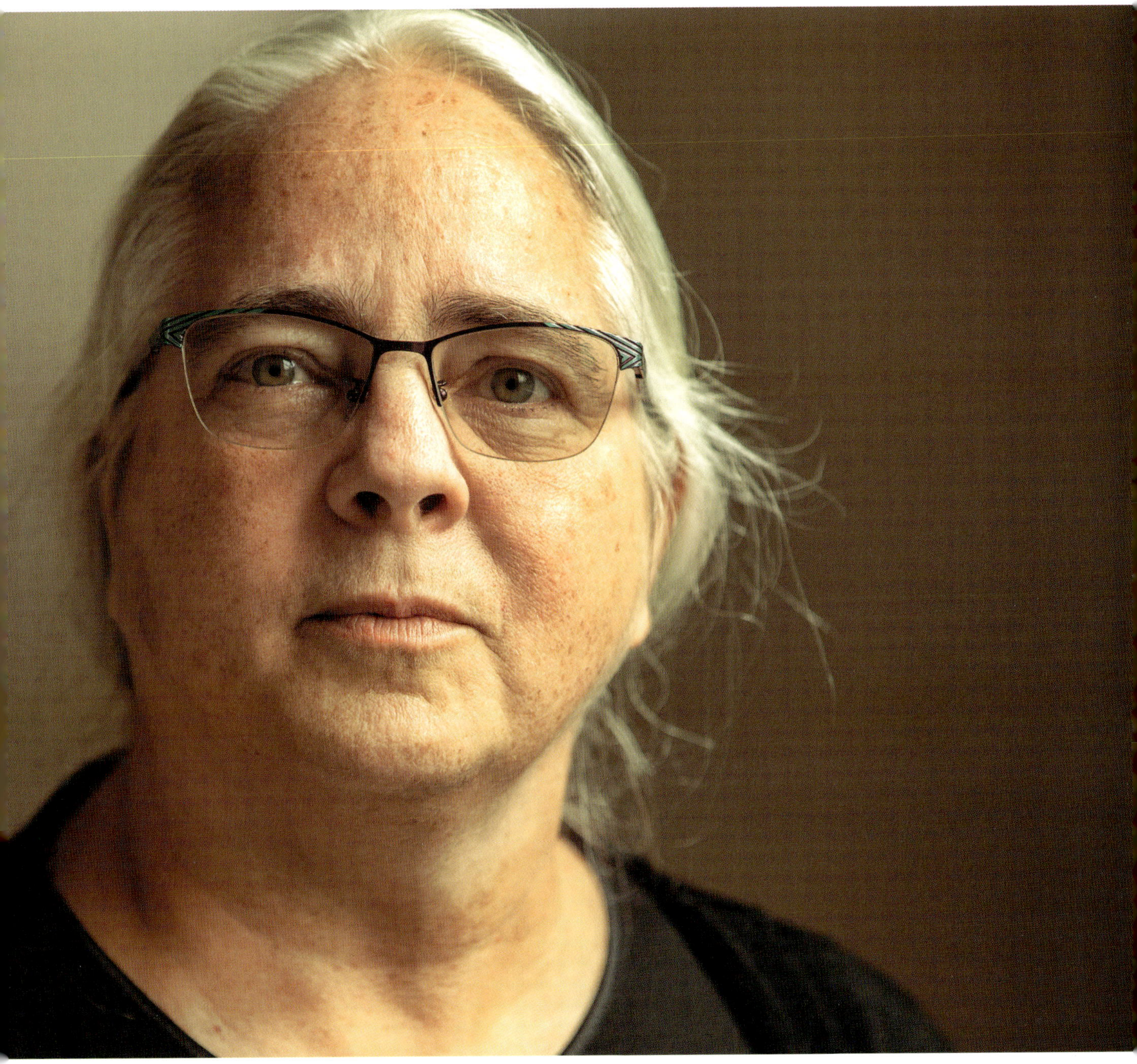

A spiritual mentor, Sister Jenna is founder and director of the Brahma Kumaris Meditation Museum and host of America Meditating Radio. She practices Raja Yoga, which invites participants to "turn inward and to look at the soul and investigate the way the soul feels and what it's going through" in order to find the vision that calls to you. She believes this practice can develop our ability to see the divine in one another.

I don't want to waste my thoughts on anything that isn't supporting the establishment of a better world. I don't want my thoughts to go into any area of my past that I have no control over. I don't want those thoughts to hold me hostage and take me away from the real purpose of my birth at this time, which is to cocreate a better world in companionship with God and God's children.

I've grown into letting go and allowing my practice to educate me more and more each day. I have learned that it is essential for me to begin to remember the nature of my soul's existence, which is very detached and yet very loving at the same time. And that's an art within itself. It will be what it is meant to be. I think that if my practice of being loving and detached will continue to help me to navigate this particular space and time, I'll be fine. We'll all be fine if we did that, actually.

> "Many of us have had this experience of divine light, but we didn't choose to hold onto it. We allow it to just come and go."
> —Sister Jenna

There are certain energies—I call it ALGAE. It's an acronym that I know is our shadow, our blockage, our limited belief systems: A for anger, L for lust, G for greed, A for attachment, and E for ego.

This is the reason why there's so much injustice and division in the world. This is why there's so much violence in the world, so much hatred, so much fear.

In the teachings of the Brahma Kumaris and meditation, it's offered that individuals have to look inside of themselves and begin to recognize their own limits and their own blockages. By doing that, you get to understand what a fellow brother must be going through. And with that understanding comes compassion, patience, understanding, perseverance, determination, and service. How can I be of service and help my brother? Not, how can I be an instrument to take my brother down and destroy him? It won't let you think that way.

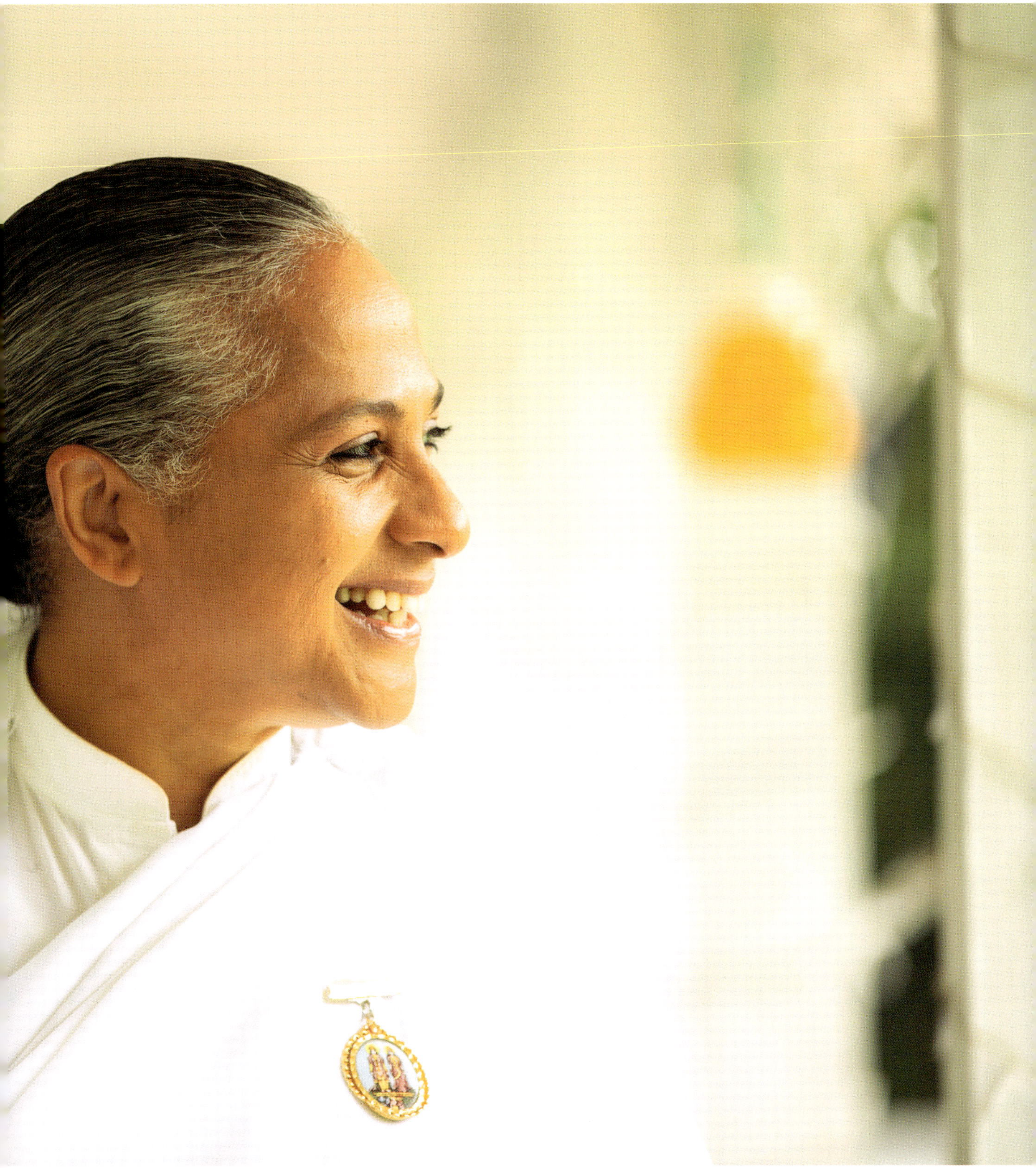

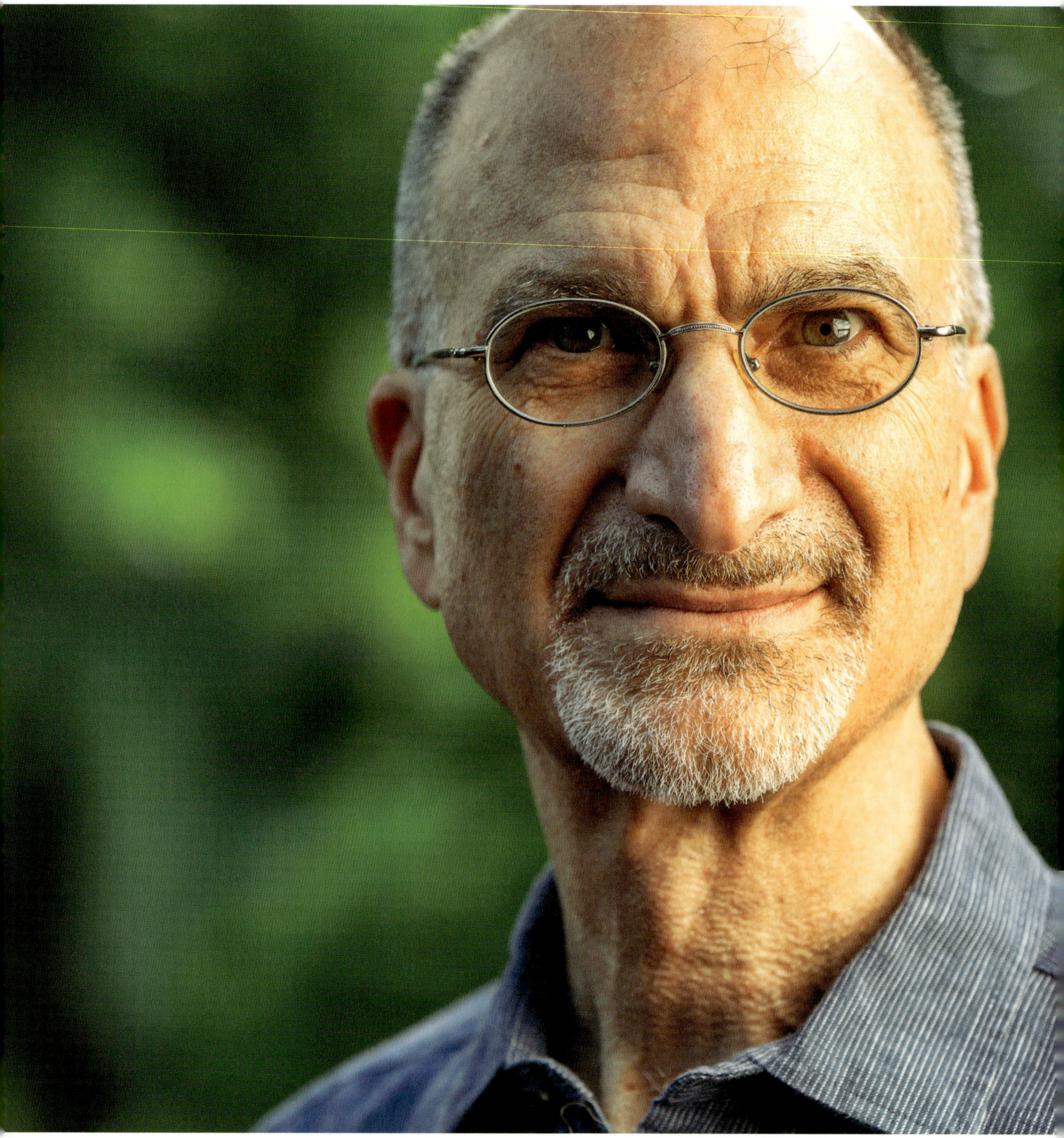

Michael Skoler describes himself as a "reformed NPR correspondent." He spent a decade working as a journalist in Nairobi, Kenya, covering the 1994 genocide in Rwanda and its aftermath. He is also a husband, a father, and a backpacker. He practices meditation. Michael is currently communications director for Weave the Social Fabric Project, an initiative of the Aspen Institute designed to address the broken social trust in America.

I covered the genocide in Rwanda. What was fascinating to me is that most journalists were telling a story that the Hutus and the Tutsis in Rwanda were age-old enemies and they could never get along. And everything I found in Rwanda told me that wasn't the case. Hutus and Tutsis had lived together as neighbors, as friends. They had intermarried so much that you could no longer look at someone and say, "Oh, they're Hutu or Tutsi."

But journalists were telling this simple conflict story. The true story was that the colonial powers had chosen one ethnic group to have power when they left. The true story was that Rwanda was one of the most populated countries on the African continent. They had an equitable way of providing inheritance to both the girls and boys in their society. As a result, farm plots were getting smaller and smaller in a mainly sustainable farming economy. And the government used that economic pressure and the threat of a Tutsi army, which the government was refusing to negotiate with, to scare their own people.

> "I'm going to care. If the world gets better, wonderful. If it doesn't get better, I'm still going to care."
> —Michael Skoler

[They told] the Hutu population, "Oh, the Tutsis are gonna kill you if you don't kill them first. And, by the way, if you do kill them, you can get that land for yourself." They distributed guns. It was an orchestrated genocide by a government that wanted to divide its people. But this wasn't Hutus and Tutsis wanting to kill each other. This was a government inciting people to do it.

I think our natural state is to care about the people we're with, and it's our structures that somehow give us another cultural message that we're in competition, that we've got scarcity and not abundance. And when that happens, it can spin out of control pretty quickly as I saw in Rwanda. I tell that story, because in many ways that realization led me to want to tell a different story of caring, of sharing more than we differ. Because if we tell stories of division, we can create division that isn't there. That's what happened in Rwanda.

> "I think we can either approach the world with fear, or we can go into the world with a sense of wonder and humility and learning, which I think helps us become a fuller human being."
> —Andrew Cheung

Andrew Cheung is the senior pastor of Washington Community Fellowship, a Protestant community located less than a dozen blocks from our nation's Capitol that strives to practice love as a lifestyle.

I'm always this person who wants to cross boundaries, being an ethnic Chinese born in the states to immigrants from Hong Kong, but all my living memory has been in Canada, until I moved to Washington, D.C., to pastor this church.

So I've always tried to understand differences and notice different ways of looking at the world and ask, "How do we find bridges?" My Chinese name, in Cantonese, means "a household or a family of peace." So this sense of peace and reconciling and bridging has always been a part of who I am.

God loves everyone. And so, if we're willing to pay attention and slow down, step away from the instinct to judge or resort to transactional relationships, then maybe we'll recognize God and become a little bit more like God in the process of that interaction.

For me, the Christian faith offers the internal strength to do that without becoming proud or self-righteous. And because of God's love for me and for the world, I get to be a part of this movement of the world toward justice and peace and flourishing and beauty and love, that the world hasn't seen enough of yet. That foundation is what I think gives me the ability to stretch out into things that I don't really know much about and I'm willing to take a risk.

[My simple message is] God loves you and God's got you and you can trust God.

Maybe more from a philosophical [view], there's more to the world than we see and know, and when things are going on, there's always something else going on. Take the time to notice those things.

The thing that's in front of us, often isn't the thing that's most important. Be willing to ask some of those questions. Do a bit of unearthing and find some wise people along the way. We're not meant to do life alone. We need others to remind us of who we are and to remind us of the good things in our lives—and, sometimes, to point out the things that we can do a little bit better.

> "I want to be a lifeboat, a safety blanket, for someone else. In a world [that] is always going to make you feel like you're not enough, or you're too much, or you're invisible, I see you."
> —Lauren Reliford

Lauren Reliford is political director for Sojourners, an organization based in Washington, D.C., that advocates for issues at the intersection of faith and justice. Her work is centered on applying social theory, spirituality, research, and practice to the political policy that guides our nation.

Lauren says she is inclined to care deeply, which can take a personal toll, but that her faith compels her to serve others.

I'll tell you it's a struggle. Christianity is peace and nonviolence, but as a Black American and a descendant of enslaved people, I don't have the luxury of being peaceful. I have always had to fight in one way or another. And if I give up, whatever God has assigned me to do is not going to get done.

A lot of this is just what it means to be a Black woman. We do not get to rest. And so I think some of this is like the Black woman trauma response—which is clearly not a healthy way of living—but it's also a culture and an identity that I've been born into. It's a core part of me.

White supremacy and the idolatry of whiteness, this need to be white-adjacent and white proximity, for me, has always created a space in which you either fight or you put down your weapons and you die by white supremacy. And I know I am here because my ancestors certainly fought.

If my ancestors did it, I can do it. You either die or you survive, but I am focused on creating a third option of thriving. I want that freedom for myself and others.

Rest is radical and I do try to get my rest. I see a therapist. I'm learning what it means to take care of myself. It matters so much and that always drives me. When I get weary, I gotta keep going.

I don't do this alone. My view of the world is more communal than individualistic. I selfishly get life from being in the presence of other people. That is how I get energized. Being with my family every weekend and being in their presence and soaking in their joy and feeling like I'm connected to something bigger than self. That is what drives me. I have a very communal core; we are part of the vine and I don't do it alone.

06.24.2022: The Dobbs ruling

The entire country had been waiting for the ruling in the *Dobbs v. Jackson Women's Health Organization* case. An unprecedented leak had tipped the Supreme Court's hand and set expectations for the result. Everyone anticipated that the decision would be released soon, but we didn't know on what day or at what time.

I had scheduled the portrait of Lauren Reliford outside the Capitol for the morning of June 24. I had scouted it the afternoon before and found the perfect spot. Walking to the location in the morning, I passed the Supreme Court. There had been protesters and onlookers gathered there all week, but today the crowd was bigger. The mood felt more tense.

When I arrived at the location I had chosen on the Capitol grounds for the portrait, it was blocked off by barricades. I found a new site and texted Lauren about the change. She arrived feeling the weight of the day. We made the portrait and on my walk back to Sojourners, I noticed that the crowd in front of the Supreme Court continued to grow. Media had arrived in large numbers. So I stayed.

People were jockeying for position. Moving their signs in front of other signs to upstage them for the cameras and showcase their position. Voices got louder. A row of bicycle cops rode into the midst of the crowd and separated—more or less—the two factions. A column of motorcycle cops followed suit, dismounted, and stood in the midst.

Decisions were expected to be released about every ten minutes, starting at 10:00 a.m., and as the time approached, the crowd grew, the anticipation spread, and the tension built.

At 10:00 a.m. I watched the police commander give a signal and the motorcycle cops and the bicycle cops mounted up and rode out of the crowd. I was astounded. I turned to another officer on the

perimeter and asked, "Why would they leave now?" and he shrugged. Maybe it was easier to control a crowd from the outside? Maybe their presence would precipitate more tension?

Moments later, at 10:10 a.m., the decision came. The *Dobbs* ruling overturned the precedent of *Roe V. Wade* established nearly 50 years earlier that granted women a constitutional right to abortion access. Half the crowd cheered. Half the crowd wailed. Politicians appeared for culture war sound bytes and photo ops. A few people moved through the crowd with the intention to agitate and antagonize. They engaged in shouting debates as others called out, "Don't give them the attention they want!"

Media pushed into the crowd and the most outrageous personalities attracted the most attention. I saw them on the news. On the internet. A young woman held a fetus figurine above her head. An older woman put a strip of duct tape over her mouth that said "2nd class citizen." I heard a commotion over my shoulder and turned to find myself a few feet away from U.S. Representative Marjorie Taylor Greene, who had shown up for the cameras. All of the press photographed the spectacle. All of the press became the spectacle, and I was a part of it.

I had spent hours there and it was time to leave. There were other things I needed to do that day. It was hard to exit the bubble. It was difficult to extract myself from the whirlpool of emotion and sense of importance at that historic moment. The energy around the Supreme Court was all-consuming, and then just a few blocks away, there was no visible indication at all of what had just occurred.

MY BODY MY CHOICE
ABORTION IS MURDER
LEGAL ABORTION ON DEMAND & WITHOUT APOLOGY
RiseUp4AbortionRights.org
FOR THE FIVE

END

2nd Class
Citizen

FORCEPS OFF MY BODY
1/3 OF MY GENERATION HAS BEEN KILLED BY ABORTION
1/3 OF MY GENERATION HAS BEEN KILLED BY ABORTION
My Body, My Choice.
why is that so hard for you?
KEEP YOUR RELIGION OUT MY VAGINA & PUSSY POSSE
VOTE
END ABORTION VIOLENCE
STUDENTSFORLIFE.ORG
POLICE
BRESNAHA

> "When we are brave enough to speak our truth, other people feel like they can claim theirs, too."
> —Katey Zeh

Katey Zeh is chief executive officer of the Religious Coalition for Reproductive Choice. She's an ordained Baptist minister and author of *A Complicated Choice, Making Space for Grief and Healing in the Pro-choice Movement*. Katey has served as an untrained abortion doula in order to accompany women through their abortion experience and offer emotional and spiritual support. I interviewed Katey just ten days before the *Dobbs* ruling from the U.S. Supreme Court struck down the precedent of *Roe v. Wade*.

I asked a local abortion clinic if I could come do a tour because I wanted to see for myself what that experience was like for people. I arrived at the clinic, and I was confronted by the protestors who were outside, trying to get me to stop, trying to give me literature. When I got out of my car, [they] were yelling at me and that was really unsettling.

And then I walked inside and was amazed at the staff there. Everybody was providing such compassionate care to the patients, some of whom were nervous or scared. I was so taken with it that I decided to volunteer there every week.

I started out in the recovery room, just helping the nurses, handing out ginger ale. And one day they were down a staff person. They needed an extra set of hands in the procedure room to help and I just said, "Yes."

It was really beautiful that these strangers allowed me in. Let me hold their hand. Just let me keep presence with them. And I thought, wow, this is really holy. I can't describe it other than feeling the presence of God in that room, which is a profound thing to say because so often abortion clinics are talked about as these godless places.

On my best days, I have compassion for people who have that certainty that abortion is wrong, because that was my approach to faith for so long. I really thought that I knew what the truth—capital T Truth—was. I thought I knew what was right and wrong and who God was and who God wasn't.

I'm grateful that I've had the opportunity to learn something different, to have an open heart, to realize maybe I don't know everything. All the patient people in my life who have had those conversations with me, challenged me, exposed me to different ideas. I'm grateful for the journey that I've been on. And I try on my best days, to remember that we are all on a journey and it's not really my place to tell someone else what their journey should be.

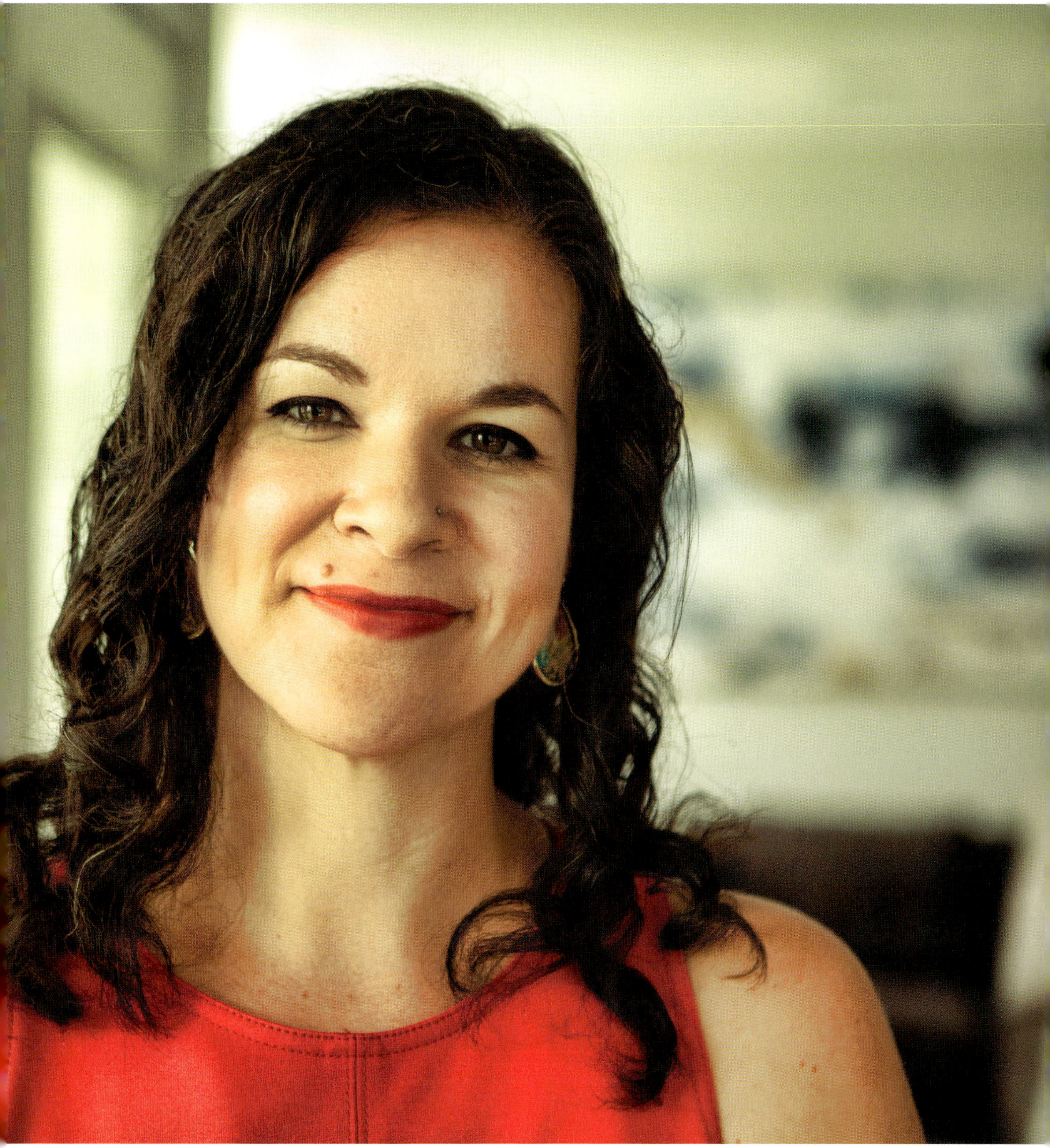

Trail magic

The weather was hot. The political tension was hot. We were hot. We found ourselves with a few weeks of down time before our next scheduled stop in North Carolina, and we called up our weather apps to see where things might be cooler. The coast of Maine looked to be in the 60s and was just a day's drive away.

"What's the one thing you'd most like to do on the way there?" I asked Karen. "Trail magic," she replied. It was an informal tradition along the 2,200-mile Appalachian Trail. People would set up beside the trail to pass out cold drinks and snacks to the through-hikers going by. A simple act of hospitality in what felt like an inhospitable world.

We did our research, made a couple calls, and found that a northbound bubble of hikers was expected to be going through New Jersey right about then. On the map, it looked like Mohican Outdoor Center could offer us a great home base, as well as the chance for some local intel about where the hikers were.

We bought a cooler, ice, drinks, hot dogs, and chips. We made a tagboard sign that rivaled any 8-year-old's lemonade stand. We parked beside the trail and set up shop.

"You need anything?" we'd call out as hikers approached. The answer was always yes. They dropped their packs. They sat on our folding chairs. They grabbed a drink. They ate a snack. They shared the stories of their journey and the reasons why they were on it.

I set up a light and invited people to have their photo taken and write a few words about what they had learned on the trail. To document that moment for them and for us. More than two dozen people walked by our spot on the trail that day. Every single person stopped to visit. It was community on a human scale. It was connection and purpose. It was a simple and tangible way to offer care. It felt good, and the simple act of giving that small gift to others was one of the best gifts Karen and I received.

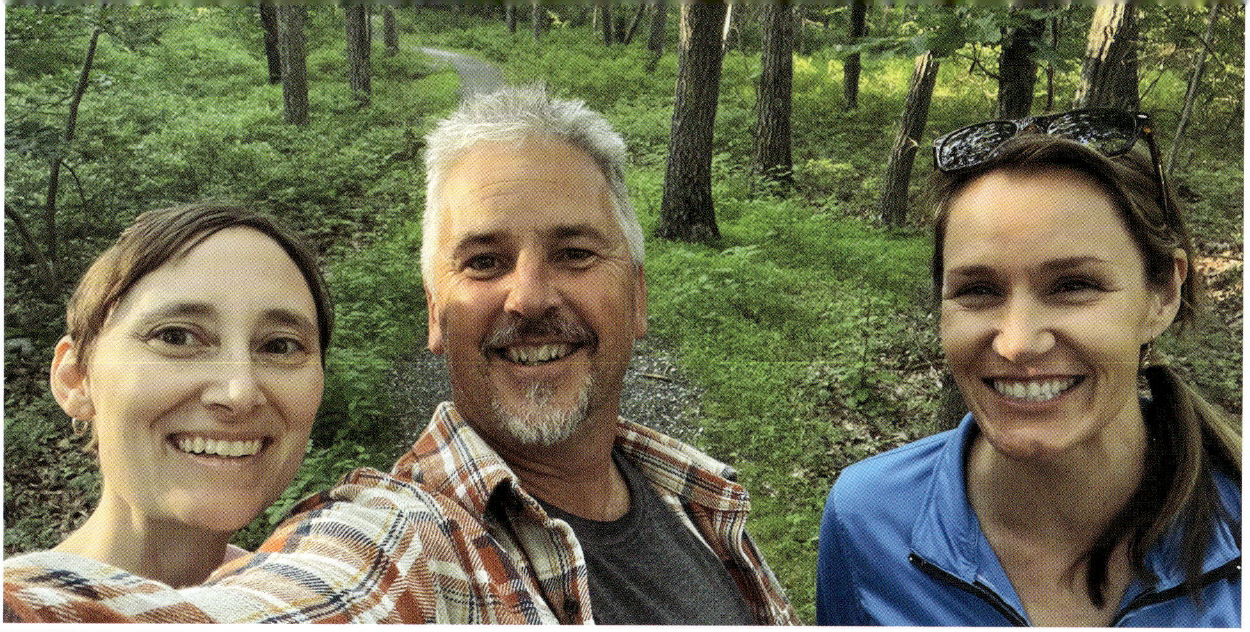

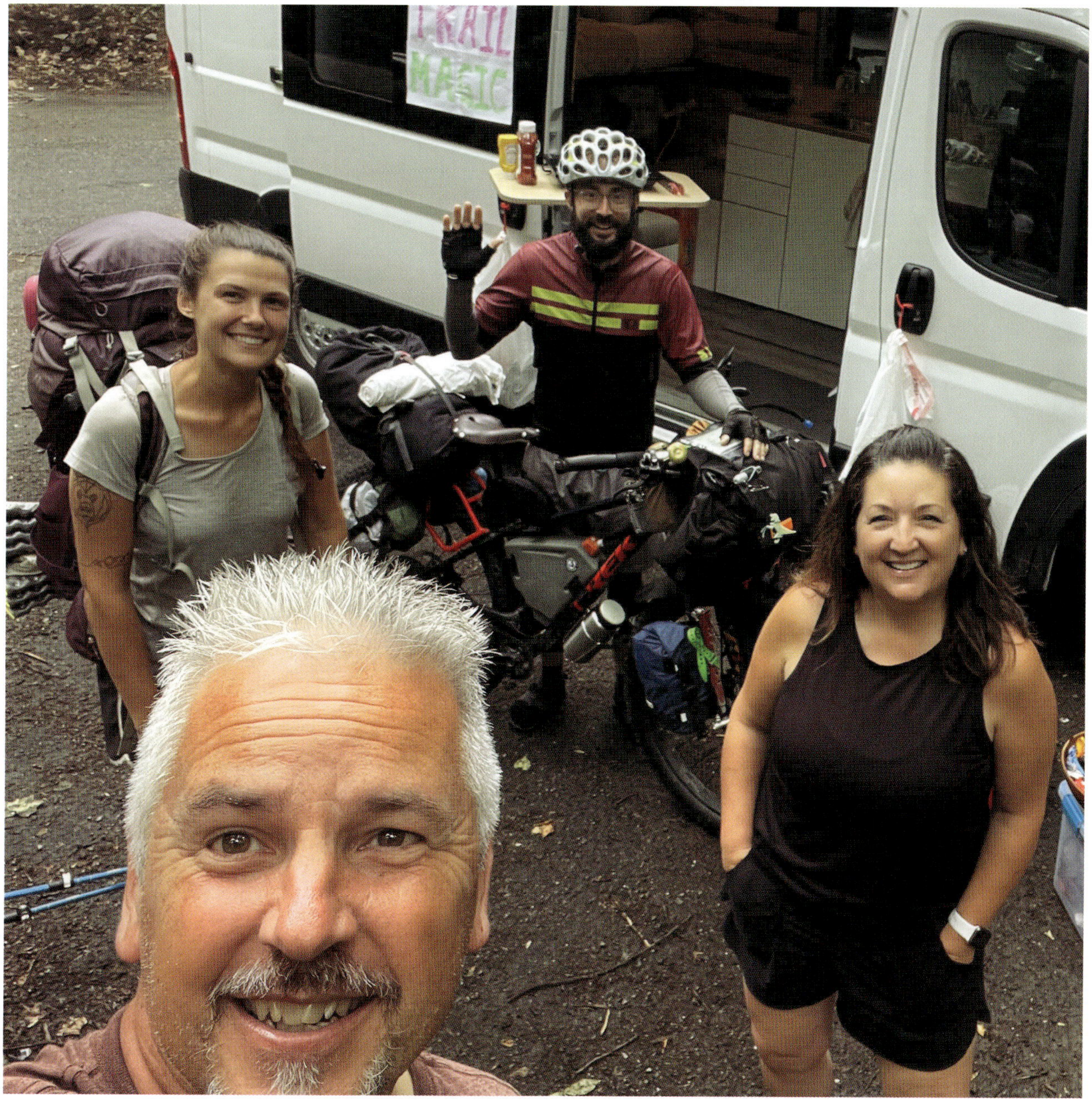
TRAIL
MAGIC

"What has the trail taught you?"

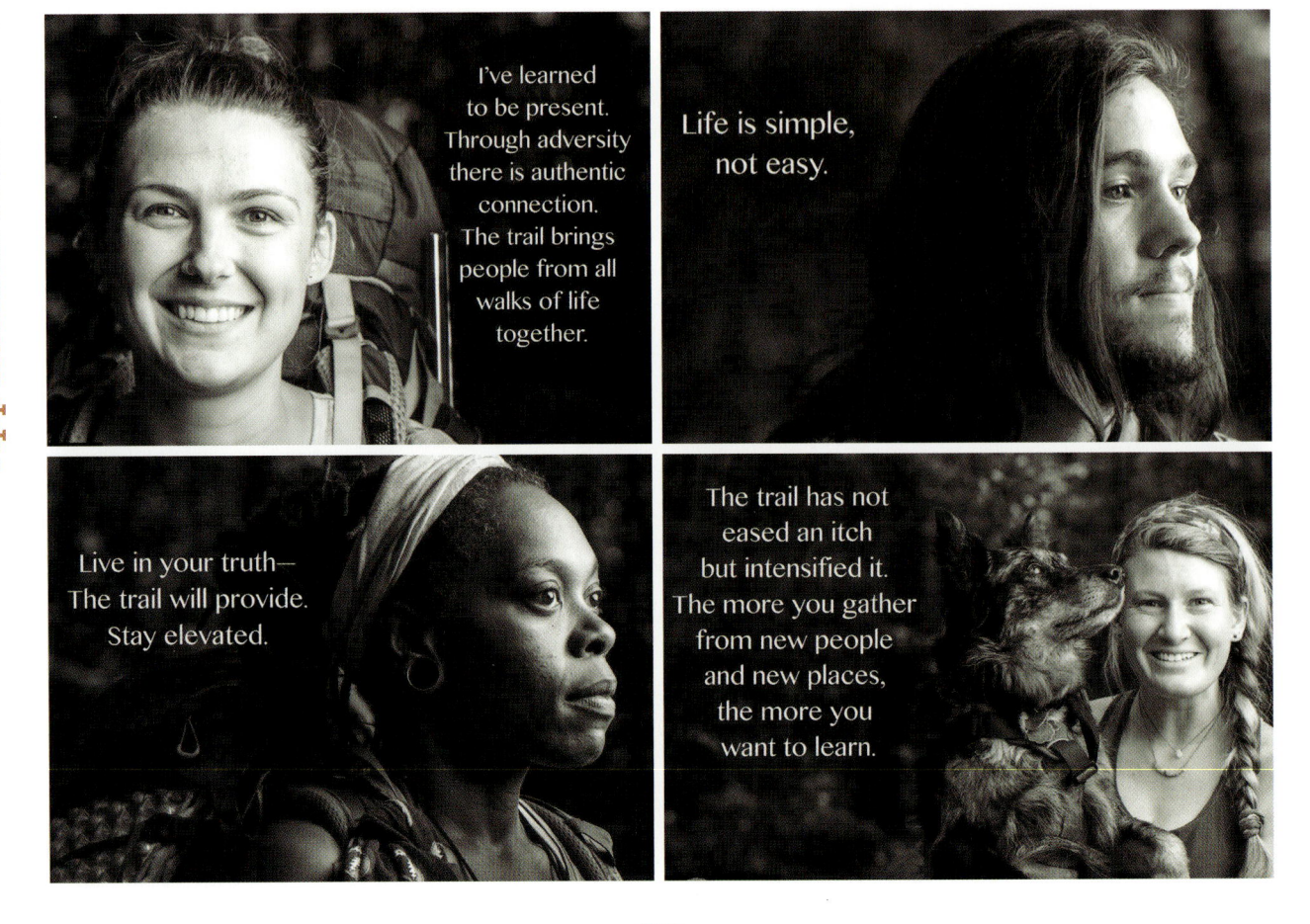

Appalachian Trail studio

I've learned to be present. Through adversity there is authentic connection. The trail brings people from all walks of life together.

Life is simple, not easy.

Live in your truth— The trail will provide. Stay elevated.

The trail has not eased an itch but intensified it. The more you gather from new people and new places, the more you want to learn.

Kindness will lift you over all obstacles. Start by being kind— to yourself and others. Then kindness will carry you everywhere.

I've learned to slow down. To sit and watch the sunrise and remember that there is always a new beginning, an inherent forgiveness. To be intentional always and love everyone around me no matter who they are.

I need very little to survive and thrive: a goal, great friends and what I can carry on my back.

Pursue your dream, no matter how hard it is. Enjoy the process, rather than focus on the end result.

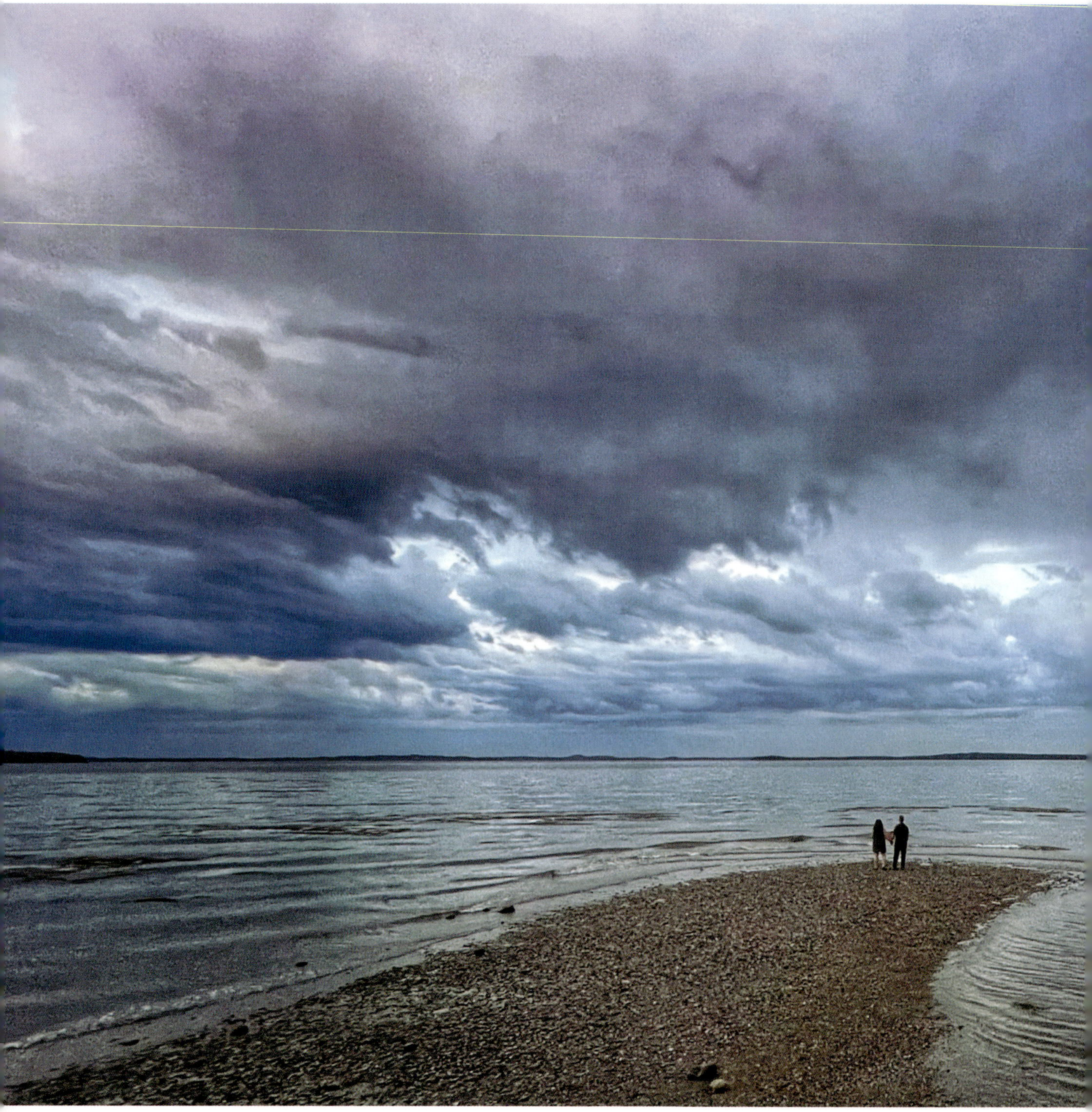

A break by the sea

We slowed down in the cool breezes of the sea. We stayed at Searsport Shores Oceanfront Camping just north of Belfast, Maine. We watched the rhythms of the tides and enjoyed live music in the evenings. There were goats and chickens on the property. Art workshops. Because we had Vinny and didn't need much for services, we took a tent site 100 feet from the water and breathed in the salty air.

We found a balance of office work in the morning and exploration in the afternoon. We started to feel like maybe we had accomplished what we set out to do. We tentatively said it out loud and to each other. Maybe it was time for a new season. We had been gathering stories for 20 months and maybe it was time to think about bringing the journey to a close and settle down to produce the next exhibit and write the next book.

We looked at our upcoming schedule and it was filled with programming. In late summer, we would install an exhibit in Orlando and slowly work our way up the East Coast, with exhibits and programming booked in Virginia, West Virginia, and New York. If everything worked just right, we might squirrel away a little free time to return to New England just as the autumn colors hit their peak, a life-long bucket list item.

We thought about how to bring the journey to an end. We considered making a mad dash to see all 50 states. Our tally was currently at 44 and there was something appealing about the idea. But Alaska and Hawaii would present certain logistical challenges, and we realized the journey was never about checking off a list.

We saw a natural arc that would bring us home by the end of the calendar year. We weren't settling on a final decision, but the idea was fully on the table and we both seemed to be on the same page. It was important that we were on the same page.

It was hard to leave the cool comfort of the Maine coast but we had an engagement at the Wild Goose festival in North Carolina and, on the way, we passed through Long Island to meet Simran.

Dr. Simran Jeet Singh is executive director of the Religion and Society Program at the Aspen Institute and the author of *The Light We Give: How Sikh Wisdom Can Transform Your Life*. Simran aspires to build a pluralistic world that allows all people to thrive. He finds joy in challenging people's assumptions of who he is in order to break down stereotypes and build new connections.

Probably the most important part of who I am is that I'm a Spurs fan. Basketball. I grew up in San Antonio. It's something people don't really expect about me. They see the turban, they see the beard, they see the brown skin. They assume me to be a foreigner who has no idea about what pop culture and sports culture in America is.

> "Life is hard and there's a lot of ugliness, but there's always more goodness. There's always more love."
>
> —Simran Jeet Singh

[I grew] up in Texas as a religious minority and as part of a faith community that really shows up visibly—we literally wear our religion on our heads. My turban announces to people that I'm different. I've been on the other side of religious intolerance for a lot of my life and I've learned firsthand how painful and exclusionary that can be.

Sometimes it's malicious in the ways that you might expect. Like people saying things to me or refusing me service. That's happened. But sometimes it's more innocuous, where people have questions or there are rules in place.

For example, uniform policies in sports and in the military: you cannot have facial hair, or in sports, especially, you can't have headwear. And I don't think people made those rules to exclude people like me. I think they just didn't have us in mind.

And so I've become really sensitive to other people's experiences that are similar to mine because of their religious difference. What does it mean to have a select few people in this country making rules for everyone based on their religious presumptions or convictions? That doesn't feel right.

You're constantly having to pick and choose where and how to fit in. And there are sacrifices that are being made. For me, the vision of religious pluralism is one where everyone gets to thrive. We can create conditions that account for everyone that are more flexible, that don't center just one community, but really make sure that everyone is set up for success in this country.

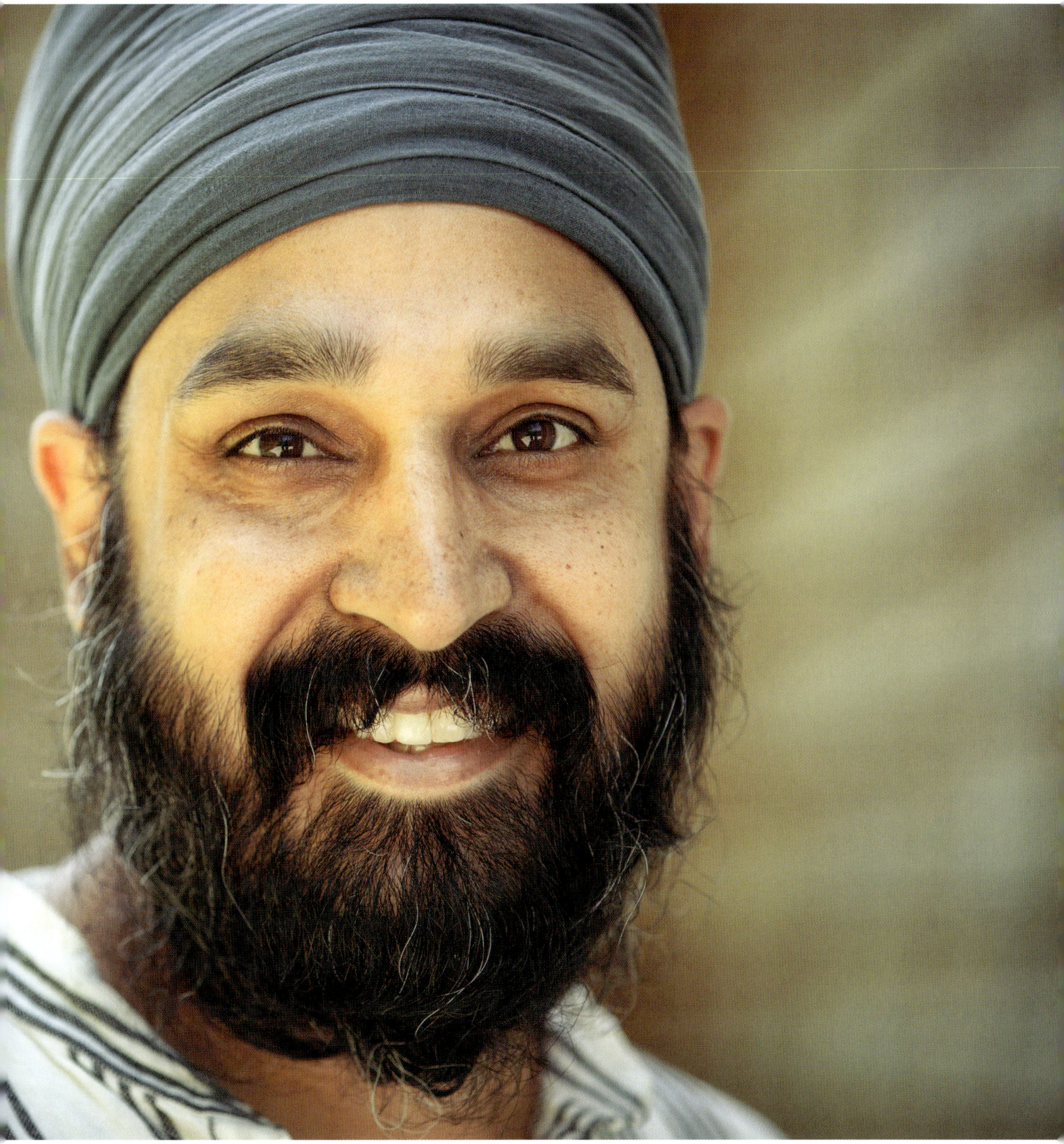

278

07.13.2022: Wild Goose Festival

I'd never been to Wild Goose Festival in North Carolina, but I'd heard about it. Imagine Woodstock for faith and justice people.

A couple thousand people camped on a big farm, with music, lectures, and art. Folks who believe they are called to make a difference in the world. Folks who've been damaged in some way by the institutional church, but they didn't want to give up on their faith.

It was hot. Sweltering. Humid. We set up a studio under a 10' x 20' tent and asked the sweaty people, "What has called you to action?"

Why have you shown up? What gets you out of bed in the morning? What inspires you? I've done dozens of these studios and I'm always worried that nobody will show up, but when you make room to listen, people always show up.

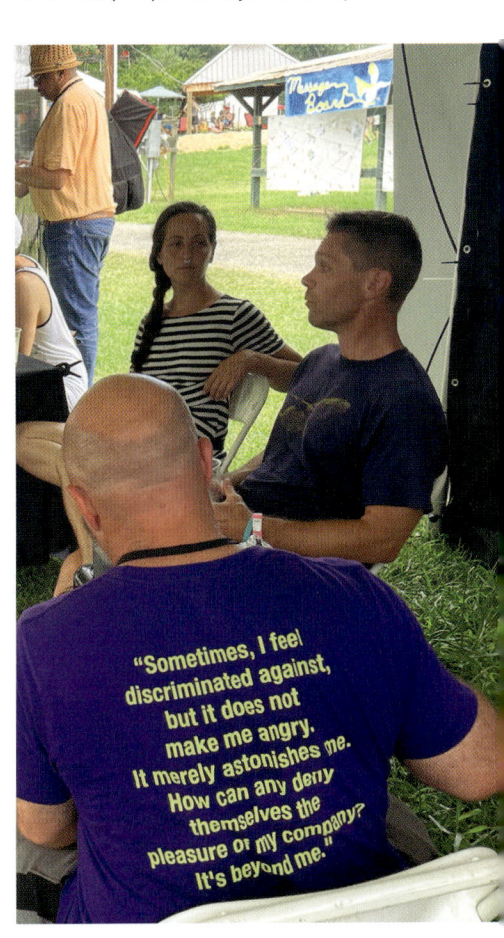

"What has called you to action?"

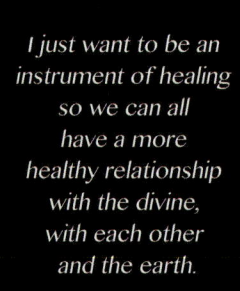

Wild Goose studio

I just want to be an instrument of healing so we can all have a more healthy relationship with the divine, with each other and the earth.

I have decided to experience the journey— seeing, hearing, feeling. Stepping up to be obedient to what I am called to do. Here I am Lord. Send me.

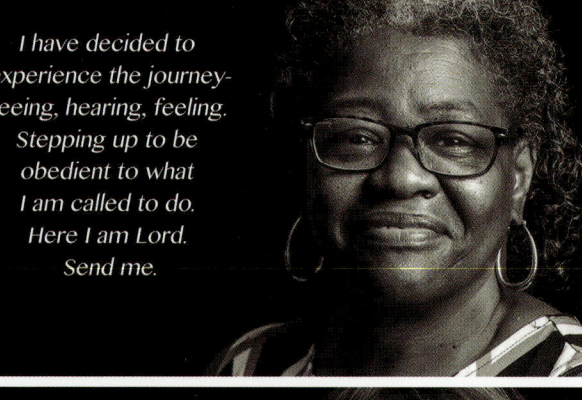

The racial, political and societal divides in this country have called me to action to believe we can do better. We have to do better.

My disgust with the continued injustices that hurt my siblings has called me to action.

In spite of myself, who prefers separation, I seek out others because I know that together we can do great things.

The spirit of the Lord is upon me, has anointed me to preach good news to the poor. Injustice is not just bad policy, it is sin.

Trust. That within EVERY thing is a good intention. And that when we rediscover our own good intentions, our actions, too, become good.

The God of my understanding has called me to practice the work of John 11… I raise the dead by the power of Christ. I pastor the Lazarus Community in Oklahoma City as a monastic community.

280

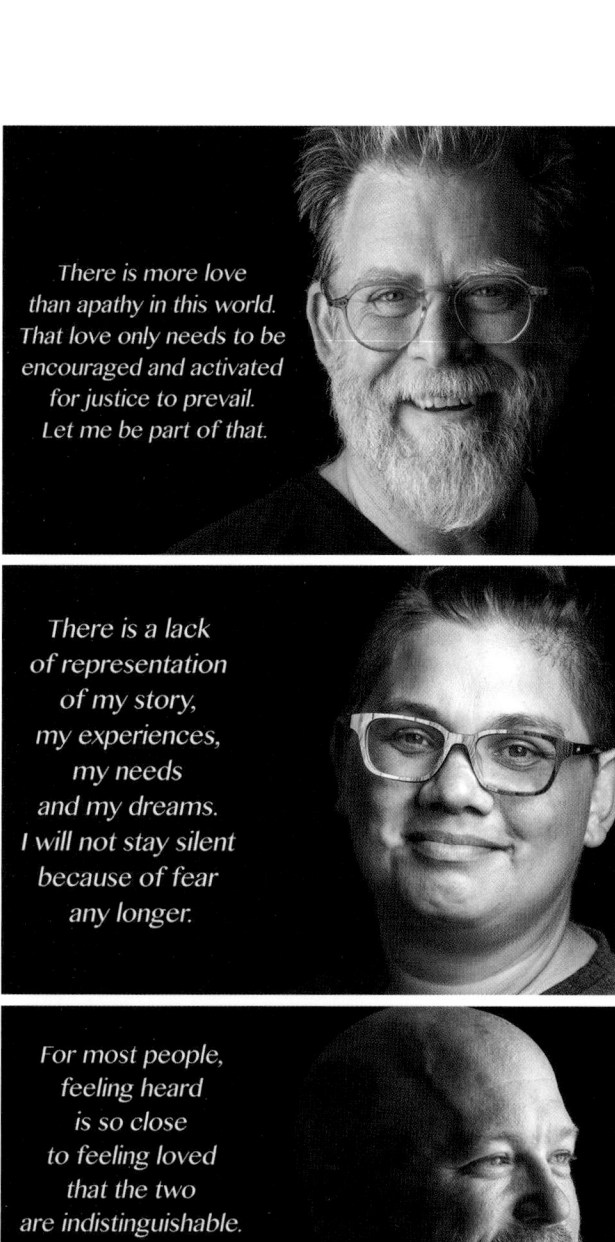

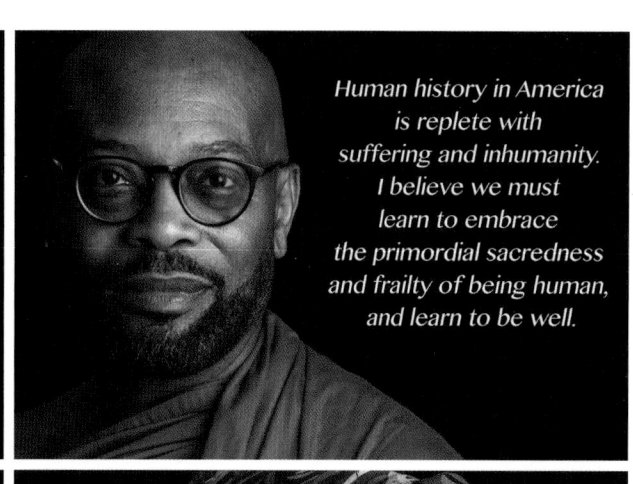

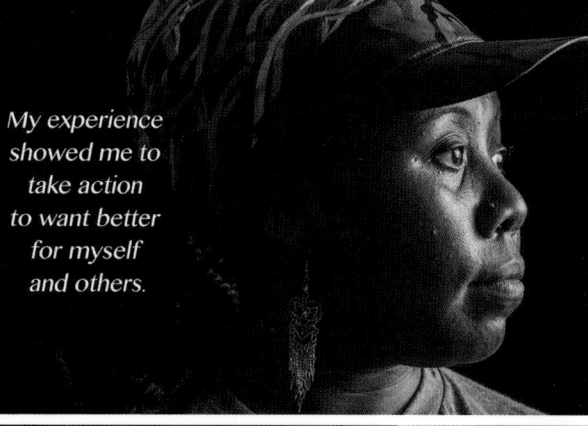

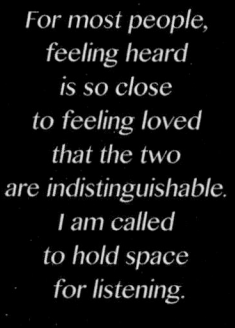

*There is more love
than apathy in this world.
That love only needs to be
encouraged and activated
for justice to prevail.
Let me be part of that.*

*Human history in America
is replete with
suffering and inhumanity.
I believe we must
learn to embrace
the primordial sacredness
and frailty of being human,
and learn to be well.*

*There is a lack
of representation
of my story,
my experiences,
my needs
and my dreams.
I will not stay silent
because of fear
any longer.*

*My experience
showed me to
take action
to want better
for myself
and others.*

*For most people,
feeling heard
is so close
to feeling loved
that the two
are indistinguishable.
I am called
to hold space
for listening.*

*I used to
run across rabid,
vicious racists.
When I quit
stumbling on them
I thought
they were gone.
I was wrong.*

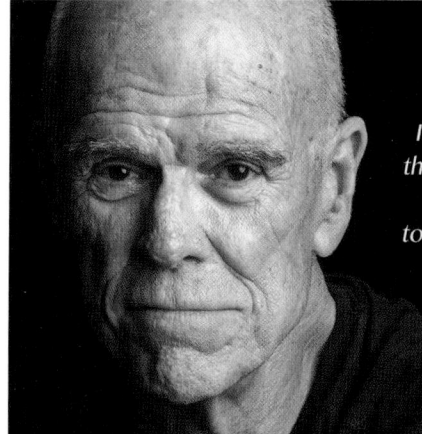

*Life's been
good to me.
I'm just lucky.
It's my privilege
that has called me
to give back
to make the world
a better place.*

*My own journey
through pain
to finding acceptance
led me to realize
so many others
share this pain.
How can I help them?*

Journey to Florida

Our fall was full. The world was coming back to life and all of the engagements that had been canceled during COVID-19 were repopulating our calendar, and then some. Our attention had shifted from gathering new stories to installing exhibits and leading workshops.

There was a good chance that our schedule would decide for us that this journey was complete. We felt the call to be back in community, but it was more than that. My regular cycle of arriving at a new place, falling in love with it, and then mourning the loss when we left was becoming increasingly difficult. The mourning process lasted longer. I found that I was reluctant to get too attached to the next place, knowing that it would be painful to leave it. I was slow to say hello to new friends in an effort to protect myself from the difficult process of saying goodbye.

Florida studio

"What does peace mean to you?"

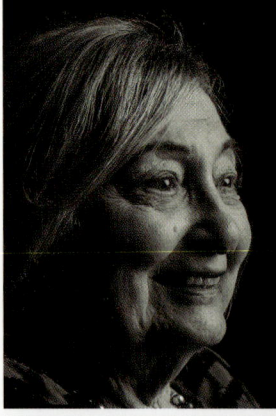

The core meaning of the familiar Hebrew word translated as "peace" -shalom- is "completeness." Peace means fitting all the pieces together.

From the Holocaust we remember the depths to which humanity might sink; but also the heights to which we might aspire.

Peace is a feeling of serenity resulting from being heard, accepted and respected within oneself, between individuals and among communities.

To me, peace is the understanding that everything within me (body, mind & spirit) has the power to consolidate into calmness even amidst chaos.

Peace means having a heart that is selfless and treating others with compassion and respect. Peace is being accepted for who we are.

Peace is when your mind and heart are aligned with love, gratitude, and compassion.

The Holocaust Memorial Resource and Education Center of Florida in Orlando hosted *A Peace of My Mind*'s original exhibit. We coordinated a studio day and invited people from their community to answer the question, "What does peace mean to you?" More than 50 people showed up to share a story and have their photo taken, including the museum's founder and Holocaust survivor Tess Wise.

Peace means holding to the dream that one day, people of color will be able to walk down the street and not fear that it might be their last, because someone fears how they look or what they represent.

Peace to me means being calm, still and reflective in nature - that's where I find and feel peace.

I believe there's a close link between peace and perception. When we truly see each other, we find common truths and less to fear.

Peace is freedom from the prison I held myself in for many years. It is love, understanding, tranquility, and the ability to love wholeheartedly.

For me peace is living in harmony and living fearlessly (nirbhau) without hatred (nirvair) and without compromising my identity or freedom. It's activism towards ending conflicts and aiding people in need.

Peace means something different than when I was with the Germans. Now, peace means freedom. I never thought I would be alive and have great-grandchildren.

Peace means knowing that your needs are met, you have value, and you belong… so much that you strive to share that feeling with others.

Peace is tranquility. Peace is contentment. Peace is accepting and being accepted. Peace is fearless. Peace is salvation.

This was our conversation earlier in the summer, before we even got out of bed:
"Another shooting."
"Where?"
"Fourth of July parade in Illinois."
"How many?"
"Seven."
Five in Colorado Springs because they were LGBTQ.

Twenty-three in El Paso because they were Latinx.

Eight in Milwaukee because they were Sikh.

At the Holocaust Center, I met and photographed the owner of the Pulse nightclub in Orlando, where 49 people were killed in a 2016 shooting. The site was not far away and I went to visit it.

And perhaps these words by Simran Jeet Singh offer some consolation: "Life is hard and there's a lot of ugliness, but there's always more goodness. There's always more love."

But that's not enough, is it? Be kind to one another. That's maybe the lowest bar. Also, make sure to show up for one another. Take a risk for one another. Advocate for one another.

Love one another.

287

A changing season

We rolled right into the fall. We set up exhibits in West Virginia, New York, Michigan, Wisconsin, and Minnesota. We parked Vinny and flew to conferences in Ohio and Nebraska.

We saw a new role for our work, to encourage small human encounters and open a space to nurture relationships. In a post-pandemic season, in many ways, we had forgotten how to be together. Each exhibit and every workshop showed us that this process of storytelling invited connection. People lingered to talk, hungry for a place to be seen and heard.

Alex remained pretty quiet during my lecture to his class. A big man with a full beard and a flannel shirt, I made certain assumptions about who he was and, as he waited to talk to me after class, I prepared to be challenged. Instead, he said this: "As I listened to you talk, I realized that I can give love. I'm just not sure I can receive it." Other students nodded as they related to his experience and appreciated his vulnerability.

Another student waited until all the others had left. "What would you say to someone who can't let down his defenses?" he asked, his eyes watering. I didn't have a good answer for him. "Look for little victories," I said. "Keep trying and be gentle with yourself in the process."

On another campus, a student shared, "My dad was killed when I was 12. I wanted to be angry, but I don't think that's what my dad would have wanted."

A woman explained, "My mom walked out of the hospital right after I was born. She abandoned me. It took a long time to forgive her."

A student couldn't make himself come out to his family. He loved his very traditional grandparents and was afraid of their reaction—and of their potential rejection.

A note on our windshield thanked us for coming to their community. An email from a Ukrainian exchange student said she was drawn to the stories of forgiveness, knowing that her country would need that lesson some day to move on.

We had spent the last two years gathering these seeds of conversation. Now it was time to plant them, water them, and watch them grow.

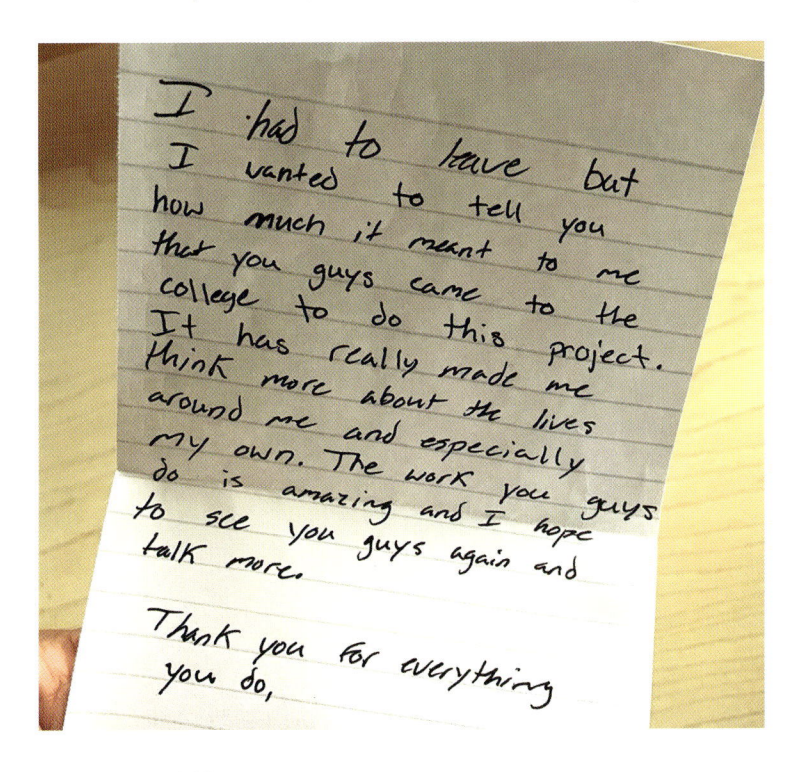

289

10.06.2022: Journey to New England

Karen and I looked at each other and said, "I think we did it." We laughed and then we cried. Life on the road was magical, but we always knew it would come to an end. It was hard to let go of this wandering exploration, but it was time. We just knew that it was time.

For every decision, there is a cost. For every gain, there is a loss. Not everything is meant to last forever and everything has its season. These are the things I kept telling myself

It was time to write the next book and produce the next exhibit, and that couldn't happen on the road. The logistics of nomadic life were all-consuming and I needed the headspace of a more stable home base to write from. We missed community, and it was time to be home again.

We offered ourselves the gift of a week in New England during peak fall colors. We hiked and paddled and let it all settle in. We started to think about what a more rooted life might look like. The destination was not at all clear, but we started moving toward it anyway.

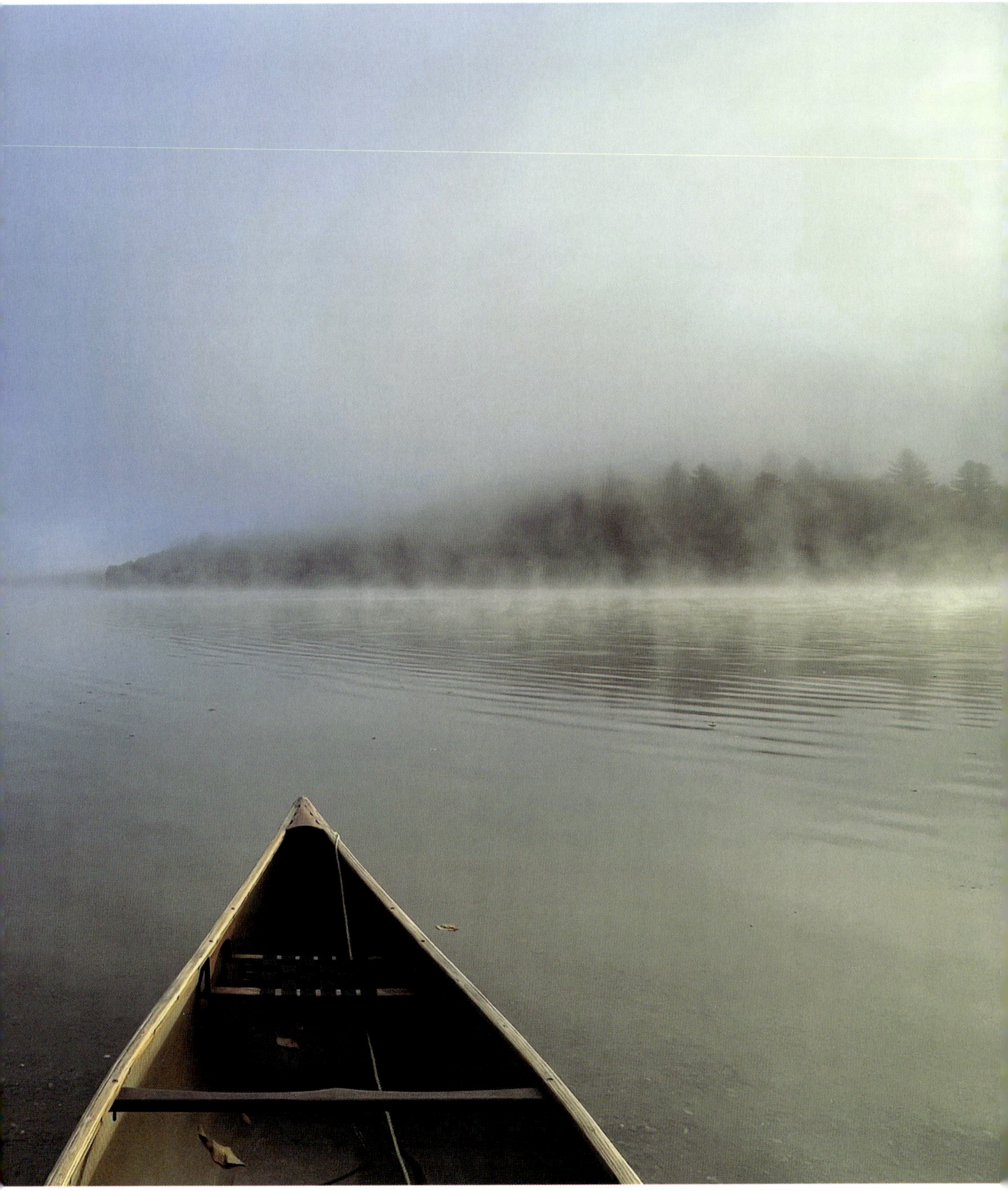

12.10.2022: Journey to Colorado

My heart still flutters when I see the mountains. "These are your mountains," my mom used to say. As a 12-year old in the back seat of our Ford LTD-II, I remember looking out the window and fretting about the day the craggy peaks would all erode down to flat plains. Nothing lasts forever.

But on this day, the corrugated backbone of Rocky Mountain National Park stood tall and proud. Snowy. Stark. Majestic. I climbed a small ridge to find a shred of cell service and didn't notice four grazing mule deer until they were right beside me. They weren't scared. They seemed unaware of the rule that told them to stay away from humans, or me away from them. They just quietly went about their work while I went about mine.

This was our final chapter. We watched the sun rise, then set, then rise again. We hiked through the snowy landscape, felt the crisp wind on our faces and tried to soak in these last, untethered days.

Coffee and breakfast on the side of the road. Reading in the front seat. Two-handed rummy played on the bed in the van.

We were in Colorado because Vinny was almost a year old and we had a few small repairs to get done at the shop before his warranty ran out. We planned on one last day of snowshoeing near Vail, but an impending storm chased us home. Our choice was to leave a day early, or hunker down and get stranded for the next four days. The prediction was for eighteen inches of snow, 50 mph winds, and sub-zero temperatures.

We rolled east. The temperature dropped, the rain started, and the wind picked up. We watched the weather minute by minute as the temperature hovered around 34 degrees, and we hoped the world wouldn't turn to a sheet of ice.

We stopped for a night in a Grand Island, Nebraska, hotel. Work boots lined the hallway outside each room. We closed our eyes for what seemed like a few minutes and left early in the morning. The interstate had been shut down at North Platte, just two hours behind us, 100 miles to the west. We'd dodged the weather before. We kept just ahead of the storm's full grip and we made it home, or at least to the city where home would be. Friends offered us a spare room, and we started putting the pieces together for the next chapter of our life.

100 days of transition

We knew that setting off on this journey would take some intention and planning. We didn't fully understand how much work it would take to return home.

We knew we wanted to return to the Twin Cities. If what we were missing was community, it made sense to come back to where our people and community already existed. Our timing was suspect. When you live in a van, you could argue that relocating to the Upper Midwest in December might be a tactical error. But it was time, regardless of the season.

We didn't want to buy a house. That seemed like too much of a commitment for a couple of vagabonds just coming off the road. We decided to rent a place and we slowly narrowed down our neighborhood options. I wanted to spend my time writing and editing, not mowing and shoveling, so an apartment or a townhome made sense. We found some townhomes across the street from a 2,500-acre nature preserve that promised to soften the blow of coming off the road with easy access to green space. And then we waited for the right floorplan to become available. And we waited. And waited some more.

It took 100 days to finally sign a lease. Friends offered us their homes as they vacationed to warmer climates, and we cobbled together an ever-evolving schedule of temporary lodging where we watered the plants and brought in the mail in exchange for a place to stay. Truth be told, none of these kind souls needed a house-sitter, they were just being generous to help us out.

We planned a "Coming Home" event and gathered friends and followers to celebrate our return as we shared stories from the road. It was good to have our people around us again.

Greg Campbell went home to die on March 8, 2023. His liver and kidneys were failing and he chose to return home to hospice care for his final days because he didn't want to die in a hospital. He chose to die at home, where he finds peace and love and safety. I interviewed Greg on March 9, 2023, and he passed away peacefully at home on March 28.

I could have probably gotten a few more months out of life, but when I go to dialysis, my blood pressure would crash. I could limp along for a couple more months, but there's no reason to do that when there's no chance of me getting better. I'm extremely comfortable with [my decision]. We're all born to die. I guess I've affected enough people here that it's time to move on. It is okay.

Do I feel cheated? No. Saddened and disappointed that I won't go back to Lake of the Woods, where I go walleye fishing every year? I'll miss that. But I actually told the guys that I fish with, "Next summer when you're fishing, I'm going to be in the front of that boat and every big fish you guys pull in, it's because I sent it to you."

> "Am I sad? Yeah. But this is the trail I'm on. And I have to finish the trail."
> —Greg Campbell

When you've had a slow burn like I have, you have an opportunity to visit with people. I found out that I have affected more people in this world than I ever knew. I didn't realize how much they loved and cherished my friendship. And to me it's stunning.

A friend is somebody that will go to bat for you. If you've broken down someplace in the middle of the night, they will get out of bed and come get you. If you're short of money, they'll give you some money. They stand by you. They cry with you. They laugh with you. That's a friend.

If you want to have friends, you have to open up. And that can be very scary because you can get hurt. But I have friends I've known for 46 years and, to this day, they're still helping me. They're shoveling my sidewalk. They're here every day asking, "What can we do?" They do it because it's right and they do it for everything I've done for them. When people talk about paying it forward in life by being kind and good and peaceful, you never know when the withdrawal comes. And the withdrawal is coming for me right now.

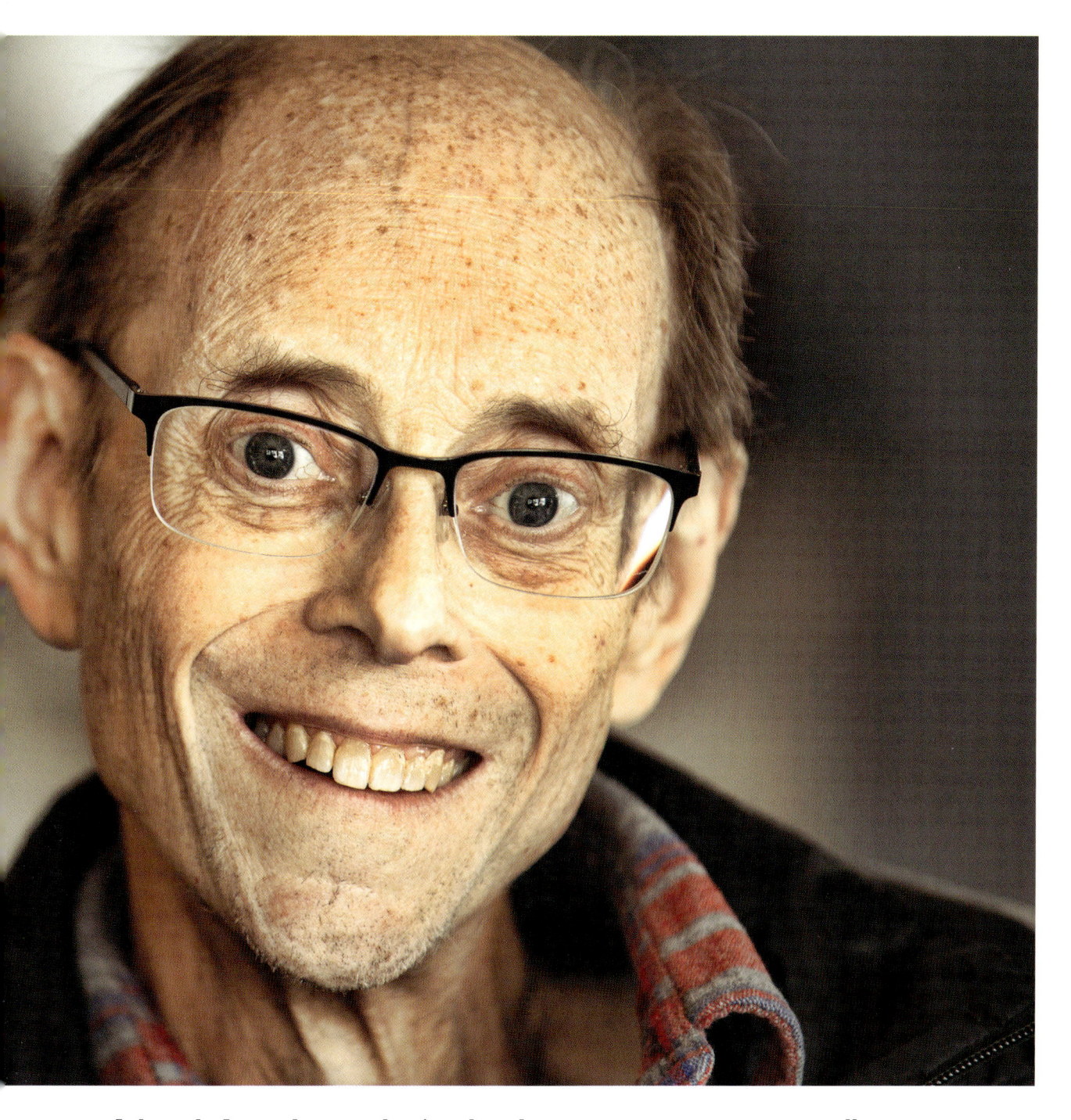

I thought I was done gathering, but there was one more story to tell.

My good friend Wade told me that his good friend Greg was dying.

Wade told me that it felt like Greg had something he wanted to say, but he didn't have a place to say it. "Does he want to sit for an interview?", I asked. I wasn't sure I had the emotional capacity to do it. Coming off the road, overwhelmed with the task ahead and feeling unsettled, I had my own sort of grief to manage.

But I also knew that if Greg wanted to do an interview, I would find a way to make it work.

Greg said yes. He only had a few good days left, so we agreed to meet the next day. I thought I was doing Greg a favor, but I'm pretty sure I'm the one who received the gift.

—John Noltner

After all those miles on the road, here's the secret answer: There is no secret answer.

There is no us and no them. We are all a part of the problem and we are all a part of the solution.

A Peace of My Mind is not an answer, it is a process. A way to model how we can be in community with one another and move toward something better together.

A Peace of My Mind is an example of how we can engage across difference and how we can hear other voices. Our history is filled with both beauty and pain woven together. They can't be separated. It's raw and messy and real. We need to address the wound if we want it to heal. We have to be brave and set our egos aside and allow ourselves to imagine new possibilities.

Maybe that's what art does best. It helps us imagine new possibilities when the path we are on fails us.

All across the country, people are lighting the way, illuminating the challenges, and offering creative solutions. Hearing those stories and sharing them with you is the only path I see forward.

I hope that *A Peace of My Mind* can offer a model of engagement that leads us toward the truth. Not because I know it, but because I have not been afraid to seek it. Actually, I have been afraid, but I have gone looking anyway.

An invitation

You don't have to drive 93,000 miles across the country to find the wisdom and beauty that is all around us. (I mean, I highly recommend it if you can, but it's definitely not the only way.) Right in your own backyard, you can choose to listen deeply, challenge your own expectations, and keep showing up for one another.

That's how we connect. That's how we build strong communities. That's how we find a path forward for one another.

We are all a little more vulnerable than we knew.

We are all a little more connected than we understood.

Have courage and love one another.

Use these questions for self-reflection or for discussion in a group.

Which of the stories in the book resonated? Why?

Which of the stories in the book challenged you? Why?

When have you taken a risk in your life?
Was it a positive or a negative experience?

Did George Floyd's death and the events that followed change the way you understood the world?
How did you respond personally, if you did?

Is there a time when you have been uncomfortable in a new situation?
What was that like?
What did you learn?

Where are your blind spots?
Where do you have work to do?

Can you identify a time of great growth in your life?
What allowed that to happen?
Who allowed that to happen?

When have you been misunderstood?

When have you tried to bridge a divide?
Was it well received?

Has someone ever reached out to you and offered healing?

Share a time when you allowed yourself to be vulnerable.

Has travel ever helped you to learn new truths?

What is the issue of the day that is closest to your heart?
What is the action that you take because of it?

These are some of the questions that I ask people during my interviews.

If I didn't know anything about you, what would you want me to know?

What kind of world do you want to live in?

When have you made your greatest impact?

What has called you to action?

What do you want the world to understand?

What gives you hope?

When have you found unexpected courage?

When have you seen a good example of peace?

Resources (in the order that they appear in the book)

A Peace of My Mind
Bridging divides and building community through storytelling and art.
www.apeaceofmymind.net

Pádraig Ó Tuama
Poet and Theologian
www.padraigotuama.com

Harvest Hosts
An RV membership club that allows free camping at unique destinations.
www.harvesthosts.com

George Floyd Global Memorial
Conserving stories of resistance to racial injustice and curating spaces for all people to grieve, pay respect, and be a voice for justice.
www.georgefloydglobalmemorial.org

The Slave Dwelling Project
Inspiring a more truthful and inclusive narrative of the history of the nation that honors the contributions of all our people.
www.slavedwellingproject.org

International African American Museum
Honoring the untold stories of the African American journey at one of our country's most sacred sites.
www.iaamuseum.org

National Action Network
One of the leading civil rights organizations in the nation with chapters throughout the entire United States.
www.nationalactionnetwork.net

Gullah Tours
Exploring the places, history, and stories that are relevant to the rich and varied contributions made by Black Charlestonians.
www.gullahtours.com

PFLAG
Creating a caring, just, and affirming world for LGBTQ+ people and those who love them.
www.pflag.org

Center of the World
A quirky roadside attraction in the southern California desert.
www.historyingranite.org

Santa Fe Ranch Foundation
Modeling and teaching sustainable ranching in the Sonoran Desert.
www.santaferanchfoundation.org

Gary Nabhan
Writer, agrarian activist and ethnobiologist conserving the links between biodiversity and cultural diversity.
www.garynabhan.com

Circles of Peace
A restorative justice program ending the cycles of abuse for individuals, families, and communities.
www.circlesofpeace.us

Voices from the Border
Responding to the needs of migrating people by providing housing, medical care, and humanitarian aid in Nogales, Sonora, Mexico.
www.voicesfromtheborder.net

Border Action Network
Working with immigrant and border communities in southern Arizona to ensure that our rights are respected, our human dignity upheld, and that our communities are healthy places to live.
www.borderaction.org

Alvaro Enciso
Contemporary artist living and working in Tucson, Arizona. exploring ideas about the American Dream, cultural identity, and crossing borders.
www.instagram.com/aencisoart/

Delta Discovery Tours
Ecotours into the Mississippi River Delta
www.deltadiscoverytours.com

The Juror Project
Working to change the makeup of juries to better represent the American population and the communities most commonly accused.
www.thejurorproject.org

Peyton Scott Russell
Graffiti artist, educator, activist.
www.houseofdaskarone.com

The Violence Project
The most comprehensive mass shooter database, dedicated to reducing violence through research.
www.theviolenceproject.org

The National Civil Rights Museum
Tracing the history of the Civil Rights Movement, located at the site of the Lorraine Motel, where Dr. King was assassinated on April 4, 1968.
www.civilrightsmuseum.org

Listen First Project
A coalition of 500 organizations combating toxic division by bringing Americans together.
www.listenfirstproject.org

Alluvial Collective
Ending inequity based on difference by cultivating belonging and wholeness in the world.
www.alluvialcollective.org

Center for the Study of Southern Culture
An academic organization dedicated to the investigation, documentation, interpretation and teaching of the Southern United States, including its culture.
www.southernstudies.olemiss.edu

Equal Justice Initiative's Legacy Museum
Providing a comprehensive history of the United States with a focus on the legacy of slavery.
https://legacysites.eji.org/

Neal Moore
A 7,500 mile paddling journey into the soul of America.
www.22rivers.com

Honor the Earth
Creating awareness and support for Native environmental issues and developing needed financial and political resources for the survival of sustainable Native communities.
www.honorearth.org

Empowerment Through Adventure
Inspiring others to scale life's mountains and obstacles, and climb beyond their own preconceived limitations.
www.lorischneider.net

Friends of the Apostle Islands National Lakeshore
Promoting an appreciation for and preservation of the natural environment and cultural heritage of the Apostle Islands National Lakeshore.
www.friendsoftheapostleislands.org

Hope of the Valley
Working to prevent, reduce and eliminate poverty, hunger and homelessness by offering immediate assistance and long-term solutions.
www.hopethemission.org

Union Rescue Mission
One of the largest rescue missions in the United States, and the oldest in Los Angeles.
www.urm.org

Circles in the Sand
Sharing love, joy and kindness by creating sand labyrinths surrounded by intricate designs and artwork.
www.sandypathbandon.com

Corvallis Daytime Drop-in Center
A community-based resource hub providing information, referral, and direct services for people experiencing homelessness and poverty in Benton County and beyond.
www.corvallisddc.org

Darcelle XV Showplace
Entertaining audiences in all walks of life for over 50 years with Las Vegas-style cabaret revues of Glitz, Glamour and Comedy.
www.darcellexv.com

Project Sanctuary
Offering a human-centered, solution-based approach to helping military families heal and move forward in life.
www.projectsanctuary.us

Dave and Matt Vans
Making van life accessible to everyone
www.dmvans.com

Glen Canyon Institute
Dedicated to the restoration of Glen Canyon and a free flowing Colorado River.
www.glencanyon.org

Conserve Southwest Utah
Advocating for conservation and stewardship of our area's natural and cultural resources and implementation of Smart Growth policies that benefit present and future generations.
www.conserveswu.org

Desert Adventures
Guiding trips in some of the harshest, most rugged terrain in the United States.
www.desert-adventures.com

Lake Mead Mohave Adventures
Exploring America's first National Recreation area.
www.lakemeadmohaveadventures.com

Living Rivers/Colorado Riverkeeper
Empowering a movement to instill a new ethic of achieving ecological restoration, balanced with meeting human needs.
www.livingrivers.org

Desert Research Institute
A world leader in basic and applied environmental research.
www.dri.edu

Southern Nevada Water Authority
Providing world-class water service in a sustainable, adaptive, and responsible manner to our customers through reliable, cost-effective systems.
www.snwa.com

Water and Tribes Initiative
Enhancing tribal capacity and supporting sustainable water use through collaboration.
www.waterandtribes.org

Sojourners
Inspiring hope and building movements to transform individuals, communities, the church, and the world.
www.sojo.net

Poor People's Campaign
A national call for moral revival.
www.poorpeoplescampaign.org

Brahma Kumaris Meditation Museum
A place of inner silence where we can learn to nurture the beautiful part of ourselves and understand the things we hold on to that disconnect us from that inner beauty.
www.meditationmuseum.org

Weave the Social Fabric Project
Addressing the crisis of broken social trust that has left Americans divided along many lines, isolated and unable to address our common needs.
www.aspeninstitute.org/programs/weave-the-social-fabric-initiative

Religious Coalition for Reproductive Choice
A multifaith, intersectional, and antiracist movement for reproductive freedom and dignity leading in spiritual companionship, curating frameworks for faith leaders, and training the next generation of activists.
www.rcrc.org

Appalachian Trail Conservancy
Protecting, managing, and advocating for the Appalachian National Scenic Trail.
www.appalachiantrail.org

Religion and Society Program at the Aspen Institute
Igniting change through convening, catalyzing, and researching the challenges and opportunities at the convergence of religion, culture, and justice.
www.aspeninstitute.org/programs/religion-society-program

Wild Goose Festival
A transformational community grounded in faith-inspired social justice.
www.wildgoosefestival.org

Holocaust Memorial Resource and Education Center of Florida
Using the history and lessons of the Holocaust to build a just and caring community free of antisemitism and all forms of prejudice and bigotry.
www.holocaustedu.org

onePULSE Foundation
Creating a sanctuary of hope to honor the 49 Angels that were taken, the 68 others who were injured and the countless first responders and healthcare professionals who treated them.
www.onepulsefoundation.org

Copyright © 2023 by John Noltner
Text and photographs by John Noltner
Top photo on page 20
taken by Jordan Noltner
Bottom photo on page 74
taken by Karen Noltner
Cover and interior design
by Barbara Koster
All rights reserved.
No part of this book may be reproduced by any means without written permission from the publisher, except brief portions quoted for purposes of review.
ISBN 979-8-218-27819-9
Printed at Sheridan-Worzalla
in Stevens Point, Wisconsin
First United States Edition

Acknowledgements

My gratitude could fill its own book. Many thanks to Teresa and Joan for their careful and critical eyes in the editing process. To Karen for proof reading. To Barbara for the beautiful design. To all of the people who shared the stories in these pages and enriched our lives through the connection. To the many new friends who took good care of us on the road and the many old friends who took good care of us when we returned to the place we will always call home. Special thanks to our kids Grey and Jordan and Tiffany for making room for us old folks to chase this dream and especially to Karen for going on this journey with me. There is no better partner I could ask to have by my side as we walk through this life.

And finally, a deep bow of gratitude to all of our donors who made this journey and this book possible. A Peace of My Mind is a 501(c)(3) organization. Donations are tax deductible and help support our mission of bridging divides and building community through storytelling and art. If these stories have inspired you and if you'd like to help pay it forward, we'd welcome you onto our small and mighty team of donors who believe that something better is possible and that we are the ones who can make it happen.

www.apomm.net

"FOR ONLY LOVE CAN CONQUER HATE"
- MARVIN GAYE